MW00995402

STATES, FIRMS, AND THEIR LEGAL FICTIONS

This volume offers a new point of entry into questions about how the law conceives of states and firms. Because states and firms are fictitious constructs rather than products of evolutionary biology, the law dictates which acts should be attributed to each entity, and by which actors. Those legal decisions construct firms and states by attributing identity and consequences to them. As the volume shows, these legal decisions are often products of path dependence or conceptual metaphors like "personhood" that have expanded beyond their original uses. Focusing on attribution, the volume considers an array of questions about artificial entities that are usually divided into doctrinal siloes. These include questions about attribution of international legal responsibility to states and state-owned entities, transnational attribution of liabilities to firms, and attribution of identity rights to corporations. Durkee highlights the artificiality of doctrines that construct firms and states and, therefore, their susceptibility to change.

Melissa J. "MJ" Durkee is Professor of Law at Washington University in St. Louis. She is an expert in international and business law and her research focuses on the public-private interactions that produce and interpret legal norms. She is an elected member of the *American Journal of International Law* and chairs the International Legal Theory interest group of the American Society of International Law. Her work appears in leading journals including the *Yale Law Journal, Stanford Law Review, Virginia Law Review,* and others.

ASIL STUDIES IN INTERNATIONAL LEGAL THEORY

Series Editors

Michael D. Cooper, American Society of International Law
Mortimer Sellers, University of Baltimore

Editorial Board

Samantha Besson, University of Fribourg
Allen Buchanan, Duke University
David Kennedy, Harvard University
Jan Klabbers, University of Helsinki
David Luban, Georgetown University
Larry May, Vanderbilt University
Mary Ellen O'Connell, University of Notre Dame
Helen Stacy, Stanford University
John Tasioulas, University of Oxford
Fernando Tesón, Florida State University

The purpose of the ASIL Studies in International Legal Theory series is to clarify and improve the theoretical foundations of international law. Too often the progressive development and implementation of international law has foundered on confusion about first principles. This series raises the level of public and scholarly discussion about the structure and purposes of the world legal order and how best to achieve global justice through law.

This series grows out of the International Legal Theory project of the American Society of International Law. The ASIL Studies in International Legal Theory series deepens this conversation by publishing scholarly monographs and edited volumes of essays considering subjects in international legal theory.

Books in the series

Rethinking the Relationship between International, EU and National Law
Lando Kirchmair

Consenting to International Law
Edited by Samantha Besson

The Death Penalty's Denial of Fundamental Human Rights
John Bessler

Theories of International Responsibility Law
Edited by Samantha Besson

Human Dignity in International Law
Ginevra Le Moli

States, Firms, and Their Legal Fictions

ATTRIBUTING IDENTITY AND RESPONSIBILITY TO ARTIFICIAL ENTITIES

Edited by

MELISSA J. DURKEE

Washington University in St. Louis

CAMBRIDGE
UNIVERSITY PRESS

Shaftesbury Road, Cambridge CB2 8EA, United Kingdom

One Liberty Plaza, 20th Floor, New York, NY 10006, USA

477 Williamstown Road, Port Melbourne, VIC 3207, Australia

314–321, 3rd Floor, Plot 3, Splendor Forum, Jasola District Centre, New Delhi – 110025, India

103 Penang Road, #05–06/07, Visioncrest Commercial, Singapore 238467

Cambridge University Press is part of Cambridge University Press & Assessment, a department of the University of Cambridge.

We share the University's mission to contribute to society through the pursuit of education, learning and research at the highest international levels of excellence.

www.cambridge.org
Information on this title: www.cambridge.org/9781009334679

DOI: 10.1017/9781009334709

First published 2024

A catalogue record for this publication is available from the British Library

A Cataloging-in-Publication data record for this book is available from the Library of Congress

ISBN 978-1-009-33467-9 Hardback

Contents

Contributors

The Editor

Melissa J. "MJ" Durkee is Professor of Law at Washington University in St. Louis.

The Authors

Olabisi D. Akinkugbe is Associate Professor and the Viscount Bennett Professor of Law at the Schulich School of Law, Dalhousie University.

Joshua Barkan is Associate Professor in the Franklin College of Arts and Sciences at the University of Georgia.

Kristen E. Boon is the Susan & Perry Dellelce Dean of the Faculty of Law at the University of Ottawa.

David Ciepley is a fellow at the Institute for Advanced Studies in Culture at the University of Virginia.

Laura A. Dickinson is the Oswald Symister Colclough Research Professor of Law and Professor of Law at The George Washington University Law School.

Benjamin P. Edwards is Professor of Law at the William S. Boyd School of Law at the University of Nevada, Las Vegas.

James T. Gathii is the Wing-Tat Lee Chair in International Law and Professor of Law at Loyola University Chicago School of Law.

Sarah C. Haan is the Class of 1958 Uncas and Anne McThenia Professor of Law at Washington and Lee School of Law.

Catherine A. Hardee is Professor of Law at California Western School of Law in San Diego.

Doreen Lustig is Associate Professor at Tel Aviv University, Faculty of Law.

Kishanthi Parella is the Class of 1960 Professor of Ethics and Law at Washington and Lee School of Law.

Dalia Palombo is Assistant Professor of Human Rights Law at the Department of Public Law and Governance at Tilburg University.

Mikko Rajavuori is Assistant Professor of Law at the Faculty of Law, University of Turku.

Acknowledgments

My first debt is due to my contributors, who had the temerity to participate in a theoretically-oriented volume seeking to bring ideas across doctrinal divides, and also the patience to see the project through to completion, which allowed each of the chapters to germinate in its own time.

The volume grew out of a workshop cosponsored by the American Society of International Law's International Legal Theory Interest Group and the University of Georgia School of Law, and thanks are due to these key supporters. A particular thanks to Georgia Law's Dean Rusk International Law Center for its logistical support of the workshop, which took place virtually at a time when many of us were new to the world of virtual exchange.

In addition to the contributors featured in this volume, the workshop benefitted from the involvement of Ingrid (Wuerth) Brunk and William C. Banks, whose helpful insights are reflected at various points in the volume. My colleague Harlan Cohen brought his characteristic generosity to the project, engaging in many generative conversations and reflecting helpfully on drafts.

Several anonymous reviewers provided thoughtful responses to the volume and a number of its chapters. I also appreciate the support of Mortimer Sellers, editor of the ASIL Studies in International Legal Theory Series, as well as Cambridge University Press editors Tom Randall and Marianne Nield.

A team of research assistants at the University of Georgia shared good insights and meticulous editorial support: Jackson R. Nock, Jack Schlafly, Christopher Webb, Savannah Grant, and Madeleine Hoss.

Finally, and most importantly, I acknowledge my family: Eva, my rock; Leonard, who was two when this project began; Philipp, who was born as it developed; and my mother, Deborah, who has consistently helped to buffer this dual-academic-career couple from the vicissitudes of life with very small children.

1

Introduction

States, Firms, and Their Legal Fictions

Melissa J. Durkee

What is a corporation? What is a state? These are not biological creatures. They do not have flesh, blood, or organic parts. They are artificial, human creations. They are also abstract. You cannot point to a thing in the world and say: "That is a state" or "that is a firm." Rather, what you see is a logo, a person in uniform, workers in a building, flashing lights. It is law that gives meaning to these objects and that tells us which people speak and act for which entity: the firm or the state. Firms and states are thus constructed objects, not natural ones. Laws imbue the collections of logos, uniforms, workers, and weapons with legal salience, assigning identity, rights, and responsibilities.

Although these legal entities are not natural, their activities nevertheless have profound consequences for people and things in the natural world. In fact, as this book explores, the artificial, legal construction of identity and responsibility has produced a Swiss-cheese pattern of rules and holes. The picture is hard to see from the vantage point of one legal regime alone: International law has certain expectations, objects, and concerns, and national laws have a separate set. The interface between the two leaves gaps. The picture is also not complete when you consider how domestic and international legal regimes apply to only one of these actors: the state or the firm.[1] Layering both actors and regimes together offers a new way of understanding what exactly the law is doing, and not doing.

The project of this book is, therefore, synthetic in that it is placing diverse things together to try to create a new form of coherence. It combines analysis of two kinds of artificial entities – states and firms – and two regimes – national law and international law – to try to better understand the way law builds and maintains the identity of entities. Specifically, it tries to better understand how this legal construction of entities leads to responsibility gaps.

---

[1] International lawyers tend to use the term "domestic" or "municipal" law to refer to the internal laws of a nation, as distinct from international laws. *See, e.g.*, John H. Jackson, *Status of Treaties in Domestic Legal Systems: A Policy Analysis*, 86 AM. J. INT. L. 310 n.2 (1992) (noting this usage).

There are many potential points of entry for such a project. Indeed, this book builds on rich literatures in corporate social responsibility,[2] business and human rights,[3] theories of the firm,[4] and conceptions of state sovereignty and responsibility.[5] Each of these addresses one or more aspects of the volume's central question about how law constructs the identities and responsibilities of firms and states.

This book begins its analysis from the concept of attribution. "Attribution" is a term of art with a defined meaning in international law, as I will review shortly.[6] "Attribution" also has a defined meaning in domestic corporate law, where it is related to the law of agency.[7] Beyond these specific doctrines, the concept itself does work that is helpful for this project. "Attribution," according to the *Cambridge English Dictionary*, is "the act of saying or thinking that something is the result or work of a particular person or thing."[8] The *Collins Dictionary* offers another formulation: "Attribution" is "the act of attributing; ascription," and, in an archaic usage, an "authority or function assigned, as to a ruler, legislative assembly, delegate, or the like."[9]

Attribution is a useful concept for the purposes of this volume because the noun characterizes an activity: the *act* of ascribing something to someone. This is helpful because the book is trying to draw attention to the idea that the law is actively constructing artificial entities. Attribution has synonyms, such as "ascription," "charge," "credit," and "blame."[10] Artificial entities do not have innate characteristics or identities, but

[2] Archie B. Carroll, *Corporate Social Responsibility: Evolution of a Definitional Construct*, 38 BUS. SOC. 268 (1999) (reviewing the literature).

[3] *See, e.g.*, GWYNNE L. SKINNER, TRANSNATIONAL CORPORATIONS AND HUMAN RIGHTS (2020); Anita Ramasastry, *Corporate Social Responsibility versus Business and Human Rights: Bridging the Gap between Responsibility and Accountability*, 14 J. HUM. RTS. 237 (2015); John Ruggie, *Business and Human Rights: The Evolving International Agenda*, 101 AM. J. INT'L L. 819 (2007); Stephen Ratner, *Corporations and Human Rights: A Theory of Legal Responsibility*, 111 YALE L.J. (2001).

[4] *See, e.g.*, FRANK H. EASTERBROOK & DANIEL R. FISCHEL, THE ECONOMIC STRUCTURE OF CORPORATE LAW (1991) (shareholder primacy); Margaret M. Blair & Lynn A. Stout, *A Team Production Theory of Corporate Law*, 85 VA. L. REV. 247 (1999) (team production theory); GRANT M. HAYDEN & MATTHEW T. BODIE, RECONSTRUCTING THE CORPORATION: FROM SHAREHOLDER PRIMACY TO SHARED GOVERNANCE (2020) (reviewing "stakeholderism" and proposing democratic participation). For theories of the firm in an international legal context, *see, e.g.*, Fleur Johns, *Theorizing the Corporation in International Law*, in THE OXFORD HANDBOOK OF THE THEORY OF INTERNATIONAL LAW 635 (Anne Orford & Florian Hoffman eds., 2016); JOSHUA BARKAN, CORPORATE SOVEREIGNTY (2013); Jose E. Alvarez, *Are Corporations "Subjects" of International Law?*, 9 SANTA CLARA J. INT'L L. 1 (2011).

[5] *See, e.g.*, André Nollkaemper, *Responsibility*, in CONCEPTS FOR INTERNATIONAL LAW 760 (Jean d'Aspremont & Sahib Singh, eds., 2019) (reviewing the literature on state responsibility).

[6] *See infra*, notes 35–38, and accompanying discussion.

[7] *See* Restatement (Third) of Agency §2 (2006) (offering "[p]rinciples of attribution," which define when an agent acts with the authority of a principal).

[8] Attribution, CAMBRIDGE DICTIONARY, https://dictionary.cambridge.org/us/dictionary/english/attribution.

[9] Attribution, COLLINS DICTIONARY, www.collinsdictionary.com/us/dictionary/english/attribution.

[10] *Id.*

ascribed ones. A person or a thing can be ascribed characteristics, activities, intentions, functions, or authority. The book considers the law's diverse ways of saying that characteristics, functions, authorities, rights, credit, or blame belong to a firm or state.

If the starting point for the book is attribution, its ending point is responsibility. That is, the book is trying to understand how law attributes various characteristics to firms and states so that it can better explain how the law assigns responsibility for harms, or fails to do so. If attribution is "saying … that something is the result or work of a particular person or thing,"[11] then attribution enables judgments about responsibility. How does the law determine that something is the work of a firm or a state, and assign consequences?

One reason for the Swiss-cheese–like legal construction of responsibility is that states and firms are both *transnational actors*. They are rooted, supposedly, within the territorial boundaries of the nation-state.[12] But their activities and effects are not so confined.[13] After all, territorial boundaries and borders are artificial creations as well.[14] The transnational activity of firms and states can fall into an interstitial space, not adequately captured by either domestic or international regimes.

Other responsibility gaps exist because of the *pliability of the entity form*, which allows states and firms to trade roles, hide behind each other, and exploit uncertainty.[15] For example, governments sometimes shrink themselves: They outsource activities to private actors, privatizing utilities, jails, border security, or even military functions.[16] Alternately, governments sometimes expand into the market, owning or controlling companies and using ownership to accomplish policy objectives.[17]

---

[11] CAMBRIDGE DICTIONARY, *supra* note 2.

[12] PETER T. MUCHLINSKI, MULTINATIONAL ENTERPRISES AND THE LAW ix (2d ed. 2007) ("[I]f one were to look at legal sources alone, the [multinational enterprise] would not exist: all one would find is a series of national companies.").

[13] Eyal Benvenisti, *Sovereigns as Trustees of Humanity: On the Accountability of States to Foreign Stakeholders*, 107 AM. J. INT'L L. 295 (2013) ("[T]oday's [sovereignty] … is more analogous to owning a small apartment in one densely packed high-rise that is home to two hundred separate families."); MUCHLINSKI, *supra* note 8, at 8 (transnational activity of multinational business enterprises can "affect the international allocation of productive resources").

[14] Gail Lythcoe, *Distinct Persons; Distinct Territories: Rethinking the Spaces of International Organizations*, 19 INT'L ORG. L. REV. 365, 367 (2022) (territory is a "socially produced space").

[15] E.g., Julian Arato, *The Elastic Corporate Form in International Law*, 62 VA. J. INT'L L. 383, 384–87 (2022) (investor–state dispute settlement tribunals address corporate formalities in an inconsistent manner that results in an "elastic" or "plastic" corporate form).

[16] See MICHAEL J. STRAUSS, HOSTILE BUSINESS AND THE SOVEREIGN STATE: PRIVATIZED GOVERNANCE, STATE SECURITY AND INTERNATIONAL LAW (2019) (describing and assessing the "massive worldwide shift of state activities to the private sector since the late 1970s"); *see generally* SUSAN STRANGE, THE RETREAT OF THE STATE: THE DIFFUSION OF POWER IN THE WORLD ECONOMY (1996) (observing the declining authority of states and a growing diffusion of power and authority to impersonal market forces and agents other than states).

[17] *See, e.g.*, Curtis Milhaupt, *The State as Owner: China's Experience*, 36 OXFORD REV. ECON. POL'Y 362, 362–65 (2020) (in the twenty-first century the state-owned entity "has proliferated and evolved into a major player in the global economy"; "many governments have 'rediscovered' [state-owned entities] as useful instruments for dealing with specific policy objectives").

The fact that governments can expand and contract in this way demonstrates the artificiality of boundaries between "state" and "firm." International law has little to say about what functions are "governmental,"[18] leaving this to domestic law. But most domestic entity laws have no special reason for concern about privatization, state ownership, or the responsibility of states for internationally wrongful acts. International law's entity agnosticism and domestic law's identity minimalism can create room for regulatory arbitrage and leave responsibility gaps.

Another explanation for responsibility gaps is the opportunistic *cocreation of firms and states*. Firms and states have constructed each other over time through facilitation and borrowing, as several chapters in this volume show,[19] and they can do so in ways that are less focused on public goods than "quelling societal conflict and securing group or class power."[20]

Because they draw on different areas of law, questions about attribution of entity identity and responsibility are often considered separately, fragmented by doctrinal boundaries. Yet, the law can function across regimes to facilitate harmful effects – the consolidation of power or resources, and the avoidance of consequences for harm. Attribution questions both broaden and narrow the aperture. They allow for a focused discussion across legal regimes: How does the law conceive of the entity of the state and of the firm? What values does it advance? Does it promote accountability and fairness? Predictability? Is it coherent enough to advance values?

The ultimate aim of the book is to highlight the potential malleability of law. Exposing the fundamental contingency of the legal construction of entities should also expose the law's vulnerability to change. That is, if the law constructs firms and states, it can also deconstruct and reconstruct them.

---

[18] *See* STRAUSS, *supra* note 11, at 5–6 (describing the "absence of an international standard for the functions that a government must exercise"); *see also* Frédéric Mégret, *Are There "Inherently Sovereign Functions" in International Law?*, 115 AM. J. INT'L L. 452, 452 (2021) ("[I]nternational law has sometimes appeared agnostic ... about ... privatization" but places some very limited constraints on functions a sovereign state can outsource.).

[19] *See, e.g.,* Doreen Lustig, "The Enduring Charter: Corporations, States, and International Law," *infra*, Chapter 5; James Gathii & Olabisi Akinkugbe, "Corporate Structures and the Attribution Dilemma in Multinational Enterprises," *infra*, Chapter 6; David Ciepley, "The Juridical Person of the State: Origins and Implications," *infra*, Chapter 12; Joshua Barkan, "Corporate Personhood as Legal and Literary Fiction," *infra*, Chapter 13; *see also* Taisu Zhang & John Morley, *The Rise of the Modern State and the Business Corporation*, 132 YALE L.J. (2023) ("[T]hroughout history, the rise of the modern state has almost always been a necessary precondition for the rise of the modern business corporation.").

[20] Joshua Barkan, "Corporate Personhood as Legal and Literary Fiction," *infra* Chapter 13. Sundhya Pahuja describes this relationship as a "rivalry over public authority." Sundhya Pahuja, *Public Debt, the Peace of Utrecht, and the Rivalry between Company and State, in* THE 1713 PEACE OF UTRECHT AND ITS ENDURING EFFECTS (Alfred Soons, ed., 2016) (characterizing the parties in this relationship as the "sovereign-territorial arrangements we now call the state" and "the commercial-political groupings of merchants associated in the juridical form of the joint-stock company").

IMAGINATION, FICTIONS, AND CONSEQUENCES

Consider some of the particular concerns that motivate the project of this book. Again, abstract entities are "things" only because the law makes them so. This requires an act of "legal imagination."[21] Attributing rights and duties to an abstract entity requires a conceptual story explaining why a set of individuals or activities belongs to a single thing. It involves a choice about how to aggregate individuals into a legally cognizable whole.

Sometimes, this choice is based on a metaphor: To structure thinking and guide decisions about rights and duties, a corporation is a "person"; a state is a "sovereign." Sometimes, the choice is the product of a set of incremental and historically contingent facts: A right or responsibility seems inherently "sovereign" because the state has generally monopolized it, or a firm is shielded from international legal obligation because it has long been considered "private." Theoretically, one could instead use first principles, or an instrumentalist approach to attributing identity and responsibility. In the case of firms and states, however, legal actors have leaned into storytelling modes of metaphors and traditions.

Each of these bases for attributing identity and responsibility – the metaphor, the historical legacy – brings a separate set of consequences. One potential consequence of a metaphor is that it can take on a life of its own in the minds of legal actors, expanding over time. Does "personhood" characterize the firm only for the purposes of legal standing in court, or does it also entitle the firm to human rights or constitutional protections? What exactly is a corporate person? The metaphor can escape the confines of a legal fiction – an untrue but legally convenient shorthand[22] – and become an organizing conceptual principle. At the same time, a potential consequence of historical tradition as a basis for attributing identity and responsibility is path dependence. The law can ossify even as the underlying context evolves.

Questions about the theoretical and conceptual bases for attribution are not purely academic. Legal choices about attribution have sweeping consequences. In international law, scholars and practitioners struggle to attribute behavior – and thus responsibility – to states in areas as diverse as military contracting, environmental accountability, human rights, international investment, and cyber espionage and warfare.[23] States can often avoid attribution of responsibility in these areas by privatizing their functions, outsourcing key responsibilities to firms.[24] Sometimes,

---

[21] Martti Koskenniemi, To the Uttermost Parts of the Earth (2021) (offering a "history of the legal imagination as it operates in relationship to the use of power").

[22] Lon Fuller, Legal Fictions 9 (1967) ("A fiction is either (1) a statement propounded with complete or partial consciousness of its falsity, or (2) a false statement recognized as having utility.").

[23] See James Crawford, State Responsibility: The General Part 205 (2013) (laying out these debates).

[24] See, e.g., Alex Mills, *State Responsibility and Privatisation: Accommodating Private Conduct in a Public Framework*, EJIL:Talk! Blog (Aug. 4, 2021) at www.ejiltalk.org/

the state outsources to a firm in which the state itself holds a significant ownership stake. Those firms, in turn, avoid responsibility under international law by operating below the level of international personhood. They are not traditionally "subjects" of international law, and so do not hold internationally recognized rights or duties.[25] At the same time, these firms avoid responsibility in national jurisdictions by organizing in complex transnational parent–subsidiary structures, creating globally dispersed families of entities and nimbly organizing and reorganizing subsidiaries to take advantage of jurisdictions with favorable laws or enforcement environments.[26] The law resists attributing responsibility to a corporate parent for acts taken by a subsidiary because veil-piercing doctrines preserve the fictitious legal separateness of entities, even while proceeds flow freely between them.[27]

Each of these exclusions of responsibility by the state and the firm is facilitated by legal doctrines that demarcate the boundaries of an artificial entity and cut off responsibility at those boundaries. Attribution doctrines allow the entities to retract into narrow, sharply drawn confines that protect them from consequences such as international responsibility or financial liability. The firm and state use attribution doctrines as shields to avoid responsibility.

The firm and the state also use attribution doctrines as swords to claim rights. The state has long relied on its status as a sovereign to claim certain prerogatives.[28] It holds territorial dominion, jurisdiction, immunities, and a monopoly on the legitimate use of force, among other rights.[29] In the United States, the corporation has been on a steady campaign to claim rights deriving from its status as a "person."[30] Most recently, corporate claims to the rights of personhood have produced

---

state-responsibility-and-privatisation-accommodating-private-conduct-in-a-public-framework/ (privatization "is often designed to transfer control and thus responsibility away from the state"); *see generally* RICHARD MACKENZIE-GRAY SCOTT, STATE RESPONSIBILITY FOR NON-STATE ACTORS (2022) (examining and critiquing the attribution of responsibility doctrines).

[25] 1 LASSA OPPENHEIM, INTERNATIONAL LAW: A TREATISE 341 (1905) ("Since the Law of Nations is a law between States only and exclusively, States only and exclusively are subjects of the Law of Nations."); *see generally* MARKOS KARAVIAS, CORPORATE OBLIGATIONS UNDER INTERNATIONAL LAW (2013).

[26] *See, e.g.,* Gwynne Skinner, *Rethinking Limited Liability of Parent Corporations for Foreign Subsidiaries' Violations of International Human Rights Law,* 72 WASH. LEE L. REV. 1769, 1799 (2015) (noting these responsibility gaps); *see also* Rachel Brewster & Philip J. Stern, *Introduction to the Proceedings of the Seminar on Corporations and International Law,* 28 DUKE J. COMP. INT. L. 413 (2018) (describing corporations as "jurisdictionally ambiguous and spatially diffuse").

[27] *See, e.g.,* Rachel Brewster, *Enabling ESG Accountability: Focusing on the Corporate Enterprise,* 2022 WISC. L. REV. 1367 (2022); Skinner, *supra* note 26; Arato, *supra* note 15.

[28] Daniel Lee, *Defining the Rights of Sovereignty,* 115 AJIL UNBOUND 322, 324–25 (2021).

[29] *See, e.g.,* Nigel D. White, *Outsourcing Military and Security Functions,* 115 AJIL UNBOUND 317 (2021) (monopoly on use of force); *see generally* OPPENHEIM'S INTERNATIONAL LAW 432 (Robert Jennings & Arthur Watts eds., 2008).

[30] *See, e.g.,* Adam Winkler, *The Long History of Corporate Rights,* 98 BOSTON U. L. REV. ONLINE 64 (2018) ("Today, corporations have nearly every right a corporation might want under the [U.S.] Constitution: free speech, freedom of religion, Fourth Amendment privacy rights, due process, equal protection, property rights.").

headlining debates among U.S. scholars and in the popular press about whether these entities can claim constitutionally protected speech rights, moral identity, and religious beliefs. Each of these claims can shift responsibility away from the firm and shield it from consequences.

Attribution doctrines and their consequences have produced extensive but siloed literatures. Scholarship on the international legal doctrine of attribution of responsibility for an internationally wrongful act is significant and continues to grow.[31] A robust business and human rights literature has scrutinized the moral hazard and human rights consequences of protecting separate entity status in the transnational context.[32] Interest in the nature and consequences of corporate personhood remains keen.[33] Notwithstanding the volume of analysis in each of these literatures – and in adjacent disciplines such as political theory, history, and international relations – they are not often in conversation, even as they increasingly intersect.

The project of this book is to bring together conversations about entity construction and its consequences in these three distinct legal spaces: international, transnational, and domestic. Contributors to this volume bring diverse kinds of expertise. The volume includes established experts and rising stars in international law, business and human rights, constitutional and corporate law, history, geography, and political theory.[34] Contributors have been invited to consider the common theme – attribution of identity and responsibility to states and firms – across these three legal domains: international, transnational, and domestic. Contributions explore the theoretical, doctrinal, and conceptual choices that drive attribution of identity and responsibility for states and firms. They focus especially on attribution questions at

---

[31] Several notable contributions on attribution of responsibility for the conduct of private actors include Marko Milanovic, *Special Rules of Attribution of Conduct in International Law*, 96 INT. L. STUD. 295 (2020); Judith Schönsteiner, *Attribution of State Responsibility for Actions or Omissions of State-Owned Enterprises in Human Rights Matters*, 40 U. PENN. J. INT. L. 895 (2019); Vladyslav Lanovoy, *The Use of Force by Non-State Actors and the Limits of Attribution of Conduct*, 28 EUR. J. INT. L. 563 (2017); Oona A. Hathaway, et al., *Ensuring Responsibility: Common Article 1 and State Responsibility for Non-State Actors*, 95 TEX. L. REV. 539 (2017); Kristen E. Boon, *Are Control Tests Fit for the Future? The Slippage Problem in Attribution Doctrines*, 15 MELB. J. INT. L. 330 (2014); *see also* André Nollkaemper et al., *Guiding Principles on Shared Responsibility in International Law*, 31 EUR. J. INT. L. 15 (2020).

[32] *See, e.g.*, Brewster, *supra* note 27; GWYNNE L. SKINNER ET AL., TRANSNATIONAL CORPORATIONS AND HUMAN RIGHTS (2020).

[33] *See, e.g.*, ADAM WINKLER, WE THE CORPORATIONS: HOW AMERICAN BUSINESSES WON THEIR CIVIL RIGHTS (2019); SUSANNA KIM RIPKIN, CORPORATE PERSONHOOD (2019); VISA A.J. KURKI, A THEORY OF LEGAL PERSONHOOD (2019); ANNA GREAR, REDIRECTING HUMAN RIGHTS: FACING THE CHALLENGE OF CORPORATE LEGAL HUMANITY (2010).

[34] To promote a dialogue between the authors and the eventual chapters, contributors to the volume were invited to a two-day conference cohosted by the Dean Rusk International Law Center at the University of Georgia, and the International Legal Theory Interest Group of the American Society of International Law. Authors were encouraged to read and discuss all the draft chapters. Each was also asked to lead discussion on a contribution from a different doctrinal or disciplinary area than the author's own.

the dividing line of these two entities, and on areas where attribution questions are currently most live in theory and practice.

The book moves through the three legal domains – international, transnational, domestic – in that order, though there are interconnections and themes that run through all three. The first part focuses on attributing responsibility for internationally wrongful acts; the second part on attributing responsibility for externalities across the conceptual boundaries of territory and separate entity status; and the third part on attribution of identity characteristics to abstract entities. The fourth part offers cross-disciplinary context. Next, we turn to a preview of the progression between these themes and the contributions within each part.

INTERNATIONAL ATTRIBUTION

In international law, attribution is associated with the law of the international responsibility of states for wrongful acts. It is the "legal fiction which assimilates the actions or omissions of state officials to the state itself and which renders the state liable for damage."[35] According to the International Law Commission's (the ILC's) classic articulation of the rule of state responsibility, the conduct of a private actor can be attributed to the state when it is performed by an agent or organ of the state, acting under the state's direction or control, performing "elements of the governmental authority," or later adopted by the state.[36] This formulation has been widely accepted as authoritative, and it was confirmed by the International Court of Justice in the *Bosnia* case.[37] However, it harbors ambiguities that even the ILC acknowledges, and offers little theoretical substance to answer newly pressing questions. For example, in the context of a state that has disaggregated and privatized many traditionally "sovereign" functions, with diverse forms of state investment in private entities, who obtains the legal rights and responsibilities of the state? How should doctrinal tests navigate increasingly murky lines of ownership and control between the state and private entities? And how and when should responsibility be shared between entities?

The book begins with a chapter by Kristen E. Boon, "Attribution in International Law: Challenges and Evolution."[38] Boon argues that the attribution doctrines within the regime of international responsibility for internationally wrongful acts are premised on a vision of the state that is both culturally embedded and increasingly outdated. Boon points out that the rules governing attribution of responsibility were developed "before the rapid hollowing out of the state" due to widespread

---

[35] MALCOLM N. SHAW, INTERNATIONAL LAW 595 (8th ed. 2017).

[36] Int'l Law Comm'n, Rep. on the Work of Its Fifty-Third Session, U.N. Doc. A/56/10, at 38–42 (2001); *see also* Kristen E. Boon, "Attribution in International Law: Challenges & Evolution," *infra* Chapter 2.

[37] Application of the Convention on the Prevention and Punishment of the Crime of Genocide (*Bosn. and Herz. v. Serb. and Montenegro*), Judgment, 2007 I.C.J. Reports at 43 (Feb. 2007).

[38] Boon, *infra* Chapter 2.

outsourcing of previously governmental functions such as "prisons, immigration services, and security," which has produced closer connections between states and corporations. The rules also imagine a "limited state," more common to western liberal democracies than other contexts, such as China and Norway, where state-owned entities proliferate. Boon explores these doctrinal limitations in the context of international investment law, where tribunals have grappled with the question of when "effective" control by the state over private conduct exists, and what functions provided by private entities are sufficiently "governmental" to pierce the veil between a private entity and the state, whose interests the private entity serves. The failure of international attribution rules to imagine the potentially extensive links between firms and states has created an accountability gap that shields state actors from international legal responsibility for private acts, protects firms from responsibility as international legal persons, and bars claimants from access to remedies.

Also drawing on the extensive jurisprudence of international investment tribunals, Mikko Rajavuori argues in "Between States and Firms: Attribution and Construction of the Shareholder State" that the attribution doctrines can influence how states organize their ownership interests in private entities.[39] Rajavuori shows that when investment tribunals are confronted with attribution questions in the context of entities with a state ownership interest, the tribunals construct a "hypothetical ordinary shareholder" and compare state behavior to that fictitious, imagined standard. The tribunals conceptualize shareholders' *"ordinary* roles, competencies, and interests, as well of those of *ordinary* company law and ... *ordinary* commercial interests," finding that the state avoids attribution of responsibility if state ownership does not stray outside of these "ordinary" roles. States, understandably, respond by organizing their ownership interests accordingly. They use the tribunals' fictitious ordinary as a "template for managing the relationship" between themselves and market actors they partially own. Over time, therefore, applying the attribution doctrines becomes an exercise in the "legal construction of state shareholders."

As Chapters 2 and 3 noted, one method by which states can avoid international responsibility is by outsourcing their agendas to private actors. The problem, as Laura A. Dickinson diagnoses it, is the law of state responsibility's "overly formalist reliance on purportedly clear dividing lines between what is state and what is non-state," which breaks down in practice.[40] In "Contractors and Hybrid Warfare: A Pluralist Approach to Reforming the Law of State Responsibility," Dickinson argues that states that do not embrace the rules-based international order can flout that order when they hire private military contractors who then "commit atrocities or flout other substantive international legal rules." Dickinson offers a case study

---

[39] Mikko Rajavuori, "Between States and Firms: Attribution and Construction of the Shareholder State," *infra* Chapter 3.

[40] Laura A. Dickinson, "Contractors and Hybrid Warfare: A Pluralist Approach to Reforming the Law of State Responsibility," *infra* Chapter 4.

focused on the Wagner Group, to which Russia has seemingly outsourced many military and security functions. Dickinson proposes a functional approach to attribution, focusing on questions such as: How is private power being used to aggrandize state power and in what ways are the state actors and the non-state actors so intertwined that they become part of the same legal activity? She proposes that the attribution rules ought to assess whether the contractor is "performing a role that is governmental – one that is considered to be in the inherent or core domain of a government." The core normative insight driving this reform is the idea that governments should not be able to evade responsibility by shifting their "inherent" or "core" activities to contractors.

One theme running through these three chapters is that the international attribution rules are based on a particular conception of the state that is overly rigid and frozen in time. Not only are these rules pinned to a fixed and outdated concept of the state, but they continue to lose ground by inadvertently disciplining future behavior by state-owned, state-controlled, or state-related entities. These entities learn to adapt to the attribution rules over time, constituting themselves and their behavior to fall on the *private* or *ordinary corporate* side of the public/private divide, thus operating below the level of international law. This is not a new phenomenon, as the next chapter shows.

In "The Enduring Charter: Corporations, States, and International Law," Doreen Lustig traces the origins and effects of what she calls the "separate spheres presumption" in international law. This is the basic presumption that states are "public" entities and business enterprises are "private" ones; the presumption is useful to "private" enterprises in that it serves to shield them from international legal scrutiny.[41] Lustig weaves together an origin story for this presumption that focuses on the end of the nineteenth century, homing in on the formal end of the corporate charter as a monopolistic device that granted corporations sovereign governance privileges in their colonies. With the end of the charter, lawyers began to view corporations as formally separated from the state. This formal legal separation obscured the persisting "deep interdependence" between the entities. Moreover, rather than producing greater regulation of private entities by governments, this formal legal separation rendered their close relationship "informal and flexible." Because corporations were identified as falling on the "private" side of the public–private divide, they became invisible under international law.

The post-charter "separate spheres" presumption has had a substantial influence on the development of international law, Lustig observes. Corporations have come to be "conceived by international law as 'nationals' in the context of diplomatic protection or 'investors' and 'individuals' in international investment law and international human rights" but "that nexus of nationality was not a sufficient basis for

---

[41] Doreen Lustig, "The Enduring Charter: Corporations, States, and International Law," *infra* Chapter 5.

state responsibility" over their activities. Moreover, corporations exercise formal and informal regulatory authority themselves, blurring "the distinction between the corporation as a private individual and the state as the architype for public governance authority." Thus, "during the post-charter era, the international legal doctrines of state responsibility, diplomatic protection, human rights, and investment law weaved a veil that concealed much of the activities of corporations from legal scrutiny and nurtured the alliance between powerful governments and commercial corporations."

The result of this historical legacy, which continues to today, seems to be overly formalist conceptions of state and firm. These operate to exclude the behavior of states from international scrutiny when states outsource that behavior to private firms, even when those firms are wholly or partially state owned. These formalist demarcations also operate to exclude the behavior of firms, as they are conceived as private and, thus, below the level of scrutiny of international law. Nevertheless, moving below the level of international law to domestic law, there is another accountability gap at the transnational level, as the next part reviews.

TRANSNATIONAL ATTRIBUTION

When an abstract entity is not held accountable under international law because, for instance, it is found to be a private company and not a state, then the relevant law will be national law, known to international lawyers as "domestic" law. In other words, moving one rung down from the international legal context to the transnational context, national laws dictate how and when to attribute conduct to abstract entities that may commit wrongful acts, even when those entities are part of sprawling multinational corporate families. This transnational attribution involves questions of jurisdiction and extraterritoriality: Will a government apply its laws to a "foreign" entity organized under the laws of a foreign jurisdiction? Will a state apply its laws to conduct occurring outside its borders?

The transnational attribution question involves another area of extreme formalism based on a legal fiction. Domestic law doctrines will almost exclusively preserve the artificial legal "separateness" of entities, resisting the call to "pierce the corporate veil" and disregard that separateness for the purposes of attributing behavior from one entity to another.[42] Thus, when entities wholly own or control each other, the law permits financial proceeds to flow up from subsidiaries to parents, while cutting off liability for torts and contractual breach at the artificial borders of each entity.[43] Entities can organize corporate children all around the world. Proceeds of actions taken in those far-flung jurisdictions flow upward from corporate subsidiaries to parents and on to their shareholders, most often from the developed world,

---

[42] Brewster, *supra* note 27; *see also* SKINNER, *supra* note 32.
[43] Skinner, *supra* note 12, at 1807–08.

while the upstream entities remain free from the burden of liability. That liability stays grounded with the often minimally funded corporate child, far from home.[44]

The result of these national law doctrines that preserve the separateness of entities despite their financial interdependence is another set of accountability gaps. Entities below the level of international law evade accountability under national law by doing business in jurisdictions unequipped to hold them to account, or at levels of capitalization that will not suffice to make victims whole. As the first chapter in this section shows, the accountability gap is complicated in the context of financial liabilities because separate entity status can also facilitate corruption.

In "Corporate Structures and the Attribution Dilemma in Multinational Enterprises," James T. Gathii and Olabisi D. Akinkugbe observe that the structural complexity of multinational enterprises operating in developing countries, particularly Africa, creates difficulties for domestic jurisdictions seeking to attribute tax responsibilities and financial liabilities to the appropriate entity.[45] Attribution of financial liabilities is particularly problematic for poorly resourced developing countries that host corporate subsidiaries. The problem is worsened in Africa by the involvement of domestic elites who complicate attribution questions through various forms of opportunistic and corrupt behavior. The story begins with colonialism, Gathii and Akinkugbe show, and specifically the strategies of transnational enterprises anxious to reinvent themselves from "guardians of the colonial order" to "partners in building the new post-colonial states." To avoid a post-colonial legitimacy crisis and curry favor with African governments, multinational corporations have adopted "Africanization" policies, such as recruiting African elites as officers and directors, which has allowed "transnational capitalist elites" to siphon public funds, block investigations, and generally create conduits for illicit financial flows. Legal rules that attribute liabilities among the members of a transnational corporate family are inadequate if they do not account for this complex post-colonial context.

Taking as a given that separate entity status produces an accountability gap in the transnational context, academic debates in this area principally focus on how to address it. Existing conversations have focused on whether entity separateness should be set aside in the context of vast corporate families, with up to thousands of subsidiaries around the world. Should entity separateness be set aside when harms are foreseeable? When conduct is particularly hazardous? When the parent meddles too much, or when it was inadequately diligent?

The following two chapters explore out-of-the-box approaches to these questions. Perhaps, Kishanthi Parella suggests, *reputational* attribution can help address the

---

[44] As Doreen Lustig observes, the governance gap results from "[t]he regulatory weakness of host states and limited to no regulatory responsibility of home states." *See infra* Chapter 5.

[45] James Gathii & Olabisi Akinkugbe, "Corporate Structures and the Attribution Dilemma in Multinational Enterprises," *infra* Chapter 6.

gap? Or perhaps, Dalia Palombo proposes, we need a new conceptual frame that binds corporations to society with a social contract? Both approaches take as an inevitable given that corporations will continue to enjoy the protection of the fiction of separate entity status – a seemingly necessary condition as a political matter, although not as a conceptual or legal one.

In "Transnational Blame Attribution: The Limits of Using Reputational Sanctions to Punish Corporate Misconduct," Parella lays out the landscape: Because attributing responsibility among members of complex transnational families of entities presents an array of difficult challenges, including home state reluctance to enforce laws over foreign domestic subsidiaries operating abroad, legal sanctions may be wholly inadequate.[46] Reputational sanctions can offer a complementary strategy, Parella proposes. She unpacks the legal difficulties by exploring a case study: a prominent recent U.S. Supreme Court case, *Doe v. Nestle*, which reflects U.S. courts' "unwillingness to recognize causation between the types of corporate decision-making that occurred in the United States and the harms suffered elsewhere." The reason is the United States' restrictive presumption against the extraterritorial application of its statutes – a presumption mirrored in the comity doctrines of other capital-exporting countries. Legal rules may, however, facilitate the operation of reputational markets, which can trigger penalties that "magnify the costs of the misconduct, thereby (hopefully) encouraging companies to alter their conduct for the better going forward." Nevertheless, reputational sanctions are not a panacea. Blame attribution is difficult in both the legal and reputational contexts for factual reasons ("lack of information concerning what happened … why it happened …, and by whose hand it happened…."), and normative reasons – neither legal systems nor reputation markets have figured out who, in complex production and consumption networks, is to blame for the externalities of this system.

In "Mind the Agency Gap in Corporate Social Responsibility," Palombo widens the aperture, looking beyond the individual doctrinal hurdles that prevent attribution of harmful conduct from subsidiaries to corporate parents.[47] These doctrinal gaps are attributable to a larger failure of law to define principles of corporate accountability to society, Palombo claims. Existing frameworks for corporate accountability are inadequate: corporate social responsibility involves only voluntary commitments, not legal obligations, and corporate accountability to shareholders does not address harms to the rest of society. For states, by contrast, social contracts embedded in constitutions and public law set the terms of the relationship between society and its government, transforming public officials into agents, and society

---

[46] Kishanthi Parella, "Transnational Blame Attribution: The Limits of Using Reputational Sanctions to Punish Corporate Misconduct," *infra* Chapter 7.

[47] Dalia Palombo, "Mind the Agency Gap in Corporate Social Responsibility," *infra* Chapter 8.

into the principal. Corporations already have important relationships with society: they accomplish public goods, control the means of production, and produce externalities. There is no principled reason why society should not have a social contract with corporate actors as it does with states, which would transform those entities into agents accountable to society, Palombo asserts. Since this framework has not yet been established, or even imagined, Palombo concludes that we are in the "prehistory of corporate social accountability."

The fiction of separate entity status creates rigid segmentation of responsibility, these chapters have observed; and the problem is compounded when that status facilitates corruption, restrictive extraterritoriality doctrines, and normative uncertainty about what responsibilities corporations should bear. The result is that harms can be externalized, with responsibility for them safely squirreled away within the confines of individual, far-flung, undercapitalized entities. While capital comes home, liabilities do not. The solution these chapters suggest is either incremental – a turn to reputational levers, or an acknowledgment of post-colonial context – or it is radical – a dismantling of separate entity status, or an entirely new social contract between firms and society.

DOMESTIC ATTRIBUTION

At the same time that corporations assert the protections of separate entity status to defend against liability for human rights violations, they have also used that entity status and its accompanying personhood metaphor to seize rights that belong to human persons. While concepts of corporate personhood reach as far back as Roman law, corporate personhood in the U.S. context expanded in the nineteenth century with the end of slavery and the passage of the 14th Amendment.[48] It originally comprised the legal right to sue and be sued, then "expanded fairly quickly until it had rendered the corporation a rights-holder, like a natural person."[49] This legal status has recently received intense academic and popular interest.

Debates about the nature and identity of a corporation have been disciplined by the compelling metaphor of personhood – which entities use as a tool to claim more rights. However, the metaphor functions imperfectly as a legal principle, that is, as a coherent rationale for assigning rights to artificial persons. A flurry

---

[48] *See infra* Chapter 12 at n38. While this portion of the book focuses principally on corporate identity debates within the United States, these relate to important discussions about corporate identity under international and European human rights law. *See, e.g.*, Silvia Steininger & Jochen von Bernstorff, *Who Turned Multinational Corporations into Bearers of Human Rights? On the Creation of Corporate "Human" Rights in International Law*, in CONTINGENCY IN INTERNATIONAL LAW: ON THE POSSIBILITY OF DIFFERENT LEGAL HISTORIES 280, 290 (Ingo Venzke & Kevin Jon Heller eds., 2021); GREAR, *supra* note 33; UPENDRA BAXI, THE FUTURE OF HUMAN RIGHTS (2008); Andreas Kulick, *Corporate Human Rights?*, 32 EUR. J. INT. L. 537 (2021).

[49] *See infra* Chapter 9 at n50.

of recent scholarship in the United States responds to the U.S. Supreme Court's recent struggles to define what, precisely, the corporate person is. This inquiry has been precipitated by corporate claims for constitutional speech rights, exemptions from regulation on the ground of moral identity, and immunity from liability for matters that require a mental state, among other matters. Each of these issues raises questions of identity attribution. What is the principle by which features of human personhood – speech, mind, moral soul – should be attributed to artificial entities? As the following chapters show, the personhood fiction and metaphor break down under scrutiny.

In "To Whom Should We Attribute a Corporation's Speech?" Sarah C. Haan handily deconstructs the "facile" metaphor of corporate personhood in the context of corporate speech. Her argument is conceptual and normative.[50] The personhood "conceit ... works poorly for speech attribution, because corporations share few of the characteristics of human persons that are relevant to speech production." Corporations produce speech through governance processes, rather than organic ones, and while human people may express themselves for the purposes of autonomy, self-realization, or "fulfillment," these concepts are meaningless in the context of corporations. "To ascribe to such artificial entities an 'intellect' or 'mind' for freedom of conscience purposes," she quotes U.S. Supreme Court Justice Rehnquist as saying, "is to confuse metaphor with reality." Nevertheless, U.S. jurisprudence on corporate speech attribution for constitutional purposes has historically done exactly that, with important implications. As Haan points out, in the realm of speech and expression, basing legal expressive rights on a concept of corporate personhood "expresses the normative judgment that corporations and human actors are functionally equal." The approach facilitates corporate power, sows confusion and distrust of corporate speech, and devalues human expression. Haan would have the law dispense with the fiction that corporate and human speakers are analogous for speech purposes, and instead base rights and responsibilities on the internal governance processes that produce corporate speech.

Benjamin P. Edwards, in "What Is a Corporate Mind? Mental State Attribution," explores an area of law where the personhood fiction appears to be useful to hold corporations to account for bad acts such as securities fraud.[51] But while the personhood fiction allows the law to bring business entities within the ambit of the criminal law, differences between human and corporate persons complicate the analysis and ultimately allow corporate persons to more easily evade scrutiny. The challenge is that attributing mental states to business entities "requires law to embrace a double fiction" that business entities "exist," and that they have the specific sorts of intent that can makes their conduct liable. Such a compound analysis

---

[50] Sarah C. Haan, "To Whom Should We Attribute a Corporation's Speech?," *infra* Chapter 9.
[51] Benjamin P. Edwards, "What Is a Corporate Mind? Mental State Attribution," *infra* Chapter 10.

challenges courts to "attribut[e] a mental state to a mindless legal fiction." The simplest approach might seem to be to locate this intent in a particular human responsible for the corporate decision, but Edwards rejects this approach. It would problematically absolve a corporation of liability for algorithmically produced decisions and fail to recognize the intentionality of the entity as a whole when bad acts are distributed across actors and cannot be traced to individuals. "Business entities today often behave more like octopi than humans.... One employee may make statements that another employee knows to be false," but "our law makes it unlikely that any mental state would be attributed to an entity for these acts – even though we would likely attribute intentionality if we understood the entity to function as a whole." The law should recognize this decentralization, but the personhood metaphor obscures it.

In "Who Is a Corporation? Attributing the Moral Might of the Corporate Form," Catherine A. Hardee observes that U.S. jurisprudence has begun to give corporations "deeply personal rights," including "the freedom of religion," while at the same time corporations face calls to express moral agency in response to societal problems like racism and climate change.[52] The result is widespread agreement from across the political spectrum that the corporation can generate and act upon moral principles. But who or what is the moral conscience of the entity? The question matters to legal rights when, for example, a corporation claims religious beliefs that exempt the entity from otherwise applicable laws regarding discrimination, or reproductive health care coverage. It may also be "desirable to ensure that those who are impacted by corporate moral decision making have a voice in the creation of the corporation's moral code." U.S. courts have nevertheless struggled to express a consistent theory of morality attribution. Here again, fictional personhood diverges from organic personhood. Only in the former instance does the question of morality attribution arise, yet the personhood, or "separate entity" construct cannot answer it. Hardee thus examines the playbill of potential individuals who may have a claim on the corporation's moral conscience – shareholders, management, employees, and consumers – and offers a nuanced analysis that would peg moral identity to different groups in different contexts. In particular, Hardee draws a distinction between "corporate ethics designed to supplant democratically imposed norms," which should require a heightened level of "true corporate democracy," and "corporate morality working within democratically set limits, [which] may raise fewer representation concerns."

Read together, these three chapters show the how the corporate personhood metaphor cannot offer a coherent rationale for corporate rights, although it has been offered as a legitimizer for them. Analogizing corporate persons to human persons would seem to suggest a "functional equality" between the two, such that

---

[52] Catherine A. Hardee, "Who Is a Corporation? Attributing the Moral Might of the Corporate Form," *infra* Chapter 11.

characteristics and rights attaching to the latter should also be attributed to the former.[53] But since personhood can create only juridical personality and not consciousness, it cannot endow corporate entities with the powers to which human rights attach, like self-expression, intention, and morality. Each of these must be traced back to individuals, a fact which the personhood metaphor obscures, rather than resolves.

POLITICAL AND CONCEPTUAL GENEALOGIES

The final section of the book develops origin stories for the current conceptual and doctrinal landscape. In particular, these chapters dig more deeply into the concept of juridical personhood to try to understand how this artificial entity status has come to carry the consequences explored in the previous chapters. The first takes a political history approach, while the second develops a conceptual genealogy. These chapters frame a poignant question: Why do lawyers keep trying to elaborate the personhood metaphor and render it knowable, when the metaphor is thin, holds limited uses, and has a distortive effect when read beyond those uses?

In "The Juridical Person of the State: Origins and Implications," David Ciepley finds the idea of juridical personhood to have been developed in the context of the Catholic church "by canon lawyers, who developed [it] into a robust body of rules for the external and internal operation of corporate bodies – a procedural and constitutional law for corporations. These rules were then applied to the largest 'corporate' bodies of all, the Church, Empire, commune, and kingdom." Two of these canonical ideas were "personification and officeholding," which allowed for the continuity of an entity beyond the lifetime or tenure of individuals. Juridical personhood expresses the concept that there is an entity, and not an individual human person, who "owns all the property, makes all the contracts, and appears in court in its own name rather than in the name of natural persons." To apply these ideas to the state, one had to square them with the idea of sovereignty. How can the state be both a sovereign maker of law and bound by the law? Ciepley says the answer is found in the Americans' experience as corporate colonies. Americans eschewed the idea of a lawless sovereign and wanted their government bound by law in the way that corporations are, so they adopted familiar corporate forms from their colonial experience: "written constitutional charters, constitutional conventions, elected executives, judicial review, and charter amendment." These allowed the American "People" itself to be the sovereign; their creation could maintain "juridicality" through the institutions of government, which they had chartered.

The chapter shows how the idea of personhood is both very old and quite new in its application to the state. It also shows, by illustration, the narrow uses to which juridical personhood can be put. There is nothing necessary about

---

[53] Haan, *infra* Chapter 9.

expanding the personhood metaphor to create a false equivalence between corporate and natural persons for the purpose of human or constitutional rights. As Joshua Barkan observes in the next chapter, however, that metaphor metastasized in the legal imagination.

Barkan's "Corporate Personhood as Legal and Literary Fiction" closes out the volume with a Foucauldian "genealogical" approach to juridical personhood. The chapter tries to understand the uses of this legal fiction in "relation to the shifting uses of corporate and state power."[54] Barkan's starting point is the difficulty personhood presents for human rights. In the context of natural persons, personhood rights protect the vulnerability of embodiment, while for corporate persons they "protect and immunize ... from regulation and legal oversight" "some of the most powerful institutions in contemporary society." There is no easy fix: Corporations, like embodied persons, can use the language of vulnerability to establish their need for protection.

While legal scholars approach this puzzle by trying to get to the *truth* of the metaphor, to understand the concept in line with some more foundational idea that would allow a pragmatic legal use, Barkan would reverse the inquiry. He proposes to ask, instead, why the law insists on recourse to this fiction, and tries so hard to refine and maintain it. The answer to this question, in Barkan's analysis, has to do with quelling societal conflict and securing group or class power. What dystopian fiction understands about corporations, but law does not, "is that central problems with corporations and corporate power are caused by, rather than resolved by, law." The solution is not "a more accurate image of the corporate person" but something more fundamental that cures the "radical dissatisfaction" of the dystopian nightmare by dismantling the formal structures of collective life.

THEMES OF THE BOOK

The multinational corporate enterprise "barely exists under international law," as John Ruggie has memorably stated.[55] Enterprises are not single actors, but families of separate legal entities organized under the national laws of individual states; these entities are "invisible" to international law[56] because they do not hold a subject status that could confer formal responsibilities on them, as states do. Nevertheless, the formal legal status of firms under international law belies a much more complex relationship between firms and states.

There has been growing and sustained interest among lawyers in the late twentieth and the early twenty-first centuries in this complex relationship. Observations

---

[54] Barkan, *infra* Chapter 13.

[55] John Gerard Ruggie, *Multinationals as Global Institution: Power, Authority and Relative Autonomy*, 12 REGUL. GOV. 317 (2018).

[56] Fleur Johns, *The Invisibility of the Transnational Corporation: An Analysis of International Law and Legal Theory*, 19 MELB. U. L. REV. 893 (1994).

in political science and international relations about the global power of multinational corporations have influenced legal inquiries about the rights and duties of the entities.[57] The United Nations has grappled with whether and how to regulate multinational entities, and has increasingly welcomed private actors as partners in global governance agendas.[58] Private market actors have increasingly sought to participate in global governance projects and have signed on in droves to Global Compact and climate change pledging platforms.[59] Literatures have flourished in law about corporate responsibilities to society and for human rights, and the rights these entities may hold within society due to their status as legal persons.[60] New projects in law have started to train their sights on the multinational or "global" corporation as a unitary actor holding various sorts of power, despite its international legal invisibility.[61] In sum, while multinational entities are murky, minimally cognizable entities from the perspective of international law, it is clear that they have various forms of global power. Both international and domestic lawyers have tried to assess the legal bases for that power, and legal means of grounding it in relevant forms of responsibility.

This book organizes these questions through the concept of "attribution," both as a doctrinal instrument and conceptual touchstone. As the chapters that follow show, law has various ways of ascribing and assigning identity and responsibility at the international, transnational, and domestic levels.

As a whole, the volume demonstrates that these ascriptions of identity and responsibility are often elastic in one direction and rigid in another. For example, there is a permeability of the boundary between firms and states, as states enter the market through ownership and retreat from governance through outsourcing. But international legal doctrines of state responsibility for internationally wrongful acts are not flexible enough to offer a nuanced appraisal of the expansion and contraction of the state in order to assign responsibility consequences to relevant actors. These doctrines operate to exclude the behavior of states from international scrutiny when they outsource activities to private firms, even when those firms are wholly or partially state owned. Responsibility doctrines are also based on a particular conception of the state that is overly rigid and increasingly outdated, and they entirely

---

[57] *See, e.g.,* Joseph Nye, *Multinationals: The Game and the Rules: Multinational Corporations in World Politics,* FOREIGN AFF. (Oct. 1, 1974); STRANGE, *supra* note 16.

[58] *See* Georg Kell, *Relations with the Private Sector, in* THE OXFORD HANDBOOK OF INTERNATIONAL ORGANIZATIONS (Jacob Katz Cogan, Ian Hurd, and Ian Johnstone, eds., 2017); *see also* Melissa J. Durkee, *Privatizing International Governance,* 116 ASIL PROC. 147 (2023).

[59] Melissa J. Durkee, *The Pledging World Order,* 48 YALE J INT. L 1 (2023).

[60] See sources cited *supra* notes 2–4, and accompanying discussion.

[61] One salient example is Sundhya Pahuja's pathbreaking Laureate Research Program in Global Corporations and International Law at Melbourne Law School, which aims "to examine the role of international law in enabling global corporate power, to identify the ways in which international law and institutions can be reformed to limit that power, and to [facilitate] a more balanced relationship between states and global corporations." *See* www.lpgcil.org/about (last accessed Apr. 12, 2023).

exclude the behavior of firms, as those entities are conceived as private, and thus unreachable by international law.

There is similarly an elasticity and rigidity in the way that corporations can use separate entity status to expand operation all over the world in corporate families of parents and far flung subsidiaries, but separate entity status is flexible in only one direction. It creates an impermeable segmentation of responsibility between those entities. The result is that harms can be externalized, with responsibility for them confined within individual undercapitalized entities in jurisdictions foreign to the parent entity. Separate entity status ensures that capital travels, not responsibility. The interventions in this book show just how difficult it is to overcome this rigidity, suggesting either minor corrections or major reforms that would create a radical reconceptualization of the role and responsibilities of firms in their relation to society.

The book as a whole also spotlights the borrowing between firms and states, and their opportunistic co-creation. These include the post-charter context where firms wrote themselves out of international law by policing the public-private divide, the post-colonial context where firms curried favor with African governments by "indigenization" strategies that increased the complexity of corporate families, the disciplining of the state into an "ordinary" market participant in the investment arbitration context, the transplantation of juridical personhood from firms to states, and the claiming of constitutional protections from states by firms, among many examples.

Ultimately, reading the chapters in this volume together shows how legal constructions ascribing entity identity and responsibilities can come to seem necessary, inevitable, and immutable. They can become invisible, woven so deeply into the legal imagination and the fabric of common life that it becomes hard to perceive them, and to perceive their artificial nature, and thus their fundamental contingency.

CONCLUSION

This volume aims to offer a new point of entry for enduring questions about how the law conceives of firms and states. The point of entry is attribution. Because firms and states are fictitious constructs rather than products of evolutionary biology, the law must make decisions about which acts it should attribute to them, and by which actors. Those legal decisions construct firms and states by attributing identity and consequences to them. And those decisions, in turn, are products of conceptual storytelling. The attribution framework allows the volume to consider together an array of problems that are usually divided into doctrinal silos, addressing particularly relevant and difficult questions about how the law should deal with artificial entities: attribution of international legal responsibility, transnational attribution of liabilities, and attribution of identity to artificial actors.

Together, the chapters in this volume show how much conceptual and theoretical work is needed to address the important responsibility challenges of our time. By highlighting the artificiality of doctrines that construct firms and states, the chapters in this volume emphasize their mutability. These doctrines exist, together with their founding metaphors and traditions, in the legal imagination. If law is to be of service to human needs, then it should create entities that reflect those needs. Perhaps those human needs might serve as a touchstone for the entities created to address them.

PART I

International Attribution

2

Attribution in International Law

Challenges and Evolution

Kristen E. Boon[*]

INTRODUCTION

The doctrine of attribution in international law has been defined, in large part, by the International Law Commission's (ILC) provisions on attribution of conduct in the Articles on State Responsibility for Internationally Wrongful Acts (ARSIWA).[1] The term "attribution" is used to denote the operation of attaching a given action or omission to a state or international organization (IO).[2] If these acts are internationally wrongful, they may create responsibility leading to an obligation to make reparations.[3] Like agency rules in tort law, the doctrine of attribution determines what degree of connectivity is required to link the act of an entity to a principal for purposes of assigning liability.

It is uncontroversial to note that despite the influence of the ILC's rules on attribution, the regime of international responsibility remains underdeveloped. This is because ARSIWA principally addresses states. Although the ILC has offered rules on attribution for IOs, and attribution in the context of international criminal law is now well developed for natural persons, there is no unified set of rules applicable to the gamut of actual actors on the global stage. For example, multinational corporations and non-state entities like rebel groups are untouched by these rules because they are not subjects of, or typically regulated by, international law.[4] ARSIWA's limited range reduces the exposure of states for potentially wrongful acts and can benefit states that are under-resourced. Moreover, a limited attribution regime can make it difficult for claimants to have access to a remedy in the international sphere.

[*] Thanks to Gregory Batt and Wolfgang Albrecht III for their research assistance.

[1] Pieter Jan Kuijper, *Introduction to Symposium on Responsibility of International Organizations and of (Member) States: Attributed or Direct Responsibility or Both?*, 7 INT'L ORG. L. REV. 9 (2010) (explaining that attribution of conduct is not based on attribution of responsibility).

[2] *Report of the International Law Commission*, 53 U.N. GAOR Supp. No. 10, at 36, U.N. Doc. A/56/10 (Nov. 2001) [hereinafter "Articles on State Responsibility"].

[3] *Id.* at 40, Ch. IV(E)(2) Part One Ch. 2 Art. 4.

[4] *But see* the discussion of effective control *infra* note 41, in which certain entities under the effective control of a state may render the state responsible for wrongful conduct.

In addition to being underinclusive, the rules of attribution in ARSIWA are beginning to appear outdated.[5] They are based on practices that predate 2000, before the rapid hollowing out of the state, the shift toward globalization, and the exponential growth of the field of human rights. They do not reflect technological changes, the Internet, or the rise of non-state actors in areas such as cyberwarfare. They are also premised on a conception of a limited state, and as such, reflect a certain cultural embeddedness that resonates more clearly in some political systems than in others. With the contemporary rise in the influence of state-owned enterprises (SOE) and sovereign wealth funds (SWF) more generally, the ILC's rules might become increasingly disconnected from the current state of play.

The central question, therefore, is whether the rules of attribution in ARSIWA are flexible enough to accommodate two disparate trends. On the one hand, we have witnessed an outsourcing of public functions to private actors in areas such as immigration, prison management, and education, whereby privatization has reduced state control and, consequently, potential state responsibility. On the other hand, there is a marked centralization of power in SOEs, some of which are now playing a global role as investors.[6] This creates tension: in some situations, states are divesting activities to the private sector, while in others, states are consolidating their influence and control through state-affiliated companies. ARSIWA, although never codified as a treaty, has been remarkably influential in creating the international legal architecture that applies to state responsibility. This contribution assesses whether the default rules on attribution are flexible enough to manage both ends of the spectrum of state activity, which will be a crucial issue for regulators going forward.

James Crawford described the control tests in the attribution rules in particular as ones of "essential ambiguity," which ILC members hoped would be fleshed out in practice.[7] The ARSIWA were commended to states in 2001. At the time of this writing, some twenty years later, the moment is ripe to assess them. This contribution offers some reflections on how the ARSIWA rules have fared in practice and identifies developments or, conversely, concerns that have led to new approaches that are

---

[5] For diverse views on this issue, *see generally* Federica Paddeu & Christian Tams, *The ILC Articles at 20: Introduction to the Symposium*, EJIL:Talk! (Aug. 2, 2021) *available at* www.ejiltalk.org/the-ilc-articles-at-20-introduction-to-the-symposium/; in particular, *see* Federica Paddeu & Christian Tams, *Dithering, Trickling Down, and Encoding: Concluding Thoughts on the 'ILC Articles at 20'* *Symposium*, EJIL:Talk! (Aug. 9, 2021) *available at* www.ejiltalk.org/dithering-trickling-down-and-encoding-concluding-thoughts-on-the-ilc-articles-at-20-symposium/ (noting that the attribution articles need a "check-in"); and Alex Mills, *State Responsibility and Privatisation: Accommodating Private Conduct in a Public Framework*, EJIL:Talk! (Aug. 4, 2021) *available at* www.ejiltalk.org/state-responsibility-and-privatisation-accommodating-private-conduct-in-a-public-framework/ (noting the difficulties with the public/private divide).

[6] On this phenomenon, *see generally* WINSTON MA & PAUL DOWNS, THE HUNT FOR UNICORNS: HOW SOVEREIGN FUNDS ARE RESHAPING INVESTMENT IN THE DIGITAL ECONOMY (2020).

[7] JAMES CRAWFORD, STATE RESPONSIBILITY: THE GENERAL Part 205 (Cambridge Univ. Press 2018).

further explored in other chapters in this book. I focus, in particular, on how doctrines of attribution have been applied to corporate actors and SOEs by investment tribunals and compare them with rules of attribution proposed in contemporary investment and trade treaties, which offer more rigid tests to determine state affiliation. I argue that the institutional and control tests continue to command a high degree of respect and adherence, but that the functional tests reflected in Article 5 of ARSIWA and applicable to SOEs have been applied in less consistent ways. This inconsistency is due to different emphases in the legal tests, different cultural approaches (within states and by arbitrators), and international law's "own concept of what is a 'public function,' its own sense of when a body 'in truth' acts as a state organ."[8] The doctrine of attribution is in a liminal state, and this has important feedback effects for state sovereignty.[9] Moreover, it shows that a fundamental premise in international law is being challenged by contemporary corporate entities that have both public and private elements.[10]

ATTRIBUTION TESTS FOR STATES

The dominant approach to attribution, as reflected in ARSIWA, has three conceptual pillars:

- institutional links (such as organs or entities of a state),
- functional links (such as parastatal entities or state corporations), and
- control (where a state controls the activity of a non-state actor).

For states, responsibility is most clearly engaged when a state organ or entity has an *institutional* link to the state. For example, under Art. 4 of ARSIWA, an organ created by law constitutes an instrumentality of the state.[11] Within this category sit ministries, armed forces and the police, courts, and any other official division of the state. This is the most direct, uncontroversial rule of attribution: the institution itself is considered part of the state.[12]

---

[8] Mills, *supra* note 6.

[9] *Id.* ("a foundational problem thus arises as to which body of law – national or international – should be responsible for determining whether an act or actor is public or private in character."). *See*, in this regard, *Mykhaylenky and others v. Ukraine*, 2004-XII ECtHR 656, at § 45 (regarding the determination that an institution was public, because it operated in the highly regulated energy sector).

[10] Freya Baetens, *Lifting the Corporate Veil between China and its State-Owned Enterprises: Revisiting the International Rules on Attribution of State Conduct* (draft on file with author).

[11] *See* CSABA KOVÁCS, ATTRIBUTION IN INTERNATIONAL INVESTMENT LAW 70 (Wolters Kluwer 2018).

[12] Articles on State Responsibility, *supra* note 3, at 40–1 ("The reference to a 'State organ' covers all the individual or collective entities which make up the organization of the State and act on its behalf.... Article 4 covers organs, whether they exercise legislative, executive, judicial or any other functions. This language allows for the fact that the principle of the separation of powers is not followed in any uniform way, and that many organs exercise some combination of public powers of a legislative, executive or judicial character. Moreover, the term is one of extension, not limitation, as is made clear by the words 'or any other functions.'") (quotations omitted).

In addition to institutional links, attribution may arise when an entity acts under the color of state authority as a de facto organ or entity under ARSIWA Article 5.[13] This second pillar is based on functional links, and this rule is supported by the policy that states should not avoid responsibility by conferring authority on an entity run by the state. It is meant, in particular, to bring parastatal entities under the umbrella of ARSIWA. Because the rules of attribution provide that "the conduct of private persons is not, as such, attributable to the state," there is much engagement in arbitral awards about whether the acts of entities with some functional connections to the state are in fact connected to those states.[14] This provision is discussed at length below.

Finally, the third pillar is one of control. Article 8 provides that acts of private entities and non-state actors can be attributed to the state if they operate under that state's direction or "effective control."[15] The general rule is that "the only conduct attributed to the State at the international level is that of its organs or government, or of others who have acted under the direction, instigation or control of those organs, that is, as agents of the State."[16] Designed to permit case-by-case assessments, the control tests focus on the nature of the relationship between a state and a private entity, rather than the function being performed, which can be public or private depending on the context.[17]

CONCERNS ABOUT ATTRIBUTION TESTS

A key issue with ARSIWA's rules on attribution is that they create an incentive to outsource state activities in order to reduce liability. This concern exists across multiple areas of law. For example, in the context of humanitarian law, Hathaway *et al.* note:

> Suppose a state supports a non-state group seeking to overthrow its government.... The state would like to assure the victory of the side it supports, but it would also like to avoid any responsibility for violations of international law.... Because of the high bar established by modern attribution doctrine, states in this circumstance may believe that they can work through non-state actors and thereby avoid legal responsibility that would be triggered if they employed their own forces.[18]

---

[13]   *Id.* at 42 ("The conduct of a person or entity which is not an organ of the State under article 4 but which is empowered by the law of that State to exercise elements of the governmental authority shall be considered an act of the State under international law, provided the person or entity is acting in that capacity in the particular instance.").

[14]   KOVÁCS, *supra* note 12 (citing Commentary to ILC Art. Ch. II ¶ 3).

[15]   Articles on State Responsibility, *supra* note 3, at Ch. IV(E) Pt. I, Ch. 2 Art. 8.

[16]   *Id.* at 38.

[17]   Kristen E. Boon, *Are Control Tests Fit for the Future? The Slippage Problem in Attribution Doctrines*, 15 MELB. J. INT'L L. 330, 334 n.17 (2014).

[18]   Oona A. Hathaway et al., *Ensuring Responsibility: Common Article 1 and State Responsibility for Non-State Actors*, 95 TEX L. REV. 539, 562 (2017).

Similarly, in the context of cyberwarfare, there is often significant involvement by non-state actors who may acquire control of state infrastructure and use it to conduct cyber operations.[19] As Finlay and Paine note: "The relative availability and cheapness of the technology necessary to mount a cyber-attack makes significant attacks launched by private individuals or corporations far more feasible compared with other types of warfare."[20] The high thresholds of control set out in ARSIWA permit states to turn a blind eye to the actions of rogue actors in many instances and avoid responsibility.[21] In the past, there was a presumption that the use of governmental assets in traditional warfare (like military equipment, tanks, or warships) constituted a nearly irrefutable indication of attribution due to the improbability of their use by persons other than state organs. Today, however, the accessibility of technology means this presumption would not make sense in cyber warfare.[22] Given these concerns and disconnects, it is noteworthy – and surprising – that The Tallinn Manual on international law governing cyber operations took a largely orthodox approach and tracked the ARSIWA standards as well as the high bar for attributing responsibility.[23] Interestingly, the gap is partially addressed by Rule 6, which creates a separate due diligence obligation for states.[24]

A slightly different concern has arisen with regard to attribution for wrongful conduct in the context of peacekeeping. Here, the issue is whether effective control is given a broad or a narrow interpretation, with a broad interpretation assigning liability to the entity which had the "power to prevent" particular acts. This alternative interpretation of control prevailed for a period in Dutch courts, which seemed

[19] Lorraine Finlay & Christian Payne, *The Attribution Problem and Cyber Armed Attacks*, 113 AJIL UNBOUND 202, 204–05 (2019) ("The principles of attribution relating to the actions of nonstate actors are particularly relevant to cyberattacks, given that the relative availability and cheapness of the technology necessary to mount a cyber-attack makes significant attacks launched by private individuals or corporations far more feasible compared with other types of warfare.") (internal quotations omitted).

[20] Christian Payne & Lorraine Finlay, *Addressing Obstacles to Cyber-Attribution: A Model Based on State Response to Cyber-Attack*, 49 GEO. WASH. INT'L L. REV. 535, 556 (2018).

[21] Finlay & Payne, *supra* note 20, at 205 ("In any event, regardless of whether 'effective control' or 'overall control' ultimately applies, the attribution threshold remains extremely high. Mere encouragement or support by a state through financing and equipping groups will be insufficient for attribution. Simply financing a cyberattack or providing a safe haven to nonstate perpetrators would not appear to meet the threshold for the state itself to be held responsible for a cyberattack.").

[22] MICHAEL N. SCHMITT ET AL., TALLINN MANUAL 2.0 ON THE INTERNATIONAL LAW APPLICABLE TO CYBER OPERATIONS 84 (Cambridge Univ. Press, 2nd ed. 2017).

[23] *Id.* at Rules 15–17.

[24] *Id.* at Rule 6 (Cyber-related acts are defined with reference to the fact that a State sometimes may bear responsibility for acts other than cyber operations that it conducts or that are attributable to it. The Manual states: "for instance, a State can make its cyber infrastructure available to non-State groups or other States, fail to take required measures to terminate cyber operations from its territory … or provide hardware or software to conduct cyber operations."); *see id.* at Rule 14 (noting that "[a]n 'internationally wrongful act' is an action or omission that both: (1) constitutes a breach of an international legal obligation applicable to that State; and (2) is attributable to the State under international law. The absence of either element precludes State responsibility with respect to the act in question.").

to open up opportunities for victims to bring claims.[25] However, as discussed further below, in the culminating appellate judgment regarding the Srebrenica massacre, the Dutch Supreme Court rejected this victim-centered interpretation, once again narrowing the basis upon which a claim could be brought.[26]

Given the wide variety of situations that attribution rules apply to, some of these concerns have been addressed by creating primary rules through treaties or other international instruments. For example, under Article 139 of the Law of the Sea Convention, a state will be responsible for acts of a subcontractor when it sponsors certain private acts in seabed mining.[27] In the context of terrorism and private military contractors, in particular, Security Council resolutions have been a source of more stringent rules of attribution.[28] Non-binding norms on attribution are emerging with regard to social corporate responsibility for human rights violations committed by corporations.[29] As discussed in more detail below, recent treaties in the trade and investment context create stricter rules for attribution for state-owned or -controlled entities than what the ILC proposed in 2000.[30] Nonetheless, since most treaties are silent on issues of attribution, the ILC's articles have gained prominence, and continue to supply the default approach to attribution.[31] Like the restatements in U.S. law, which are not binding but have persuasive authority, ARSIWA are secondary, background rules that constitute (for the most part) customary international law and exist by default. The next sections will explore alternative tests for attribution, and then analyze the jurisprudence involving corporate actors.

ATTRIBUTION TESTS FOR INTERNATIONAL ORGANIZATIONS

About a decade after the General Assembly commended ARSIWA to states, the ILC proposed a set of attribution rules for IOs. These rules are similar, but not identical,

---

[25] Tom Dannenbaum. *Killings at Srebrenica, Effective Control, and the Power to Prevent Unlawful Conduct*, 16 INT'L & COMP. L. Q. 713 (2012).

[26] In the case Mothers of Srebrenica, the Dutch Supreme Court set aside the power-to-prevent interpretation of ARSIWA, holding instead that under Article 8 of ARSIWA, effective control exists in the event of "[a]ctual participation of and directions given by that state. The decision demonstrates that ARSIWA continue to enjoy greater authority than ARIO, while marking a retreat from accountability: it reduced plaintiff's damages and made it harder for plaintiffs to sue peacekeepers for wrongful actions." *Mothers of Srebrenica Assoc. et al. v. Netherlands*, Sup. Ct. Neth. 17/04567 (July 19, 2019), ¶ 3.5.3; *Netherlands v. Mustafić-Mujić*, Sup. Ct. Neth. 12/03329 (Sept. 6, 2013) ¶ ¶ 3.11.2–3.12.3.

[27] U.N. Convention on the Law of the Sea, *opened for signature* Dec. 10, 1982, 1833 U.N.T.S. 397 (entered into force Nov. 16, 1994), art. 139.

[28] *Discussed in* CRAWFORD, *supra* note 8, at 205.

[29] Judith Schonsteiner, *Attribution of State Responsibility for Actions or Omissions of State-Owned Enterprises in Human Rights Matters*, 40 U. PA. J. INT'L L. 895 (2019).

[30] *See* discussion *infra* notes 93–94.

[31] David Caron, *The ILC Articles on State Responsibility: The Paradoxical Relationship Between Form and Authority*, 96 AM. J. INT'L L. 857 (2002).

to those applicable to states.[32] The ILC's work on responsibility of IOs has been criticized for lack of underlying practice and over-similarity to ARSIWA.[33] While the Articles on the Responsibility of International Organizations (ARIO) have not commanded the same level of authority as ARSIWA, it stands as a useful point of comparison. In particular, ARIO is relevant to the present conversation because IOs are a form of corporations.[34] Specifically, IOs are distinct legal entities in law, with many exhibiting a separate legal personality from their members in the form of corporate structures, including an executive board and voting members.[35] Corporate law analogies, such as piercing the corporate veil, have been proposed as a way to close the accountability gap.[36] Ahlborn, in particular, notes that "it is significant that courts, tribunals, and scholars dealing with international organizations have used corporate law to discuss their legal personality for purposes of their responsibility."[37]

Under ARIO, institutional links remain central, with acts of organs of an IO considered to be acts of the IO.[38] ARIO integrates the control test as well. Article 7, the key provision in ARIO on attribution of conduct between IOs and states, provides: "The conduct of an organ of a State or an organ or agent of an international organization that is placed at the disposal of another international organization shall be considered under international law an act of the latter organization if the organization exercises effective control over that conduct."[39]

The test of effective control is explicitly adopted in Article 7 of ARIO, whereas ARSIWA is silent on the level of control required for attribution leaving it to judicial

---

[32] The legal status of ARIO is less clear than ARSIWA. The former constitutes progressive development of the law, whereas the latter is generally considered as customary international law.

[33] Niels Blokker & Ramses A. Wessel, *IOLR* (2012) – *Introduction: First Views at the Articles on the Responsibility of International Organizations*, 9 INT'L ORG. L. REV. 1, 8 (2012).

[34] Wojciech Morawiecki, *Functions of International Organizations*, 3 POLISH ROUND TABLE 147, 157 (1969).

[35] *Id.* at 167 (In particular, the specialized agencies of the United Nations: the IMF, the World Bank, IFC, and IDA were created according to a model of capitalist business corporations in which a decisive role in policy making is played by major shareholders according to rules of weighted voting.) (quotations omitted).

[36] Ki-Gab Park & Kyongwha Chung, *Responsibility of International Organizations*, 2 KOR. U. L. REV. 67, 87 (2007) ("Some … have advanced the view that IO members assume unlimited responsibility for their IOs' obligations because, as of date, there is no set theory of limited responsibility in international law. [Others] have compared the shareholders of a corporation in domestic law to an IO.").

[37] CHRISTIANE AHLBHORN, LIFTING THE CORPORATE VEIL: THE RESPONSIBILITY OF INTERNATIONAL ORGANIZATIONS AND THEIR MEMBER STATES (Universiteit van Amsterdam, 2020).

[38] *Report of the International Law Commission*, 63 U.N. GAOR, U.N. Doc. A/66/10, Ch. V(E) Art. 6 (2011) *available at* https://legal.un.org/ilc/texts/instruments/english/commentaries/9_11_2011.pdf ("The conduct of an organ or agent of an international organization in the performance of functions of that organ or agent shall be considered an act of that organization under international law, whatever position the organ or agent holds in respect of the organization."). The International Court of Justice and the UN Secretariat would, for example, be considered organs of the UN based on the UN Charter.

[39] *Id.* at Chapter V(E) Art. 7.

determination.[40] An important difference between the control tests in ARSIWA and ARIO is that under the former, the control test is used to determine whether acts of individuals or groups of individuals that do not have status under international law are attributable to the state. The answer to that question will either be yes or no. In this way, the attribution rules define the limits of state responsibility, potentially creating an accountability gap if actors are not sufficiently connected to the state. In the latter case, however, effective control is part of a comparative inquiry: "Assuming states and IOs are both involved, which entity (or both) exercises effective control?"[41] As such, ARIO approaches the question of attribution from a different angle. The rules on state responsibility envision many situations in which attribution thresholds will not be met, whereas under ARIO it is an either/or question. Put differently, the question under ARIO is not if conduct is attributable, but rather to which entity it should be attributed: the IO or the state, which serves to close the accountability gap as a matter of law.[42]

ARIO also presupposes that conduct is prima facie attributable first to the state, and secondarily to the UN. As Crawford explained:

> [T]o determine whether an unlawful act is imputable to the UN, the fundamental rule of [the] international law of responsibility … should be applied, ie the international responsibility should be borne by the state whose organ or agent had committed the wrongful act. The UN may be held responsible for the unlawful act committed by a member of its force so long as this member could be considered [as] acting as an organ or agent of the UN…. The UN should not be held responsible for activities carried out by a member state using its own organs and under its full organic jurisdiction, even if those activities were in application of a decision [taken] by the UN.[43]

As such, ARIO closes a legal gap, potentially tightening the accountability regime.

The differences between the approaches of ARSIWA and ARIO came to the forefront in a series of cases before Dutch courts involving the Srebrenica massacre of 1995. The decisions involved issues of international responsibility for the conduct of peacekeepers – in particular, attribution of conduct to the United Nations and its member states, and immunity of international organizations. The 2019 decision of

---

[40] The effective control standard is specific in Art. 7 of Articles on the Responsibility of IOs, unlike Art. 8 of the Articles on State Responsibility, which refers generically to control. These different approaches were put to the test in recent cases in the Netherlands involving the Srebrenca massacre of 1995. In Nuhanović, the Supreme Court, applying Article 7 of ARIO and Article 8 of ARSIWA, held that it was possible that both the Netherlands and the United Nations had effective control over the same wrongful conduct, indicating that attributing the conduct to the Netherlands did not determine whether the United Nations also had effective control, and that the entity with the power to prevent was in effective control.

[41] Boon, *supra* note 18, at 354.

[42] Id.

[43] CRAWFORD, *supra* note 5, at 190.

The State of the Netherlands v. Respondents & Stichting Mothers of Srebrenica was the culmination of this long litigation, and the Supreme Court of the Netherlands found the state partially responsible (10 percent) for the damages arising from the conduct of Dutch peacekeepers.[44] It was significant that the Court analyzed both Article 7 of ARIO and Article 8 of ARSIWA in its reasoning. Ultimately, it upheld a lower court decision that the state had no effective control over the acts of Dutchbat. In so doing, the court emphasized ARSIWA over ARIO, which resulted in a narrow approach to shared responsibility and the attribution of wrongful conduct.[45]

The three pillars of attribution that underpin ARSIWA – institutional links, functional links, and control – continue to dominate legal thinking with regards to how conduct should be attributed at the international level. ARSIWA has provided a code and a system of thinking about international responsibility.[46] However, ARIO's rules demonstrate that different approaches to the topic of attribution exist.[47] I will suggest in the section below that the ARIO structure could provide a conceptual point of departure in cases involving SOEs.

SPECIAL CHALLENGES: ATTRIBUTION TESTS AND CORPORATE CONDUCT

I have argued elsewhere that the rules on attribution create a "slippage" problem because they appear to offer objective standards that operate across various issue areas in international law but, in fact, are premised on the concept of a limited state.[48] While this model has currency in the context of western liberal democracies, it is far from universal. Many formerly communist Eastern European states continue to be heavily involved in commercial enterprises. In other countries, firms prosper because of their close connection with the state. Companies like TikTok and Huawei made front page news because of their deep connections with the Chinese government, which in turn created diplomatic wars over access to data by the Chinese government.[49] As Curtis Milhaupt writes: "Functionally, state owned entities [SOEs] and large publicly owned entities [POEs] in China share many similarities in the areas commonly thought to distinguish state-owned firms from

---

[44] *See generally* Kristen E. Boon, *International Decisions: The State of the Netherlands v. Respondents & Stichting Mothers of Srebrenica*, No.17/04567, 144 AM. J. INT'L LAW 479 (2020).

[45] *Id.*

[46] Federica Paddeu & Christian Tams, *Dithering, Trickling Down, and Encoding: Concluding Thoughts on the 'ILC Articles at 20' Symposium*, EJIL:Talk! (Aug. 9, 2021) *available at* www.ejiltalk.org/dithering-trickling-down-and-encoding-concluding-thoughts-on-the-ilc-articles-at-20-symposium/.

[47] Another approach to the topic of attribution was developed by TAL BECKER, TERRORISM AND THE STATE: RETHINKING THE RULES OF STATE RESPONSIBILITY (2006) (setting out the legal duties of States to prevent, and abstain from supporting, terrorist activity and exploring how to maximize State compliance with these obligations.).

[48] Boon, *supra* note 18, at 334.

[49] Harlan Cohen, *Nations and Markets*, 23 J. INT'L ECON. L. 793 (2020).

privately owned firms: market access, receipt of state subsidies, proximity to state power, and execution of the government's policy objectives."[50] Some of the founding assumptions of the ILC's approach to attribution, therefore, are put to the test in complex corporate settings where states are closely connected with markets.

The ILC anticipated the power of transnational corporations in the commentary to Article 5. Nonetheless, their influence has far outstripped predictions. Today, some companies are wealthier than states.[51] The influence of sovereign wealth funds and public pension funds in particular, is transforming the global economic landscape. In the following discussion, I demonstrate the evolution in application of Article 5, and compare it to the more static effective control test under Article 8, in investor-state tribunals. In my view, the doctrine of effective control continues to be quite settled, whereas "functional" approaches to attribution under Article 5 are more varied. Although separate legal personality in theory insulates the state from claims by investors, as a practical matter, tribunals consider the extent to which those entities are controlled by the state, regardless of the nature, function, or strategic importance of the conduct.[52] This is important because the boundary between public and private is contested, and international arbitral tribunals are increasingly opinionated on when the acts of ostensibly private actors are public and hence regulated by international law.[53] This discussion focuses on attribution in the context of responsibility, as distinct from the procedural question of whether an entity has standing to bring a claim.

Article 5: Governmental Authority

ARSIWA Article 5: Conduct of persons or entities exercising elements of governmental authority states:

> The conduct of a person or entity which is not an organ of the State under article 4 but which is empowered by the law of that State to exercise elements of the governmental authority shall be considered an act of the State under international law, provided the person or entity is acting in that capacity in the particular instance.

The goal of Article 5 is to provide rules on attribution that apply where an entity not designated in domestic law as an organ *in fact* exercises elements of government authority. The ILC commentary designates these as "parastatal" entities.[54] One of the most active areas of application of this article is in the investor-state arbitration

---

[50] Curtis Milhaupt & Wentong Zheng, *Beyond Ownership: State Capitalism and the Chinese Firm*, 108 Stan. L. Rev. 660, 660–68 (2015).

[51] *See, e.g.*, Milan Babic et al., *Who Is More Powerful: States or Corporations?*, The Conversation (July 10, 2018) https://theconversation.com/who-is-more-powerful-states-or-corporations-99616.

[52] Kovács, *supra* note 12, at 30.

[53] Mills, *supra* note 6.

[54] Kovács, *supra* note 12, at 129.

context, where arbitral tribunals assess what constitutes governmental authority and sovereign power.[55] As Mills notes, privatization has been a touchstone because the state seeks to regulate an entity which is operating in a newly constructed market space and issues arise such as whether human rights obligations follow.[56] Another common issue is whether a state is responsible for the acts of a private entity that is exercising "truly" governmental authority.[57]

The commentaries are clear that the ambit of Article 5 is potentially very broad: it applies to "public corporations, semi-public entities, public agencies of various kinds and even, in special cases, private companies, provided that in each case the entity is empowered by the law of the State to exercise functions of a public character normally exercised by State organs."[58] Often, Article 5 is invoked when the entity in question has separate legal personality.[59] Even if governmental authority in the context of Article 5 ARSIWA encompasses those traditional powers that undergird the state's existence as a public authority, it is far from easy, in practice, to identify where exactly the boundaries lie.[60] A central issue in the jurisprudence, as noted in the Noble Ventures award, is that there is no

> [C]ommon understanding in international law of what constitutes a governmental or public act. Otherwise there would not be a need for specified rules such as those enunciated by the ILC in its Draft Articles, according to which, in principle, a certain factual link between the State and the actor is required in order to attribute to the State acts of that actor.[61]

The dominant judicial approach to determining whether an entity is an SOE, and hence has conduct attributable to a state, has been to create presumptions of attributability based on ownership and function. More recent jurisprudence, however, has loosened these tests, with authorization being emphasized rather than ownership or control.

One of the early awards to set out criteria for when an entity was acting under the color of governmental authority was *Maffezini v. Spain,* which involved the creation of a chemical production company, Emilio A. Maffezini S.A. (EAMSA). To start the company, Mr. Maffezini procured an investment from the Sociedad para el Desarrollo Industrial de Galicia (SODIGA) in Spain. A dispute ensued over how to distribute the company's assets and settle debts when Mr. Maffezini decided to shut

---

[55] *Mesa Power Group LLC v. Canada,* 2016 PCA No. 2012-17 (Mar. 24, 2016), at ¶ 367 (citing Jan de Nul at ¶ 170 as "prérogatives de puissance publique").

[56] *Id.*

[57] *Id.*

[58] Articles on State Responsibility, *supra* note 3, at 43.

[59] *See generally* Kovács, *supra* note 12.

[60] Jennifer Maddocks, *Outsourcing of Governmental Functions in Contemporary Conflict: Rethinking the Issue of Arbitration,* 59 Va. J. Int'l L. 47, 76 (2019).

[61] *Noble Ventures, Inc. v. Romania,* ICSID Case No. ARB/01/11 (Oct. 12, 2005), at ¶ 82 (citing ILC commentary).

the company down. Here, the tribunal set out structural and functional tests involving ownership and control:

> [T]he question of whether or not SODIGA is a State entity must be examined first from a formal or structural point of view. Here a finding that the entity is owned by the State, directly or indirectly, gives rise to a rebuttable presumption that it is a State entity. The same result will obtain if an entity is controlled by the State, directly or indirectly. A similar presumption arises if an entity's purpose or objective is the carrying out of functions which are governmental in nature or which are otherwise normally reserved to the State, or which by their nature are not usually carried out by private business or individuals.[62]

Ultimately, the tribunal found that SODIGA was a state entity because it was created by governmental decree, discussed and approved by the Council of Ministers, and because under that decree the government would own no less than 51 percent of the entity's capital.[63] This test became the clearest early articulation, forming a rebuttable presumption, regarding attribution to governmental entities that are not formal organs of the state.

More recent cases demonstrate an evolution and loosening of standards under Article 5. In *Mesa Power Group v. Government of Canada* (2016), for example, the tribunal dealt with whether the actions of the Ontario Power Authority (OPA) were attributable to Canada.[64] The tribunal found that "by preparing the FIT (Feed-in-tariff) Rules and setting out the ranking and evaluation criteria for the applications to the FIT Program, the OPA was acting in the exercise of delegated governmental authority."[65] As a result, the tribunal held that the OPA, Hydro One, and Independent Electricity System Operator are state enterprises and that the OPA's acts were attributable to Canada, since they were done in the exercise of regulatory, administrative, or other governmental authority.[66] Canada argued that

> [T]he acts by the OPA, while carried out for the public good and in furtherance of the policy objectives of the government, cannot be considered to be the exercise of delegated governmental authority ... [because] it did not make any decisions on permits, licenses, approvals or anything that would have involved governmental authority.[67]

However, the tribunal rejected this argument, and established attribution not because the OPA was doing something that is traditionally done by a government

---

[62] *Maffezini v. Spain*, ICSID Case No. ARB/97/7, Award on Jurisdiction (Jan. 25, 2000), at ¶ 77.

[63] Baetens, *Lifting the Corporate Veil between China and its State-Owned Enterprises, supra* note 11, at nn. 72–79.

[64] The Electricity Act in Canada allowed the OPA to create a feed-in-tariff (FIT) program and rules that proponents would have to follow.

[65] *Mesa Power Group LLC v. Canada*, 2016 PCA No. 2012-17 (Mar. 24, 2016), at ¶ 371.

[66] *Id.* at ¶ 377.

[67] *Id.* at ¶ 305 (Canada's counter-memorial on jurisdiction).

agency but because OPA was doing something that the government specifically authorized it to do. As such, whereas *Maffezini* calls for the organization to carry out a function that is typical of the government or otherwise reserved to the state, in *Mesa*, the tribunal begins and ends the analysis with the fact that the government *authorized* the OPA to carry out a function. Although it did not comment on whether that function was governmental in nature, and hence appeared to defer to the state's own internal structure, in fact, the tribunal ventured into the gray space between authorization and regulation – despite the ILC's commentary to the contrary.[68]

There is a long line of awards that look at three different factors: ownership, function, and authorization, but weigh them differently. In *Gustav F W Hamester GmbH & Co KG v. Republic of Ghana* (2010), an ICSID tribunal articulated a two-part test for attribution with regard to an entity named Cocobod. First, the tribunal noted: "It is clear that two cumulative conditions have to be present [for attribution]: an entity empowered with governmental authority; and an act performed through the exercise of governmental authority."[69] The tribunal then assessed whether Cocobod was entrusted with governmental functions, answering this question in the affirmative on the basis that: "[I]t has the mission to regulate the marketing and export of cocoa, coffee and sheanuts; to encourage the development of all aspects of cocoa production and transformation; and to fight diseases of cocoa beans. In order to fulfil these functions, Cocobod was granted governmental powers."[70] It also noted it had the power to enact regulations by legislative instruments and impose penalties for their violation.[71]

The tribunal was also careful to emphasize, however, that "it is not enough for an act of a public entity to have been performed in the general fulfilment of some general interest, mission or purpose to qualify as an attributable act."[72] Indeed, not

---

[68] See Mills, *supra* note 6 ("The internal law in question must specifically authorize the conduct as involving the exercise of public authority; it is not enough that it permits activity as part of the general regulation of the affairs of the community. It is accordingly a narrow category.") (quoting ARSIWA Commentary, Article 5, (7)). Canada also pushed back against the finding in Bilcon that a Joint Review Panel (JRP) constitutes part of the 'apparatus of Canada.' Canada stated this term has "no basis in customary international law, is not found in the ILC's Articles themselves, their commentaries, any jurisprudence of the International Court of Justice or any other legal authority." See Bilcon of *Del. et al. v. Canada*, 2009 PCA No. 2009-04, Award on Jurisdiction (Mar. 17, 2015), ¶ 321 ("Even if the JRP were not, by its nature, a part of the apparatus of the Government of Canada, the fact would remain that federal Canada and Nova Scotia both adopted its essential findings in arriving at the conclusion that the project should be denied approval under their environmental laws."). However, the Tribunal determined that the acts were attributable on the basis of ratification: "Even if the JRP were not, by its nature, a part of the apparatus of the Government of Canada, the fact would remain that federal Canada and Nova Scotia both adopted its essential findings in arriving at the conclusion that the project should be denied approval under their environmental laws." *Id.*

[69] *Hamester v. Ghana*, ICSID Case No. ARB/07/24, Award (June 18, 2010), ¶ 176.

[70] *Id.* at ¶ 190.

[71] *Id.*

[72] *Id.* at ¶ 202.

all actions are governmental in nature, even if an entity exercises some aspects of governmental authority.[73] Thus, if a state instrumentality acts like any private party under a contract, their conduct is not attributable to the state.[74] Ultimately, the tribunal decided that the actions of the Ghana Cocoa Board were not attributable to the Republic of Ghana under Article 5.[75] Although the Cocoa Board was empowered to exercise some elements of government authority (e.g., regulation of export of cocoa, fighting disease of cocoa beans, and the ability to impose penalties on violations of its regulations), the Cocoa Board was acting as a private economic actor with regards to the action in question in this instance: negotiating a joint venture agreement (JVA) with a private company.[76]

It is interesting to contrast this holding with *Kardassopoulos/Fuchs v. Georgia*, which came to a different outcome on attribution. This case involved whether Georgia could be held responsible for contractual commitments made by two SOEs, SakNavtobi and Transneft.[77] The tribunal noted that the evidence demonstrated that both SakNavtobi and Transneft were incorporated within the structure of the Ministry of Fuel and Energy.[78] Also, it held that both SakNavtobi and Transneft clearly operated under its auspices and exercised (or purported to exercise) governmental authority because it was a JVA that was fully owned and controlled by the government of Georgia, and was authorized to exclusively represent Georgia in oil and gas and energy matters.[79] Ultimately, the tribunal found that the actions of the two SOEs could be attributed to Georgia, although it stated that Articles 4, 5, 7, and 11 were all applicable in the case.[80] It agreed with the claimants that attribution was appropriate because the companies were wholly owned by the state, and the actions taken in a JVA were as organs of a state, not as a commercial enterprise.[81] Despite the fact there was no direct governmental acknowledgement in the JVA, the JVA was supported by government officials.[82] In Ghana, the tribunal emphasized the function, and in Georgia the tribunal emphasized ownership, which it equated with governmental authority.

The 2016 case of *Saint-Gobain Performance Plastics Europe v. Bolivarian Republic of Venezuela* also determined that acts of an entity should be attributed to the state under Article 5. Here, an ICSID tribunal considered whether the acts of

---

[73] *Id.* at ¶ 194–98.
[74] KOVÁCS, *supra* note 12, at 153 ("This conclusion is not altered by the fact that the State instrumentality is empowered by law to carry out those commercial activities.").
[75] *Hamester v. Ghana*, ICSID Case No. ARB/07/24, Award (June 18, 2010), ¶ 255.
[76] *Id.* at ¶ 232.
[77] *Kardassopoulos v. Georgia*, ICSID Case Nos. ARB/05/18, ARB/07/15, Award (Mar. 3, 2010), ¶ 271.
[78] *Id.* at ¶ 275.
[79] *Id.* at ¶ 276.
[80] *Id.* at ¶ 279.
[81] *Id.* at ¶ 271 (note this is a near identical argument that was made by the Claimants in the *Hamester* case).
[82] *Id.* at ¶ 278.

Petróleos de Venezuela, S.A. (PDVSA), a state-owned gas company, were attributable to Venezuela under Article 5. PDVSA was given authority by the government to head the transition of a plant that produced ceramic proppants to State controlled operations. The tribunal found that PDVSA's actions were aimed at carrying out that mandate, and therefore, its acts were properly attributable to Venezuela under Article 5.[83] The tribunal wrote:

> [A]lthough PDVSA is a State-owned company with distinct legal personality, its conduct is attributable to [the] Respondent pursuant to Article 5 of the ILC Draft Articles.... [Because] [b]oth in its alleged function as a "caretaker" and its capacity as supervisor and promoter of the nationalization of the plant, PDVSA was vested with governmental authority.[84]

Although the Article 5 test has remained largely static, there have been some important variations.[85] First, despite a similarity in factual circumstances in *Hamester* and *Kadassopoulus* – whether or not a state is responsible for a JVA negotiated by SOE – the tribunals reached opposite conclusions.[86] The commentary to the ARSIWA is clear that what is considered governmental authority depends on the society, traditions, and history of a state.[87] The inconsistency in holdings of *Hamester* and *Kordassopoulos* might, therefore, be approached from the perspective that this is actually the proper application of Article 5: the tribunals were given the leeway that what might have been the exercise of government authority in Georgia does not necessarily constitute an exercise of government authority in Ghana. In effect, these are issues of domestic law. However, it is noteworthy that the reasoning in the awards did not mention the history, society, or traditions, and focused instead on whether the state imbued the entities in question with authority. As such, on the one hand, tribunals strive to provide an "international" view of what is a public act to ensure consistency in the international regulatory framework. On the other hand, ARSIWA permits internal differentiation based on the political and legal culture. In this regard, the definition of public power and the limits on what public powers can

---

[83] *Saint-Gobian v. Venezuela*, ICSID Case No. ARB/12/13, Decision on Liability and the Principles of Quantum (Dec. 30, 2016). ¶ 457–60.

[84] *Id.* at ¶ 457–58; *see also Flemingo DutyFree v. Poland*, PCA No. 2014-11, Award (Aug. 12, 2016), ¶ 439 (holding that "[t]he Ministry of Transport, by statutory provisions, delegated to PPL the task of modernising and operating Polish airports, controlled PPL, and held it accountable for the exercise of its powers. It is thus an entity exercising governmental authority, as envisaged by Article 5 of the ILC Articles.").

[85] *See, e.g., UAB E Energija v. Republic of Latvia*, ICSID Case No. ARB/12/33, Award (Dec. 22, 2017), ¶ 816 (describing a three, rather than a two-part test: "There are thus three aspects to the analysis: (i) the Regulator must have exercised elements of governmental authority; (ii) it must have been empowered by the Respondent's law to do so; and (iii) it was acting in that capacity in regulating tariffs and granting or revoking licenses.").

[86] Michael Feit, *Attribution and the Umbrella Clause – Is There a Way Out of the Deadlock*, 21 MINN. J. INT'L L. 21, 28 (2012).

[87] *Id.*

be delegated is particularly important. Mills argues that the range of possible actors and ownership structures is complex as a matter of attribution:

> Sometimes privatisation is merely a change in ownership of a market participant— this might occur, for example, where a state-owned airline which is already subject to free competition is privatised. Sometimes, however, privatised entities carry with them expressly public regulatory power—where, for example, an airline exercises delegated powers of immigration control or quarantine (Commentary, Article 5, (2)). Between these examples lie a wide variety of situations in which the entity may not have public power as defined in domestic law, but may nevertheless exercise regulatory authority (for example, through contracts, or licences, or defining industry standards) with the express or tacit support of the state.[88]

A final area in which there has been debate about the ILC's articles is the extent to which the articles on attribution apply as general rules, for example, in the case of contracts.[89] The heart of the question is whether SOEs that are set up by governments to operate on a commercial basis and that undertake contractual obligations implicate the responsibility of the parent state. Governments often deny liability for their acts, and this has been a source of considerable litigation in the investor-state arbitration context.[90] As Kaj Hobér explains, "if the ILC Articles are not applied to attribute contractual undertakings, 'it would seem that this would allow states to do precisely what the rules of state responsibility were intended to prevent, namely to avoid responsibility by delegating responsibilities, to allow states to "contract out" of state responsibility.'"[91]

A number of new treaties in the trade and investment area propose different rules for control which, when they enter into force, will resolve some of the ambiguities in ARSIWA's current structure. A particularly interesting convention is the Comprehensive Investment Agreement between the EU and China, currently in draft form, which sets out specific criteria for ownership and control. Given the significance of SOEs to China's economy – estimated at 30 percent – these rules

---

[88] *See also* Mills, *supra* note 6 (noting that it is unclear whether a contract that specifies a broad delegated function will suffice, or whether the instrument must detail the precise activities that the private military security company or other private entity is authorized to carry out in performance of that function. The commentary to Article 5 ARSIWA suggests that the delegated public powers must be specified within the authorization.).

[89] *See* discussion of *Hamester v. Ghana, supra* note 70–77; *see also* Feit, *supra* note 87, at 21 (noting that some tribunals and legal writers reject the idea that legal undertakings assumed by the SOE are attributable to the state under the ILC Articles. They take the stance that the ILC Articles are not general rules of attribution and cannot be used to attribute conduct, which does not constitute a breach of an international obligation).

[90] Srilal M. Perera, *State Responsibility: Ascertaining the Liability of States in Foreign Investment Disputes*, 6 J. WORLD INV. TRADE 499, 514 (2005).

[91] Feit, *supra* note 87, at 31 (citing Kaj Hobér, *State Responsibility and Attribution, in* THE OXFORD HANDBOOK OF INTERNATIONAL INVESTMENT LAW 575, 575 et seq. (Peter Muchlinski et al. eds., 2008)).

move away from the nature/function test noted above toward concrete ownership requirements. The CAI defines a covered entity as an entity or enterprise in which a Party directly or indirectly

i. owns more than 50 percent of the share capital;
ii. controls, through ownership interests the exercise of more than 50 percent of the voting rights;
iii. holds the power to appoint a majority of members of the board of directors or any other equivalent management body; or
iv. holds the power to control the decisions of the enterprise through any other ownership interest, including minority ownership.[92]

This fact-based approach to determining whether an entity is an SOE envisions situations in which control might arise from minority ownership with a golden share, or control through an appointment authority, in addition to setting a hard 50 percent threshold for more traditional tests. The effect of this treaty will be to take away some of the discretion accorded to arbitral tribunals that flows from the more fluid rules of ARSIWA and address the dilemma posed by the current rules over whether tribunals should defer to a national standard or emphasize an international one.[93]

Article 8: Applications

The second article on attribution treated in the Chapter, Article 8, addresses when acts of non-state entities are attributable to the state through its instructions, direction, and control:[94]

ARSIWA Article 8: Conduct directed or controlled by a State

> The conduct of a person or group of persons shall be considered an act of a State under international law if the person or group of persons is in fact acting on the instructions of, or under the direction or control of, that State in carrying out the conduct.

Typically, claimants will allege attribution under Article 4 and 5 first, before moving to Article 8 due to its high threshold. Different approaches emerged in courts. The

---

[92] *See* Comprehensive Agreement on Investment, China-E.U., art. 3bis § 1(a), Jan. 22, 2021, *available at* (https://trade.ec.europa.eu/doclib/docs/2021/january/tradoc_159343.pdf).

[93] Mills, *supra* note 6.

[94] Instructions refer to situations where state organs supplement their own action by recruiting or instigating private persons or groups who act as auxiliaries outside of the official state structure. CRAWFORD, *supra* note 8, at 145. Directions typically require the showing of a situation where corporations attempt to achieve a particular result. *See EDF v. Romania*, ICSID Case No. ARB/05/13, Award (Oct. 8, 2007), ¶ 201 (where an ICSID Tribunal found that Romania was using its ownership interest in and control of the corporations AIBO and TAROM to 'achieve a particular result,' namely bringing the contractual arrangements to an end with two entities, which met the art 8 test).

ICJ identified the appropriate standard of control in Nicaragua, Armed Activities (the Congo), and the Bosnian Genocide case as effective control, which requires evidence of specific conduct over operations. Alternatively, the International Criminal Tribunal for the former Yugoslavia in Tadic advocated the lower "overall control" test in the context of international humanitarian law.[95] As I have previously noted, however,

> [T]he elements developed by the ICJ were intended to apply to the determination of effective control during a military operation subject to the laws of war. This approach meant that the portability of the effective control test has been problematic in the corporate context, because the test is tied to violations of [international humanitarian law].[96]

Indeed, in the majority of investment cases in which Article 8 has been litigated, the test has not been met. Tribunals have been consistent in finding that although a state owns a separate entity and perhaps exercises overall control, this will not suffice to render its conduct attributable to the state.[97] Moreover, tribunals have consistently found that majority ownership is not enough to meet the Article 8 test.[98] Unlike Article 4, which is based on institutional links, or Article 5, which requires governmental authority, Article 8 employs a private law fact-based assessment of agency.[99] This solidifies the centrality of the Article 5 analysis for the majority of parastatal entities.

Three awards bear this trend out. First, in *MNSS B.V. and Recupero Credito Acciaio N.V. v. Montenegro* (2016) the issue arose as to whether Prva Banka's actions were attributable to Montenegro under Article 8. Prva, a private bank under the supervision of the government's Central Bank, was alleged to have refused to execute payments made by MNSS (a private holding company) in furtherance of a government privatization agreement.[100] The Tribunal held that other than a specific scenario where Prva Banka was acting under the direct supervision of the Central Bank, the actions of a private company, even under the supervision of a governmental authority, cannot be attributed to the state under Article 8 without evidence of specific instructions demonstrating control of the private company.[101] The emphasis

---

[95] Boon, *supra* note 18, at 346 (citing Military and Paramilitary Activities in and Against Nicaragua (*Nicar. v. U.S.*), Judgment, 1986 I.C.J. Rep. 14, ¶ 190 (June 27); Armed Activities on the Territory of the Congo (*Dem. Rep. Congo v. Uganda*), Judgment, 2005 I.C.J. Rep. 168 (Dec. 19); Application of the Convention on the Prevention and Punishment of the Crime of Genocide (*Bosn. & Herz. v. Serb. & Montenegro*), 2007 I.C.J. Rep. 43, Judgment (Feb. 26), ¶ 413).

[96] *Bayindir Insaat Turizm Ticaret Ve Sanayi AŞ v. Islamic Republic of Pak.*, ICSID Case No. ARB/03/29, Award (Aug. 27, 2009), ¶ 130.

[97] Baetens, *supra* note 11, at n.131.

[98] CARLO DE STEFANO, ATTRIBUTION IN INTERNATIONAL LAW AND ARBITRATION 172 (Oxford Univ. Press, 2020).

[99] *Id.* at 127.

[100] *MNSS B.V. v. Montenegro*, 91 ICSID Case No. ARB(AF)/12/8, Award (May 4, 2016), at ¶ ¶ 46, 223.

[101] *Id.* at ¶ ¶ 299, 331 (The Central Bank mandated the liquidity ratio of Prva, required daily and weekly reports on the bank's operations, and demanded that it make improvements to comply with guidelines.).

on specific instructions is consistent with the ICJ's approach, lending consistency to the application of the test across different fields of international law.

Second, in *Georg Gavrilović and Gavrilović d.o.o. v. Republic of Croatia*, a holding company in Croatia established nine limited liability companies (LLCs) in 1991, but three months later, after Holding d.o.o. began experiencing financial trouble, the Croatian agency placed an emergency board in the company that declared five of the nine LLCs bankrupt.[102] Mr. Gavrilović bid on the companies at the bankruptcy sale, and the subsequent Purchase Agreement served as the basis of his claim.[103] At issue was whether conduct of the liquidator, the Bankruptcy Council, the Bankruptcy Court, the Bankruptcy Judge, and the Croatian Privatisation Fund could be attributed to Croatia in order to found a claim for breach of the fair and equitable treatment standard through violations of the investor's legitimate expectations.[104] The Tribunal posited that in order to satisfy Article 8, it must be shown that the state had both general control over the non-state actor and specific control over the acts in question.[105] The Tribunal, in this instance, found that even if the placement of the emergency board within Holding d.o.o. was sufficient to prove general control over the company, specific control over the alleged acts would also need to be proven for attribution to be appropriate.[106] As such, attribution was not established under Article 8.

Finally, in 2016, *Mr. Kristian Almås and Mr. Geir Almås v. The Republic of Poland* involved a dispute over the termination of a lease agreement between the Almas and the Agricultural Property Agency (ANR), a Polish organization under the supervision of the Ministry of Agriculture and Rural Development. Here, despite the fact the ANR was under the supervision of the government, the court noted that it would need to see specific instruction by the government or of any other Polish State organ in order to attribute the actions of ANR with regard to the lease to Poland.[107] As such, the acts were once again found not to be attributable to the state. While privatization of entities may take away profits for a state, it does not always enable the avoidance of legal responsibility. Nonetheless, it is clear that in most instances, such liability will be based on Article 5.

There have been a handful of very fact-specific cases in which the test under Article 8 was met in the investment context. An example is *Ampal-American Israel Corporation and others v. Arab Republic* of Egypt. In that case, the tribunal cited Articles 4, 5, 8, and 11 and

---

[102] *Gavrilovic v. Croatia*, ICSID Case No. ARB/12/39, Award (July 26, 2018), ¶ ¶ 89, 95.

[103] *Id.* at ¶ ¶ 97, 105.

[104] Csaba Kovács, *Attribution in Investment Arbitration: From Stricto Sensu to Lato Sensu*, KLUWER ARBITRATION BLOG (Oct. 29, 2018), http://arbitrationblog.kluwerarbitration.com/2018/10/29/attribution-from-stricto-to-lato-sensu/?doing_wp_cron=1594339108.5734190940856933593750.

[105] *MNSS B.V.*, ICSID Case No. ARB(AF)/12/8 at ¶ 828.

[106] *Id.* at ¶ 829. A similar case is White Indus. *Australia Ltd. v. Republic of India*, UNCITRAL, Final Award (Nov. 30, 2011), ¶ ¶ 82, 86–7.

[107] *Almås v. Poland*, PCA No. 2015-13, Award (June 27, 2016), ¶ 270–71.

[F]ormed the view that the acts or omissions of EGPC [Egyptian General Petroleum Corporation] or EGAS [Egyptian Natural Gas Holding Company] relevant to the conclusion and termination of the GSPA [Gas Sale Purchase Agreement] are attributable to the Respondent under the relevant provisions of the ILC Draft Articles on State Responsibility, which form part of the applicable customary international law.[108]

With reference to Article 8, the tribunal noted that EGPC and EGAS "were 'in fact acting on the instructions of, or under the direction or control of' the Respondent in relation to the particular conduct."[109] Nonetheless, Article 8 continues to be regarded as an "exceptional mechanism, which requires a high threshold based on the two alternative prongs of instructions or authorization, on the one hand, and director or control on the other."[110]

In the human rights context, it is interesting to note that the Article 8 test has tended to be applied with a lower evidentiary threshold than in commercial cases. Taking a step back, this trend could suggest that a graver harm (human rights abuses) should have a lower threshold for responsibility than economic harm. Or, it could suggest that in areas where a state has positive obligations under human rights treaties or other legal instruments, courts and tribunals are more willing to assign responsibility. Two examples demonstrate this trend: in *Catan v. Moldova*, for example, the European Court of Human Rights found that Russia exercised effective control over the Moldovan Republic of Transdniestria (MRT) because of a strong dependency that the organization had on the Russian government.[111] While the Court did not specifically cite Article 8, it referenced the concept of effective control, and based its finding on Russia's continued economic, political, and military support for "MRT." Importantly, it made no mention of specific instructions Russia gave to the group or the lack thereof.[112] Second, in a number of cases involving the determination of whether separate legal entities bore a responsibility for debt, tribunals have noted that, notwithstanding the company's status as a separate legal entity, the municipal authority, and hence the state, is to be held responsible under the European Convention for the judgment debt in the applicant's favor. Here, courts have determined that the Article 8 control criteria were met.

Although tribunals demonstrate a high degree of support for the Article 8 test, and follow the holding in the ICJ's Bosnian Genocide decision requiring "effective,"

---

[108] *Ampal-American Israel Corp. v. Egypt*, ICSID Case No. ARB/12/11, Decision on Liability and Heads of Loss (Feb. 21, 2017), at ¶ 135.

[109] *Id.* at ¶ 146 (the tribunal went on to find that the acts were ultimately ratified by the state, and thus Art. 11 carried the holding.).

[110] De Stefano, *supra* note 99, at 172.

[111] *Catan and others v. Moldova & Russia*, App. Nos. 43370/04, 8252/05 & 18454/06, Eur. Ct. H.R., Judgment (Oct. 19, 2012), ¶¶ 121–22.

[112] *Id.*

specific control rather than "overall" control, there are few instances in which it has been applied in the commercial context. Moreover, it is significant that the commentary to Article 8 emphasizes that the terms "instructions," "direction," and "control" are disjunctive; that any one of these three elements would be sufficient to establish control for Article 8. However, a close reading of the awards discussed above shows that tribunals still require a separate showing of instructions, which goes farther than the commentary. This was the case in *Almås v. Poland,* where the tribunal stated that there needed to be specific instructions from the government to the Agricultural Property Agency in addition to their general control over the organization.[113]

In reality, tribunals appear to work around the difficult questions of attribution by focusing on omissions (finding states responsible for their failure to reign in the conduct of third parties where the primary rules or treaties permit this approach). In particular, there have been efforts to develop more fulsome interpretations of the duty to prevent, which creates an obligation on all states within the jurisdictional reach of a primary rule to curb the effects of conduct of private parties that may breach an international obligation.[114] The duty to prevent is dependent on the due diligence rule. While no precise definition of due diligence exists, three factors have been suggested to determine its applicability to a situation: "(i) the degree of effectiveness of the state's control over territory, (ii) the degree of predictability of harm, and (iii) the importance of the interest to be protected."[115] Due diligence is typically understood to be an objective, international standard rather than a subjective, domestic one.[116] Due diligence also requires that "a state is ... obliged to use all the means at its disposal in order to avoid activities which take place in its territory ... causing significant damage to the environment of another state."[117] Both norms are relevant to attribution because they place additional positive obligations on states, cover a state's relations with non-state actors, and, hence, serve as alternative means for closing the accountability gap if a state fails to fulfil the duty. These developments may ultimately have a halo effect, influencing the interpretation of attribution in international law and building bases for a more complete system of responsibility.

---

[113] *Almås v. Poland,* PCA No. 2015-13, Award (June 27, 2016), ¶ 270–71.

[114] Boon, *supra* note 18.

[115] J. Giorgio Gaja, The Relations between the European Union and Its Member States from the Perspective of the ILC Articles on Responsibility of International Organizations, SHARES Lecture at the University of Amsterdam (Apr. 11, 2013), *in* AMSTERDAM CENT. FOR INT'L L. SHARES RES. PAPER SERIES 25 (2013).

[116] Boon, *supra* note 18.

[117] Vassilis P. Tzevelekos, *Reconstructing the Effective Control Criterion in Extraterritorial Human Rights Breaches: Direct Attribution of Wrongfulness, Due Diligence, and Concurrent Responsibility,* 36 MICH. J. INT'L L. 129, 153 (2014); *see* Responsibilities and Obligations of States Sponsoring Persons and Entities with Respect to Activities in the Area, Advisory Opinion, ITLOS Case No. 17, Rep. 10 (Feb. 1, 2011).

CONCLUSION: CLOSING THE ACCOUNTABILITY GAP

Disputes involving SOEs operate in the contested space between domestic and international rules, between privatization and assertion of state control, and between divergent models of the state. It is perhaps no surprise that there is considerable engagement by regulators and disputing parties alike with norms of attribution today. Due to the changing global landscape and the inherent difficulties of developing general rules of attribution for application in varying circumstances, new approaches are emerging in primary rules including treaties such as CETA, the CPP, and CAI.

Another approach to closing the accountability gap involves building on ARSIWA through principles related to shared responsibility. As noted in the 2020 Principles of Shared Responsibility: "The defining feature of shared responsibility is that multiple international persons, by committing one or more internationally wrongful acts, contribute to an indivisible injury."[118] Although the principles note that their scope "is limited to states and international organizations … but the entitlement to invoke responsibility under the Principles extends to all persons that have rights under international law."[119] This includes individuals or other entities, such as corporations, that have rights under investment laws. The framework of shared responsibility and the principles proposed therein are of great significance to corporate actors that operate globally because they address a central limitation in ARSIWA, namely that multiple international legal persons may jointly commit a wrongful act, and the existing international rules do not provide solutions to address them.

In conclusion, cases involving SOEs appear to be on the rise. However, ARSIWA was not drafted with SOEs in mind, and tribunals are now being invited to apply them by analogy to a new commercial reality. Although the rules on attribution have fared well in practice, it is time to revisit the rules on attribution and to bring them into the conversation today. A revision of the rules would serve to right the balance between state autonomy and international standards.

---

[118] Andre Noellkaemper et al., *Principles of Shared Responsibility in International Law*, 31 EJIL 14, 24 (2020).
[119] *Id.* at 67.

3

Between States and Firms

Attribution and Construction of the Shareholder State

Mikko Rajavuori

INTRODUCTION

State ownership of private firms was revitalized in the early twenty-first century. Government bailouts and equity injections in the wake of the financial and COVID-19 crises, the aggressive expansion of state-owned national champions, and the emergence of sovereign wealth funds investing in private companies have recalibrated states' ownership functions across the world. As state ownership grows, morphs, and globalizes, states increasingly channel their influence through the financialized markets. The ensuing merger of the state's commercial and sovereign roles suggests that state ownership is, again, becoming a vector of sovereign authority.

Unsurprisingly, the global reconfiguration of state ownership is also reflected in the rules by which the contemporary "shareholder state" organizes and operates. This chapter analyzes the international legal system that has developed around surging state ownership. It suggests that the legal construction of distinctive "shareholder identities" in international economic law plays a key role in this complex regulatory matrix. Specifically, the chapter focuses on how arbitral tribunals adjudicating claims arising from international investment treaties use *attribution*, a doctrine of customary international law, in creating, maintaining, and disciplining state shareholders. Arbitral tribunals use the analytical category of the state shareholder in order to delineate and construct state and company identities and to understand the economic, political, and legal implications of those identities in the global economy. Accordingly, the interactions between substantive international economic law and the law of state responsibility form important, but underappreciated, elements of this constitutive process, which comes to affect the institutional design of state shareholding and disincentivize hands-on control over state-owned entities.

The argument proceeds in three steps. Part 1 provides a concise history of state ownership with a focus on its current permutations. Building on the rich multidisciplinary scholarship on state capitalism that has emerged over the past decade, the part traces the institutional evolution of state ownership from archetypical state-owned entities to the contemporary forms, thus identifying the state shareholder as an analytical category that mediates the state's direct market participation through the corporate form. Part 2 analyzes how the rise of the shareholder state is reflected in contemporary international economic law. In particular, the part examines how substantive trade and investment treaty provisions and the law of state responsibility conceptualize and govern the relationship between state-owned companies and their state shareholders. Against this backdrop, Part 3 analyzes recent arbitral awards that focus on the organization and operative logic of state shareholders. The part suggests that the ways arbitral tribunals use doctrines of attribution show how the state shareholder is legally constructed and, moreover, how the adjudicators put forward an idealized shareholder template that pivots on the concept of the "ordinary" shareholder. This concept mirrors the thrust of other domestic and transnational normative projects, including investment screening legislation and corporate governance codes, that are involved in disciplining state capitalism.

The chapter thus embeds the doctrine of attribution as a distinctive response to the emergent shareholder state. Moreover, the legal construction of the state shareholder through attribution highlights the significance of customary international law as a site for managing state-company relationships amid the fast-paced development of novel disciplines against state-owned companies.

THE RISE OF THE SHAREHOLDER STATE

State ownership has been an essential component of the world economy throughout the modern era. States' direct market participation, most prevalent in Europe, Asia, Africa, Latin America, and even the United States, forms one of the core instruments of their economic policies. While the rationales for, and applications of, state ownership have varied over time, its common uses have been to overcome undeveloped capital markets, organize natural monopolies, produce public goods, account for strategic interests, and pursue social policy.[1] The past decades have witnessed rapid internationalization of state ownership, once initially confined mostly within national jurisdictions, along with its extreme politicization in international economic relations, primarily due to the expansion of Chinese state-owned enterprises (SOEs).[2] However, the current debates on the effects of hybrid forms of state capitalism, such as economic statecraft, only become understandable against the complex economic, political, and legal history of state ownership.[3]

By most accounts, the heyday of state ownership was the 1960s and early 1970s, a period characterized by the completion of postwar nationalizations, the ascendancy

[1] *See, e.g.,* THE ROUTLEDGE HANDBOOK OF STATE-OWNED ENTERPRISES (Luc Bernier et al. eds., 2020).
[2] *See, e.g.,* Milan Babic et al., *The Rise of Transnational State Capital: State-Led Foreign Investment in the 21st Century,* 27 REV. INT'L POL. ECON. 433 (2020).
[3] *See, e.g.,* Robert Loring Allen, *State Trading and Economic Warfare,* 24 L. CONTEMP. PROBS. 256 (1959).

of the socialist economic model, and massive expropriations brought about by the decolonization movement.[4] During this period, the functions of state ownership were both numerous and pervasive, leading commentators to consider "public ownership ... the main mode of economic regulation," as it enabled the state "to impose a planned structure on the economy and at the same time to protect the public interest against powerful private interests."[5] From the mid-1970s onward, the state ownership model, as a catalyst of economic development, quickly fell from grace. State ownership was increasingly viewed as an inefficient burden for public finances, as a barrier to flourishing private enterprise, and as a site for elite expropriation.[6] Notwithstanding the prominent position of privatization in the Washington Consensus policy bundle, however, state ownership proved sticky in the 1990s and 2000s, particularly in Asia, Europe, and South America.[7] The continuing relevance of state ownership became particularly acute after the 2008 financial crisis. Following the bailouts of key financial companies in the United States and across Europe, and the capital provided by sovereign wealth funds, heavy-handed state intervention was, at least for the moment, again a legitimate course of economic policy.[8] More recently, the growth and internalization of state ownership have rendered hybrid state capitalism a pertinent issue of economic innovation and security policy and revitalized the debate on the pros and cons of direct state intervention.[9] The effects of the COVID-19 pandemic on the macro trends of state capitalism are still inconclusive, but initial reactions suggest that policy responses to the pandemic resulted in the growth of direct state control over companies.[10]

The ebb and flow of state ownership policy is inextricably linked to its evolving institutional arrangements. During the 1960s, for example, the dominant mode of state capitalism centered on wholly owned companies. As the sole owner, the state could essentially arrange many facets of economic and social life through its

---

[4] *See, e.g.,* Pier Angelo Toninelli, *The Rise and Fall of Public Enterprise: The Framework, in* THE RISE AND FALL OF STATE-OWNED ENTERPRISE IN THE WESTERN WORLD (Pier Angelo Toninelli ed., 2000).

[5] Giandomenico Majone, *From the Positive to the Regulatory State: Causes and Consequences of Changes in the Mode of Governance,* 17 J. PUB. POL'Y 139, 144 (1997).

[6] *See, e.g.,* WORLD BANK, BUREAUCRATS IN BUSINESS: THE ECONOMICS AND POLITICS OF GOVERNMENT OWNERSHIP (1995); WILLIAM L. MEGGINSON, THE FINANCIAL ECONOMICS OF PRIVATIZATION (2005).

[7] *See, e.g.,* ALICE AMSDEN, THE RISE OF "THE REST": CHALLENGES TO THE WEST FROM LATE-INDUSTRIALIZING ECONOMIES (2001); Bernardo Bortolotti & Mara Faccio, *Government Control of Privatized Firms,* 22 REV. FIN. STUD. 2907 (2009).

[8] *See, e.g.,* William Megginson, *Privatization, State Capitalism, and State Ownership of Business in the 21st Century,* 11 FOUNDS. TRENDS FIN. 1 (2017).

[9] *See, e.g.,* Andreas Nölke, *Introduction: Toward State Capitalism 3.0, in* MULTINATIONAL CORPORATIONS FROM EMERGING MARKETS: STATE CAPITALISM 3.0 (Andreas Nölke ed., 2014).

[10] *See, e.g., Equity Injections and Unforeseen State Ownership of Enterprises during the COVID-19 Crisis,* OECD (2020), https://read.oecd-ilibrary.org/view/?ref=131_131932-wjo71ujbxy&title=Equity-injections-and-unforeseen-state-ownership-of-enterprises-during-the-COVID-19-crisis.

entrepreneurial, not regulatory, roles. Operationally, this was achieved by maintaining administrative controls over SOEs, for instance, through using sectoral ministries to accomplish extensive direction of business operations.[11] By contrast, the current organizational models are often built around minority ownership, centralization of the state ownership in dedicated ownership entities, and the emergence of novel types of state-owned asset and investment vehicles, which create additional institutional boundaries between politicians, state officials, and company management.[12] In China, for instance, the move from direct government control to a centralized ownership entity-driven model, with the State-owned Assets Supervision and Administration Commission (SASAC) of the State Council on top of the pyramid, was part of a broader financialization policy whereby "the Chinese state transform[ed] its management of the economy from administrative intervention and fiscal allocation to supervising its massive state assets according to shareholder value."[13] In France, the creation of Agence des participations de l' État (APE) in the early 2000s was motivated by similar outcomes – professionalization of asset ownership – but was more limited in scope.[14]

Each of these examples indicates institutional evolution in the policy frameworks that hinge on the separation between the state's regulatory function and its shareholder function. Instead of pervasive and direct control by ministries or other governmental agencies, state ownership interests are increasingly ring-fenced in distinctive shareholder entities, including state holding companies or various investment vehicles. This broad shift – while diverse in its particular instantiations – hints at the emergence of a distinct organizational paradigm, *the shareholder state*.

Under this emergent model – which the existing scholarship often compares to that of an asset manager or institutional investor – the state ownership function deviates from many prior eras in its organization, operation, rationality, and geographical scope.[15] Rather than viewing the state as a dirigiste sovereign administrator, able

---

[11] *See, e.g.*, Aldo Musacchio and Sergio Lazzarini, Reinventing State Capitalism. Leviathan in Business, Brazil and Beyond (2014).

[12] *See, e.g.*, Dag Detter & Stefan Fölster, The Public Wealth of Nations: How Management of Public Assets Can Boost or Bust Economic Growth (2015); Aldo Musacchio et al., *New Varieties of State Capitalism: Strategic and Governance Implications*, 29 Acad. Mgmt. Perspectives 115 (2015).

[13] Yingyao Wang, *The Rise of the "Shareholding State": Financialization of Economic Management in China*, 13 Socio-Econ. Rev. 603 (2015).

[14] Hadrien Coutant & Scott Viallet-Thévenin, *The State as an Eager Shareholder*, 30 Revue de la Régulation [Rev. Regul.] (2021) (Fr.).

[15] *See, e.g.*, Junmin Wang et al., *The Rise of SASAC: Asset Management, Ownership Concentration, and Firm Performance in China's Capital Markets*, 8 Mgmt. Org. Rev. 253 (2012); Adam Dixon, *The State as Institutional Investor: Unpacking the Geographical Political Economy of Sovereign Wealth Funds*, in Handbook on the Geographies of Money and Finance (Ron Martin & Jane Pollard eds., 2017); Roberto Cardinale & Emanuele Belotti, *The Rise of the Shareholding State in Italy: A Policy-Oriented Strategist or Simply a Shareholder? Evidence from the Energy and Banking Sectors' Privatizations*, 62 Strucl. Chan. Econ. Dynamics 52 (2022).

to coordinate and dictate corporate decision-making using regulatory authority, it is positioned as a shareholder whose power is channeled transnationally through the investee company's investor relations and ultimately exercised in the general meeting of shareholders. Even though the policy objectives traditionally associated with the regulatory use of SOEs have not disappeared, they are increasingly mediated through professionalized shareholder entities and deployed through established company decision-making structures.

The new geographical and institutional set-up of the shareholder state is underwritten by a complex, diffuse, and multitiered governance framework. Much of the regulatory infrastructure in which state shareholders operate is of domestic origin. In particular, national administrative, corporate, competition, and constitutional laws provide the basic structure and the general parameters for state shareholding, often as a reflection of the domestic legal traditions and varieties of capitalism.[16] In a process mirroring the rise of the shareholder state paradigm, most legal systems have opted to limit the government's abilities to exert undue influence over its investee companies through public listings and corporate law reforms,[17] thus essentially transforming the earlier paradigm of "ownership as regulation" into "regulation of ownership."[18] Moreover, specific ownership and foreign investment statutes, such as the recent crop of investment screening laws that create additional hurdles for corporate acquisitions by foreign SOEs, also illustrate the expanding domestic regulation of internationalizing state capitalism.[19]

Many of these national law and policy choices are embedded in international regulatory arrangements that enable, constrain, and shape the broad parameters of state shareholding. On the regional level, the European Union is known for maintaining state aid and free movement of capital provisions, which regulate the conduct of states when they intervene in the market economy through shareholder positions.[20] On the transnational level, several prominent soft law codes, such as the Organization for Economic Cooperation and Development (OECD) Guidelines for Corporate Governance of State-owned Enterprises, provide a robust set of best practices for organizing the state shareholder function. These codes have

---

[16] *See, e.g.*, Benjamin Templin, *The Government Shareholder: Regulating Public Ownership of Private Enterprise*, 62 ADMIN. L. REV. 1127 (2010); Mariana Pargendler, *State Ownership and Corporate Governance*, 80 FORDHAM L. REV. 2917 (2012).

[17] Curtis J Milhaupt & Mariana Pargendler, *Governance Challenges of Listed State-Owned Enterprises around the World: National Experiences and a Framework for Reform*, 50 CORNELL INT'L L. J. 473 (2017).

[18] Ian Thynne, *Ownership as an Instrument of Policy and Understanding in the Public Sphere: Trends and Research Agenda*, 32 POL'Y STUD. 183 (2011).

[19] *See, e.g.*, Mikko Rajavuori & Kaisa Huhta, *Investment Screening: Implications for the Energy Sector and Energy Security*, 144 ENERGY POL'Y 111646 (2020).

[20] *See, e.g.*, Andrea Biondi, *When the State Is the Owner – Some Further Comments on the Court of Justice "Golden Shares" Strategy*, in COMPANY LAW AND ECONOMIC PROTECTIONISM: NEW CHALLENGES TO EUROPEAN INTEGRATION (Ulf Bernitz & Wolf-Georg Ringe eds., 2010).

proliferated over the past decades.[21] On the international level, trade and investment treaties increasingly register the impact of SOEs and their owner states.[22] The proliferation of various supranational regulatory mechanisms targeted at the rise of the shareholder state exposes the significance of state ownership on global economic governance and draws attention to regional and international economic law as key domains for structuring its normative and operative conditions.

Thus, the reinvigorated state shareholders are subject to domestic regulation consisting of both public and private law, and they garner increasing global attention through specialized regional, transnational, and international regimes. Due to the rapid internationalization of state ownership, international economic law in particular has emerged as a vital piece in this global regulatory infrastructure. Given how equity ownership continues to encroach on the exercise of sovereign authority and plays a significant role in the world economy, the next part focuses, first, on the governance of state shareholders in substantive international trade and investment law and, second, on their characterization under customary international law.

GOVERNING THE SHAREHOLDER STATE IN INTERNATIONAL ECONOMIC LAW

This part discusses the international economic law setting in which the contemporary shareholder state operates. First, the part introduces primary trade and investment treaty law provisions that relate to state ownership, with a focus on recent treaty practice. Next, the part identifies customary international law as a key, but underappreciated, site for managing the relationship between state shareholders and their investee companies.

State Shareholders under International Trade and Investment Law

State involvement in the market through ownership has been a staple issue in international economic law for over a century. In the mid-twentieth century, for instance, the toughest legal conundrums related to whether and how to apply the law of state immunity to SOEs operating outside their home jurisdictions.[23] By contrast, in the decolonization era the most topical issues were nationalizations and the respective protections allotted to foreign companies under state contracts.[24]

---

[21] *See, e.g.,* Mikko Rajavuori, *Governing the Good State Shareholder: The Case of the OECD Guidelines on Corporate Governance of State-Owned Enterprises,* 29 Eur. Bus. L. Rev. 103 (2018).

[22] *See, e.g.,* Petros Mavroidis & Merit Janow, *Free Markets, State Involvement, and the WTO: Chinese State-Owned Enterprises in the Ring,* 16 World Trade Rev. 571 (2017).

[23] *See, e.g.,* Vernon Setser, *The Immunities of the State and Government Economic Activities,* 24 L. Contemp. Probs. 291 (1959).

[24] *See, e.g.,* Robert von Mehren & Nicholas Kourides, *International Arbitrations between States and Foreign Private Parties: The Libyan Nationalization Cases,* 75 Am. J. Int'l L. 476 (1981).

International economic law has never, however, tackled state ownership in a comprehensive way. For example, a few isolated references to state trading enterprises aside, early trade regimes refrained from explicitly singling out SOEs.[25] Even the current World Trade Organization system tackles state ownership mostly indirectly through subsidy regulation.[26] In the same vein, most bilateral investment treaties (BITs) omit specific references to SOEs or to the conduct of states as their shareholders. While there are many reasons for the lack of explicit legal control of state ownership, perhaps the most compelling argument builds on the dynamics of the post-World War II economic architecture. On the one hand, the Soviet bloc insisted on deference to SOEs in their international operations, blocking various regulatory instruments.[27] On the other hand, the Bretton Woods institutions that provided the basic framework for international economic governance in the West operated under the paradigm of embedded liberalism, which allowed a great deal of domestic flexibility in pursuing different modes for economic development.[28] The effects of these historical bargains remain visible to this day.

Whether the silence of international economic law on state ownership was based on comity or on the inability to negotiate effective multilateral rules, the relevant treaty law remains skeletal. The most prominent early example of a highly specific SOE provision was the Energy Charter Treaty's Article 22(1), which stipulates that "[e]ach Contracting Party shall ensure that any state enterprise which it maintains or establishes shall conduct its activities in relation to the sale or provision of goods and services in its Area in a manner consistent with the Contracting Party's obligations under … this Treaty."[29] Some BITs also contain special measures targeting SOEs. According to the US-Ukraine BIT Article II(2)(b), for example, "[e]ach Party shall ensure that any State enterprise that it maintains or establishes acts in a manner that is not inconsistent with the Party's obligations under this Treaty."[30] Likewise, Article 10.1.2 of the US-Oman free trade agreement stipulates that a "Party's obligations … shall apply to a state enterprise or other person when it exercises any regulatory, administrative, or other governmental authority delegated to it by that Party."[31] Despite their ambiguity, these treaty provisions extend obligations to arrange and

---

[25] *See, e.g.,* Roy Baban, *State Trading and the GATT*, 11 J. WORLD TRADE 334 (1977).

[26] *See, e.g.,* Ming Du, *China's State Capitalism and World Trade Law*, 63 INT'L & COMPAR. L. Q. 409 (2014).

[27] *See, e.g.,* Rosanne Thomas, *Host State Treatment of Transnational Corporations: Formulation of a Standard for the United Nations Code of Conduct on Transnational Corporations*, 7 FORDHAM INT'L L. J. 467 (1983).

[28] *See, e.g.,* John Ruggie, *International Regimes, Transactions, and Change: Embedded Liberalism in the Postwar Economic Order*, 36 INT'L ORG. 379 (1982).

[29] Energy Charter Treaty art. 22(1), *opened for signature* Dec. 17, 1994, 34 I.L.M. 360 (entered into force Apr. 1998).

[30] Treaty Concerning the Encouragement and Reciprocal Protection of Investment, U.S.–Ukr., art. II(2)(b), T.I.A.S. No. 96-1116 (1996).

[31] U.S.-Oman Free-Trade Agreement, U.S.–Oman, art. 10.1.2 120 Stat. 1192 (2016).

control the behavior of "state enterprises" to match the state party's own obligations. The provisions are, however, typically limited in scope to the most obvious
arrangements where SOEs assume distinct public functions. As the existing treaty
provisions mostly predate the rise of state capitalism in the early twenty-first century,
they do not seem to regulate the changing institutional structures of the shareholder
state, such as those that are most acutely reflected in the organization and practices
of Chinese state capitalism.

Against this backdrop, it is no surprise that trade and investment treaties drafted
and negotiated from the 2010s onward have taken a more comprehensive approach to
state ownership, both in terms of definitions and substantive obligations. The evolving treaty practice emphasizes competitive neutrality – fair competition between
firms regardless of their ownership structure or nationality – and it builds on a mix
of provisions tackling issues ranging from coordination to covert state aid, subsidies,
and transparency.[32] An influential early example is the Trans-Pacific Partnership
(TPP), a U.S.-driven mega-regional trade agreement that included a distinct SOE-
chapter, but was promptly abandoned by the Trump administration.[33] Several major
trade and investment agreements have since included SOE provisions. The successor of the TPP – the Comprehensive and Progressive Agreement for Trans-Pacific
Partnership – for example, extended state obligations to SOEs. Moreover, SOEs are
explicitly defined in that agreement. They are companies in which the state party
directly owns more than 50 percent of the stock, controls the enterprise through the
ownership of more than 50 percent of its voting rights, or has the right to appoint
the majority of the members of the executive board or any other decision-making
body.[34]

The EU-Japan Free Trade Agreement opts for a similar definition, but also
covers situations where the state has the power to "legally direct the actions of
the enterprise or otherwise exercises an equivalent degree of control in accordance with its laws and regulations."[35] By contrast, the EU-Vietnam Free Trade
Agreement expands the definition of state-owned enterprises beyond the ownership stake by reference to the state party's ability to "exercise control over the strategic decisions of the enterprise."[36] The EU-UK Trade and Cooperation Agreement
opts for a formulation whereby an SOE is defined by whether the state party has

[32] *See, e.g.*, Mitsuo Matsushita & Chin Leng Lim, *Taming Leviathan as Merchant: Lingering Questions about the Practical Application of Trans-Pacific Partnership's State-Owned Enterprises Rules*, 19 WORLD TRADE REV. 402 (2020).
[33] *See, e.g.*, Julien Sylvestre Fleury & Jean-Michel Marcoux, *The US Shaping of State-Owned Enterprise Disciplines in the Trans-Pacific Partnership*, 19 J. INT'L ECON. L. 445 (2016).
[34] Comprehensive and Progressive Agreement for Trans-Pacific Partnership (CPTT) art. 17(1)(3), *opened for signature* Mar. 8, 2018 (entered into force Dec. 30 2018) *available at* www.dfat.gov.au/trade/agreements/in-force/cptpp/comprehensive-and-progressive-agreement-for-trans-pacific-partnership (last visited March 6, 2023).
[35] European Union-Japan Economic Partnership Agreement, Japan-E.U., art. 13(1)(h), Feb. 1, 2019.
[36] European Union-Vietnam Free Trade Agreement, Viet.-E.U., art. 11(1)(g), Aug. 1, 2020.

"the power to exercise control over the enterprise," with "all relevant legal and factual elements [to] be taken into account on a case-by-case basis" in establishing control.[37] The European Union's recent major trade agreement, the EU-China Comprehensive Agreement on Investment (CAI, Agreement in Principle), combines the two special rules, although the relevant provision refrains from using SOE terminology, opting instead for a similar formulation through the term "covered entity."[38]

The most comprehensive rules are included in the Agreement between the United States of America, the United Mexican States, and Canada (USMCA), which define SOEs expansively to cover companies with more than 50 percent of state ownership or the power to control the enterprise through any other ownership interest, including indirect or minority ownership.[39] This form of control is further detailed as an ownership interest through which the state party can determine or direct important matters affecting the enterprise, excluding minority shareholder protections. In assessing control, "all relevant legal and factual elements shall be taken into account on a case-by-case basis," including "the power to determine or direct commercial operations."[40]

Taken together, recent trade and investment treaty practice makes several innovations that seek to accommodate the changes in the operating conditions of state ownership. On the definitional side, the new provisions result in quantifiable bright-line tests as to what constitutes an SOE, often detaching the definition from abstract notions of governmental authority. Compared to prior, and often elliptic treaty language, new definitional attempts can be seen to better cover the state's commercial and regulatory roles even when it operates as a minority shareholder or exercises control over the company's strategic decisions in other ways. By focusing on the organization and intensity of state shareholding, rather than the overt exercise of governmental authority, the new provisions are an indication of a concerted, if largely Western-driven, response to the evolution of the shareholder state. Notwithstanding the explicit expansion of SOE obligations to cover the state's minority shareholding and the attempted changes in state shareholder rationality, however, the new provisions are unlikely to provide a comprehensive international regime to manage state capitalism.[41] While the geographical coverage of the treaties is wide, the new trade and investment regimes remain binding only on the signatory states and thus lack

---

[37] Trade and Cooperation Agreement between the European Union and the European Atomic Energy Community, of the one part, and the United Kingdom of Great Britain and Northern Ireland, of the other part, art. 4.1, Jan. 12, 2021.

[38] U.S.-Mexico-Canada Agreement part II, art. 3bis, Dec. 13, 2019, OFFICE U.S. TRADE REP., https://ustr.gov/trade-agreements/free-trade-agreements/united-states-mexico-canada-agreement/agreement-between.

[39] *Id.*, art. 22(1)–(2).

[40] *Id.*, art. 22(1), n. 8.

[41] *Cf.* Weihuan Zhou et al., *Building a Market Economy through WTO-Inspired Reform of State-Owned Enterprises in China*, 68 INT'L & COMPAR. L. Q. 977 (2019).

global applicability. In addition, even the recent treaties contain numerous exceptions that carve out significant portions of the SOE-sector from the reach of the new disciplines.[42]

State Ownership under Customary International Law

The continuing absence of a comprehensive regime to discipline SOEs under international economic law is, however, mitigated by a branch of customary international law, the law of state responsibility, and specifically its doctrine of attribution. In essence, attribution refers to a process which demarcates the exact boundaries of the state for the purpose of triggering state responsibility. Attribution in the context of state ownership is of practical importance, as it is frequently relied upon in international adjudication to establish if the state is responsible for the conduct of a state-owned or controlled company. This is especially so in international investment law, a regime fragmented into thousands of individual investment treaties. In this regime, the law of state responsibility and the doctrine of attribution provide a unifying framework used to distinguish permissible state behavior from conduct that infringes a BIT's substantive guarantees. In this way, attribution emerges as a key doctrinal pathway to structure and align the operation of shareholder states with their existing treaty obligations.

The attribution doctrine of the law of state responsibility is most commonly discussed with reference to the International Law Commission's (ILC) Articles on Responsibility of States for Internationally Wrongful Acts (ARSIWA), a codification of customary international law completed in 2001.[43] Even though the ARSIWA is not binding as such, it is widely accepted as an accurate representation of the customary standards of state responsibility, which international adjudicators use to assess claimed breaches of international law.[44] While some international treaty regimes contain special rules of attribution, the ARSIWA's universally applicable "transubstantive" rules influence international adjudication across different branches of international law, spanning from human rights to international humanitarian law.[45]

---

[42] *See, e.g.,* Leonardo Borlini, *When the Leviathan Goes to the Market: A Critical Evaluation of the Rules Governing State-Owned Enterprises in Trade Agreements,* 33 LEIDEN J. INT'L L. 313 (2020); Jaemin Lee, *The "Indirect Support" Loophole in the New SOE Norms: An Intentional Choice or Inadvertent Mistake?,* 20 CHINESE J. INT'L L. 63 (2021).

[43] Int'l L. Comm'n, *Draft Articles on Responsibility of States for Internationally Wrongful Acts,* U.N. Doc. A/56/10 (Oct. 24, 2001) [hereinafter "ILC Articles"].

[44] *See, e.g.,* Luigi Condorelli & Claus Kress, *The Rules of Attribution: General Considerations, in* THE LAW OF INTERNATIONAL RESPONSIBILITY (James Crawford et al. eds., 2010); JAMES CRAWFORD, STATE RESPONSIBILITY: THE GENERAL Part (2013).

[45] Compare with David Caron, *The Basis of Responsibility: Attribution and Other Transubstantive Rules, in* THE IRAN-UNITED STATES CLAIMS TRIBUNAL: ITS CONTRIBUTION TO THE LAW OF STATE RESPONSIBILITY (RB Lillich & DB Magraw eds., 1998); Marko Milanovic, *Special Rules of Attribution of Conduct in International Law,* 96 INT'L L. STUD. 1 (2020).

International investment arbitration has historically been one of the most active forums for applying the doctrines of attribution in concrete disputes involving state-owned entities. This is because typical large-scale investment projects, particularly in Global South and transition economies, are often arranged with foreign investors contracting, interacting, and cooperating with SOEs or other separate instrumentalities rather than the state itself. From the perspective of the state, this allows flexibility and other advantages of the corporate form, such as segmentation and limitation of potential liabilities. If, however, the investment project faces obstacles, such as governmental interference, undercapitalization, or contractual breaches, questions often emerge as to the responsibility and, with that, the liability of the shareholder state.[46] State shareholders are thus subject to scrutiny when claimants seek to construe SOEs and other state-owned entities either as functional parts of the state or its instrumentalities. The issue of attribution often emerges as the focal point of litigation.[47]

ARSIWA contains three primary attribution rules that delineate whether a state is internationally responsible for the conduct of a state-owned company in the light of the substantive obligations of a given treaty. These basic rules, found in Articles 4, 5, and 8 of the ARSIWA and the ILC's commentary, provide a framework where markedly private arrangements can trigger state responsibility. The rules cover the instances where an entity is considered an organ of the state, where it is empowered to exercise elements of the governmental authority, and where it is acting under instructions or under the direction or control of the state.[48] All three of these relevant rules are usually pursued in litigation involving private parties. From the perspective of the foreign investor litigating against a state under international investment law, for example, the optimal outcome is usually to equate an SOE with a state organ under Article 4. Under that rule, all conduct of a separate entity, irrespective of its regulatory or commercial nature, shall be considered an act of that state.[49] Alternatively, the foreign investors can also seek to demonstrate, under Article 5, that an SOE was exercising elements of governmental authority when breaching a substantive provision of a BIT.[50] Finally, under Article 8, the conduct of a company may be attributed to the state if there is "evidence that the corporation was exercising public powers, or that the State was using its ownership interest in or control of a corporation specifically to achieve a particular result."[51] The threshold for attributing conduct under Article 8 is very high because of the

---

[46] *See generally*, ALBERT BADIA, PIERCING THE VEIL OF STATE ENTERPRISES IN INTERNATIONAL ARBITRATION (2014).

[47] *See, e.g.*, Mikko Rajavuori, *Making International Legal Persons in Investment Treaty Arbitration: State-Owned Enterprises along the Person/Thing Distinction*, 18 GERMAN L. J. 1183 (2017).

[48] For a more comprehensive analysis, see the chapter by Kristen E. Boon in this volume.

[49] ILC Articles, *supra* note 43, art. 4, 6.

[50] *Id.* at art. 5.

[51] *Id.* at art. 8.

evidentiary difficulties claimants face when trying to establish state direction and control over an SOE.[52]

Together, the rules articulated in ARSIWA cover instances where SOEs have, for example, been established as standalone companies with separate legal personalities in their domestic jurisdictions, but nevertheless have been entrusted with carrying out governmental policies. This is usually in sensitive fields such as energy, telecommunications, infrastructure, or finance. Another typical situation involves state-owned companies that clearly operate outside any governmental prerogative, but in which states retain a high degree of influence and control. That influence and control is then used to breach the shareholder state's treaty commitments.[53] From a practical perspective, the law of state responsibility thus is instrumental in probing the conduct of state shareholders in order to enforce the substantive guarantees arising from individual treaties. At the same time, however, the law of state responsibility – through the doctrine of attribution – also plays a key role in shaping and channeling the wider international economic law responses to the rise of the emergent shareholder state.

ATTRIBUTION AND LEGAL CONSTRUCTION
OF THE SHAREHOLDER STATE

This part analyzes how investment arbitration tribunals use doctrines of attribution to construe the shareholder state. First, the part discusses how attribution may be understood as a regulatory technique that frames legitimate state shareholder power. Next, the part analyzes five arbitral awards that focus on the organization and operation of the state shareholder. The part suggests that the analysis of attribution by the tribunals in these cases pivots on the concept of the "ordinary" shareholder, which forms a key element in the legal construction of the state shareholder.

Attribution as a Regulatory Technique

The way investment tribunals interpret and apply the doctrines of attribution greatly affect the outcome of investment treaty arbitration. In some concrete disputes involving state-owned entities, the tribunals' interpretive standards may lead to establishing attribution and state responsibility. In others, the facts of the case and the conduct of shareholder states do not meet the necessary control threshold. While analysis of the technical operation of attribution in the case of state-owned

---

[52] *Cf.* Thomas Wälde, *Equality of Arms in Investment Arbitration: Procedural Challenges*, in ARBITRATION UNDER INTERNATIONAL INVESTMENT AGREEMENTS: A GUIDE TO THE KEY ISSUES (Katia Yannaca-Small ed., 2010).

[53] *See, e.g.*, Michael Feit, *Responsibility of the State under International Law for the Breach of Contract Committed by a State-Owned Entity*, 28 BERKELEY J. INT'L L. 142 (2010).

companies is already well-rehearsed in scholarly commentary,[54] significantly less emphasis has been placed on its system-level ramifications for the emergent shareholder state. This is a significant omission because the doctrines of attribution can form trans-substantive and universally applicable techniques that frame and sustain the legitimate exercise of state shareholder power. This applies particularly "in the foggy borderland between the worlds of public and private" where the doctrines of attribution enable international adjudicators to demarcate the exact boundaries of the state regardless of its domestic administrative traditions and institutional arrangements.[55]

In principle, attribution doctrines perform a highly specialized function. According to ARSIWA, the purpose of attribution is to define "the conditions under which conduct is attributable to the State" and thus the rules ought not to be used "for other purposes for which it may be necessary to define the State or its Government."[56] Notwithstanding such a clear position, ARSIWA's rules of attribution are regularly used in multiple roles and at multiple stages of international adjudication. The doctrine appears, for instance, when investment tribunals analyze the proper authors of a particular representation and the attribution of contractual obligations, both of which clearly deal with attribution of internationally *lawful* acts.[57] Similarly, rules of attribution often appear at the jurisdictional stage when tribunals examine their competence over disputes involving state-owned entities.[58] Accordingly, international courts and tribunals also use the attribution doctrine in ways that extend their scope and applicability beyond what the ILC's conceptualization of them would suggest, with important ramifications.

---

[54] *See, e.g.,* Mikko Rajavuori, *How Should States Own? Heinisch v. Germany and the Emergence of Human Rights-Sensitive State Ownership Function,* 26 Eur. J. Int'l L. 727 (2015); Simon Olleson, *Attribution in Investment Treaty Arbitration,* 31 ICSID Rev. 457 (2016); Judith Schönsteiner, *Attribution of State Responsibility for Actions or Omissions of State-Owned Enterprises in Human Rights Matters,* 40 U. Penn. J. Int'l L. 895 (2019); Jorge Viñuales, *Attribution of Conduct to States in Investment Arbitration,* 20 ICSID Rep. 13 (2022).

[55] Gus van Harten, *The Public-Private Distinction in the International Arbitration of Individual Claims Against the State,* 56 Int'l & Comp. L. Q. 371, 371–94 (2007).

[56] ILC Articles, *see supra* note 43, Ch. II, ¶ 5.

[57] *See, e.g.,* Csaba Kovács, Attribution in International Investment Law (2018).

[58] It is important to note that state-owned entities can also appear as claimants in investment treaty arbitration. In these cases, the tribunals often rely on the so-called *Broches* test, which suggests that claims under the ICSID Convention by government-owned corporations should not be disqualified unless they act as agents for the government or discharge essentially governmental functions. *See* Aron Broches, *The Convention on the Settlement of Investment Disputes between States and Nationals of Other States, in* 136 Collected Courses of the Hague Academy of International Law, Part II, 334–335 (1972). These conditions closely resemble those under ILC Articles 8 and 5, and their parallels are frequently discussed both in arbitral case law and legal commentary. *See, e.g.,* Mark Feldman, *State-Owned Enterprises as Claimants in International Investment Arbitration,* 31 ICSID Rev. 24 (2016); Anran Zhang, *The Standing of Chinese State-Owned Enterprises in Investor-State Arbitration: The First Two Cases,* 17 Chinese J. Int'l L. 1147 (2018). Due to space constraints, however, this article does not address these jurisdictional issues in greater detail.

In the context of international investment law, the practical "distributive effects of extending attribution rules" on the host state's political economy are clear, given that triggering state responsibility over the acts of separate entities can lead to awarding substantial pecuniary compensation to private investors.[59] Volatile and potentially costly outcomes of attribution can, already by themselves, incentivize states to limit the use of state-owned entities, but attribution also has more constitutive effects.[60] Thus, this chapter suggests that attribution forms a key, but underappreciated, component in shaping, nudging, and defining the ways in which states organize themselves when they operate as shareholders in the global economy. Specifically, the malleability of the attribution doctrine enables adjudicators to create and maintain powerful templates to manage and discipline the relationship between the state shareholder and the investee company. Often, these templates privilege institutional arrangements where the state commits to being an "ordinary" shareholder. The construction of such a shareholder identity is visible both in the tribunals' analysis of the organizational set-up of the state shareholder function and in its substantive operation. Crucially, this image is vital for legal construction of the state shareholder, and it connects the doctrine of attribution with the other major regulatory and normative projects, such as domestic investment screening or transnational corporate governance, that have developed to temper the rise of contemporary state capitalism.

To support this idea, the following part focuses on the doctrinal analysis performed in five recent arbitral awards involving state-owned companies. Naturally, the awards give only a fleeting overview of the complex arbitral case law that consists of dozens of awards ranging from the conduct of national oil companies to that of privatization funds.[61] Because the specific language of different BITs can vary – as can the different tribunals' interpretation of customary law relating to state responsibility – providing a coherent doctrinal exposition of the heterogeneous case law is a task that goes beyond this chapter. For this reason, the awards discussed here were selected due to their explicit, and often careful, analysis of the organizational and operative conditions in which state shareholders interact with their investee companies and foreign investors.

Making "Ordinary" State Shareholders in Investment Treaty Arbitration

When assessing the conduct of state-owned entities, arbitral tribunals frequently focus on the broader organizational setting of state ownership in a given country.

---

[59] James Crawford & Paul Mertenskötter, *The Use of the ILC's Attribution Rules in Investment Arbitration*, in BUILDING INTERNATIONAL INVESTMENT LAW: THE FIRST 50 YEARS OF ICSID 33 (Meg Kinnear et al. eds., 2015).

[60] Compare with the established debates on regulatory chill, *see, e.g.*, Kyla Tienhaara, *Regulatory Chill in a Warming World: The Threat to Climate Policy Posed by Investor-State Dispute Settlement*, 7 TRANSNAT'L ENV'T L. 229 (2018); Carolina Moehlecke, *The Chilling Effect of International Investment Disputes: Limited Challenges to State Sovereignty*, 64 INT'L STUD. Q. 1 (2020).

[61] For a different set of cases, *see* Boon in this volume.

This prong of the analysis is primarily interested in how state shareholding has been institutionally arranged and how it interacts with the overall exercise of public authority. Doctrinally, this scrutiny is embedded in Articles 4 and 5 of the ARSIWA.

Flemingo v. Poland

Flemingo v. Poland, a case arising out of the Polish Airports State Enterprise's (PPL) termination of lease agreements for retail stores at the Warsaw airport, illuminates the operation of these Articles.[62] PPL was a company separate from the state, established in 1987 pursuant to special legislation, whose sole shareholder was the Polish State Treasury. The respondent state argued that the company formed "an independent, self-governing and self-financing entrepreneur with legal personality" and conducted "its business activities 'independently of the Polish authorities and on the same principles as any other business entity'."[63] In the claimant's view, however, PPL was a direct successor of Poland's Air Traffic and Airport Management Board, a governmental agency, pursuing a clear governmental task and factually immersed in the Ministry of Transport. The Tribunal agreed with the claimant, deeming PPL a de facto state organ under Article 4 of the ARSIWA and, in any case, an entity exercising governmental authority in the sense of Article 5 of the ARSIWA. While the analysis was informed by specific legislation on the PPL and the company's ownership structure, crucial factors in establishing attribution related to the institutional and practical arrangements through which the state interacted with the SOE. The fact that PPL was, according to relevant evidence, "an enterprise which is functioning within the structure of the Ministry" and that "[w]hen it comes to questions on investments ... the supervision over PPL's action is exercised by the minister responsible for transport" was enough to convince the Tribunal of the PPL's status as a de facto organ of the state.[64]

By foregrounding the company's persistent legacy as an administrative agency, the Tribunal essentially highlighted the limited transformation of state institutions despite corporatization. While the state efforts to insulate PPL from state machinery by turning it into a company with a separate legal personality and independent decision-making structure, the dynamics of the shareholder-company-relationship, which blended shareholder control with persistent governmental oversight, enabled the Tribunal to construe the institutional set-up of the state shareholder to jeopardize the neat separation between the Ministry and the company.

Staur Eiendom v. Latvia

Another investment Tribunal reached a different outcome in *Staur Eiendom v. Latvia*, a case where the claimants entered into a contract with the Latvian

---

[62] *Flemingo DutyFree Shop Private Ltd. v. Republic of Poland*, PCA Case No. 2014-11, Award (Aug. 12, 2016).

[63] *Id.* at ¶¶54–55.

[64] *Id.* at ¶¶434–435.

state-owned company SJSC Airport Riga (SJSC) to develop land adjacent to the airport.[65] Over the course of the project, SJSC initiated numerous amendments to the development plan which, ultimately, meant significant downsizing of the planned airport, to the detriment of the foreign investors. The Tribunal had to assess if the SJSC's conduct in revising the development plans was attributable to the state for the purposes of triggering state responsibility over breaches of a fair and equitable treatment provision in the relevant treaty. As in *Flemingo*, the claimants sought to establish attribution by pursuing Articles 4 and 5 of the ARSIWA, thus focusing on the organization of the state shareholder. In their view, SJSC was "an instrument of the Latvian State, with no real autonomy of its own, notwithstanding its separate legal personality" and the Ministry of Transport exerted significant control of "SJSC Airport's decision-making and operations."[66] The claimants heavily relied on the separate legal framework governing the operation of the airport, the general provisions on state-owned companies, the OECD reviews of the general Latvian policy on the corporate governance of state-owned enterprises, as well as the involvement of the Ministry in "nearly all decisions by [SJSC] Airport."[67]

The respondent, in turn, emphasized the separate legal personality of SJSC, the general nature of the "so-called instructions," and the independence of the company to "determine its own strategy in line with … broad objectives."[68] The government further argued that "the Latvian State as Shareholder of SJSC Airport, represented by the Ministry of Transport, consistently made it clear that, in accordance with Latvian law, it could not interfere with the operation of the company."[69] By contrast, the "State shareholder was only responsible" for regular functions under the Latvian corporate law such as:

> approval of the annual accounts, the decisions on the use of profits from the previous year, the appointment of the members of the Supervisory Council and the auditor, the approval of the articles of association, acquisition or disposal of a business and abandoning existing activities and initiating new activities, and decisions relating to the winding up of the company.[70]

The Tribunal agreed, ruling that by limiting its role to "that ordinarily played by the shareholder of any private company"[71] and refraining from "day-to-day governance decisions,"[72] the actions of the state shareholder were "not sufficient … for

[65] Staur Eiendom AS, *EBO Invest AS & ROX Holdings AS v. Latvia*, ICSID Case No. ARB/16/38, Award (Feb. 28, 2020).

[66] *Id.* at ¶258.

[67] *Id.* at ¶¶259–264.

[68] *Id.* at ¶¶279–292.

[69] *Id.* at ¶282.

[70] *Id.* at ¶325.

[71] *Id.* at ¶332.

[72] *Id.* at ¶329.

SJSC Airport's separate legal personality to be disregarded and for SJSC Airport to be treated as an organ of the State."[73] Compared to *Flemingo*, the *Staur Eiendom* award illustrates how a stable regulatory environment, where the roles and procedures for exercising shareholder power are clear and firmly established, can absolve the state shareholder even when circumstantial evidence supports attribution.

Tenaris and Talta v. Venezuela

In *Tenaris and Talta v. Venezuela*, the Tribunal rendered a similar conclusion. This case dealt with national expropriation and the state's pre-nationalization interference with an investment in a steel company.[74] As a part of their argument, the claimants suggested that a raw materials company, CVG FMO, whose majority shareholder was a state-owned company (CVG), discriminated against the foreign investor in the supply of raw materials for the benefit of another state-owned company.[75] The claimants further argued that CVG FMO formed "part of the 'functionally decentralized public administration' of the Government of Venezuela and that the company is subject to the control of the Ministry of Industry by reason of CVG's shareholding."[76] By contrast, the respondent argued that "the powers of CVG over CVG FMO are no more than those of a shareholder."[77] The Tribunal agreed with the respondent, thus accepting that the company's obligations toward foreign investors were contractual and not in any way connected to exercising governmental authority. In this context, the Tribunal also determined that "to the extent that the actions of its principal shareholder CVG might be said to be relevant, there is nothing in the evidence to suggest that its oversight of CVG FMO went beyond the exercise of general supervision."[78]

Unlike in *Flemingo*, the *Staur Eiendom*, and *Tenaris and Talta* Tribunals thus emphasized how the state's efforts to confine its interaction with the investee companies to standard corporate law mechanisms could provide institutional insulation around the organization of the state shareholder function. As a result, the latter two cases show how tribunals can interpret the attribution doctrines in such a way as to shield the shareholder state from responsibility when its exercise of public authority is isolated from its shareholding functions via intuitional design, thus encouraging this kind of organizational arrangement.

Tulip v. Turkey

While state commitment to the "ordinary" shareholder role is most often discussed with reference to the organizational set-up of state shareholding, a similar analysis

---

[73] *Id.* at ¶332.
[74] *Tenaris S.A. & Talta v. Bolivarian Republic of Venezuela*, ICSID Case No. ARB/11/26, Award (Jan. 29, 2016).
[75] *Id.* at ¶323.
[76] *Id.* at ¶400.
[77] *Id.* at ¶401.
[78] *Id.* at ¶417.

also emerges with respect to the substantive and operative aspects of shareholder conduct. *Tulip v. Turkey* provides an illustrative example of such an analysis.[79]

The case arose from the termination of a real estate development contract by Emlak, a Turkish real estate investment trust owned by TOKI, a state organ responsible for Turkey's public housing. The claimant argued, based on Article 8 of ARSIWA, that TOKI had maintained an "extraordinary level of control over every aspect of Emlak's operations" through the control of voting shares and members of the board, and thus furthered interests alien to Emlak's genuine business interests.[80] As part of its defense, the respondent contended that the termination of the contract did not go "beyond the legitimate exercise of the rights of a majority shareholder to manage the company's affairs in furtherance of those perceived interests."[81] The Tribunal agreed, noting how the evidence suggested "ordinary control exercised by a majority shareholder acting in the company's perceived best interests" rather than specific activity "in the sense of sovereign direction or control."[82] On this point the minority of the Tribunal dissented, suggesting that Emlak's decision to terminate the contract was, both in terms of the company's organizational structure and the substance of the decision, "guided – if not fully directed – by the sovereign's hand."[83] For the majority, however, the "plain documentary," including Emlak's board of directors' minutes and agenda papers, did not support outsized substantive instruction by the state shareholder in the company's "decision-making process."[84]

EDF (Services) v. Romania

A different verdict was reached in *EDF (Services) v. Romania*, a case concerning an arbitrary taking of a concession to provide duty-free services at Romanian airports and particularly the role of two Romanian SOEs, which together participated in the joint venture companies, in the process.[85] Relying on Articles 4, 5, and 8 of ARSIWA, the claimant argued the conduct of both entities was attributable, as they acted "as agents of the Romanian State."[86]

The Tribunal rejected the claimant's position with regard to Articles 4 and 5, holding the Romanian SOEs were separate legal persons "in pursuit of the corporate objects of a commercial company with the view to making profits, as any other commercial company operating in Romania."[87] A more detailed examination

---

[79] *Tulip Real Est. Inv. & Dev. Netherlands BV v. Republic of Turkey*, ICSID Case No ARB/11/28, Award (Mar. 10, 2014).

[80] *Id.* at ¶243.

[81] *Id.* at ¶307.

[82] *Id.* at ¶¶309–11.

[83] Tulip, ICSID Case No. ARB/11/28, Separate Opinion of Michael Evan Jaffe ¶8.

[84] *See supra* note 79, ¶¶311, 314.

[85] *EDF (Serv.) Ltd. v. Romania*, ICSID Case No. ARB/05/13, Award (Oct. 8, 2009).

[86] *Id.* at ¶102.

[87] *Id.* at ¶198.

was conducted under Article 8 of ARSIWA. As part of its defense, the Romanian government argued that the Ministry of Transportation, the sole shareholder of the SOEs in question, only provided rough mandates to the companies, consistent with its significant shareholder role. Thus, the government "did not exercise control … beyond its role as shareholder."[88] Examining the evidence, the Tribunal noted that the mandates the Ministry gave to the SOEs were not as general as they were depicted to be. Instead, the instructions contained concrete instructions impinging on the relationship between the SOEs and the claimant, leading the Tribunal to an:

> understanding that the corporate bodies of companies under the authority of the Ministry of Transportation had [no] initiative to originate, in full independence, proposals to the Ministry concerning the kind of decisions to be taken, much less that such bodies were free to decide other than as provided by the mandates.[89]

Even though the ownership mandates were deployed through proper channels and operationalized by both the joint venture companies' boards of directors and the general meeting, the directives emanating from the Ministry were considered compelling in achieving the particular result of bringing the contractual arrangements to an end.[90] Unlike *Tulip*, the *EDF (Services)* award thus showcases how the specificity of shareholder communication and the tight limits posited on the company may trigger attribution despite the shareholder state's reliance on standard influence mechanisms provided by domestic corporate law.

The Making of the State Shareholder under Investment Law

Two key findings arise from the discussed arbitral case law. First, the category of the "state shareholder" emerges as the analytical linchpin when applying the doctrines of attribution in concrete cases. Whether the issue is the institutional set-up of ownership functions across ministries and various holding companies or the substantive elements of shareholder communication, the parties' arguments and the tribunals' analyses focus on the state shareholder's organization and operation. In *Flemingo*, for example, the fact that SOE operations were physically run by the Polish Ministry of Transport – the company's sole shareholder – was crucial for attributing the conduct of the company to the state. Similarly, the *EDF (Services)* Tribunal considered the specificity of mandates given by the Romanian Ministry of Transportation to amount to detailed micromanagement, which jeopardized the neat separation between the shareholder and the company. Thus, these mandates injected elements of governmental authority into the shareholder–investee company relationship that was otherwise arranged to preserve each entity's unique competency under corporate law. Focusing on the organizational structure and operation of shareholding

---

[88] *Id.* at ¶171.
[89] *Id.* at ¶205.
[90] *Id.* at ¶209.

institutions enables tribunals to largely disregard the domestic variations of state capitalism and concentrate on the processes that mediate the state's market participation. As with the law of state responsibility, more generally, the making of the state shareholder under investment law is a matter of international law rather than national law.

Second, the interpretative practices in the arbitral case law also propound on the normative elements of state shareholder behavior. In particular, the concrete techniques used to employ doctrines of attribution to legally construe state shareholders expose how deeply international investment law enmeshes with other regulatory projects focused on the rise of the shareholder state. The examined cases underscore how concepts of shareholders' *ordinary* roles, competences, and interests, as well of those of *ordinary* company law and the *ordinary* commercial interests of state-owned companies are profoundly featured in tribunals' analytical processes. In each case, the malleable doctrine of attribution seems to extend a template for managing the relationship between the state shareholder, the rest of the state apparatus, and other market actors by rationalizing institutional arrangements, practices, and the state shareholder's behavior. The outcome, which brings forward the distinction running through most SOE-related legal regimes, is that by deviating from the standard shareholder competencies and behavior underwritten by corporate law, the state exposes itself to a high risk of responsibility and liability. As such, the tribunals' use of attribution under the law of state responsibility imbues an "ordinary" shareholder logic on state shareholders, suggesting that the organization and operation of state shareholders is increasingly compared to that of a hypothetical ordinary shareholder.

In sum, the concept of the "ordinary" shareholder emerges as a crucial analytical tool used by tribunals to put forward an idealized shareholder template which privileges separation of regulation and ownership via institutional design, portrays the state shareholder as any other private shareholder, and provides a robust set of legal disciplines that disincentivize hands-on control over state-owned entities. While fragmented, this notion emerges as a touchstone that frames both the regulatory and the normative dimensions of international investment law. Relatedly, the doctrinal operation connects attribution to other international, regional, and domestic legal regimes that attempt to manage the relationship between state shareholders and their investee companies.

While it is possible to make a normative case both for and against such a hypothetical comparator, this regulatory image comes to influence the identity of the state shareholder, as well as how it mediates interactions between states and companies in the aggregate. Through customary international law's doctrines of attribution, investment tribunals partake in a larger regulatory undertaking that has developed around the rise of the shareholder state. Beyond this, the heavy emphasis on the category of the "state shareholder" as an analytical lens may have a broader impact on international economic governance. For one example, the doctrinal construction of state-company relationship could be informative for future trade and investment treaties as state ownership is increasingly channeled through minority, rather than majority, positions and organized through complex holding company structures or sovereign wealth funds.[91] The covert legal construction of shareholder identities may also have more drastic implications. Given the ubiquity of state ownership in several sectors critical to the sustainability transition, for instance, the doctrinal templates that arise from investment treaty arbitration will likely come to influence both the use of SOEs as vehicles of energy policy and the international legal challenges to climate policy by private investors in general.[92]

CONCLUSION

State shareholding has grown in significance with the rise of state capitalism in the early twenty-first century, but it has long implicated questions of law, economics, and political philosophy. State control over the economy is also a key area of political contestation, and the state shareholder's constitution, operation, and legitimacy are, as a result, moving targets. Over the past decades, the practice and regulation of public intervention in the private market have experienced major shifts that have transformed the earlier dominant paradigms of "ownership as regulation" into "regulation of ownership."[93] Most recently, the internationalization of state ownership, and varied responses to its economic, political, and intellectual underpinnings, has put forward a distinctive model of the shareholder state.

This chapter has examined the legal construction of state shareholders as a part of this diffuse regulatory system addressing state shareholding. Focusing on international economic law, the chapter identified state shareholders as key targets in the evolving international regulatory framework that shapes the parameters of state ownership. In this context, the chapter suggested that the law of state responsibility forms a crucial, but underappreciated, fulcrum in the international legal framework that has developed around state capitalism.

Specifically, the chapter concentrated on the shareholding institutions that mediate the state's market participation, focusing on investment arbitration tribunals' use of the doctrines of attribution when they analyze the organization and operation of state shareholders. Through these doctrinal operations, investment arbitration tribunals can be seen to construe a particular state shareholder identity centered on the notion of the "ordinary shareholder." When states deviate from this hypothetical category – either through the organizational structure of their ownership or control or their intervention in a company's operations – they increase their risk of responsibility and liability for breaches of investment treaties' substantive guarantees.

---

[91] Compare with Borlini, *supra* note 42.
[92] *See, e.g.*, Kyla Tienhaara et al., *Investor-State Disputes Threaten the Global Green Energy Transition*, 376 SCI. 701 (2022).
[93] Thynne, *supra* note 18.

Beyond this specific context, the "ordinary" shareholder template also shapes, nudges, and defines the ways in which states organize themselves when they operate through shareholder positions more broadly. While the law of state responsibility and its doctrine of attribution cannot be solely responsible for the governance patterns of state shareholders – these doctrines form too slender of a support for that – their universal applicability and doctrinal malleability not only compensate for the dearth of primary investment treaty law, but also connect the operation of customary international law with many other regulatory projects. These include the new forms of transnational corporate governance and invigorated investment screening procedures, which have emerged to rein in the rise of the shareholder state. In this way, the legal construction of the state shareholder through attribution also highlights the dynamics and persistent significance of customary international law – a branch of law that often receives less attention than novel treaty regimes or specific SOE-disciplines – for international economic law.

4

Contractors and Hybrid Warfare

A *Pluralist Approach to Reforming the Law of State Responsibility*

Laura A. Dickinson

INTRODUCTION

When Russian troops moved into the Crimean Peninsula in 2014 and joined forces with local groups stirring up unrest in Ukraine's eastern Donbas region, Russia initially denied its military involvement. Moscow claimed that armed groups in the region were local forces with no ties to the Kremlin. These flat denials were belied by the fact that the forces on the ground were speaking Russian, operating Russian weaponry, and describing casualties on Russian social media.[1] And long before these forces arrived, a series of cyber intrusions weakened Ukraine's financial institutions, and an information campaign stirred up ethnic Russians against the new Ukrainian government. Russia did not acknowledge its involvement in these events either. Russia subsequently launched a full-scale invasion of Ukraine and is currently using private military and security companies (PMSCs) in the territory yet again.[2]

These multifaceted tactics, deployed in combination even as officials denied state involvement, proved quite potent, and they prompted foreign policy experts to give this type of mix a new moniker: "hybrid warfare." Frank Hoffman, of the U.S. National Defense University, defined this approach to warfare as "[a]ny adversary that simultaneously employs a tailored mix of conventional weapons, irregular tactics, terrorism, and criminal behavior in the same time and battlespace to obtain their political objectives."[3] And though that category has at times been criticized

---

[1] STEVEN WOEHREL, CONG. RSCH. SERV., RL33460, UKRAINE: CURRENT ISSUES AND U.S. POLICY, 4 (2014).

[2] See Christopher Faulkner & Marcel Plichta, *Win, Lose, or Draw, the Wagner Group Benefits from the War in Ukraine*, LAWFARE (Oct. 23, 2022), www.lawfareblog.com/win-lose-or-draw-wagner-group-benefits-war-ukraine. For a discussion of the global reaction to Russia's 2022 invasion and the potential to strengthen trans-regional alliances of liberal democratic states, *see* Laura A. Dickinson & David Sloss, *The Russia-Ukraine War and the Seeds of a New Plurilateral International Order*, 116 AM. J. INT'L L. 798 (2022).

[3] Frank Hoffman, *On Not-So-New Warfare: Political Warfare vs. Hybrid Threats*, WAR ON THE ROCKS (July 28, 2014), http://warontherocks.com/2014/07/on-not-so-new-warfare-political-warfare-vs-hybrid-threats/.

as overly amorphous,[4] the U.S. National Defense Strategy has made it clear that such hybrid warfare is one of the most important national security challenges the United States now faces: "In competition short of armed conflict, revisionist powers and rogue regimes are using corruption, predatory economic practice, propaganda, political subversion, proxies, and the threat or use of military force to change facts on the ground."[5]

Despite this emerging focus on hybrid warfare and its legal dimensions, relatively little attention has been paid to an important element of the hybrid strategies used by Russia and other countries: PMSCs. By hiring or encouraging these contractors, states can often evade responsibility as a matter of international law even when these actors commit atrocities or flout other substantive international legal rules. Thus, such intrusions present enormous challenges for targeted states that abide by international law, while allowing greater scope for states such as Russia that do not embrace the rules-based international order. When such states operate below these legal thresholds, international law limits the available responses of targeted states and therefore reduces deterrence and undermines the strength of the rule of law.[6]

Accordingly, this chapter focuses on governmental use of PMSCs to evade the law of state responsibility, using as a case study Russia's deployment of the shadowy corporation known as the Wagner Group.[7] This chapter then suggests ways in which we might rethink the law of state responsibility in order to respond to the increasing threat of this sort of hybrid warfare.

---

[4] *See, e.g.,* Michael Kofman & Matthew Rojansky, *A Closer Look at Russia's "Hybrid War,"* 7 KENNAN CABLE 2 (2015) ("Even those who have put forward such a definition must admit that the combination of war across domains is not new, but in fact is as old as warfare itself.").

[5] U.S. DEP'T OF DEFENSE, SUMMARY OF THE 2018 NATIONAL DEFENSE STRATEGY, SHARPENING THE AMERICAN MILITARY'S COMPETITIVE EDGE 5 (2018). The Council of Europe has also drawn attention to the legal challenges posed by hybrid warfare in a strongly worded resolution adopted in March, 2018. The Council identified a core feature of hybrid war as "legal asymmetry," in which

> Hybrid adversaries, as a rule, deny their responsibility for hybrid operations and try to escape the legal consequences of their actions. They exploit the lacunae in the law and the complexity of legal systems, and operate across legal boundaries and in under-regulated spaces, exploit legal thresholds, are prepared to commit substantial violations of the law and generate confusion and ambiguity to mask their actions. EUR. PARL. ASS. DEB. 17th Sitting, Resolution 2217 (2018).

[6] Aurel Sauri, *Legal Aspects of Hybrid Warfare*, LAWFARE (Oct. 2, 2015) ("Serious and blatant violations of international law, and attempts to cover them with legal fig leaves, expose and deepen the international legal order's structural weaknesses. All the more so if such violations involve a permanent member of the Security Council."); *see also* Shane Reeves, *The Viability of the Law of Armed Conflict in the Age of Hybrid Warfare*, LAWFARE (Dec. 5, 2016) (calling for significant changes to the law to reduce the ability of states to take advantage of hybrid war).

[7] This chapter was written prior to the 2023 failed coup against Vladimir Putin that was organized by Wagner's leaders, Yevgeny Prigozhin, and Dmitri Utkin, as well as their subsequent deaths after a plane crash that may have been orchestrated by the Russian government. However, in the future, either the Wagner Group itself (operating under new leadership) or similar PMSCs are likely to remain an important part of Russia's imposition of force abroad.

Drawing from scholarship on global legal pluralism, I argue for a less formalist and more functionalist analysis of the law of state responsibility. Legal pluralists have long contended that analyses of law focus too much on the acts of formal governmental entities, thereby ignoring the crucial norm-creating and norm-enforcing roles frequently played by less formal authorities and non-state actors. According to legal pluralists, the overly rigid distinction between what is state and what is non-state, or what is law and what is not-law, impoverishes our understanding of those forces that actually impact behavior on the ground in everyday life. In the context of hybrid war, formalist conceptions of the state allow governments such as Russia to skirt state responsibility solely because there may be no formal contract between Russia and a PMSC such as the Wagner Group.

One possible response then is to reinterpret Article 8 of the Articles of State Responsibility so that it looks at the real functional ties between a state actor and a PMSC, along with the "governmentality" of the function performed by the PMSC. Such a change would look behind the formal legal relationship in order to assign state responsibility, and instead would ask about the web of connections and communications between members of the state bureaucracy and the leadership of PMSCs, the degree of coordination, the use of arms supplied by the government, and so on. This functionalist approach would more easily allow the acts of PMSCs to be deemed within the ambit of state responsibility.

RUSSIA'S PRIVATE ARMIES

From Ukraine to Syria to Africa, Russia has been deploying private military and security contractors to engage in activities in support of its foreign policy interests, whether below or above the armed attack or armed conflict threshold. Probably the dominant company playing this role is the Wagner Group. Employees of this shadowy company are fighting on foreign soil in battles that serve Russian interests, guarding oil fields and mines in countries where Russia seeks influence, providing military advice and assistance to Russian military, economic, and political partners, and gathering information wherever they operate. Despite many demonstrated links, the Russian government for many years denied a direct connection to the activities of the Wagner Group, enabling it to enhance military involvement overseas without the political costs of deploying uniformed troops and also allowing the Kremlin to create confusion and plausible deniability regarding its involvement in extraterritorial activities. Thus, the use of PMSCs in this way bears all the hallmarks of hybrid war: an irregular tactic that enables the Russian government to exploit ambiguity and sow confusion in the pursuit of its foreign policy objectives.[8]

---

[8] Anna Maria Dyner, *The Role of Private Military Contractors in Russian Foreign Policy*, 64 POLISH INST. MIL. AFF. BULL. 1135 (2018).

The Russian use of PMSCs also demonstrates some of the specific legal challenges posed by hybrid war. By deploying security contractors to engage in combat activities without clearly acknowledging them, Russia can disguise its involvement in the use of force and exploit legal rules about the armed attack and armed conflict thresholds. Similarly, by providing contracted military trainers and advisers to partner with states which themselves are engaging in armed conflicts, Russia can disguise its involvement in those armed conflicts and reduce its legal exposure. And in areas where there is no armed conflict, Russian contractors who provide security for natural resources evade human rights obligations by hiding behind the cloak of the private sector.

Research on this topic is difficult because there is relatively little public information, and Russia in most cases officially denies its link to contractors. Indeed, the use of extraterritorial PMSCs is largely illegal in Russia. As a result, many "Russian" PMSCs are incorporated in other countries. And the Kremlin denies governmental relationships, including funding of the companies' activities. Yet from Ukraine to Syria to Africa, the role of Russian PMSCs such as the Wagner Group is undeniable.

The Wagner Group is by no means the only Russian PMSC operating globally, but is rather a relative newcomer to a group of companies that have operated for decades. Although Russian law has long prohibited mercenary activities,[9] Russia has "actively used military 'volunteers' since at least 1992, when members of the 'Rubicon' group … were sent to Bosnia … to take part in local hostilities."[10] Since 2008, approximately ten Russian PMSCs have been active. Probably the most notorious company was, until recent years, Slavonic Corps Limited, an organization that employed primarily former members of the Russian riot police and whose two founders ultimately were tried and convicted for mercenary activity in Russian courts in 2013. A failed operation in Syria that year led to the demise of the company, which paved the way for the rise of the Wagner Group.[11]

Wagner, a Russian chVK (or private military company) registered in Hong Kong,[12] emerged in 2014 as an actor in Ukraine and subsequently grew to be the dominant Russian PMSC.[13] It is not a Russian company in the sense that it is registered overseas on account of Russian law's ban on mercenaries, but it is "Russian funded, Russian-commanded, and largely Russian-manned."[14]

[9] Ugolovnyĭ Kodeks Rossiĭskoĭ Federatsii [UK RF] [Criminal Code] art. 359 (Russ.).
[10] Sergey Sukhanin, *War, Business and 'Hybrid' Warfare: The Case of the Wagner Private Military Company* (Part One), 15 Eurasia Daily Monitor (2018).
[11] *Id. See also* Dyner, *supra* note 8.
[12] Tim Hume, *Nobody Wants to Talk about the Russians Killed by U.S. Airstrikes in Syria*, Vice News (Feb. 14, 2018), www.vice.com/en/article/evmpnk/russians-killed-syria-us-airstrikes.
[13] Sergey Sukhanin, *War Business and 'Hybrid' Warfare: The Case of the Wagner Private Military Company* (Part Two), 51 Eurasia Daily Monitor (2018).
[14] Neil Hauer, *Russia's Favorite Mercenaries*, The Atlantic (Aug. 27, 2018), www.theatlantic.com/international/archive/2018/08/russian-mercenaries-wagner-africa/568435/; *see also* Mark Galeotti, *Moscow's Mercenaries Reveal the Privatisation of Russian Geopolitics*, Open Democracy (Aug. 29, 2017), www.opendemocracy.net/en/odr/chvk-wagner-and-privatisation-of-russian-geopolitics/.

Operations of the company were for a long time difficult to document because, as the *Washington Post* noted, "[e]ven by the poor standards of transparency in today's Russia," Wagner is "clouded in unusual secrecy."[15] Indeed, journalists who have written about Wagner's activities have met with mysterious, fatal accidents. For example, the Russian journalist Max Borodin, who helped break stories about Wagner's activities, died in April 2018 after "mysteriously falling from a balcony."[16] Three more Russian journalists making a documentary about Wagner's activities in the Central African Republic died there in an ambush. And another journalist who covered the company is reportedly in hiding.[17]

The firm was long headed by Dmitri Utkin, who served as a lieutenant colonel of the GRU, Russia's military intelligence agency. Reportedly, the name "Wagner" derives from Utkin's self-chosen code name and reflects Utkin's homage to Nazi culture.[18] The Kremlin-linked Russian oligarch Yevgeny Prigozhin provided financial backing and on-the-ground leadership for the company, although his involvement for many years was difficult to pin down.[19] Known as "Putin's chef," Prigozhin ran a lucrative catering company and had a close relationship with the Russian President. (Prigozhin also supervised the St. Petersburg "Internet troll factory" involved in interfering in the U.S. election in 2016.)[20]

Prior to the Ukraine invasion of 2022, Wagner employed between 1,350 and 2,000 armed contractors, many of whom trained in Krasnodar Krai, a military-style compound near Ukraine.[21] Employees consisted of a mix of elite professionals, "apparently recruited through channels controlled by the security services, or 'siloviki,'" and "semiprofessionals (recruited via war veteran and Cossack organizations)," along with "former criminals, amateurs, and persons with a shady past."[22] They earned up to 240,000 Russian rubles, or roughly $3,550 per month.[23] Interviews with family members indicate the "monetary allure" of working for Wagner was significant, although many were also motivated by ideological reasons to support Russia.[24] And they have fought in military operations in zones as diverse as Ukraine, Syria,

---

[15] Vladimir Kara-Murza, Opinion, *The Kremlin's Mysterious Mercenaries and the Killing of Russian Journalists in Africa*, WASH. POST, Aug. 21, 2018.

[16] Daniel Brown, *Russian Journalist Who Covered Wagner Group Mercenary Deaths in Syria Dies After Falling from Balcony*, BUSINESS INSIDER, Apr. 15, 2018.

[17] Hauer, *supra* note 14.

[18] Kara-Murza, *supra* note 15.

[19] Sukhanin (Part Two), *supra* note 13.

[20] Kara-Murza, *supra* note 15.

[21] Oliver Carroll, *Russia's Private Mercenaries and the Lengths Russia Goes to Deny Them*, THE INDEPENDENT, Feb. 17, 2018.

[22] Sukhanin (Part Two) *supra* note 13; *see also* S. A. Cavanagh, *SWJ Factsheet: Observing Wagner Group, an Open Intelligence Study*, SMALL WARS J.

[23] Carroll, *supra* note 21. Reports indicate that the wages may have dropped somewhat, to 160,000 rubles per month, a sum that still "far outpaces the typical wages in provincial Russia." Neil Hauer, *Russia's Favorite Mercenaries*, THE ATLANTIC, Aug. 27, 2018.

[24] Hauer, *supra* note 14.

the Central African Republic, and Sudan. The Wagner Group's tactical capabilities include "infantry, heavy artillery, air defense, armoured tanks, training advisory and intelligence."[25] In particular, the company is known for the "relatively high quality of their weaponry," as well as the "quantity of their personnel" and their organized command structure.[26] In addition, unlike other Russian PMSCs, which tend to play a support role, the Wagner Group is known for direct combat operations.[27]

Even before the Ukraine invasion, Wagner and Utkin had fallen into the crosshairs of the United States. For example, in June of 2017, the U.S. Treasury Department placed the Wagner Group and Utkin on its sanctions list. Specifically, the department included the company and Utkin on its Office of Foreign Assets Control (OFAC) Specially Designated Nationals List of entities subject to sanctions related to Russia/Ukraine events.[28] Russia, however, denied its link to the company and indeed denied that the company was even a private military and security company. In response to inquiries about the sanctions, Russian Federation Council defense and security committee head Viktor Ozerov said that there were no private military companies in Russia's jurisdiction.[29] Yet, Utkin received the Russian Order of Courage honor, apparently for his role in Wagner.[30]

The Russian annexation of the Crimean peninsula in Ukraine in the spring of 2014 and its subsequent support for the armed conflict in eastern Ukraine illustrates the potency of the hybrid war threat, in general, and the role of PMSCs like the Wagner Group, in particular. After the fall of Ukrainian Russia-allied President Viktor Yanukovich, Russia deployed thousands of troops across the border into Crimea and took control of strategic positions and infrastructure within the territory. The troops, who did not bear the insignia of the Russian military, were dubbed the "little green men." Russia initially denied involvement, claiming that the troops were indigenous militias who supported Russia – despite numerous reports that they were, in fact, Russian soldiers.[31] Ultimately, protests by ethnic Russians within Crimea against the Ukrainian government prompted a referendum in which Crimeans voted to join the Russian Federation.[32] Russia then officially annexed the Crimean peninsula.

---

[25] *Id.*

[26] Sukhanin (Part Two), *supra* note 13.

[27] *Id.*

[28] *U.S. Treasury Puts Private Military Company Wagner on Sanctions List*, INTERFAX, RUSSIA & CIS MILITARY NEWSWIRE, June 21, 2017, at 1.

[29] *Id.*

[30] Alexander Gostev, *Russia's Paramilitary Mercenaries Emerge from the Shadows*, RADIO FREE EUROPE, Dec. 16, 2016.

[31] *Russia Says Cannot Order Crimean 'Self-Defense' Units Back to Base*, REUTERS (Mar. 5, 2014), www.reuters .com/article/us-ukraine-crisis-lavrov-spain/russia-says-cannot-order-crimean-self-defense-units-back-to-base-idUSBREA240NF20140305.

[32] Many international entities questioned the fairness of the referendum, which garnered 95 percent of the vote.

After the referendum, Russia finally acknowledged its support for the annexation of Crimea, stating in April 2014 that it had backed Crimean separatist militias in order to "ensure proper conditions for the people of Crimea to be able to feely express their will."[33] A majority of world leaders condemned the annexation as a violation of article 2(4) of the United Nations Charter and the Budapest Memorandum on Security Assurances, which provided for the territorial integrity of Ukraine. The United Nations General Assembly rejected the referendum and Russia's annexation as invalid, adopting a non-binding resolution by a vote of 100 to 11, with 58 countries abstaining, affirming the "territorial integrity of the Ukraine within its internationally recognized borders."[34] In December 2016, the General Assembly voted 70 to 26, with 77 countries abstaining, to condemn "the temporary occupation" of Crimea and reaffirmed nonrecognition of its annexation.[35] Many states, including the United States, imposed sanctions on Russia for its actions in Ukraine at that time.

After annexing the Crimean peninsula, Russian energy then shifted to eastern Ukraine, where similar tactics prompted ongoing hostilities in the Donbas region. As in Crimea, despite numerous contrary reports,[36] Russia denied that its troops were active in the region, although President Putin has now admitted to the presence of Russian intelligence officers. The Organization for Security and Cooperation in Europe (OSCE), which established an observer mission in the region, reported hundreds of civilian deaths and other significant human rights abuses after the hostilities began – even before the 2022 Russian invasion.

The strategy that Russia used in Ukraine at the time of the 2014 annexation included not only the "little green men" – Russian soldiers without insignia – but also a series of other measures that long preceded these boots on the ground. Such measures encompassed extensive information operations and cyber intrusions to interfere with the new Ukrainian government, and to whip up ethnic Russian sentiment and expand Russian economic influence.[37] For example, beginning in late November 2013, reports surfaced that "Russian hacker groups were defacing and executing [denial-of-service] attacks on websites critical of the Yanukovich government's relationship with Russia."[38] "This period was characterized by low-level hacking targeting highly visible websites, either rendering

---

[33] *Direct Line with Vladimir Putin* (Apr. 17, 2014), http://en.kremlin.ru/events/president/news/20796. On this same date, however, the Russian Foreign Minister Sergei Lavrov denied direct Russian military involvement. Speech by Sergey Lavrov, Russian Foreign Minister, Geneva (Apr. 17, 2014).

[34] G.A. Res. 68/262, at 2 (Apr. 1, 2014).

[35] G.A. Res. 71/205 (Dec. 19, 2016).

[36] Organization for Security and Co-operation in Europe [OSCE], *Spot Report by the OSCE Special Monitoring Mission to Ukraine (SMM)* (Nov. 8, 2014).

[37] Patrick J. Cullen & Erik Reichborn-Kjennerud, MCDC COUNTERING HYBRID WARFARE PROJECT: UNDERSTANDING HYBRID WARFARE (2017).

[38] *Id.*

them unavailable or changing their content."[39] After Yanukovich was forced out of office and fled the country, Russia continued its disinformation campaign. The "little green men" tampered with fiber optic cables, "raiding the facilities of Ukrainian telecom firm Ukrtelecom, which stated afterward that it had 'lost the technical capacity to provide connection between the peninsula and the rest of Ukraine and probably across the peninsula too.'"[40] In addition, cell phones of Ukrainian members of parliament were hacked "and the main Ukrainian government website was shut down for 72 hours after Russian troops entered Crimea."[41]

This combination of measures is emblematic of hybrid warfare, where a state (or non-state actor) "synchronize[s] multiple instruments of power simultaneously and intentionally ... below obvious detection and response thresholds, and often rel[ies] on the speed, volume, and ubiquity of digital technology that characterizes the present information age."[42] This broad spectrum of means, unleashed together in ways that are difficult to attribute, can leave the targeted state flatfooted. In Ukraine during this time period, Russia deployed all of these measures "in ambiguous ways, hidden from view or conducted with unclear intentions, making it difficult for the Ukrainians to understand and respond to [them]."[43]

While many sources described Russia's hybrid approach to Ukraine at the time of the 2014 invasion as deploying a mix of proxies, information warfare, cyber intrusions, and economic influence, few homed in on the role of PMSCs in particular. Yet, sources indicate that Wagner emerged on the scene as a potent PMSC force when its contractors took "active part in the hostilities in the Donbas region" in Ukraine in 2014.[44] Reportedly, between 2,000 and 5,000 Wagner contractors set foot in Ukraine during this period, engaging in direct combat.[45] Moreover, 1,570 of those who operated in the region have since been identified by the SBU, the security service of Ukraine.[46] They played a "pivotal" role, "working closely alongside Russian military forces and their separatist proxies."[47]

Wagner head Utkin himself apparently commanded a contingent of his PMSCs in Luhansk, in Ukraine, beginning in 2014. His unit reportedly trained at the 10th

[39] Tim Maurer & Scott Janz, *The Russia-Ukraine Conflict: Cyber and Information Warfare in a Regional Context*, ISN (Oct. 17, 2014).

[40] *Id.*

[41] *Id.*

[42] Cullen & Reichborn-Kjennerud, *supra* note 37, at 2–3.

[43] *Id.* at 19–20.

[44] Sukhanin (Part Two), *supra* note 13; *see also* Sergey Sukhanin, *Making War Profitable Again: PMCs as Russia's "Key" to Africa*, INT'L CTR. DEF. SEC. J. (Aug. 17, 2018); Cavanagh, *supra* note 22.

[45] Cavanagh, *supra* note 22.

[46] *Id.*

[47] Neil Hauer, *Wagner, Russian Private Military Company, Goes to Africa*, THE ATLANTIC (Aug. 27, 2018).

Spetsnaz Brigade's base at Molkino, in the south of Russia, and "was far more carefully prepared and well paid than the typical adventurers in the Donbas."[48]

An account from the Russian website *Military Arms* described Wagner forces at the time as "distinguished by their very high percentage of losses, which is not characteristic of private military companies."[49] The account further stated that in the Donbas region, as well as Syria, Wagner contractors "work[ed] in the most dangerous situations, often moving out in the first wave of an attack and storming population centers and enemy positions."[50]

Experts argue that Wagner was deployed in Ukraine to enable Russia to maintain "plausible deniability" about its military involvement there.[51] At the same time, the Russian government was better able to control the Wagner contractors than the irregular bands of criminals it also reportedly sponsored in the region.[52] Indeed, Utkin reportedly killed one of these criminals, known as "Batman," on orders from the Russian government, because the gang member had gotten out of control.[53]

Moreover, Wagner's success in Ukraine reportedly increased support within the Russian government for the use of contractors. As far back as 2011, Putin suggested that "these kind of companies are a way of implementing national interests without the direct involvement of the state."[54] Two years later, Deputy Prime Minister Dmitry Rogozin embraced this concept: "from the outset, it was clear that the aim was a structure financed through private contracts, but essentially there had to be a deniable instrument for the state."[55] Yet at the time, the Russian Defense Ministry and General Staff were "fiercely opposed."[56] Wagner's successes in Ukraine after the 2014 annexation, however, prompted a shift in thinking and a willingness to deploy these shadowy forces in many other contexts, such as Syria, the Central African Republic, and Sudan.[57] And Russia again deployed PMSCs inside Ukraine following its full-scale invasion of the country in 2022.

HYBRID WARFARE AND THE LAW OF STATE RESPONSIBILITY

Hybrid war allows states to exploit existing international legal regimes by operating below legal thresholds or taking advantage of ambiguities or gray areas in the

---

[48] Mark Galeotti, *Moscow's Mercenaries in Syria*, WAR ON THE ROCKS (Apr. 5, 2016).

[49] Aleksandr Gostev, *Russia's Paramilitary Mercenaries Emerge from the Shadows*, RADIO FREE EUROPE (Dec. 16, 2016).

[50] *Id.*

[51] Sukhanin, *supra* note 13.

[52] Galeotti, *supra* note 48.

[53] *Id.*

[54] Galeotti, *supra* note 14.

[55] *Id.*

[56] *Id.*

[57] Federica Saini Fasanotti, *Russia's Wagner Group in Africa: Influence, Commercial Concessions, Rights Violations, and Counterinsurgency Failure*, BROOKINGS (Feb. 8, 2022), www.brookings.edu/blog/order-from-chaos/2022/02/08/russias-wagner-group-in-africa-influence-commercial-concessions-rights-violations-and-counterinsurgency-failure/.

law.[58] For example, hybrid measures are often designed to fall below the thresholds for what constitutes an armed attack or a use of force under the *jus ad bellum*, thereby limiting the lawful responses a targeted state may take under the UN Charter.[59] Thus, scholars and policymakers have debated under what circumstances cyber intrusions could qualify as an armed attack.[60] Other measures, such as coercive economic interventions and campaigns to influence elections, as well as broader information operations, raise similar issues, even if it is clear they do not cross the higher armed attack threshold.[61] Likewise, if the hybrid measures do not amount to armed conflict, then the range of measures available to the state being attacked under the *jus in bello* would also be constrained, particularly with regard to whom that state could then target or detain in retaliation. Finally, as the Ukraine example makes clear, hybrid tactics often use proxies to obscure the involvement of an external state, helping to turn what would otherwise be an international conflict into one seemingly being fought by factions within a state. By transforming the conflict into one that is categorized as a non-international armed conflict, hybrid war again ties the hands of the targeted state.[62]

With regard to the use of contractors in particular, however, the key international law question concerns state responsibility. By using contractors instead of acting directly, states can deny their involvement and potentially evade

---

[58] Sauri, *supra* note 6 ("[H]ybrid warfare seeks to exploit … legal thresholds, fault-lines, and gaps.").

[59] Under the *jus ad bellum* as laid out in the U.N. Charter and customary international law, a targeted state may use force on the territory of another state in the absence of that state's consent or a Security Council Resolution only in response to an armed attack or imminent armed attack. States can exploit this threshold in part because there is uncertainty and disagreement about when certain types of measures cross the threshold. *See* UN Charter art. 2(4).

[60] *See, e.g.*, Michael N. Schmitt, *"Attack" as a Term of Art in International Law: The Cyber Operations Context*, in PROCEEDINGS OF THE 4TH INT'L CONF. ON CYBER CONFLICT 283 (Christian Czosseck, Rain Ottis & Katharina Ziolkowski eds., 2012).

[61] *See, e.g.*, CHRIS DONNELLY, TOWARD THE NEXT DEFENCE AND SECURITY REVIEW: Part Two— NATO. https://publications.parliament.uk/pa/cm201415/cmselect/cmdfence/1127/112705.htm#n11 (citing Donnelly). Donnelly uses the example of Russia in Ukraine to show how hybrid operations are designed to "break the integrity of the state … before there is any need to cross its borders with an invasion force." *Id.* As he puts it, "we are seeing a form of warfare that is operating under our reaction threshold." *Id.*

[62] Although the law of armed conflict would clearly govern, expanding the range of responses available to the targeted state beyond those permitted in peacetime, some recent judicial decisions arguably require states to obey international human rights law when acting in NIACs (as compared to international armed conflicts). *See, e.g.*, Joined cases of *Serdar Mohammed v. Ministry of Defence* and *Qasim et al. v. Secretary of State for Defence* [2014] EWHC 1369 (QB). To be sure, the import of these decisions is disputed, as is the relationship between human rights law and the law of armed conflict more broadly. *See* Sean Aughey & Aurel Sauri, *Targeting and Detention in Non-International Armed Conflict, Serdar v. Mohammed and the Limits of Human Rights Convergence*, 91 INT'L L. STUD. 60 (2015). Nonetheless, with respect at least to some targeting and detention issues, the targeted state might (under some interpretations) be obligated to observe principles that are closer to the more stringent rules of international human rights law in NIACs as opposed to the freer hand the state would have in responding to international armed conflicts.

international law obligations.[63] The law of state responsibility, therefore, is central to this problem.

Although not set forth in any clear treaty, this body of law finds its most comprehensive articulation in the International Law Commission's draft Articles of State Responsibility.[64] Culled from decisions of international tribunals, the principles contained in these articles provide an important framework for assessing the responsibility of states, including for the action of non-state actors such as PMSCs linked to them. Hybrid war scenarios involving PMSCs expose the limits of this body of law as it addresses the links between states and non-state actors.

Indeed, two of the potentially relevant provisions, Articles 4 and 5, require such formal, direct, and close links to the state that PMSCs such as Wagner would likely never fall within their ambit. Article 4(2) provides that a state is responsible for its "organs," including "any person or entity which has that status in accordance with the internal law of the state."[65] As Lindsay Cameron and Vincent Chetail observe in their comprehensive work on PMSCs and the law of state responsibility, this threshold is very high.[66] Without a formal legal relationship between the PMSC and the state under domestic law defining that PMSC as a state organ – a relationship comprising more than a mere contract for services – a state would incur responsibility for the PMSC under this article only in "exceptional" circumstances.[67] Those circumstances would require the "complete ... dependence" of the PMSC on the state, and such a degree of planning and coordination by the state that the PMSC can be viewed as a state "instrument."[68] Therefore, Article 4 takes a largely formalist, quite strict approach.

Article 5 is similarly formalist. Although it sweeps somewhat more broadly than Article 4, it likely still would not cover most scenarios involving the deployment of PMSCs to conduct "hybrid war." Article 5 provides that the conduct of "a person or entity which is not an organ of the state under article 4 but which is empowered by the law of that state to exercise elements of ... governmental authority shall be considered an act of the state." Although a state could be responsible for entities such as PMSCs that act functionally with an element of governmental authority, the phrase "empowered by the law of the state" requires a formal legal relationship between the entity and the state. A formal contract might suffice to meet this element, but this language would seem to preclude state responsibility in scenarios such as Russia's use of Wagner, where no such formal legal relationship exists.

---

[63] Sauri, *supra* note 6 (quoting Richard Gross) ("'[D]enial of their involvement in hybrid operations is one of the primary methods for States to avoid crossing their adversary's reaction threshold.'").

[64] *Draft Articles on Responsibility of States for Internationally Wrongful Acts with Commentaries in Report of the International Law Commission*, 53rd sess., Apr. 23–June 1 and July 2–Aug. 10, 2001, 56 U.N. GAOR Supp. No. 10, 30, at 132, A/56/10 (2001) [hereafter "Articles of State Responsibility"].

[65] *Id.* at art. 4(2).

[66] Lindsay Cameron & Vincent Chetail, Privatizing War, Private Military and Security Companies under Public International Law (2013).

[67] *Id.* at 152–55.

[68] *Id.*

Article 8 supplies the most plausible form of state responsibility that could apply to PMSCs deployed in hybrid warfare. This article provides that "[t]he conduct of a person or group of persons shall be considered an act of a State under international law if the person or group of persons is in fact acting on the instructions of, or under the direction or control of, the State in carrying out that conduct."[69]

The fundamental principle embodied in this rule for our purposes is the notion that states do bear responsibility for persons or entities working for them, provided that the state is exerting sufficient control over those persons or entities. (Although the article would also permit a finding of a sufficient nexus between a state and a non-state entity if the state issues instructions or direction, these require a very tight relationship of command[70] that go beyond the kind of hybrid war context that is the subject of this chapter). Furthermore, this standard allows for a functional approach that would turn on how the entity actually behaves in relationship to the state, rather than resting on formal legal ties.

The challenge here, however, is that the threshold for establishing responsibility is quite high, and therefore it is one that is ripe for states to exploit. States engaging in hybrid warfare take advantage of this legal boundary by engaging with the PMSCs in ways that fall short of the conditions that establish state responsibility. In other words, they engage with PMSCs in ways that do not amount to the degree of "control" that is the lynchpin of state responsibility under this article.

The ability of a state to take advantage of this threshold is enhanced by the ambiguity in the meaning of "control." There are at least two competing legal interpretations of the requisite degree of "control" to trigger this type of state responsibility. The first is generally understood to be the more stringent "effective control" test articulated by the International Court of Justice in the *Nicaragua* case, where the court was evaluating the relationship between the United States and the Nicaraguan Contras.[71] The court noted that a state should be deemed responsible for the actions of a non-state group it supports only if it exerts "effective control" over the non-state actors in question.[72] The second is generally understood to be the less demanding "overall control" test set forth by the International Criminal Tribunal for the Former Yugoslavia in *Tadić*, a case in which the court was assessing whether the Federal Republic of Yugoslavia maintained sufficient control over the military forces operating in Bosnia to be deemed a party to the armed conflict.[73] The court in that context rejected *Nicaragua's* stringent test and concluded that the state need only exercise "overall control" of the non-state actor to trigger responsibility.[74]

---

[69] Articles of State Responsibility, *supra* note 64, at art. 8.

[70] *See* Cameron & Chetail, *supra* note 66.

[71] International Court of Justice (ICJ), Military and Paramilitary Activities in and against Nicaragua (*Nicar. v. U.S.*), Judgment, 1986 I.C.J. Rep 14 (June 27).

[72] *Id.*

[73] *See, e.g., Prosecutor v. Tadić,* Case No. IT-94-1-A, ¶ 4-32 (separate Opinion of Judge Shahabuddeen).

[74] *Id.*

Some scholars have suggested that the degree of control necessary to establish state responsibility for non-state actors might differ depending on the type of underlying legal issue involved. Ryan Goodman, for example, has argued that in determining whether a state is simply a party to an armed conflict, a lesser degree of control over a paramilitary organization might be sufficient.[75] However, in determining whether a state is guilty of war crimes based on the *specific acts* of that paramilitary organization, a greater degree of state control might be necessary. Indeed, one could potentially read *Nicaragua* itself to support this distinction. On this reading, *Nicaragua's* more stringent conception of control applies only to the allegations that the United States should be responsible for the specific wrongful acts of the contras, rather than the more general claim that the United States crossed the use of force threshold by providing support to the contras.

For our purposes, this potential distinction is quite significant. A looser nexus of control may be more appropriate to demonstrate state use of force or involvement in an armed conflict via a non-state group. In such circumstances, indicia of "overall control" of the group by the state rather than specific, effective control of the group's individual actions may be sufficient to satisfy state responsibility. This broader approach is more likely to encompass states' deployment of PMSCs in hybrid war.

Returning to Wagner's role in eastern Ukraine after Russia's 2014 annexation of Crimea, we can see how the doctrine of state responsibility can be subverted. Russia generally denied its involvement in eastern Ukraine altogether. But to the extent that the Kremlin admitted at least some link to the contractors (and other fighters) there, it argued that it had no control over them. Journalists attempted to demonstrate links between Wagner and the Kremlin, but such connections were difficult to prove (especially because many of the journalists died in mysterious incidents). Moreover, even if connections had been shown between Putin and Wagner's corporate leadership, such connections might still not have satisfied the requirements of Article 8 because it would have been difficult to establish the requisite degree of control, at least as that Article is traditionally understood.

Facts on the ground – which are difficult to obtain in conflict zones – would have been needed as well. It is true that there is evidence that Wagner forces trained alongside Russian special forces, that many former special forces were then employed by Wagner, and that Wagner was reportedly using sophisticated weaponry similar to the weapons used by the Russian military. Such facts provide some evidence that move closer to satisfying the "control" tests for Article 8, but even if all of those facts could have been shown, it is still unclear whether Russia would have been deemed in control for the purposes of Article 8.

---

[75] Ryan Goodman, *Legal Limits on Military Assistance to Proxy Forces: Pathways for State and Official Responsibility*, JUST SECURITY (May 14, 2018) www.justsecurity.org/56272/legal-limits-military-assistance-proxy-forces-pathways-state-official-responsibility/.

The use of PMSCs, therefore, provides a convenient tool for states who want to engage in hybrid warfare. Even if the contractors' presence is known, it is difficult to demonstrate the kinds of links required to establish state responsibility under Article 8. The difficulty of establishing state responsibility, in turn, insulates the aggressor state both from legal responsibility under the *jus ad bellum* and from having a direct link to an armed conflict under the *jus in bello*.

REFORMING THE LAW OF STATE RESPONSIBILITY

The case of the Wagner Group illustrates the many ways in which military and security contractors can be deployed by states that seek to wage hybrid warfare. Moreover, by using these contractors, states can skirt the existing frameworks for assigning state responsibility under international law. In the face of this challenge, how can the law of state responsibility be adjusted and reformed? Here, I argue that one problem with the law of state responsibility is its overly formalist reliance on purportedly clear dividing lines between what is state and what is non-state. Yet, as the hybrid war paradigm makes clear, such formal lines are impossible to maintain and indeed they play directly into the hands of those who would use the letter of the law to defy its core aims.

Thus, we must consider expanding the reach of the state responsibility doctrine by taking a more functional approach to PMSCs operating in armed conflict zones. Drawing on the theoretical framework of global legal pluralism, we can eschew the idea that formal state actors are the only sorts of actors who serve as the instruments of state power and instead see the state and its law enforcement and military power amassed over a much broader array of actors, certainly including PMSCs. This approach, I argue, provides a useful interpretive pathway for rethinking the law of state responsibility so that it can better address the hybrid war challenge.[76]

Global Legal Pluralism

Legal pluralists have long recognized that law is not found only in the formal instruments of treaties, legislation, or judicial pronouncements.[77] Instead, pluralists look to the wide variety of legalities that course through daily life and that end up actually affecting behavior. For example, scholars studying colonialism noticed that even when the imperial power purported to impose an entirely new legal

---

[76] In this discussion my focus is on PMSCs specifically, both because they form a leading prong of the hybrid war strategy and because of distinctions in how they operate due to their corporate form and enhanced legitimacy on the global stage as compared to other types of proxies and irregular forces. The implications of my approach for those other categories of non-state actors is beyond the scope of this paper.

[77] See, e.g., Sally Engle Merry, *Legal Pluralism*, 22 L. SOC'Y REV. 869, 869–75 (1988).

system, the preexisting legal system was never banished entirely, leading to strategic maneuvering and jurisdictional contestation among the systems.[78] Likewise, both religious law and indigenous systems of order can persist in opposition to formal law and, in many cases, have far more impact on daily life.[79] Finally, non-state actors such as corporations, industry-standard-setting bodies, norm-generating communities, ethnic and religious group leaders, local warlords, and so on can all articulate and impose norms that govern behavior as much as, or more than, formal law.[80] Accordingly, pluralists argue that if one wants to understand law in any given social field, one needs to look beyond the formal pronouncements of official governmental actors. Most famously, John Griffiths argued against what he described as "legal centralism," the tendency of scholars only to focus on the state and its formal mechanisms of law, while ignoring all the other ways in which legality operates in daily life.[81]

Global legal pluralism took those insights of legal pluralism and applied them to the global arena. In doing so, scholars of global legal pluralism asked us to turn our gaze away from abstract debates about, for example, whether international law is truly law or not and instead examine on-the-ground questions of efficacy.[82] From this perspective, law is not law just because some authority says it is or because it is formally linked to the state. Likewise, the state is not only found in the formal levers of the state. Rather, just as legal realists and critical legal studies scholars have for decades challenged the artificial distinctions between state and non-state implicit in the U.S. Supreme Court's state action doctrine,[83] legal pluralists likewise view the seemingly sharp divide between state and non-state along a continuum. States are not monolithic. Many actors both within and without a state bureaucracy may articulate norms or take action that enlarge the power of the state. Those norms and actions cannot slip from view just because they are not officially designated as state action or taken by official state actors.

Thus, global legal pluralists would not stop at the formal delineations between state and non-state, or between public and private. Rather, the key question from a pluralist perspective becomes: How is private power being used to aggrandize state power and in what ways are the state actor and the non-state actor so intertwined that they become part of the same legal activity? And, in this inquiry, the key is to look at the real impacts of acts on the ground regardless of the formal legal category used.

[78] *See, e.g.*, LEGAL PLURALISM AND EMPIRES 1500–1850 (Lauren A. Benton & Richard J. Ross eds., 2013).

[79] *See, e.g.*, OXFORD HANDBOOK (collecting essays).

[80] *See, e.g., id.; see also* Laura A. Dickinson, *Regulating the Privatized Security Industry: The Promise of Public/Private Governance*, 63 EMORY L.J. 417–454 (2013).

[81] John Griffiths, *What is Legal Pluralism?*, 24 J. *Legal Pluralism & Unofficial L.* 1 (1986).

[82] *See, e.g.*, Paul Schiff Berman, *Seeing Beyond the Limits of International Law*, 84 TEX. L. REV. 1265 (2006).

[83] *See, e.g.*, MARK TUSHNET, WEAK COURTS, STRONG RIGHTS 161–62 (2008).

A Pluralist, Functional Approach to Article 8 as It Applies to PMSCs

What is a pluralist approach to state responsibility for the actions of PMSCs operating in armed conflict zones? At its core, such an approach focuses not on formal legal ties or rules, but on the functions that the PMSCs perform and the practical ties between those PMSCs and the state in question. For this reason, I focus my analysis on Article 8, which is most oriented around such functional relationships, as opposed to Articles 4 and 5, which contain in their terms the formalist links discussed above. That being said, the concept of "governmentality" in Article 5 provides a useful analogy for the functional approach I am advocating for Article 8.

The lynchpin of Article 8 in a hybrid war setting is the concept of control by the state over the non-state actor. As discussed above, there are two approaches to the requisite level of control required to establish a link to the state: the slightly lower threshold of "overall" control or the higher standard of "effective" control that would mandate a tighter nexus between the state and the non-state actor in question. As noted earlier, the case law provides some support for the idea that the lower "overall control" standard is more appropriate for an evaluation of state responsibility when evaluating whether a state has crossed the thresholds of the *jus ad bellum* and the *jus in bello*, as opposed to whether the state should bear responsibility for the specific wrongful acts committed by individual members of the group. In other words, "overall control" by the state of the non-state group arguably is the more appropriate framework for determining whether the state is participating in an armed conflict or has crossed the use of force or armed attack thresholds in the *jus ad bellum*. It would be difficult to conclude unequivocally that the "overall control" standard has attained the status of customary international law, but in my view it is probably the better approach. (And states could adopt it as a matter of policy.[84])

It is my contention, further, that an analysis of the precise function the group is performing should be relevant to the "overall control" analysis. Specifically, whether a PMSC is performing a role that is governmental – one that is considered to be in the inherent or core domain of a government – should be a relevant factor in finding "overall control." In effect, I am suggesting that, when a PMSC is acting like a government actor based on the specific functions it pursues, it should be easier to establish the requisite tie between a government that is affiliated with that PMSC and the PMSC itself in order to trigger state responsibility for the purposes of determining whether the state has crossed the *jus in bello* or *jus ad bellum* thresholds. Of course, this inquiry raises a difficult definitional question concerning what should count as acting "like a government actor." But certain activities would easily qualify, and even in the gray area cases, we would at least be discussing the core issues of

---

[84] *See, e.g.,* Laura A. Dickinson, *National Security Policymaking in the Shadow of International Law,* 2021 UTAH L. REV. 629 (2021).

function and control, rather than the formalistic – and easily skirted – categories of the current state responsibility doctrine.

Lindsay Cameron and Vincent Chetail make a somewhat similar argument in the context of interpreting Article 5. Article 5 specifically permits a finding of state responsibility for an entity exercising "elements of governmental authority" that are "empowered by the law of the state" in question. Article 5 contains a formalist prerequisite, however, that is not met in the typical hybrid war scenario because often there is no formal contract between the state in question and PMSCs operating on its behalf. Yet, Cameron and Chetail's analysis of the circumstances in which PMSCs exercise elements of governmental authority is potentially quite relevant in the Article 8 context as well. They argue that certain functions of PMSCs can be clearly defined as governmental: the use of force and activities which, in armed conflict, would constitute taking a direct part in hostilities. They also suggest that the concept of "inherently governmental functions" in U.S. law and policy provides an additional framework for defining this category of governmental activity. They contend that the "governmental" character of the PMSC turns on the type of work a PMSC actually performs.

In my view, this analysis should also be relevant to the interpretation of Article 8. When a PMSC acts in a functionally governmental role and holds significant ties to a government, it bears the imprimatur of that government even if there is no formal contract or tight nexus of direction or control. Such functionally governmental roles would include the use of force in the form of private security, as well as military advice or training on the use of force. A private contractor performing such functions would be taking a direct part in hostilities under the Law of Armed Conflict, and if the functions entailed the offensive or defensive use of force in a high-threat situation, they would likely qualify as "inherently governmental" under U.S. policy. When a PMSC exercises such functions, it is my contention that a somewhat looser web of ties between the state and the PMSC could trigger state responsibility, at least for determining whether the state has crossed *jus ad bellum* and *in bello* thresholds. Such ties might include, for example, shared training of PMSC and governmental personnel, a common background of personnel, shared reward systems, shared weapons systems, and common strategy. In such contexts, it should not be necessary to delineate as tight a tie between the state and the PMSC because the PMSC role is inherently governmental in nature.

The operations of Wagner group described above could satisfy such a standard. The role of Wagner easily qualified as functionally governmental, given that Wagner provided offensive and defensive security as well as military advice and training on direct combat. Furthermore, Wagner hired many of its employees from the Russian military, trained them alongside Russian forces, and equipped them with Russian weapons. Also, Wagner employees were rewarded with Russian military orders. Available evidence suggests that Wagner conducted its activities pursuant to a strategy dictated by the Russian government, even if the specific actions of Wagner may not have been directed or controlled by Russian military forces. In such circumstances, a more functionalist understanding of Article 8 would mean that its criteria for state responsibility would be satisfied.

CONCLUSION

The phenomenon of hybrid war presents new and important challenges to the categories and definitions of international law, including the law of state responsibility. As we consider possible reforms, we should not forget about the important role private contractors, such as the Wagner Group, play in enabling states to both engage in and disguise their participation in armed conflict, often with devastating consequences. The law of state responsibility lies at the heart of the matter because this body of law enhances states' capacity to exploit other international legal thresholds. A broad, functionalist interpretation of the state responsibility framework as it applies to PMSCs can, therefore, help address the challenge of hybrid war. Even if states such as Russia will almost certainly refuse to adhere to any such rules, those rules can nonetheless help thwart Russia's efforts to use PMSCs to deny involvement in armed attacks and armed conflicts, thereby creating a context for possible responses by the international community.

5

The Enduring Charter

Corporations, States, and International Law

Doreen Lustig

INTRODUCTION: CORPORATIONS, STATES, AND THE
QUESTION OF RESPONSIBILITY IN INTERNATIONAL LAW

The corporation as a legal entity and a form of governance has no innate conceptual identity; rather, its legal identity is the product of historical developments. During the nineteenth century, a corporation came to be considered a private entity formed for the purpose of pursuing commercial ends. Prior to that time, the identity of corporations was less clearly defined, and they owed their existence to the governments that chartered them. They were frequently granted monopolistic privileges and tasked with building infrastructure projects, such as roads and canals. As noted by Philip Stern, during the early modern period "[i]ncorporation ... had nothing to do with the nature of the business at hand. It was a legal and political institution that allowed groups of students, merchants, townsmen, or monarchical subjects to make claims on property, rights, and privileges, and to pass these on to later generations in perpetuity."[1] Over the course of the nineteenth century, the corporation gradually came to be governed by private and contract law principles.[2]

---

[1] Philip J. Stern, *The Corporation in History, in* THE CORPORATION: A CRITICAL, MULTI-DISCIPLINARY HANDBOOK 21, 24 (Grietje Baars & Andre Spicer eds., 2017). For further discussion on the history and theory of corporate–state relations, *see* David Ciepley, *Beyond the Public and Private: Toward a Political Theory of the Corporation*, 107 AM. POL. SCI. REV. 139 (2013).

[2] For literature distinguishing corporations as governed by private and contract law principles, *see generally* Ron Harris, *Spread of Legal Innovations Defining Private and Public Domains, in* THE CAMBRIDGE HISTORY OF CAPITALISM VOLUME 2: THE SPREAD OF CAPITALISM: FROM 1848 TO THE PRESENT, 127, 142–43 (Larry Neal & Jeffrey G. Williamson eds., 2014); Gregory A. Mark, *The Personification of the Business Corporation in American Law*, 54 CHI. L. REV. 1441 (1987); William W. Bratton, Jr., *The New Economic Theory of the Firm: Critical Perspectives from History*, 41 STAN. L. REV. 1471 (1989); Ron Harris, *The Transplantation of a Legal Discourse: Corporate Personality Theories from German Codification to British Political Pluralism and American Big Business*, 63 WASH. LEE L. REV. 1421 (2006); S.K. RIPKEN, CORPORATE PERSONHOOD (2019); D. Millon, *Theories of the Corporation*, 39 DUKE L.J. 201 (1990); S.K. Ripken, *Corporations Are People Too: A Multi-Dimensional Approach to the Corporate Person Puzzle*, 15 FORDHAM J. CORP. FIN. L. 97, 107 (2009); E. Pollman, *Reconceiving Corporate Personhood*, 2011 UTAH L. REV. 1629 (2011).

In the context of international law, this transition would gain prominence in the latter part of nineteenth century in debates among scholars in the field about the involvement of chartered companies in the scramble for Africa. During this period, scholars of international law scrutinized the involvement of business corporations in Africa and ultimately criticized the use of the chartered company for colonial purposes. As the nineteenth century drew to an end, most chartered companies dissolved. Consequently, the international legal debate over the legitimacy of using companies as governing authorities in Africa was put to rest. In the following decades, international legal scholars rarely considered the private business corporation an issue of concern or subject for examination in key treaties or other works.

Yet, the *formal* dissolution of the charter hardly put an end to the close relationship between governments and corporations. That relationship continued to have far-reaching implications for international law with respect to corporations and the question of corporate responsibility. Legal scholars frequently perceived formal dissolution of the charter as a *normative* dissolution of the dependence of private business corporations on governments in order to survive and thrive. That normative dissolution is a central feature of the legal rules of attribution on state responsibility. The following analysis reveals the gap between the legal assumption that corporations and governments are formally separated and the reality of deep interdependence between governments and corporations in colonial settings. This situation provided private business corporations with the legal infrastructure they needed to leverage their position to thrive in the colonization of Africa. I then explore related doctrines of international law – diplomatic protection, human rights, and investment protection – as additional aspects of the international legal infrastructure that protected corporate actors from responsibilities while granting them significant benefits as individual rights bearers. This chapter chronicles the lingering presence and influence of international law on the regulatory options available for corporations operating both within and outside state borders.

The Separate Spheres Presumption in the Articles on Responsibility of States for Internationally Wrongful Acts

The Articles on Responsibility of States for Internationally Wrongful Acts (ARSIWA) are the primary source for defining the doctrine of attribution in international law. Of particular interest here is their definition of the circumstances under which "conduct consisting of an act or omission or a series of acts or omissions is to be considered as the conduct of the State."

As noted in the ILC commentaries, "the conduct of private persons or entities is not attributable to the State under international law."[3] While the ILC has presented

---

[3] *Report of the International Law Commission*, 53 U.N. GAOR Supp. No. 10, at 47, U.N. Doc. A/56/10 (Nov. 2001) *available at* https://bit.ly/39T3EHB [hereinafter "Articles on Responsibility of States 2001"].

rules for entities, or organizations,[4] and international criminal law has developed rules for holding natural persons responsible,[5] the responsibility of non-state actors in international law remains underdeveloped.[6]

In the context of state responsibility, the circumstances for imputing the acts of corporate actors to a state are limited to situations in which the private corporation is operating *as a state organ* (Article 4), *like a state organ* (Article 5), or in cases when it is *directed or controlled by the state* (Article 8). This approach to attribution presumes a clear distinction between the private sphere of the corporation and the public sphere of the state as the underlying logic for defining the extent of state responsibility. As the ILC commentary explains:

> In theory, the conduct *of all human beings, corporations or collectivities* linked to the State by nationality, habitual residence or incorporation might be attributed to the State, whether or not they have any connection to the Government. In international law, such an approach is avoided, both *with a view to limiting responsibility to conduct which engages the State as an organization,* and also *so as to recognize the autonomy of persons acting on their own account* and not at the instigation of a public authority.[7]

In his article *The Articles on State Responsibility and the Guiding Principles of Shared Responsibility: A TWAIL Perspective*, B.S. Chimni criticized the implications of this approach to postcolonial states. According to Chimni, by adopting this approach, the "ILC was able to ignore the history of the *symbiotic relationship between the corporation and the capitalist state*, including their role *in the shaping of particular international law obligations*."[8]

Indeed, the above paragraph from the ILC commentaries reiterates a prevailing international legal approach to the relationship between the corporation and the state, perceiving them as separate entities. As the following analysis suggests, the demise of the chartered company and the transition to privately incorporated business enterprises toward the end of the nineteenth century ushered in the end of the *recognized* symbiotic relationship between the state and the corporation and gave rise to the presumption of separate spheres between the public state and the privately incorporated corporation (hereinafter: the separate spheres presumption).

---

4   *Report of the International Law Commission,* 63 U.N. GAOR, U.N. Doc. A/66/10 (2011) *available at* https://legal.un.org/ilc/texts/instruments/english/commentaries/9_11_2011.pdf [hereinafter "Articles on Responsibility of States 2011"].

5   Rome Statute of the International Criminal Court, *opened for signature* July 17, 1998, 2187 U.N.T.S. 3 (entered into force July 1, 2002).

6   For an elaborate discussion on the deficiencies in the current responsibility regime for corporations in international law, *see* Kristen E. Boon, *Attribution in International Law: Challenges & Evolution,* Ch. 1.

7   Articles on Responsibility of States 2001, *supra* note 3, at 38 (emphasis added).

8   B.S. Chimni, *The Articles on State Responsibility and the Guiding Principles of Shared Responsibility: A TWAIL Perspective,* 31 EJIL 1211 (Nov. 2020).

Section II describes the early colonial corporations and Adam Smith's eighteenth-century critique of the use of chartered companies for colonial ends. Smith's influential analysis would have a lasting impact, as evident in the commentaries of the late nineteenth-century international lawyers' discussions on the chartered companies involved in the scramble for Africa, which are analyzed in Section III. International lawyers condemned what they considered the illegitimate use of corporations for colonial ends and focused their attention on the charter as a prominent manifestation of that illicit relationship. Section IV is dedicated to the aftermath of the chartered company. I argue that the international legal approach to the corporation after the revocation of the charter, rather than putting an end to the close relationship between companies and states, made the relationship invisible in ways that improved the position of corporations in colonial and postcolonial settings. Section V demonstrates how the *separate spheres presumption* shaped other facets in the meaning of attribution in international law in the context of diplomatic protection, human rights, and international investment law, and analyzes how these doctrinal developments contributed to the propensity of limiting corporate accountability in international law. Section VI concludes the chapter.

THE COLONIAL CORPORATIONS AND ADAM SMITH'S CRITIQUE

Background: The Early Colonial Corporations

Before the nineteenth century, corporations operating beyond imperial borders enjoyed special relationships with imperial authorities. The prerogatives of the United East India Company (Verenigde Oostindische Compagnie, VOC) to wage war and forge alliances with local leaders were meticulously documented and justified by Hugo Grotius (1583–1645).[9] The VOC remained more successful than the contemporaneous English East India Company (EIC) for almost two hundred years after their parallel establishment.[10] Like the early Dutch ventures, the first English trading companies enjoyed trade monopolies and trading zones.[11] While other monopoly-based companies declined between

---

[9] Martine Julia van Ittersum, *Introduction* to Hugo Grotius, Commentary on the Law of Prize and Booty (Knud Haakonssen ed., Liberty Fund 2006) (1603).

[10] The VOC was a limited liability company, but the meaning of this feature wasn't clear in its founding. For further discussion, *see* Jan de Vries and Ad van der Woude, The First Modern Economy: Success, Failure, and Perseverance of the Dutch Economy, 1500–1815 (1997); Julia Adams, *Principals and Agents, Colonialists and Company Men: The Decay of Colonial Control in the Dutch East Indies*, 61 Am. Soc. Rev. 12 (1996); Femme S. Gaastra, *Competition or Collaboration? Relations between the Dutch East India Company and Indian Merchants around 1680*, *in* Merchants, Companies and Trade: Europe and Asia in the Early Modern Era 189 (Suchil Chaundhury & Michel Morineau eds., 1999); Ron Harris, *Law Finance and the First Corporations*, *in* Global Perspectives on the Rule of Law (James J. Heckman et al., eds., 2009).

[11] These early corporations were granted monopolistic privileges in return for payments to the Crown. Whether the colonial corporation which settled Virginia, Massachusetts, and other areas in North

the 1630s and the Glorious Revolution (1688),[12] the EIC was exceptional in its rise to prominence during this period. Philip Stern's early history of the EIC, *The Company-State*, invites us to think of the EIC as a form of early modern government from its inception. During the second half of the seventeenth century, the EIC became a colonial proprietor, doing "what early modern governments did: erect and administer law; collect taxes; provide protection; inflict punishment; perform stateliness; regulate economic, religious and civic life; conduct diplomacy and wage war; make claims for jurisdiction over land and sea; cultivate authority over and obedience from those people subject to its command."[13] Surveying broader mercantilist practices, Stern observed how "English merchants routinely appealed to the sovereignty of the Crown and its infrastructure – courts, customs officials, diplomatic corps, naval power, among others – while also attempting with varying degree of success to keep the state from interfering too much in its affairs, especially overseas."[14]

The Glorious Revolution gradually challenged the legitimacy of the EIC, a corporation that was constitutionally rooted in royal grants at home and provided with prerogatives abroad.[15] During the eighteenth century, the EIC became a de facto sovereign power in India, with its administrative center in London and a complex management system for long-distance trade. The EIC's growing involvement in armed conflicts and direct control of India was a subject of heated debate and criticism. The words of the eighteenth-century theorist Thomas Pownall – "The merchant is become the sovereign" – became a slogan frequently applied to the EIC's activities.[16]

Adam Smith and the Critique of Colonial Corporations

Perhaps the most influential and memorable among the EIC's critics was Adam Smith, as set forth in *An Inquiry into the Nature and Causes of the Wealth of*

America should be regarded as part of the history of the business corporation is yet unresolved; *see* RON HARRIS, INDUSTRIALIZING ENGLISH LAW 25–43 (2000); FERNAND BRAUDEL, THE WHEELS OF COMMERCE 445–47 (1982); Ann M. Carlos and Stephen Nicholas, *Agency Problems in Early Chartered Companies: The Case of the Hudson's Bay Company*, 50 J. ECON. HIST. 853, 854–56 (1990); Ann M. Carlos & Stephen Nicholas, *Theory and History: Seventeenth Century Joint-Stock Chartered Trading Companies*, 56 J. ECON. HIST. 916 (1996); NICHOLAS CANNY, THE ORIGINS OF EMPIRE (1998).

[12] HARRIS, *supra* note 11, at 50.

[13] PHILIP STERN, THE COMPANY-STATE: CORPORATE SOVEREIGNTY AND THE EARLY MODERN FOUNDATIONS OF THE BRITISH EMPIRE IN INDIA 3 (2011).

[14] Philip Stern, *Companies: Monopoly, Sovereignty and the East India*, in MERCANTILISM REIMAGINED: POLITICAL ECONOMY IN EARLY MODERN BRITAIN AND ITS EMPIRE 177–181 (Philip Stern & Carl Wennerlind eds., 2014).

[15] STERN, *supra* note 13, at 143 (explaining that the EIC had strong relations to the Crown (King James was invested in the Company) but it was not institutionally tied to the Crown).

[16] 3 THOMAS POWNALL, THE RIGHT, INTEREST AND THE DUTY OF GOVERNMENT, AS CONCERNED IN THE AFFAIRS OF THE EAST INDIES 26–27 (J. Almon rev. ed. 1781) (1773).

Nations.[17] Smith considered mercantilism an assault on "the most sacred rights of mankind,"[18] going on to explain why mercantilist policies were less profitable,[19] doomed to failure, and highly disadvantageous to the interests of the colonies.[20] Smith considered the merchant as the – highly problematic – navigator of the colonial system.[21] Indeed, according to Smith's view of joint-stock companies, the entire colonial project was essentially a corrupt endeavor, led by commercial agents for the sake of their advantage and commercial survival and contrary to the interests of colonial subjects.[22] "To promote the little interest of one little order of men in one country, it hurts the interest of all other orders of men in that country, and of all men in all other countries."[23]

Smith accused the joint-stock companies of subjecting the people in the colonies to great suffering and misfortune.[24] "[A] company of merchants," he wrote, "regard the character of the sovereign as but an appendix to that of the merchant, as something which ought to be made subservient to it."[25] The companies' charters went so far as to grant them the right to possess forts and garrisons, enabling them to make peace and war in areas they controlled. "How unjustly, how capriciously, how cruelly they have commonly exercised it, is too well known from recent experience."[26] The local population, conscious of being robbed and ignored, expressed its resentment through violence and protests. In response, the company then exerted military and other measures of control. "Such a council [of merchants] can command obedience only by the military force with which they are accompanied, and their government is therefore necessarily military and despotical."[27]

As thoroughly analyzed by the political scientist Sankar Muthu,[28] Smith also criticized colonial corporations for seizing control of imperial governments by

---

[17] ADAM SMITH, AN INQUIRY INTO THE NATURE AND CAUSES OF THE WEALTH OF NATIONS 489, IV.iii.C.2 (R.H. Campbell & A.S. Skinner eds., W.B Todd, textual ed., Oxford Univ. Press 1976) [hereinafter "WN"].

[18] *Id.* at vii.b.44/582.

[19] *See id.* at IV.vii.c.9/592 (discussing trade restrictions in the context of the American colonies).

[20] *Id.* at IV.vii.c.80/626.

[21] *Id.* at IV.vii.b 49/584.

[22] *Id.* Furthermore, "[a]ll the original sources of revenue, the wages of labour, the rent of land, and the profits of stock, the monopoly renders much less abundant than they otherwise would be. To promote the little interest of one little order of men in one country, it hurts the interest of all other orders of men in that country, and of all men in all other countries." *Id.* at IV.vii.c. 60/612.

[23] *Id.*

[24] *Id.* at IV.vii.c.104/638. In a later passage Smith vividly described the indifference of the company managers to the fate of the colonies. *Id.* at IV.vii.c.106/640. He further conceded that on some occasions managers of such companies acted honorably, but this was not expected of those "who have been bred to professions very different from war and politicks." *Id.* at IV.vii.c.107/641.

[25] *Id.* at IV.vii.c.103/637.

[26] *Id.* at V.i.e.29/754.

[27] *Id.* at IV.vii.c.104/638.

[28] Sankar Muthu, *Adam Smith's Critique of International Trading Companies: Theorizing Globalization in the Age of Enlightenment*, 36 POL. THEORY 185 (2008).

compelling them to subsidize and secure global trade and pursue wasteful policies that were incompatible with national concerns: "raising the rate of profit both in the new market and in the new employment, draws produce from the old market and capital from the old employment."[29] Furthermore:

> To found a great empire for the sole purpose of raising up a people of customers, may at first sight appear a project fit only for a nation of shopkeepers. It is, however, a project altogether unfit for a nation of shopkeepers; but extremely fit for a nation whose government is influenced by shopkeepers.[30]

Smith further criticized companies' limited liability. "This total exemption from trouble and risk [of the company proprietors], beyond a limited sum, encourages some people to become adventurers in joint stock companies, who would, upon no account, hazard their fortunes in any private country."[31] These shortcomings led companies to seek the help and favor of governmental benefits in the form of monopoly charters. "They have, accordingly, very seldom succeeded without an exclusive privilege; and frequently have not succeeded with one."[32]

As noted by H.V. Bowen, "[t]his strain of criticism endured for decades ... there was a residual sense of unease about leaving an empire in the hands of traders."[33] While the phenomenon of chartered companies for the purpose of colonialism diminished, and despite the anti-corporate critique in Britain and the United States, the number of corporations increased. As noted by Pauline Maier, writing on the American context, "Americans in the 1780s and 1790s elaborated the ideals of the Revolution, and gathered them into what Louis Hartz called 'an anti-charter doctrine.'" Yet, "[t]he anticharter doctrine that took form in states such as Pennsylvania soon after Independence persisted into the nineteenth century but failed to undercut Americans' enthusiasm for corporations."[34] Corporations were conceived, like incorporated cities, as aristocratic and anti-republican because they gave privileges to the few at the cost of the many. "Critics also attacked the creation of business corporations, like that of municipal corporations, because it implied 'granting ... an inherent right of sovereignty to individuals and thus reduced the power of the people.'"[35] This line of criticism would become quite central in the work of international lawyers writing about the chartered company toward the end

---

[29] WN *supra* note 17, at IV.vii.c.49/608; for further discussion of this aspect, *see* Muthu, *supra* note 28, at 196–98.

[30] WN *supra* note 17, at IV.vii.c. 63/613.

[31] WN *supra* note 17, at V.i.e.18/741.

[32] *Id.* In the following passages, Smith described in some detail the failing experiences of the Royal African Company, the Hudson Bay Company, the South Sea Company, and the English East India Company.

[33] H.V. Bowen, The Business of Empire 14 (Cambridge Univ. Press, 2006).

[34] Pauline Maier, *The Revolutionary Origins of the American Corporation*, 50 Wm. Mary Q. 51, 52 (1993).

[35] *Id.* at 68.

of the nineteenth century. These scholars considered the corporation an inappropriate vehicle for the exercise of sovereign authority. Yet, their theoretical exclusion
of the corporation from the realm of politics and their conceptualization of it as a
vehicle suited for economic activity ultimately insulated the corporation from legal
and political scrutiny for years to come.

International lawyers focused their attention on the harmful consequences of the
charter device for the colonized as well as for the fate of the colonial project.[36]
However, as the following analysis suggests, notably absent from their discussions is
Smith's critique of the undue influence of trading companies on imperial governments' colonial policies[37] and how they used that influence to reduce their risks and
enhance their position in colonial settings. More broadly, in the early decades of the
twentieth century, lawyers would show limited interest in scrutinizing the practices
of privately incorporated companies. Yet, the contours of the international legal
order that emerged in the aftermath of the chartered companies' rise and fall was
frequently shaped by the influence of business interests, and would prove beneficial
for these companies. During this post-charter era, companies continued to flourish
in colonial and postcolonial settings. The marginalization of the issue of corporate
responsibility in international law during this period should not be mistaken for its
irrelevance. Rather, the key elements of the international legal architecture that
would emerge in lieu of the chartered era imperial regime would be highly beneficial for corporate actors operating globally and would often facilitate their involvement in dubious practices with limited to no accountability.

INTERNATIONAL LAWYERS' CRITIQUE OF THE LATE NINETEENTH-CENTURY CHARTERED COMPANIES

The Late Nineteenth-Century Modality of the Chartered Company

From 1879 to 1882 onward, European powers increasingly sought colonial control
over Africa. Their colonial presence on the continent gradually evolved from that
of a powerful influence primarily along the coast into full colonial governance
within the hinterland. This transition was accompanied by mounting tensions
among European powers, which formed the backdrop to the Berlin West Africa
Conference of 1884–1885.[38] Amid these tensions, most industrialist economies of

---

[36] *See infra* § III (2).

[37] For example, "particular companies of merchants have had the address to persuade the legislature to
entrust to them the performance of this part of the duty of the sovereign, together with all the powers
which are necessarily connected with it." (WN *supra* note 17, at 733.)

[38] For general accounts of the conference, *see* J. KELTIE, THE PARTITION OF AFRICA (1893); S.E.
CROWE, THE BERLIN WEST AFRICA CONFERENCE, 1884–85 (1942); R. GAVIN & J. BETLEY,
THE SCRAMBLE FOR AFRICA: DOCUMENTS ON THE BERLIN WEST AFRICA CONFERENCE AND
RELATED SUBJECTS 1884/1885 (1973); R. ROBINSON ET AL., AFRICA AND THE VICTORIANS:

the time – for example, those of Britain, Germany, and Belgium – were reluctant to bear the financial burdens of establishing territorial authority on African soil. It is therefore not surprising that the parties to the Berlin Act that emerged from the conference opted for limited requirements for the establishment of sovereignty in Africa.[39] Imperial powers applied the Berlin Act very loosely, claiming chartered companies with a limited administrative presence were sufficient to establish sovereignty claims. This conveniently loose interpretation is evident in King Leopold's colonization of the Congo[40] and Bismarck's choice to use the charter model for his colonial endeavors in Africa.[41] Both cases demonstrate the potential of using private entities to establish sovereign claims in Africa. To these we may add Portugal, which sought to control large parts of Mozambique through two chartered companies.[42]

In the course of the nineteenth century, the joint-stock company re-emerged in non-colonial settings (initially with the charter) to carry out industrial projects, such as the construction of canals and railways.[43] In the colonial context,

THE OFFICIAL MIND OF THE VICTORIANS (2015); A.G. HOPKINS, BISMARCK, EUROPE AND AFRICA: THE BERLIN AFRICA CONFERENCE 1884–1885 AND THE ONSET OF PARTITION (Stig Förster et al., eds., Oxford Univ. Press 1988); THOMAS PAKENHAM, THE SCRAMBLE FOR AFRICA: WHITE MAN'S CONQUEST OF THE DARK CONTINENT FROM 1876 TO 1912 (1991); M. EWANS, EUROPEAN ATROCITY, AFRICAN CATASTROPHE: LEOPOLD II, THE CONGO FREE STATE AND ITS AFTERMATH (2002); R. LOUIS, ENDS OF BRITISH IMPERIALISM, 26–77 (2007); Matthew Craven, *Between Law and History: The Berlin Conference of 1884–1885 and the Logic of Free Trade*, 3 LONDON R. INT'L L. 31 (2015).

39 General Act of the Berlin Conference concerning the Congo, Feb. 26, 1885, 3 AJIL SUPP. 7 (1909), art. 34–35. For further discussion, *see* J.D. Hargreaves, *The Berlin Conference, West African Boundaries, and the Eventual Partition, in* BISMARCK, *supra* note 38. On the ways in which the instability and open-endedness of the categories in arts. 34–35 for sovereignty structured the architecture of Africa's partition, *see* Craven, *supra* note 38, at 44–46; Andrew Fitzmaurice, *The Genealogy of* Terra Nullius, 129 AUSTL. HIST. STUD. 1, 10–11 (2001); M. KOSKENNIEMI, THE GENTLE CIVILIZER OF NATIONS: THE RISE AND FALL OF INTERNATIONAL LAW 1870–1960 150–51 (2010); ANDREW FITZMAURICE, SOVEREIGNTY, PROPERTY AND EMPIRE 1500–2000 285–90 (2015).

40 The AIC was an offshoot of the Comité d'études du Haut-Congo, the executive arm of a syndicate set up by Leopold in 1878, financed by private subscription, which included William Mackinnon, the later founder of the Imperial British East Africa Company. For an elaborate discussion, *see* Andrew Fitzmaurice, *The Justification of King Leopold II's Congo Enterprise by Sir Travers Twiss, in* LAW AND POLITICS IN BRITISH COLONIAL THOUGHT: TRANSITION OF EMPIRE 109 (Shaunnagh Dorsett & Ian Hunter eds., 2010); ADAM HOCHSHILD, KING LEOPOLD'S GHOST 75–82 (1998); Pakenham, *supra* note 38, at 11–29, 239–255.

41 On February 27, 1885, one day after the Berlin West Africa Conference ended, Bismarck wrote a *Schutzbrief* (royal charter) for the Gesellschaft für Deutsche Kolonisation (GfdK) East African possessions. The charter enabled Bismarck to recognize an area in East Africa as a German protectorate, and to grant its administration to the German East Africa Company (Deutsch-Ostafrikanische Gesellschaft, DOAG). Bade, *supra* note 38, at 124–25; *see also* SEBASTIAN CONRAD, GLOBALIZATION AND THE NATION IN IMPERIAL GERMANY 119–24 (2006).

42 Leroy Vail, *Mozambique's Chartered Companies: The Rule of the Feeble*, 17 J. AFR. HIST. 389 (1976).

43 For a discussion of the British context, *see* HARRIS, *supra* note 11, at 217–93. For a classic discussion of the American context, *see* JAMES WILLARD HURST, LAW AND THE CONDITIONS OF FREEDOM IN THE NINETEENTH-CENTURY UNITED STATES (1956); *see also* LAWRENCE FRIEDMAN, A HISTORY OF AMERICAN LAW 390–403 (2005); WILLIAM G. ROY, SOCIALIZING CAPITAL: THE RISE OF THE LARGE INDUSTRIAL CORPORATION IN AMERICA 42–77 (1997).

the British chartered companies were initiated by British businessmen working in commerce.[44] The British revival of the chartered company began with the North Borneo Company in 1881.[45] This precedent was soon followed in Africa with the Royal Niger Company (1886–1900), the Imperial British East African Company (1888–96), and Cecil Rhodes's BSAC (1889–1923). Free incorporation only became a central feature of business organizations operating transnationally toward the end of the nineteenth century and even later.[46] The free incorporation of these chartered companies proved critical to their success in the aftermath of the dissolution of their original charters.

This new modality of the charter contained a peculiar blend of features from the early colonial company (reflecting the territorial aspirations of these companies) without the formal monopoly or state funding that was characteristic of sixteenth- and seventeenth-century trade companies. The rationale for their introduction, however, was quite reminiscent of earlier British trading companies. The charters of earlier centuries were often justified in terms of efficiency (allocation of cost between the Crown and the merchant) and ideology (as epitomizers of a mercantilist order). Their late appearance in Africa was similarly related to the British government's attempt to minimize the cost of colonization and the aspiration of businessmen to gain advantages over their competitors through benefits potentially derived from the charter. In terms of ideology, this later generation of chartered companies presented itself as compatible with contemporary sensibilities of free trade (the charters prohibited monopolies) and as bearers of the civilizing mission. As the debate among international lawyers of the time demonstrates, the practices of this new generation of chartered companies evoked tension and public dismay virtually from their inception, and they failed to eradicate common associations of them with the notorious legacy of their sixteenth- and seventeenth-century predecessors.

---

[44] John Flint, *Chartered Companies and the Transition from Informal Sway to Colonial Rule in Africa*, in BISMARCK, *supra* note 38.

[45] The North Borneo Charter did not grant governmental powers to the company, and prohibited any trading monopoly. Like the African chartered company, the North Borneo Company was incorporated under the Companies Act and could have operated in North Borneo independently of the royal charter. John Galbraith described how the British government used the charter as "an effective means of fencing off North Borneo from the intrusion of other powers without itself accepting direct responsibility, and the Company enabled it to do so." John S. Galbraith, *The Chartering of the North Borneo Company*, 4 J. BRIT. STUD. 102, 125 (May 1965). Galbraith further argues that while the founders of the British African chartered companies cited the North Borneo Company as a precedent, the company's charter conferred no governmental powers, and was therefore an unsatisfactory precedent. "Its main significance was as a forerunner" to the chartered companies in Africa. *Id.* at 125.

[46] The period between 1870 and 1914 saw particularly rapid levels of business creation. From the 1880s, the numbers and scale of multinationals grew rapidly. European companies dominated the world stage during this period. For an overview of this period, *see* GEOFFREY JONES, MULTINATIONALS AND GLOBAL CAPITALISM: FROM THE NINETEENTH CENTURY TO THE TWENTY-FIRST CENTURY 18–29 (2005) (drawing attention to the limited reliable data on this period).

International Lawyers' Critique

International lawyers devoted parts of their early treatises to the involvement of chartered companies in the scramble for Africa. Earlier accounts of the chartered companies in Africa appear in the works of Henry Maine and John Westlake, with Maine emphasizing the meaning of sovereignty as territoriality, and Westlake drawing on the distinction between public rule (imperium) and private property (dominium) to distinguish between the state and other actors. Their analyses provided the rationale for preferring formal state territorial control of imperial governments rather than a control through chartered companies. In slightly later writings, Rolin-Jaequemyns and Thomas Joseph Lawrence, and Gaston Jèze and Charles Salomon would use these conceptual distinctions to develop arguments against colonial governance by chartered companies.

Sovereignty as Territoriality

In 1887, Henry Sumner Maine (1822–1888) delivered the Whewell lectures on international law at the University of Cambridge, which included one of the early international legal accounts of the revival of the chartered company.[47] Maine dedicated his discussion to a shift from defining the sovereign as an individual to identifying sovereignty's link to a specific territory as the defining feature of contemporary international law (from individuality to territoriality): "Sovereignty was not always territorial."[48] He concluded that, "[e]vidently the fundamental conception was that the territory belonged to the Tribe, and that the Sovereign was the Sovereign of the Tribe."[49] Only after feudalization of Europe ended did it become possible to associate sovereignty with a defined portion of soil. Thus, sovereignty in its early form was associated with the individuals who exercised it. Maine relied on this shift to distinguish between the age of discovery during the seventeenth and eighteenth centuries and contemporary claims of colonial control. In the age of discovery, international law attributed "exaggerated importance to priority of discovery."[50] In current times…

> Some kind of formal annexation of new territory is now regarded as the best source of title. It is still allowed that prior discovery, if established, may give legal importance to acts and signs otherwise ambiguous or without validity…. [A]cts showing an intention to hold the country as your own, the most conclusive of these acts being the planting upon it some civil or military settlement.[51]

---

[47] Henry Sumner Maine, KCSI, Lecture at the University of Cambridge: International Law (1887). For further discussion on Maine's work, *see* Karuna Mantena, Alibis of Empire: Henry Maine and the Ends of Liberal Imperialism 56–88 (2009).

[48] Maine, *supra* note 47, at 56.

[49] *Id.*

[50] *Id.* at 66.

[51] *Id.* at 67.

This distinction and the emphasis on territoriality as a defining feature of sovereignty proved highly influential for future debates.

Maine's analysis alluded to the growing preference for formal territorial control. An intriguing example of this trend is captured in the writings of John Westlake (1828–1913).[52] Westlake's distinction between *dominium* and *imperium* further crystallized the meaning of the transition from individuality to territoriality as representing a distinction between the private and the public in international law.[53] Westlake conceived chartered companies as a bridgehead to formal colonial control,[54] asserting that they held their acquired territories while the international sovereignty over them belonged to the Crown.[55] In distinguishing between the age of discovery and contemporary expeditions ("now that the world has been so fully discovered"),[56] Westlake based his analysis on the nature of companies as organs of the government. His interpretive framework ignored the hybrid nature of many companies during this era as well as their organizational complexity.

Against de facto Sovereign Authority of Companies: The Argument for Formal Control

The revival of the chartered company as a colonial vehicle was a very short episode in imperial history. With the exception of the British South Africa Company, by 1900, none of the British chartered companies existed. Writing in 1889, Gustave Rolin-Jaequemyns (1835–1902) sought to explain the recent failures of the German and British chartered companies in Africa,[57] referring to a long passage from Montesquieu's *Spirit of the Laws* to make his point. For Montesquieu, writing in 1748, the use of chartered companies reflected a transition in the purpose of colonialism from conquest to commerce: "It has been established that only the mother country can trade with the colony, and this was done with very good reason, for the goal of the establishment was to extend commerce, not to found a town or a new empire."[58]

These lines, concluded Rolin-Jaequemyns, explain why the colonial system of the chartered companies was suited for earlier times, but not for the present times. He did not consider America, Africa, and Asia as mere instruments to be used by empires. Colonization could no longer be conceived of without duties toward indigenous

---

[52] On Westlake, *see* Editorial Comment, *In Memoriam: Professor John Westlake (1828–1913)* 7 Am. J. Int'l L. 582 (June 1913).

[53] Collected Papers of John Westlake on Public International Law 135–38 (Lassa Oppenheim ed., Cambridge Univ. Press 1914).

[54] *Id.* at 159.

[55] John Westlake, Chapters on the Principles of International Law 190–92 (Cambridge Univ. Press 1982).

[56] *Id.* at 160.

[57] Gustave Rolin-Jaequemyns, *L'année 1888 au point de vue de la paix et du droit international*, 31 Revue Internationale de Droit Comparé [R.I.D.C.] 189, 189–190 (1889) (Fr.).

[58] For Rolin-Jaequemyns translated quote from French, *see* Montesquieu, The Spirit of the Laws XXI 391 (Cambridge Univ. Press 1989).

peoples, its meaning having been transformed to include humanitarian tasks that the trading companies could not fulfil.[59] The changing spirit of the times, he argued, alluding to the words of Montesquieu, rendered the use of the chartered company *unwise* ("ne peut plus aujourd'hui être considéré comme un 'act de sagesse'").[60] For Rolin-Jaequemyns, the changing purpose of the colonial endeavor (its civilizing mission) created practical challenges for companies. Contemporary chartered companies were primarily interested in their profits, and their quest-for-profits-only bias triggered the military resistance of the local community. Although the sovereign, or the empire, merely delegated its authority to the company and retained its *imperium*, the use of the chartered companies' mechanism proved to be dangerous. Their biased considerations in favor of market interests and profits created serious difficulties. These, in turn, led empires to assume their formal responsibility.[61]

Other international lawyers expressed similar critiques, emphasizing the tension between the companies' commitment to profit maximization and the humanitarian obligations toward the local population. "Companies were always very influential," concluded F. E. Smith, an Oxford professor writing in 1900, "[t]he temptation to employ chartered companies is obviously great." Yet, Smith further argued that even if "pioneer work of incalculable value" had been done by such companies in the past, "imperial and economical tastes are not gracefully associated and the era of chartered companies should at most be a phase in the work of reclamation."[62] Smith, like Westlake, relied on the grant theory and concluded that "[a] nation cannot commit political functions to associations of its citizens and then disclaim responsibility for their abuse."[63]

During that same year, 1900, Thomas Joseph Lawrence (1849–1919) published his influential *Principles of International Law* and issued a fierce admonishment of corporate practices and influence. Lawrence distinguished between corporations, which are considered owners of property and are, therefore, treated like individual subjects of international law, and the practices of chartered companies involved in colonial endeavors:

> [W]e enter upon a sphere of great complexity when we endeavor to describe the international position of those great chartered companies called into existence within the last few years by some of the colonizing powers, especially Great Britain and Germany, to open up enormous territories recently brought within the sphere of their influence.[64]

---

[59] Rolin-Jaequemyns, *supra* note 57, at 190–91 [trans. by author].

[60] *Id.* at 191.

[61] *Id.* at 192.

[62] F.E. Smith & J. Wylie, International Law 37 (J.M. Dent & Sons, Ltd. 1911).

[63] This view was codified in Article IV of the Brussels Act (1890): "The Signatory Powers, however, emphasized the principle of international law that a state is responsible for its own acts and cannot contract itself out of its engagements by delegating its authority to any corporate body." General Act of the Brussels Conference relative to the African Slave Trade, July 2, 1890.

[64] T.J. Lawrence, The Principles of International Law 79 (Macmillan & Co., Ltd. 1895).

To illustrate his point, Lawrence chose the example of the British South Africa Company. He described its extensive rights: "Within this enormous territory the company possesses by royal grant the liberty to acquire by concession from the natives 'any rights, interests, authorities, jurisdictions, and powers necessary for the purposes of government.'"[65] This right was subject to the approval of the Secretary of State for the Colonies:

> The company may establish a police force and use a distinctive flag indicating its British character. It is bound not to set up any monopoly of trade, nor to allow the sale of intoxicants to the natives, nor to interfere with their religious rights except for purposes of humanity. It must establish courts for the administration of justice and pay due regard therein to native laws and tribal customs. The discouragement and gradual abolition of the slave-trade and domestic servitude are made obligatory upon it.[66]

At the same time, "it is subject to comply with the suggestions of the Colonial Secretary, perform all obligations contracted by the Imperial governments. The Crown reserves a right to revoke its charter at any time."[67] For the natives, concluded Lawrence, the company "must be all-powerful. He [the Colonial Secretary] is thousands of miles from the scene of action.... Practically the company rules its territories in so far as they are ruled at all. It legislates, it administers, it punishes, it negotiates, it makes war, and it concludes peace."[68] Like Janus, it had two faces: "On that which looks towards the native tribes all the lineaments and attributes of sovereignty are majestically outlined. On that which is turned towards the United Kingdom is written subordination and submission."[69] The problematic history of the East India Company, concluded Lawrence, "confirms in a striking manner this view of the position [in] International Law of its imitators and successors. They are altogether abnormal; and many complications are likely in future to arise from the peculiar conditions of their existence."[70] Control exercised over these companies by the "mother-country can hardly be very real or very continuous; and ... in her effort to escape responsibility by throwing it upon the shoulders of an association, she may often involve herself in transactions more dubious in character and more burdensome in execution than would have been possible had her control been direct."[71]

Failure was a key element in the critique of international lawyers. The outbreak of "natives of the German sphere of influence in East Africa" who "attacked the stations of the German East Africa Company in 1889 and required the imperial

---

[65] *Id.* at 80.
[66] *Id.*
[67] *Id.* at 80–81.
[68] *Id.* at 81.
[69] *Id.* at 82.
[70] *Id.*
[71] *Id.* at 166.

government's forceful intervention" was a case in point. Lawrence attributed the failings of the German East Africa Company to the reluctance of the German empire to bear the costs of administration.[72] In the crisis of the British East Africa Company in Uganda the "[r]esponsibilities it [the British government] did not seek, but wished to avoid, have been thrust upon it." He similarly described how the British South Africa Company's involvement in the territory of the Transvaal Republic in 1895 led the British government into "a maze of complications and helped bring about the Boer War of 1899–1900."[73] "There is doubtless much fascination in the idea of opening up new territories to the commercial and political influence of a country," concluded Lawrence, "and at the same time adding nothing to its financial burdens or international obligations. But experience shows that the glamour soon wears off, and the state which seeks to obtain power without responsibility obtains instead responsibility without power."[74] Chartered companies were criticized because they would not or could not provide order and stability.

Sovereign Authority Cannot Be Conferred on Private Corporations

The liberal French academic Gaston Jèze (1869–1953) shifted the criticism away from chartered companies to the imperial government that exercised its chartering authority. Jèze articulated a civic and constitutional argument against the possibility of conferring colonial authorities to private corporations. According to him, a state could not delegate its sovereign rights.[75] Since the people of France were sovereign in a democratic regime with sole political power, the state could not delegate sovereignty to private entities.[76] He further discussed economic and political arguments against full delegation of state power and the possibility of some limited form of delegation. Another French author, Charles Salomon (1862–1936) complemented Jèze's normative challenge by describing the distinctive *private* character of the late nineteenth-century chartered companies and the incompatibility between their profit-seeking nature and the colonial endeavor.[77]

Gaston Jèze and Charles Salomon advocated moving beyond the limited requirement of effective and territorial control as a condition for sovereign authority to a constitutional conception of constrained, limited government that draws its authority from the people. "The people" in their analysis refers to the people of France. While other international lawyers of the late nineteenth century were critical of chartered companies exercising sovereign authority in Africa, the critique of Charles

---

[72] *Id.* at 166–67.
[73] *Id.* at 167.
[74] *Id.*
[75] Gaston Jèze, Étude théorique et pratique sur l'occupation: comme mode d'acquérir les territoires en droit international 342–87 (1896) (Fr.).
[76] *Id.* at 354.
[77] Charles Salomon, L'Occupation des territoires sans maître 128–88 (V. Giard & E. Brière eds., Prix du Ministre de l'Instruction 1895) (Fr.).

Salomon and Gaston Jèze went even further and argued that representative governments cannot delegate their authorities to private entities.

International lawyers argued against the use and misuse of company charters for
the pursuit of narrow economic interests without consideration of broader humanitarian concerns. But they also criticized imperial governments' choice of the chartered company mechanism and their attempt to pursue colonial endeavors without
bearing the costs. A recurring motif their arguments share with later historical
accounts is the important role *failure* played in ushering chartered companies outside the colonial scene. The following sections complicate their narrative of failure.

STATES AND CORPORATIONS IN THE POST-CHARTER ERA

Mounting costs and competition over trade and territories drove the British government officials and businessmen to enter into the late nineteenth-century charter
deal. The same motives ultimately led to the dissolution of the charter and shaped
the post-charter alliance between governments and businessmen. Corporations of
the post-charter era enjoyed multiple advantages that enhanced their position and
enabled them to amass great fortunes while exploiting the indigenous population.
The contours of international legal scholars' analysis focused their critique on these
companies' entanglement in public affairs through the vehicle of the charter. Their
critique assumed that if only governments would exclude corporations from handling public affairs, the "problem" of the chartered company would be solved. Like
Adam Smith, they objected to the *inherent conflict of interests* between the political
commitment to the local population and the commercial interest of companies. For
them, this conflict not only explained the companies' failures, but also justified the
companies' departure from the colonial scene. Yet, their critique markedly ignored
another aspect in Smith's critique: the influence of commercial actors on imperial
governments' policies. As the following analysis suggests, that influence not only
ushered in the chartered companies to Africa, but it also played an important role
in the dissolution of the charter. While different commercial actors were interested
in the demise of the charter device, the economic actors behind the chartered companies frequently enjoyed a privileged and close relationship with politicians in the
corridors of power. These relationships could explain the beneficial arrangements
some of them were granted after the revocation of the charter. Yet, beyond specific
incidents of capture and corporate influence, the international legal architecture of
the post-charter era offered important advantages for corporations interested in commercial endeavors in colonial settings. As the following analysis suggests, the combination of free incorporation and the conception of the corporation as a commercial,
private individual, together with the law of treaties, the status of concessionary agreements in international law, and developments in diplomatic protection constituted
an international legal infrastructure with clear benefits for commercial corporate
actors. The following section offers the short case study of the Royal Niger Company

to illustrate the implication of the revocation of the charter for business corporations in Africa. I then turn to explain the legal architecture of the post-charter era.

The Case of the Royal Niger Company

In June 1899, the Foreign Office initiated procedures to revoke Royal Niger Company's charter. The company's charter was formally revoked as of January 1, 1900, and the Royal Niger Company, Chartered and Limited, became the Niger Company, Limited. The government agreed to pay the company a half of all royalties on minerals produced in much of the former Niger territory for a period of ninety-nine years. The company was relieved of all its administrative powers and duties and assigned the government all the benefits of its treaties, with the exception of "its plant and trading assets, and its stations and waterside depots, with customary rights of access, building, wharves, workshops and the sites thereof."[78]

As analyzed in the previous section, the use of chartered companies in the colonization of Africa was harshly criticized by international lawyers. Similar criticisms were raised in parliamentary debates.[79] Yet, while the emphasis of these debates on the failings of the charter attracted significant attention, the implications of the charters' revocation were *not* addressed by international lawyers. As one could learn from parliamentary debates, the benefits of the charter's revocation were quite evident to contemporary policymakers. In his concluding remarks in support of the Royal Niger Company Bill, the Conservative leader, James Edward Hubert Gascoyne-Cecil stated:

> They [the Royal Niger Company] risked their money enormously, a mere accident might have destroyed it, and it was only fair that they should receive a handsome and sufficient price such as Parliament has given them … I think we cannot part with them without recognising the enormous benefit which the civilising of those countries has received from their exertions, exertions which did a work that no mere political reform could have done.[80]

Indeed, the revocation of the charter was compatible with commercial interests, and, in the case of the Niger Company, Limited, actually proved favorable to its interests. "The terms of the charter's revocation," argued *The Economist* in 1899, reduced the company's risks "by the certainty that if they fail the British Government will help them out of their scrape, and if they succeed will buy their possessions at twice the value of the capital invested."[81] Historian Scott Pearson describes how

---

[78] Royal Niger Company Bill (H.C. Deb., July 27 1899) cols. 521–41, § 260 (UK).

[79] Parl. Deb. H.L. (4th ser.) (1899) § 73, cols. 1389–1401 (UK); Parl. Deb. H.L. (4th ser.) (1899) § 74, cols. 861–63 (UK); Parl. Deb. H.C. (4th ser.) (1899) § 74, cols. 1269–1344 (UK); Parl. Deb. H.C. (4th ser.) (1899) § 75, cols. 365–432 (UK); Parl. Deb. H.L. (4th ser.) (1899), § 75, cols. 965–1013 (UK).

[80] Parl. Deb. H.L. (4th ser.) (1899) §75, cols. 965–1013 (UK).

[81] *Nigeria*, THE ECONOMIST (July 8, 1899).

"[i]nstead of falling like a house of cards after 1900, the Niger Company turned advantages obtained and secured during the chartered period into a near monopolistic control of trade under early British colonial administration."[82] By contrast, the revocation had a detrimental effect on the coastal African brokers.[83]

In the following years, the Niger Company flourished. Its business consisted of buying local produce (primarily palm oil and palm kernels) and importing whatever was demanded by local markets. It conducted its business from a growing number of trading stations while production remained in the hands of local cultivators.[84] It engaged in agreements, contracts, and negotiations with colonial governments and shippers to defend its monopoly over the river communications secured pre-1900.[85] Its agents also expanded the geographical areas and commercial operations it was involved with (to include, inter alia, mining). In 1920, the company was taken over by the Lever Brothers.[86] In 1929, it was re-formed as the United African Company, a merger between the Niger Company and the African and Eastern Corporation, and became by far the largest single commercial organization in the West and Equatorial Africa – and thus central to modern African economic history. It was later absorbed into the Unilever multinational corporation.[87]

Toward a Legal Architecture of the Post-Charter Era

By the end of the nineteenth century, Africa was partitioned by new political boundaries, which was mirrored by economic partition. The relationship between the two is mostly studied in key turning points, such as the abolition of the slave trade or the failure of chartered companies in the scramble for Africa.[88] The history of the rise and fall of the chartered company as told by international lawyers of this era is a history with a clear position: against the chartered company. It is also a history with a markedly positive trajectory toward a normative divide between politics (the sovereign) and the market (the corporation). While charters were dissolved and, thus, can be said to have failed, private business corporations continued to flourish without their charters in the forthcoming decades. The shift from chartered to private business corporations was not a transition from an informal empire (through

---

[82] Scott R. Pearson, *The Economic Imperialism of the Royal Niger Company*, 10 FOOD RES. INST. STUD. 69 (1971).

[83] M. LYNN, COMMERCE AND ECONOMIC CHANGE IN WEST AFRICA: THE PALM OIL TRADE IN THE NINETEENTH CENTURY 187 (1997).

[84] A.G. Hopkins, *Imperial Business in Africa: Part II. Interpretations*, 17 J. AFR. HIST. 267, 277 (1976); JONES, *supra* note 46, at 77.

[85] Colin Newbury, *Trade and Technology in West Africa: The Case of the Niger Company 1900–1920*, 19 J. Afr. Hist. 551 (1978).

[86] Newbury attributes this development to slow organizational adjustments. *Id.* at 551, 553.

[87] For a comprehensive study, *see* DAVID. K. FIELDHOUSE, MERCHANT CAPITAL AND ECONOMIC DECOLONIZATION: THE UNITED AFRICA COMPANY 1929–1987 (1994)

[88] On the two partitions and the studies related to their relationship, *see* A.G. Hopkins, *Big Business in African Studies*, 28 J. AFR. HIST. 119, 129–33 (1987).

the chartered company) to a formal empire (governmental colonial rule); it was a transition to an informal and flexible alliance between governments and private corporations.

As the nineteenth century ended, governments were using the mechanism of the inter-sovereign treaty more frequently to divide territorial control and coordinate trade in Africa. Imperial governments' introduction of an extensive network of inter-imperial treaties facilitated the allocation of cost away from commercial agents to imperial governments. Concession agreements between imperial governments and companies were used to grant land and resources to the post-chartered companies and other economic agents. The recognition of inter-imperial treaties as valid sources of international law, combined with the nonrecognition of concession agreements with indigenous communities and companies, created a legal space that frequently favored commercial interests. This legal space frequently emerged from the real-life practical concerns of interest groups operating in Britain and in Africa. These groups pressured the British government to assume control over the territories previously controlled by the chartered companies and coordinate trade relations to avoid continuing clashes between competing commercial and political actors.[89]

THE POSITIVIST TURN IN CORPORATE RESPONSIBILITY AND THE SEPARATE SPHERES PRESUMPTION

The international law of the post-charter era not only leveraged the commercial interests of business corporations, it also further contributed to the insulation of corporations from legal scrutiny when they operated in colonial settings. Once the charters of these companies were revoked, they were legally considered private corporations. As the last vestiges of the chartered corporation disappeared, corporations, as such, would no longer be subjects of international legal scrutiny. The classic public–private distinction situated corporations on the private side of that divide. The fact that at this point (the 1880s onward) corporations could be freely incorporated made this transition from chartered to private companies relatively easy, with little or no negative impact on the businesses or the businessmen involved.

In an interstate legal order, concerns over corporate involvement in dubious practices translated to positivist concerns over the obligation of the state to regulate such practices. But the demand that powerful imperial governments assume control over their territories did not result in an attempt to regulate the conduct of corporations. Almost to the contrary, historical accounts of this period in the African context document how the close collaboration between colonial officials and African authorities

---

[89] For further discussion, *see* Doreen Lustig, *From Chartered to Privately Incorporated Companies in International Law* (on file with author).

"formed a patriarchal alliance to bolster their respective power and control over younger men, women and children."[90]

Amid the end of imperial governments' control over foreign territories, the involvement of corporations in the exploitation of labor and resources, as well as their destabilizing effect on political communities in postcolonial settings, remained invisible to international legal scrutiny for decades to come. Until recently, even though the home state of transnational corporations usually had the regulatory capacity to hold such corporate actors accountable, it could only be held *internationally responsible* in the exceptional circumstance of having effective control over the territory in which the corporation operates. States had no international responsibility to regulate corporate actors operating outside their national territory, even in situations where the corporate actor had the nationality of the state concerned.[91] As noted by Cristina Lafont:

> [T]he "veil of sovereignty" gives rise to the "veil of ignorance" that allows other states to single-mindedly protect and promote the interests and rights of those under their jurisdiction while disclaiming that they have any obligation to be aware of, let alone to take into account, the impact that their actions might have upon the human rights of those outside their jurisdiction. Such impacts are simply conceptualized as someone else's responsibility.[92]

While home states were conceived as having limited to no responsibility to regulate the conduct of corporations beyond their borders, governments of host states are often unwilling or unable to provide their citizens with access to remedies for international legal violations caused by corporations, either as direct perpetrators or as possible accomplices to such violations.[93] The regulatory weakness of host states and limited to no regulatory responsibility of home states is often viewed as a governance gap.[94] Indeed, applying the nineteenth-century shift to territoriality as a defining feature of sovereignty in a world of uneven regulatory capacities proved particularly consequential in the context of private corporations. Global value chains (GVCs) enable the coordination of production across

---

[90] Sacha Hepburn & April Jackson, *Colonial Exceptions: The International Labour Organization and Child Labour in British Africa, c.1919–1940*, 1 J. CONTEMP. HIST. 6 (2021).

[91] For a comprehensive analysis, *see* OLIVIER DE SCHUTTER, INTERNATIONAL HUMAN RIGHT LAW 188 (2d ed. 2014).

[92] CRISTINA LAFONT, SOVEREIGNTY AND THE INTERNATIONAL PROTECTION OF HUMAN RIGHTS 427, 437–38 (2015).

[93] *See* A. Ramasastry, *Corporate Complicity: From Nuremberg to Rangoon—An Examination of Forced Labor Cases and Their Impact on the Liability of Multinational Corporations*, 20 BERKELEY J. INT'L L. 91, 92 (2002); A. Clapham & S. Jerbi, *Categories of Corporate Complicity in Human Rights Abuses*, 24 HASTINGS INT'L COMP. L. REV. 339, 341 (2001).

[94] *See Report of the Special Representative of the Secretary-General on the issue of human rights and transnational corporations and other business enterprises*, 8 U.N. HRC at ¶ 3, U.N. Doc. A/HRC/8/5 (Apr. 2008); Florian Wettstein, *The History of "Business and Human Rights" and Its Relationship with "Corporate Social Responsibility,"* in RESEARCH HANDBOOK ON HUMAN RIGHTS AND BUSINESS (Surya Deva ed., 2020).

national borders while maintaining their high-value activities in affluent countries.[95] Since the early 2000s, a series of gradual legal developments has challenged these limitations on the responsibility of the home state for the conduct of private corporations beyond its borders.[96] Cases such as *Vedanta v. Lungowe* suggest the tide may be changing toward a greater recognition of the relationship between the home state and the corporation in establishing international responsibility.[97]

While international lawyers' opposition to the legitimacy of corporate actors exercising sovereign authority continued to shape the law on state responsibility in the post-charter era, freely incorporated corporations were conceived as nationals and could use the doctrine of diplomatic protection to call upon their incorporating (powerful) governments to protect their interests if such were undermined by, frequently, less powerful governments.[98] Yet, as noted in the landmark 1970 *Barcelona Traction* decision,

> [T]he process of "lifting the corporate veil" or "disregarding the legal entity" has been found justified and equitable in certain circumstances or for certain purposes. The wealth of practice already accumulated on the subject in municipal law indicates that the veil is lifted, for instance, to prevent the misuse of the privileges of legal personality, as in certain cases of fraud or malfeasance.[99]

---

95 The literature on GVCs is immense and cannot be cited here in full. *See, e.g.*, G. Gereffi, J. Humphrey & T. Sturgeon, *The Governance of Global Value Chains*, 12 Rev. Int'l Pol. Econ. 78–104 (2005); G. Gereffi & J. Lee, *Why the World Suddenly Cares about Global Supply Chains*, 48 J. Supply Chain Mgmt. 24–32 (2012); Peter Gibbon et al., *Governing Global Value Chains: An Introduction*, 37 Econ. Soc. 315 (2008); Sarah E. McWilliam et al., *Global Value Chain Governance: Intersections with International Business*, 55 J. World Bus. (2020); IGLP Law and Global Production Working Group, *The Role of Law in Global Value Chains: A Research Manifesto*, 4 London R. Inter'l L. 57 (2016). For an elaborate discussion on the meaning of global value chains to the theory of the multinational enterprise, *see* Peter Muchlinski, Multinational Enterprises and the Law 1–166 (2021).
96 *See, e.g.*, U.N. Comm. on Econ., Soc. & Cultural Rts., *General Comment No. 14: The Right to the Highest Attainable Standard of Health* (Art. 12 of the Covenant) (Aug. 2000) E/C.12/2000/4, ¶ 39; UN Comm. on Econ., Soc. & Cultural Rts., *General Comment No. 15: The Right to Water* (Art, 11–12 of the Covenant) (Nov. 2002), E/C. 12/2002/11, ¶ 31. U.N. Comm. on Econ., Soc. & Cultural Rts., *Statement on the Obligations regarding the Corporate Sector and economic, Social and Cultural Rights* (May 20, 2011) E/C.12/2011, ¶ 5. In September 2011 a range of experts and organizations endorsed the Maastricht Principles on Extraterritorial Obligations of States in the area of economic, social, and cultural rights, which are an attempt to systematize the case law of human rights courts and treaty bodies in this area. For a reproduction of the text, *see* Olivier De Schutter et al., *Commentary to the Maastricht Principles on Extraterritorial Obligations of States in the Area of Economic, Social and Cultural Rights*, 34 Hum. Rts. Q. 1084 (2012).
97 For a survey of the cases, *see* Axel Marx et al., *Study: Access to Legal Remedies for Victims of Corporate Human Rights Abuses in Third Countries*, Eur. Parl. Pol'y Dep't External Rel. (Feb. 2009) *available at* www.europarl.europa.eu/thinktank/en/document.html?reference=EXPO_STU(2019)603475.
98 For an elaborate historical account on the history of the doctrine of diplomatic protection, *see* Christopher A. Casey, Nationals Abroad: Globalization, Individual Rights, and the Making of Modern International Law (2020).
99 Barcelona Traction, Light & Power Co., Ltd. (*Belg. v. Spain*), Judgment, 1970 I.C.J. Rep. 3 (Feb. 5), ¶ 56.

The incorporation of the corporate actor by the same (powerful) government "was not sufficient as a basis for the attribution to the state of the subsequent conduct of that entity."[100] Thus, while a corporation could be protected as a national of a particular state under the doctrine of diplomatic protection and, later, under the regulatory umbrella of bilateral investment treaties and international human rights, that nexus of nationality was not a sufficient basis for state responsibility.[101]

While corporations are conceived by international law as "nationals" in the context of diplomatic protection or "investors" and "individuals" in international investment law and international human rights, the practice of corporations in the post-charter era often blurs the distinction between the corporation as a private individual and the state as the archetype for public governance authority. The influence of corporations on governmental lawmaking and their prominent role as regulators and lawmakers in global governance are prominent challenges to such public/private distinctions. As noted earlier, international lawyers of the late nineteenth century ignored Adam Smith's critique of the influence of chartered companies as interest groups who shaped governmental positions to advance their limited interests. Even in later periods, long after the revocation of the charter, scholars continued to criticize the failure to regulate the significant role of corporations as inhibitors or influential interest groups in international lawmaking processes.[102] *Corporations not only exercise their influence on global regulation as lobbyists and interest groups. They also exercise regulatory functions themselves.* The literature on global private authority, transnational private regulation, voluntary sustainability standards, and corporate social responsibility offers different conceptual framings for their regulatory influence.[103] Beyond the new governance context, corporations could be conceived as lawmakers in the context of concessionary agreements and

---

[100] Articles on Responsibility of States 2001, *supra* note 3, at 48.
[101] Silvia Steininger & Jochen von Bernstorff, *Who Turned Multinational Corporations into Bearers of Human Rights? On the Creation of Corporate "Human" Rights in International Law*, in Contingency in International Law: On the Possibility of Different Legal Histories 280, 290 (Ingo Venzke & Kevin Jon Heller eds., 2021); *see also* M. Emberland, The Human Rights of Companies: Exploring the Structure of ECHR Protection (2006); P.J. Oliver, The Fundamental Rights of Companies: EU, US and International Law Compared (2017); A. Grear, *Challenging Corporate "Humanity": Legal Disembodiment, Embodiment and Human Rights*, 7 Hum. Rts. L. Rev. 511 (2007); Anna Grear, Redirecting Human Rights: Facing the Challenge of Corporate Legal Humanity (2010); Andreas Kulick, *Corporate Human Rights?*, 32 EJIL 537 (2021); Jose Alvarez, *Are Corporations Subjects of International Law?*, 9 Santa Clara J. Int'l L. 1 (2011); Roland Portmann, Legal Personality in International Law (2010).
[102] *See* Melissa J. Durkee, *The Business of Treaties*, 63 UCLA L. Rev. 264, 268 (2016); *see also* Melissa J. Durkee, *International Lobbying Law*, 127 Yale L.J. 1742 (2018); Melissa J. Durkee, *Astroturf Activism*, 97 Stan. L. Rev. 201 (2017).
[103] Tim Bartley, *Transnational Corporations and Global Governance*, 44 Ann. Rev. Soc. 151 (2018); Neli Frost, *Out with the "Old," in with the "New": Challenging Dominant Regulatory Approaches in the Field of Human Rights*, 32 EJIL 507 (May 2021); Tim Büthe & Walter Mattli, The New Global Rulers: The Privatization of Regulation in the World Economy (2011).

international investment law.[104] Such non-statist regulatory perspective on the role and influence of corporations undermines the presumption of separateness between the public and the private, and marks *a transition* to a theory of international legal ordering in which the state is but one regulator among others.[105]

CONCLUSION

This chapter sought to offer an alternative to the conventional history positing the irrelevance of international law to the question of business corporations. It analyzed the facilitative role of international law in constituting a post-charter economic order that proved highly beneficial to corporate interests. Indeed, the legitimacy crisis over the use and misuse of chartered companies for the colonization of Africa probably conveyed the genuine approbation of international lawyers over the private exercise of colonial authority. Yet, reading the commentaries of these international lawyers along with the experience of the post-charter legal order exposes how the presumption of separate spheres between the public (authority of governments) and the private (authority of firms) did not necessarily result in the resumption of responsible governance on the part of the imperial state. Nor did business enterprises make a radical shift away from the practices associated with the charter era. Rather, during the post-charter era, the international legal doctrines of state responsibility, diplomatic protection, human rights, and investment law weaved a veil that concealed much of the activities of corporations from legal scrutiny and nurtured the alliance between powerful governments and commercial corporations.

---

[104] Julian Arato argues that since states and corporations "share authority over the contract's disposition, and the state cannot unilaterally terminate or vitiate the agreement without committing an internationally wrongful act" corporations impose "an enormous hindrance on the capacity of the state party to govern, they affect the rights and capacities of the citizenry as a whole" and should therefore be conceived as lawmakers. Julian Arato, *Corporations as Lawmakers*, 56 Harv. Int'l L. J. 229, 241 (2015).

[105] For a general theory of international law that challenges the interstate perspective, *see* Benedict Kingsbury, *International Law as Inter-Public Law*, 49 Nomos 167 (2009).

PART II

Transnational Attribution

6

Corporate Structures and the Attribution Dilemma in Multinational Enterprises

James T. Gathii and Olabisi D. Akinkugbe

INTRODUCTION

This chapter will explore how multiple corporate structures[1] in multinational enterprises operating in developing countries in general, and in Africa in particular, make determinations of responsibility among the members of such corporate families difficult. In doing so, it illustrates one of many possible challenges attendant to attributing identity and responsibility within and among corporate structures. Specifically, this chapter challenges the assumption that the end of colonial rule and the founding of African states threw off the economic subordination that characterized colonial-era corporate activity in Africa. In our view, the end of colonial rule was accompanied by a desire on the part of multinational corporations to re-legitimize their activities in service of the newly independent governments. These multinational corporations no longer wanted to be seen as extractive actors for the primary benefit of their European investors. A principal method of this re-legitimization by these multinational corporations was the adoption of Africanization.[2] This involved hiring African directors and officers as well as establishing domestic subsidiaries with African directors and officers. These strategies, together with the indigenization policies of postcolonial governments, in part account for the emergence and proliferation of multiple corporate structures in postcolonial African countries.

The increased use of multiple corporate structures opened the doorway for multinational enterprises operating in these newly independent countries to evade customs duties and taxes through shell companies. This arose because developing countries have difficulties attributing responsibility among members of these transnational corporate families. The transactions through which multinational enterprises evade

---

[1] By multiple corporate structures, we mean, for example, a situation where a parent company holds ownership in or controls separate companies or entities such as subsidiaries.

[2] We acknowledge that the concept of "Africanization" has been used in different contexts. For example, in international investment law context, *see* Olabisi D. Akinkugbe, *Africanization and the Reform of International Investment Law*, 53 CASE W. RES. J. INT'L L. 7 (2021).

taxes constitute illicit financial flows that drain revenue otherwise due to African governments.

Another effect of the prevalence of multiple corporate structures in the postindependence era is that it blurred the boundary between the public and the private. This is because multinational corporations welcomed many local elites, including local government officials, as directors and officers in their domestic subsidiaries. Multinational corporations labeled this re-legitimation strategy as Africanization. This widely used strategy in part accounts for the emergence and stickiness of multiple corporate structures within multinational corporations in Africa to date. The indigenization policies of postcolonial governments also contributed.

Further, international investment law has delocalized the responsibility of multinational corporate families. This delocalization has effectively removed dispute settlement from domestic courts to investor-state and commercial arbitration outside Africa. This makes it difficult to hold members of transnational corporate families, including African directors and officers, responsible for their conduct under domestic law. Finally, it is also important to consider that many of these corporations are far more wealthy than African governments and, therefore, have access to very sophisticated advisory services that far outmatch those of many African governments.

Finally, attribution of responsibility for financial liabilities between members of a corporate family cannot be understood without grounding the analysis in the duty and responsibility that multinational enterprises have to be accountable to developing countries for their conduct.

This chapter proceeds as follows: Part I sets the stage by discussing multiple corporate families in Africa. Part II discusses how indigenization complicates responsibility in multiple corporate structures. Part III illustrates the arguments in Parts I and II with examples from Kenya and Nigeria.

PART I

SETTING THE STAGE: MULTIPLE CORPORATE FAMILIES IN AFRICA

In October 2021, the International Consortium of Investigative Journalists disclosed a treasure trove of data that showed in detail how political leaders, judges, celebrities, and even business leaders used shell companies to hold assets that were often pilfered from public coffers. These included incognito bank accounts, looted antiquities, and other assets often held in what *The Guardian* newspaper described as "labyrinth corporate structures" whose true owners were identified for the first time because of a massive leak of financial data.[3] This leak, which became known as the "Pandora

---

[3] Investigations Team, *Pandora Papers: Biggest Ever Leak of Offshore Data Exposes Financial Secrets of Rich and Powerful*, THE GUARDIAN (Oct. 3, 2021), www.theguardian.com/news/2021/oct/03/ pandora-papers-biggest-ever-leak-of-offshore-data-exposes-financial-secrets-of-rich-and-powerful.

Papers," inspired more than 600 journalists around the world to sift through the leaked documents.[4] The records demonstrated how the rich and famous, as well as individuals who did not want to be in the public limelight, established not merely shell companies, but also foundations and trusts to hide their wealth. At times, these individuals used the shell companies to avoid paying taxes or to conceal crimes.

It is in this context of secrecy that the nonpayment of their fair share of customs duties and taxes by multinational enterprises in Africa must be understood.[5] Beyond leaks like the Pandora papers, a formidable body of research shows that these enterprises evade duties and taxes through shell companies that are a part of their corporate families.[6] These transactions are also facilitated by tax havens.[7] As Steven Dean and Attiya Waris have shown, tax havens are spread across the global north and global south and not merely in black and brown jurisdictions.[8] This is contrary to

[4] International Consortium of Investigative Journalists, *Pandora Papers: An Offshore Data Tsunami*, PANDORA PAPERS (Oct. 3, 2021), www.icij.org/investigations/pandora-papers/about-pandora-papers-leak-dataset/.

[5] *See generally*, Jia Liu & Olatunde Julius Otusanya, *How Multinationals Avoid Taxes in Africa and What Should Change*, THE CONVERSATION (Apr. 5, 2022), https://theconversation.com/how-multinationals-avoid-taxes-in-africa-and-what-should-change-179797 (demonstrating that "tax havens and offshore financial centres, shaped by globalisation, facilitate the sophisticated tax schemes of highly mobile transnational corporations. The effect of low-tax jurisdictions ('tax havens') hampers the social and economic development of poorer states.").

[6] "Despite the important and legitimate roles that corporate vehicles play in the global economic system, these entities may, under certain conditions, be misused for illicit purposes, including money laundering, bribery/corruption, improper insider dealings, illicit tax practices, and other forms of illicit behaviour." ORGANIZATION FOR ECONOMIC CO-OPERATION AND DEVELOPMENT, BEHIND THE CORPORATE VEIL: USING CORPORATE ENTITIES FOR ILLICIT PURPOSES 13 (2001) www.oecd .org/daf/ca/43703185.pdf [hereinafter "OECD"]. See also the study from the Financial Action Task Force, an intergovernmental body that focuses on these issues, titled THE MISUSE OF CORPORATE VEHICLES, INCLUDING TRUST AND CORPORATE SERVICE PROVIDERS (2006); Rena S. Miller & Liana W. Rosen, CONG. RSCH SERV., R45798, BENEFICIAL OWNERSHIP TRANSPARENCY IN CORPORATE FORMATION, SHELL COMPANIES, REAL ESTATE, AND FINANCIAL TRANSACTIONS (2019), https://fas.org/sgp/crs/misc/R45798.pdf; Carlos Berdejó, *Oligarchs, Foreign Powers, and the Oppressed Minority: Regulating Corporate Control in Latin America*, 30 DUKE J. COMP. INT'L L. 1 (2019) (undertaking an examination of the shareholder structure of Latin American companies, which are characterized by high levels of ownership concentration); Economic Commission for Africa Conference of Ministers of Finance, Planning and Economic Development, *Track it! Stop it! Get it! Report of the High Level Panel on Illicit Financial Flows from Africa*, AFRICAN UNION/ UNITED NATIONS (2015).

[7] Vanessa Ogle, *'Funk Money': The End of Empires, The Expansion of Tax Havens, and Decolonization as an Economic and Financial Event*, 249 PAST & PRESENT SOC'Y 213, 217 (2020), https://doi .org/10.1093/pastj/gtaa001 (arguing in the context of decolonization and the capital flight which it necessitated that "a significant share of funds was moved to an emerging system of offshore tax havens. Low-tax jurisdictions offering opportunities to avoid and evade taxation in countries with regular higher tax rates were not new at this point, but, owing to the influx of funds from the imperial and colonial world, expanded significantly during the years of decolonization"). *See also* Steven Press, *Sovereignty and Diamonds in Southern Africa, 1908–1920*, 28 DUKE J. COMP. INT'L L. 473 (2018), https://scholarship.law.duke.edu/djcil/vol28/iss3/6.

[8] Steven A. Dean & Attiya Waris, Ten Truths about Tax Havens: Inclusion and the "Liberia" Problem, 70 EMORY L. J. 1659 (2021).

the assertions of the Western-centric Organization for Economic Cooperation and Development (OECD).[9] In fact, the ability of multinational enterprises to engage in illicit financial flows is evidence of their "global footprint and influence"[10] in a manner that has real-life impacts on the economies and peoples of Africa. While the role of multinational corporations in illicit financial flows has received considerable attention,[11] only recently has there been increasing attention paid to issues of attribution of responsibility among family members of multiple corporate structures.[12]

The task of allocating where responsibilities lie in the ladder of corporate families or subsidiaries can be difficult in complex corporate structures. This is a problem that is not unique to illicit financial flows. It also includes accountability gaps for environmental disasters as well as human rights violations.[13] In the law of tort, this category of disputes is premised on a dereliction of the duty of care and negligence in the management of oil exploration and mining. One response to this issue in national courts is to inquire whether the corporate veil could be lifted in order to make the directors personally liable for these violations, or whether to make corporate parents liable for the tortious violations of their subsidiaries.[14]

Attributing tax responsibilities – and understanding the ways that multiple corporate structures enable illicit financial flows – presents complicated legal questions. For example, corporate structures often include multiple "shell" companies incorporated in different jurisdictions, making it difficult to establish attribution for tax purposes. The ownership structure of the multinationals doing business in developing states takes many complex forms. Many have the corporate parent in a non-African jurisdiction but operate through subsidiaries that are in turn connected to complex webs of their own subsidiaries, in different jurisdictions, and sometimes, with anonymous ownership structures.[15] This makes the allocation of responsibilities among these entities difficult. Attribution becomes particularly difficult where

---

[9] *Id.*

[10] Rachel Brewster & Philip J. Stern, *Introduction to the Proceedings of the Seminar on Corporations and International Law*, 28 DUKE J. COMP. INT'L L. 413, 413 (2018).

[11] *See generally* ALEX COBHAM & PETR JANSKÝ, *International Corporate Tax Avoidance*, ESTIMATING ILLICIT FINANCIAL FLOWS: A CRITICAL GUIDE TO THE DATA, METHODOLOGIES, AND FINDINGS 81, 83 (2020) (using the phrase "profit shifting" to capture "debt shifting through loans within one MNE group; location of intangible assets and intellectual property, and strategic transfer pricing" as three main recognized profit shifting channels). *See also* Sergio Puig, *The Internationalization of Tobacco Tactics*, 28 DUKE J. COMP. INT'L L. 495 (2018); Fola Adeleke, *Illicit Financial Flows and Inequality in Africa: How to Reverse the Tide in Zimbabwe*, 26 S. AFR. J. INT'L AFF. 367, 369 (2019) (analyzing the question: "Can regulation serve as an effective mechanism to sufficiently tackle illicit financial flows and break the extractive-inequality link that is common across resource rich African countries?").

[12] On the closely related issue of beneficial ownership, *see* Jeffrey Owens & Joy Ndubai, *Why and How to Effectively Implement Beneficial Ownership Regulations*, 103 INT'L TAX NOTES 12 (2021).

[13] Esther Hennchen, *Royal Dutch Shell in Nigeria: Where Do Responsibilities End?*, 129 J. BUS. ETHICS 1 (2015).

[14] *Delizia Ltd. v. Nevsun Resources Ltd.*, 2017 FCA 187 (Can. 2017).

[15] Sharman J.C., *Shopping for Anonymous Shell Companies: An Audit Study of Anonymity and Crime in the International Financial System*, 24 J. ECON. PERSPECTIVES 127 (2010).

"shell" companies disproportionately reap high premiums or other public assets from developing country governments.[16]

One avenue for tracing responsibility in multiple corporate structures is through establishing beneficial ownership. As the OECD observed in its *Report on the Misuse of Corporate Vehicles for Illicit Purposes*, "uncovering the beneficial owner may involve piercing through various intermediary entities and/or individuals until the true owner who is a natural person is found."[17] In the case of corporate families, the primary question is not always answered by establishing who exercises legal control. This is because anonymity may make it difficult to establish the identities of the shareholder or shareholders who exercise effective control over these corporations.[18]

Multiple corporate, trust, foundation, and partnership structures present particular difficulties for national revenue authorities that have little investigatory capacity.[19] The complex and opaque architecture of global tax regimes that characterize multinational enterprises also make it difficult for developing countries to meet their revenue collection goals.[20] That said, disentangling multiple corporate structures to uncover proceeds of corruption, crime, or tax evasion is now widely recognized as a goal not only for developing countries but also in global efforts to address issues such as money laundering and terrorism.[21]

---

[16] O. E. Udofia, *Imperialism in Africa: A Case of Multinational Corporations*, 14 J. BLACK STUD. 353 (1984) (examining the primary question: How far do multinational corporations promote imperialism in Africa?).

[17] OECD, *supra* note 6, at 14.

[18] In the context of anonymous shell structures, Sharman observed that

> In six cases, service providers recommended holding the ownership of the shell company in an overarching common law trust or civil law foundation. Either legal structure would present investigating authorities with one more obstacle in seeking to find the beneficial owner: tracking the bank account to the company, the company to the trust or foundation, and then control of the trust or foundation to me via the service provider, presumably with each link in a different jurisdiction. Following the money trail in such cases would be difficult, time-consuming, and expensive.

Sharman, supra note 15, at 132–33. Sharman argues further that "[e]ven if the legal trail is complex, as long as the service provider has proof of the identity of the ultimate beneficiary of a firm, the veil of secrecy is vulnerable to being pierced." Sharman identifies four reasons as the basis for this assertion: (i) "hosting jurisdictions are often vulnerable to pressure from outsiders to hand over client identity documentation …" (ii) "financial intermediaries can also be vulnerable to outside pressure …" (iii) "service providers may disregard their own advice about keeping confidential documents …" and (iv) "rogue employees of the service provider … may steal and sell sensitive material." *Id.* at 133.

[19] John Kamau, *ANC Leader Ramaphosa and the Tidy Legacy of Lonrho's Rowland*, NATION (Dec. 23, 2017), https://nation.africa/news/africa/anc-Ramaphosa-and-the-tidy-legacy-of-Lonrho-s--Rowland/1066-4240214-sj9t1c/index.html.

[20] Maya Forstater, *Illicit Financial Flows, Trade Misinvoicing, and Multinational Tax Avoidance: The Same or Different?*, CENT. GLOBAL DEV. CGD POL'Y PAPER 123 (Mar. 2018), www.cgdev.org/publication/illicit-financial-flows-trade-misinvoicing-and-multinational-tax-avoidance; James Thuo Gathii, *Recharacterizing Corruption to Encompass Illicit Financial Flows*, 113 AJIL UNBOUND (2019).

[21] Jason Rosario Braganza, *Beneficial Ownership: To Tell or Not to Tell?*, AFRONOMICSLAW BLOG (Oct. 15, 2019), www.afronomicslaw.org/2019/10/15/beneficial-ownership-to-tell-or-not-to-tell/.

PART II

HOW INDIGENIZATION COMPLICATES ATTRIBUTION IN MULTIPLE CORPORATE FAMILIES

To the literature seeking to properly establish attribution within multiple corporate families, this chapter adds an important dimension: the role that African elites play in camouflaging their illicit financial activities in concert with multinational firms. Multiple corporate structures create pathways for transnational capitalist elites in developing countries to get a toehold within these multiple and often opaque corporate structures that are involved in business relationships with multinational enterprises.[22] These transnational capitalist elites often become the in-betweens or brokers between transnational enterprises and national political elites responsible for handing out contracts and access to the resources sought by the multinational enterprises.

The problem arises when nationals of developing countries are appointed to the boards of multinational enterprises with multiple corporate structures – either by the government or by the multinational corporation. In principle, these appointments may be motivated by well-intentioned objectives such as the indigenization of ownership of enterprises in key economic sectors.[23] At times, these indigenization policies are justified as necessary for economic and social development, national growth and attaining self-sufficiency or as motivated by a desire for transfer of technology from Western investors to African governments. Whatever the motivation, the placement of transnational capitalist elites or national political elites on the boards of local subsidiaries adds another layer of complexity to answering questions of attribution for harms occasioned by family members of multinational enterprises, because it offers room for corruption and collusion. This is heightened by the complex contractual arrangements between multinational enterprises and developing country governments. The ensuing lack of transparency often has adverse implications for the development objectives set by developing countries. This problem arises both in the context of foreign and locally owned firms.

Indigenization policies through which local elites are appointed to the boards of multinational corporations – or that allow these elites to establish corporate vehicles, such as joint ventures or subsidiaries to contract with multinational corporations – have generated more inequality and worked to the disadvantage of the majority

---

[22] An example of this case which we will analyze in the substantive aspect of this paper is the notorious case of a former Nigerian oil Minister, Dan Etete, and various charges of corruption that add up to $1.3 billion arising from OPL245 oil deal. See Lionel Faull & Margot Gibbs, *Nigeria Seizes Luxury Private Jet Linked to OPL245 Money Laundering in Montreal*, FINANCE UNCOVERED (June 6, 2020), www.financeuncovered.org/investigations/nigeria-seizes-luxury-private-jet-linked-to-opl245-money-laundering-in-montreal/.

[23] Stephanie Decker, *Africanization in British Multinationals in Ghana and Nigeria, 1945–1970*, 92 BUS. HIST. REV 691 (2018).

of Africans.[24] Contrary to the benefits that governments and investors claim that such arrangements produce, these arrangements are also associated with negative externalities such environmental degradation as a result of pollution, and gas flaring in the oil sector. Further, many of the key positions in joint venture arrangements are filled by expatriates, and consequently, the promise of transfer of knowledge and technology is jeopardized. Consequently, rather than advance the cause of the majority of African peoples, indigenization policies often became a political tool to reward party officials with key appointments as directors and distributors in multinational corporate families. Further, the returns on investment in these arrangements are rigged in favor of shareholders of the parent corporation outside Africa, even while the directors and officers of the subsidiaries are located in African countries.

This is well illustrated in our discussion of the Nigerian Oil and Gas Industry Content Development Act in Part III. In short, through this law, Nigerian elites enter into partnerships with multinationals or foreign investors with a view of qualifying to bid for oil blocks. At times, these oil blocks are sold to new companies that simply retain the local elites as directors to enhance the legitimacy of the corporation and to comply with local laws. With strategic partners spread across different regions of the world, multiple corporate structures are adopted to facilitate this. These multiple structures create conduits for the flow of funds to the Nigerian elites when the oil blocks are in operation.[25] When liability issues arise, these complex corporate structures stand in the way of definitively attributing liability for the pilfering of public assets.

Before discussing this case study in detail, let us consider the historical roots of indigenization. Without this kind of historical contextualization, the attribution of responsibility in multiple corporate families would likely be bare-bone abstractions.[26]

---

[24] *Id.* (drawing on international business and organization theory to analyze the historical evolution of MNCs in Ghana and Nigeria based on historical case studies of five companies, including three regional multinationals).

[25] The Malabu Scandal in Nigeria is a very good example of the complexity of corporate structure, corruption, IFFS, and more. *See: Shell and ENI's Misadventures in Nigeria: Shell and ENI at Risk of Losing Enormous Oil Block Acquired in Corrupt Deal*, GLOBAL WITNESS (Nov. 2015), www .globalwitness.org/documents/18122/Shells_misadventures_in_Nigeria.pdf; *The Scandal of Nigerian Oil Block OPL 245*, GLOBAL WITNESS (Briefing Document, Nov. 25, 2013) (describing how secrecy in the oil & gas sector and the use of anonymous shell companies led to hundreds of millions of dollars being diverted away from Nigeria's citizens and into the hands of a convicted money-launderer), www.globalwitness.org/en/archive/scandal-nigerian-oil-block-opl-245-o/; *Middlemen Leave Statoil on Edge in Nigeria*, 51 PETROLEUM INTEL. WKLY 4 (June 25, 2012).

[26] In this regard, we agree with Kai Koddenbrock, Ingrid Havold Kvangraven, and Ndongo Samba Sylla that understanding the politics of late colonization and the logics of imperialism is critical to understanding contemporary financial imperialism in Africa. Kai Koddenbrock et al., *Beyond Financialisaion: The Need for a Longue Dureé Understanding of Finance in Imperialism*, 44 CAMBRIDGE J. ECON. 703 (2022); *see also* Geoffrey Jones, *Multinational Strategies and Developing Countries in Historical Perspective* (Harv. Bus. Sch. Working Paper 10-076, 2010), www.hbs.edu/ris/ Publication%20Files/10-076_0f98ff7b-1d22-4090-b621-f1a45036a6db.pdf (arguing that the strategies of multinationals in developing countries were shaped by the trade-off between opportunity and risk: triad of prevailing political economy – host and home governments and the international legal framework; the market and resources of the host country; competition from local firms).

Specifically, transnational enterprises anxious to reinvent themselves from being regarded as guardians of the colonial order and to be seen as partners in building the new postcolonial states established multiple corporate structures.

This historical context begins with colonialism and its legacies.[27] Colonialism was central in constructing the economies of the Global South and African countries. Multinational enterprises were a central pillar of the colonial order. Colonial trading companies like the Imperial British East Africa Company had royal charters to govern British colonial possessions.[28] These colonial multinational corporations were extractive in their nature. They extracted African resources and sent them to Europe.[29] In many parts of the Third World, decolonization, especially by the 1970s amidst increasing poverty and unemployment in Africa, produced backlash against the colonial-era multinational corporations. This backlash against multinational corporations was not new. It was foreshadowed by an upswell in criticism of the monopoly role of multinational enterprises in the 1930s and 1940s – at the height of colonization – that indicated the deeply contested futures of the multinational corporations in the postcolonial era.[30]

Decolonization set off a legitimacy crisis for multinational enterprises whose role until this point was closely tied to meeting the profit goals of their European shareholders.[31] To overcome this legitimacy crisis, colonial-era multinational enterprises sought to distance themselves from their "old imperial identity" by redefining themselves as development partners of the newly independent African states.[32] Multinational corporations engaged in a variety of strategies with a view to achieving this objective. For example, in Kenya, a British-owned multinational renamed its newspaper to suggest that its role was no longer to be the mouthpiece of white settlers and their business interests. Instead, its new name, *The Nation*, indicated that its role in the newly independent Kenya was to support the new government

---

[27] In the context of currency in former French colonies, the influence of France's monetary policy as an important factor in constituting the economic relationship of France and the former colonies in contemporary Africa illustrates a critical example of the legacies of colonialism. *See:* FANNY PIGEAUD AND NDONGO SAMBA SYLLA, AFRICA'S LAST COLONIAL CURRENCY: THE CFA FRANC STORY (2020).

[28] *See, e.g.,* SIBA GROVOGUI, SOVEREIGNS, QUASI SOVEREIGNS, AND AFRICANS: RACE AND SELF-DETERMINATION IN INTERNATIONAL LAW (1996).

[29] WALTER RODNEY, HOW EUROPE UNDERDEVELOPED AFRICA (1971).

[30] *See generally,* Stephanie Decker, *Corporate Legitimacy and Advertising: British Companies and the Rhetoric of Developments in West Africa, 1950–1970,* 81 BUS. HIST. REV. 59, 59 (In the 1930s and 1940s, "closely associated with the British Empire, imperial companies were attacked for monopolizing lucrative trades, discriminating again Africans, and colluding with colonial governments.").

[31] As Decker notes, "major transitions in the institutional environment are likely to affect the way in which organizations and organization practices are judged in terms of their legitimacy." Decker, *supra* note 23, at 694. "Legitimacy challenges usually emanate from wider societal changes; the most dramatic shifts in organizational legitimacy are cases of sudden regime change, such as military coups, but there are also more gradual ones arising from the transition from colonialism to independence." *Id.* at 695.

[32] PIGEAUD AND SYLLA, *supra* note 27, at 63 (2007).

in its post-independence goals.[33] Multinational corporations that had good relations with imperial interests in the colonial era sought to rebrand themselves as agents of "progress and civilization."[34]

Colonial-era multinational enterprises also sought to reinvent themselves by recruiting African elites as officers and directors.[35] The idea of appointing African elites as officers and directors was not simply a consequence of decolonization. Rather, it was, in part, a strategy to "maintain [the] acquiescence of colonial subjects in the British Empire, and to increase the empire's economic value" as the political objectives of development backfired.[36] This strategy was particularly useful because the economic downturns of the 1970s coincided with agenda of the New International Economic Order that included the goals of Africanizing or indigenizing economies. Multinational corporations sought to reinvent themselves to fit the goals of African governments in this heady era of economic self-determination. Thus, as African countries sought to control the activities of multinational corporations, and in some countries, to nationalize the assets of multinational corporations, multinational corporations embraced indigenization strategies in response.[37]

---

[33] James Gathii, *Freedom of Expression without a Free Press: An Inquiry into a Kenyan Paradox* (Apr. 1995) (LL.M. Thesis, Harvard L. Sch.).

[34] PIGEAUD AND SYLLA, *supra* note 27, at 62 (2007).

[35] In this regard, we agree with Decker that "[f]or former colonies in Africa and elsewhere, decolonization and the aftermath of independence can be described as a period of 'postcolonial transition,' when institutional arrangements were in a state of flux and required firms to adapt very quickly to new political, social, and economic contexts." Id. at 695.

[36] Decker, *supra* note 23, at 698. According to Decker, "[f]or British businesses operating in the Gold Coast and Nigeria, it became paramount to repair their organizational legitimacy, as they had no intention of leaving with the British Empire, which had essentially guaranteed their 'license to operate.' Id. at 700. Unless companies could convince the new African elites that they remained legitimate forms of organization in a fundamentally changed institutional environment, their future appeared to be in question."

[37] As Decker explains,

> The Gold Coast government was vulnerable to nationalist labor politics both as colonial rulers and as the largest employer in the country. While officials feared being seen as closely allied to private business, the complexity of political and social issues made both British officials and companies vulnerable to anticolonial attacks. This undermined their legitimacy at a moral level and offered few potential solutions for compromise. More challengingly, this meant that companies' ability to independently negotiate and resolve issues with their workforce was affected by a political process over which they had little control.

Decker, *supra* note 23, at 704. *See also* p. 706, stating:

> Nationalists began to prioritize industrialization and Africanization, in order to ensure greater local autonomy. Throughout the 1950s, foreign companies developed networks with African politicians and businesspeople, and they began to understand that the development and promotion of African staff sent a powerful signal that they were indeed sympathetic to the aspirations of new nations. Africanization turned out to be a more effective legitimization strategy, although tokenism and window-dressing were common, especially in the early stages.

PART III

ILLUSTRATING HOW THE INVOLVEMENT OF AFRICAN
ELITES AS MULTINATIONAL CORPORATE DIRECTORS AND
OFFICERS COMPLICATES ATTRIBUTION ANALYSIS

In this section, we now turn to illustrating the difficulties that arise in attribution analysis as a result of the involvement of African elites as directors and officers in corporate structures, participating in the business of multinational corporations.[38] We draw on examples from Nigeria and Kenya. The Nigerian example, in this chapter, demonstrates the complicity and capture of the local content regime by Nigerian national elites who act as directors, officers, and partners with multinational corporations investing in Nigeria. It also illustrates how transactions are structured in ways that complicate attribution of responsibility among various members of the corporate family structure when things go wrong. We will begin by discussing an example from Kenya, which illustrates how multiple corporate structures can shield the identities of those who profit from major transactions, such as a transaction that privatizes a public asset.

Privatization of Telkom Kenya

This first example comes from Kenya's privatization of its telecommunications industry in 2017. To privatize Telkom Kenya, the then government-owned giant telecommunications firm, Kenya sought a foreign investor to buy about a 30 percent stake in the privatized entity. The government planned to have Kenyans retain a 70 percent stake in the privatized entity, a goal it sought to achieve through an initial public offer. The entire privatization process was handled by the Minister of Finance, who declined to bring into force a privatization law that would have governed the entire process. Instead, the Minister brought that law into force after the privatization of Telkom Kenya closed pursuant to a shareholders' agreement between the government of Kenya and Vodafone Group Plc of the United Kingdom.

As part of the privatization process, Vodafone Kenya Limited was incorporated as a wholly owned local subsidiary of the multinational Vodafone Group Plc of the United Kingdom. Vodafone Kenya Limited in turn held a 30 percent stake in Safaricom, the entity created as a result of Telkom Kenya's privatization. Later in the privatization process, the government sold 10 percent of its share to Vodafone

---

[38] *See, e.g.*, Winnie Byanyima, *A Powerful and Corrupt Elite is Robbing Africa of Its Riches*, WORLD ECONOMIC FORUM (Aug. 19, 2016), www.weforum.org/agenda/2016/08/a-powerful-and-corrupt-elite-is-robbing-africa-of-its-riches/ (noting, correctly in our view, that "so much of the tax avoidance or criminal movement of finance on the continent is made possible by a system propped up by a number of banks, law firms, and other outfits based outside of Africa, working in collusion with African economic and political elites. It is a system designed in the Global North that helps Africa's few wealthy and powerful elites to cheat the rest of us.")

Kenya Limited, thereby reducing the government's shareholding in Safaricom from 70 to 60 percent.

What is of particular interest for our purposes is that a mysterious investor, Mobitelea Ventures, incorporated in Guernsey, was offered a 25 percent stake in Vodafone Kenya Limited by the Vodafone Group Plc of the United Kingdom. Mobitelea's real owners were undisclosed at the time, and have never been disclosed to date. Instead, two nominee firms, Guernsey-registered Mercator Nominees Ltd and Mercator Trustees Ltd were listed as Mobitelea shareholders. The directors were named Anson Ltd and Cabot Ltd, based in Anguilla and Antigua.[39]

This 25 percent stake owned by Mobitelea Ventures represented almost half of Vodafone Group Plc of the United Kingdom's holdings in the privatized entity. The 2002 transaction with Mobiltea was justified on the premise that Mobitelea had offered Vodafone Group Plc of the United Kingdom advisory services in the privatization process. Eventually, Vodafone Group Plc of the United Kingdom repurchased all of Mobitelea Ventures' shares through transactions that raised the question of who the ultimate beneficial owners of this faceless entity really were. This is particularly significant given that Mobitelea had effectively made a huge windfall from the privatization process. Parliamentary investigations and audit inquiries by the government of Kenya to identify who stood behind Mobitelea Ventures came to naught. Not even the UK's Serious Fraud Office that was requested to investigate the identity of those that stood behind Mobitelea Ventures produced any results. Vodafone Kenya Limited argued that the identity of those that stood behind Mobitelea was an issue for Vodafone Group Plc of the United Kingdom. None of the members of this corporate family were willing to disclose the identities of those that stood behind Mobitelea.

Ultimately, it proved impossible to establish the beneficiaries of a lucrative set of shares hewed from a state enterprise without required authorizations from the government of Kenya. Kenya's parliament concluded in 2007 that the transaction involving Mobitelea's purchase of shares from Vodafone Group Plc of the United Kingdom and then Vodafone Group Plc of the United Kingdom's purchase of these shares from Mobitelea Ventures was characterized by an effort to defraud the public and the Kenyan government of their shares in the privatized entity.[40]

Thus, the privatization of Telkom Kenya and the resulting transactions relating to its shares demonstrates the difficulty of legally establishing to whom to attribute responsibility for profiting from the sale of the very lucrative shares of a public entity upon privatization. Here, complex corporate structures layered with

[39] Leo Odera Omolo, *Kenya: Chemelil is Insolvent and on the Verge of Total Collapse Exposing its 850 Workers to Extreme Danger of Hunger and Starvation*, JALUO DOT KOM (March 21, 2013), http://blog.jaluo.com/?cat=45&paged=32.

[40] AFRICA CENTRE FOR OPEN GOVERNANCE, DELIBERATE LOOPHOLES: TRANSPARENCY LESSONS FROM THE PRIVATISATION OF TELKOM AND SAFARICOM 18 (2011) https://africog.org/reports/Deliberate_loopholes.pdf.

anonymity made it difficult for regulators to find out who really stood behind Mobitelea Ventures.[41] Although the beneficial owners of Mobitelea Ventures have never been fully disclosed, it is widely believed that they were powerful government officials who were shepherding the privatization process hidden under the guise of anonymity provided by a foreign incorporated entity. It was precisely because of the partnership that Vodafone Group Plc of the United Kingdom had with Mobitelea Ventures that Vodafone Group Plc of the United Kingdom succeeded in breaking through into the Kenyan market. To pay off Mobitelea Ventures for making this deal possible, Vodafone Group Plc of the United Kingdom sold some of its shares to Mobitelea Ventures Limited and then bought them back from Mobitelea Ventures at what many regarded a significant premium.

In sum, the anonymity behind Mobitelea Ventures made it impossible to credibly establish the true identity of its beneficial owners. Without definitively establishing who stood behind Mobitelea Ventures, it became impossible to attribute responsibility to those who benefited from the privatization of a public asset. In late 2020, Kenya enacted a beneficial ownership registry that will require Kenyan companies to disclose their owners to national regulators – perhaps a step toward avoiding a repetition of the Mobitelea Ventures saga.[42]

Indigenization in Oil Licensing in Nigeria

We next turn to several examples from Nigeria. Our first of these arises from the Malabu Oil saga.[43] At the heart of the dispute was the ownership of a highly prized oil block, OPL 245.[44] OPL 245 was a deep-water offshore oil field covering an area of over 1,000 square meters, with a proven reserve of approximately nine billion barrels of oil and a daily production capacity of 170,000 barrels. A suit by the Nigerian

---

[41] *Mobitelea Sells Stake in Safaricom for Sh6 Billion*, Business Daily (July 7, 2009) www .businessdailyafrica.com/markets/539552-620880-v37n60/index.html.

[42] The Companies Act of 2015, Beneficial Ownership Information Regulations § (2020) (Kenya) (http://kenyalaw.org/kl/fileadmin/pdfdownloads/LegalNotices/2020/LN12_2020.pdf). *See also* Will Fitzgibbon, *Cyprus, Ghana and Kenya Join Growing List of Countries to Create Beneficial Ownership Registries*, International Consortium of Investigative Journalists (Apr. 13, 2021), www.icij .org/investigations/panama-papers/cyprus-ghana-and-kenya-join-growing-list-of-countries-to-create-beneficial-ownership-registries/.

[43] The Malabu Oil Scandal has generated significant international litigation. In 1996, OPL 245 was awarded to Malabu Oil for $20million. Malabu Oil was controlled by Mr. Dan Etete, the then Minister of Petroleum, and some of the closest allies of late General Sani Abacha – Nigeria's Head of State at the time. Since 2001, the Malabu Oil saga has cascaded into several disputes not only between Nigerian national elites, but also between these elites and Western multinationals, directors and officials as well as with officials of the federal government of Nigeria. For the timeline of the several lawsuits that arose from the Malabu Oil deal, *see* Staff, *Timeline: Nigeria's OPL 245 Oilfield Licence Bribery Cases*, Reuters (Mar. 17, 2021, 12:30 PM), www.reuters.com/article/ uk-eni-shell-nigeria-timeline-idUSKBN2B92EA.

[44] *Id.* (A rich oil well that has been the subject of significant international controversy marred in accusations of bribery and corruption on the part of government, investors, and political elites).

government before the Canadian Federal High Court in 2020 revealed how shell companies were deployed to profit from the sale of this lucrative oil block.

The Nigerian government initiated a suit in Canada[45] seeking to seize a luxury private jet owned by a powerful Nigerian politician, Mr. Etete. The suit alleged that the politician had illegally used proceeds from the sale of the oil block to purchase the luxury jet. The oil block had been sold in 2011 at $1.3 billion to two multinationals, Shell and ENI.[46] The Canadian suit sought orders to seize the luxury jet to recoup monies paid to Etete by these multinationals. The Nigerian government claimed that these illegal payments were due to it, not to the politician.

The registered owner of the luxury jet was Tibit Limited – an anonymously owned company incorporated in the British Virgin Islands (BVI).[47] According to media reports, although one Ms. Giuseppina Russa of J. Russa Consultants, a company based in Montreal, was listed as a sole director of Tibit Limited, this was in fact untrue. Ms. Russa was an executive assistant of sales for Bombardier and was only hired to decorate the jet interior and had nothing to do with Tibit's affairs at the relevant times. According to evidence in the case, Mr. Etete paid a total of $57million for the luxury jet in 2011 from the proceeds of the sale of OPL 245.[48] The plane had initially been grounded in Dubai pursuant to proprietary injunction following an action brought by the government of Nigeria. However, under the guise of testing, the luxury jet found its way to Montreal, Canada, thereby triggering the case in Canada. The intervention of Canadian courts highlighted how those who stood behind the purchase and ownership of the luxury jet had been concealed.

The Malabu saga, therefore, reveals how the pilfering of public assets is often layered in anonymous corporate entities incorporated abroad that make it difficult without expensive litigation to expose those who stand behind these transactions.[49] As such, disguising ownership or using a corporate shell such as Tibit to avoid disclosing the true identity of those involved complicates the analysis of to whom to

---

[45]   See *Federal Republic of Nigeria v. Tibit Ltd.* (2020) CanLII 2410 (Montreal Sup. Ct, Civ. Division) ("The former minister is alleged to have acquired the private jet through illicit gains from the Malabu scheme where he allegedly transferred valuable petroleum assets for his personal benefit in a series of fraudulent and corrupt transactions carried out during his time as minister.")

[46]   See Lionel Faull & Margot Gibbs, *Exclusive: Malabu Scandal: Nigeria grounds Dan Etete's $57million jet in Canada*, PREMIUM TIMES NIGERIA (June 6, 2020), www.premiumtimesng.com/news/headlines/396290-exclusive-malabu-scandal-nigeria-grounds-dan-etetes-57million-jet-in-canada-1.html.

[47]   *Id.*

[48]   *Id.*

[49]   For example, when agreement was reached between Nigeria, Shell, and Malabu Oil that the sum of $1.092 billion be paid to Malabu oil by the Federal Government of Nigeria in settlement of the revocation and award of OPL 245 to Shell, "...other parties [shareholders] suddenly showed up to make claims on the money: Energy Venture Partners Limited (a British Virgin Island Company), International Legal Consulting (a Russian Company), Pecos Energy Limited and Mohammed Sani." See, Reuben Abati, *OPL 245: The Most Popular Oil Block*, THE CABLE NIGERIA (May 8, 2018, 7:25 AM), www.thecable.ng/opl-245-popular-oil-block.

attribute the conduct of these anonymous entities without expensive investigations and litigation.[50]

Our next example foregrounds another complicating factor for attributing responsibility for the pilfering of public assets in oil block allocations. This has to do with the direct involvement of national-level leadership in shepherding indigenization initiatives. When Nigeria returned to democratic governance in 1999, President Olusegun Obasanjo also doubled up as the Minister of Petroleum. He had an infrastructural development policy that prioritized diversifying the transnational actors in the oil and gas sector.[51] In April 2000, he set up the Oil and Gas Reform Implementation Committee.[52] He approached Asian investors (national oil companies) from China, India, South Korea, and Taiwan to counter the dominance of Western transnational corporations in the oil and gas extractive sector (oil for infrastructure).[53] These Asian firms were granted oil blocks in exchange for their promise to invest in the downstream oil sector and in related infrastructure projects.[54] In this respect, this approach was different from prior military administrations in Nigeria that handed over oil blocks to national elites who subsequently sold them to investors as discussed in the Malabu example above.[55] The 2005 licensing round brought the Asian National Oil Companies (ANOCs) into the fray. Many of the Western transnational corporations (TNCs), such as Shell, Total, and others, did not participate in the round. This was the first time ANOCs participated in oil block licensing in Nigeria.

---

[50] As one of the paragraphs from the Affidavit of Mr. Babatunde Olabode Johnson at the trial reveals:

> What is clear from my investigations into this transaction is that there were several 'professional frontmen' who traded on their ability to hide assets. Borgas is a dishonest enabler, and Ickonga, his codirector, was shrewd enough to take Tibit's records to Brazzaville to block any attempt to have them disclosed by order of this court. When Borgas stepped down as a director, Etete found Russa, another proxy, to step in.

> See *Malabu: Canadian Court Dismiss Etete's Appeal on Seizure of Private Jet by Nigerian Government.*, SAHARA REPORTERS (Sep. 4, 2020), http://saharareporters.com/2020/09/04/malabu-canadian-court-dismiss-etete's-appeal-seizure-private-jet-nigerian-government.

[51] President Olusegun Obasanjo's two-term tenure began in 1999 and ended in May 2007.

[52] This Committee provided the first draft of the Petroleum Industry Bill, 2008.

[53] ALEX VINES ET AL., THIRST FOR AFRICAN OIL: ASIAN NATIONAL OIL COMPANIES IN NIGERIA AND ANGOLA 1 (2009), www.chathamhouse.org/sites/default/files/r0809_africanoil.pdf.

[54] See generally Dunia Prince Zongwe, *Ore for Infrastructure: A Contractual Model for the Optimization of China's Investments in the Mining Sectors of Africa* (Aug. 2011) (Ph.D. Dissertation, Cornell Univ.).

[55] The military era decision to indigenize the oil and gas industry in Nigeria was not gazetted. As such, there was no way to ascertain the criteria for the implementation of the policy. As Mark Amaza notes:

> [Nigeria's] 1990 indigenisation policy was not published in an official gazette, and its vagueness created the possibility of the policy being abused by those charged with its implementation.
>
> …
>
> The first set of discretionary awards was made in 1991 and then a second one in 1993, with many of the recipients influential Nigerians who had never been in the oil industry before but, were well-connected to the government and especially the president, General Babangida.

> Mark Amaza, *Discretionary Awards of Oil Blocks in Nigeria: A State Capture Culture Passed Down from the Military Government*, HEINRICH BÖLL STIFTUNG, CAPE TOWN, SOUTH AFRICA (Aug. 21, 2019). https://za.boell.org/index.php/en/2019/08/21/discretionary-awards-oil-blocks-nigeria-state-capture-culture-passed-down-military.

The 2005 round was unique in two respects. First, there was a requirement of a local content vehicle having at least 10 percent equity control by an indigenous company.[56] This means that at least 10 percent of shares of such an entity had to be owned by Nigerians. Second, a right of first refusal in favor of the ANOCs was put in place to govern oil block licensing.[57] To meet the first requirement, the Nigerian government sought indigenous participation in the oil and gas industry by requiring foreign investor consortia to have a 10 percent indigenous equity participation undertaken through a Local Content Vehicle (LCV). Local elites capitalized on this requirement by creating shell or paper companies, lacking the technical and financial expertise to undertake the oil and infrastructural projects.[58] One consequence of the LCV requirement was that these shell or paper companies became vehicles for siphoning off Nigeria's oil wealth without paying taxes otherwise due to the Nigerian government.

South Korea's Korean National Oil Company (KNOC), in partnership with Equator Exploration, emerged from the 2005 licensing round with the two best deep offshore blocks on offer.[59] Equator Exploration, however, had its own challenges that go to the

---

[56] Unlike the 2000 round, local content was given a weight of twenty percent (20 percent) in the 2005 Round. *See* Inam Wilson & Dayo Okusami, *Nigeria 2005 Bid Round: Interesting Times are Coming*, MONDAQ (Mar. 21, 2005), www.mondaq.com/nigeria/oil-gas-electricity/31591/ nigeria-2005-bid-round-interesting-times-are-coming.

[57] "Prior to the auction, President Obasanjo had entered into strategic deals with South Korea, Taiwan, China, India and most recently Malaysia, offering them lucrative blocks in return for the promise of strategic investments." VINES ET AL., *supra* note 53, at 14. "The government's use of RoFR – introduced one week before allocation round – which was not clearly defined in the guidelines and, as a result, led to the subversion of due process." *See* Ben Ezeamalu, *Special Report: How Corruption Fuelled Allocation of Nigeria's Oil Blocks?*, PREMIUM TIMES NIGERIA (Jan. 8, 2018), www.premiumtimesng .com/news/headlines/254760-special-report-corruption-fuelled-allocation-nigerias-oil-blocks.html.

[58] The requirement that indigenous companies own 10 percent equity in a consortia

> [P]roduced a rash of shell or paper companies, causing bidders serious difficulty with due diligence. Of the 100-plus LCVs which pre-qualified, only 10% had previous experience in oil exploration and development. The ANOCs, new to Nigeria, would have had particular difficulty choosing the mandatory LCVs. President Obasanjo argued that the LCV scheme would develop local expertise in the oil business. Its critics pointed to the success of the existing Marginal Fields policy, which did precisely that. Many therefore dismissed the LCV scheme as a mechanism to reward cronies with a slice of the action. The evidence points in that direction. The outcome suggests that the ANOCs were steered in their choice of LCV. For instance, NJ Exploration Services, owned by Emmanuel Ojie (a well-known and close business associate of President Obasanjo) was the approved LCV on one of the Korean blocks awarded. Another LCV, Southland, which teamed up with KNOC, is owned by Andy Uba, then the President's closest adviser and gatekeeper.

> (In the 2006 round – see below – another of Ojie's companies, Emo Oil, was the approved LCV for the two blocks awarded to India. Another, Shore Beach Exploration, owned jointly by Ojie and Emeka Offor, a key financier of the ruling party, was the approved LCV for blocks awarded to China in 2006). VINES ET AL., *supra* note 53, at 13.

[59] India' Oil and Natural Gas corporation – Videsh Ltd (ONGC-VL) and China missed out on this round, while Taiwan also emerged with oil blocks. Taiwan's Chinese Petroleum Corporation (Taiwan CPC) deal also went sour after they were awarded two oil blocs. Taiwan CPC had entered into partnership with Chrome Oil to fulfil its indigenous equity component of the 2005 round. Emeka Offor, a Nigerian elite and ally of President Obasanjo, owned Chrome Oil. Chrome Oil failed to pay the signature bonus as such the deal was left uncompleted.

heart of our argument. In particular, it had no assets in the oil extractive industry.[60] Further, although ONGC Videsh Ltd (ONGC-VL), a rival of KNOC, had offered to pay the signature bonus of $485 million, the Nigerian government awarded the blocks to KNOC on the basis of pre-negotiated strategic commitments.[61] KNOC and its partners, however, missed the payments deadline for the signature bonus and did not eventually make this payment. The mystery that surrounded where and how much was paid by the KNOC is further evidence of the lack of transparency that characterizes deals struck by politicians – including the President. The fact that KNOC paid reduced signature fees to qualify for the award of the oil blocks suggests that such investors did not have the necessary capital needed to develop the blocks to produce new oil.[62] The secrecy with which discretionary discounts were made as well as the lack of accountability provided a perfect opportunity for national elites to enrich themselves all covered up under the cloak of complex transactions from the award of the oil block.[63]

The Nigerian local content requirement requiring partial ownership of these oil and gas ventures by indigenous firms may very well be good for the eventual development of this sector, especially when those firms are owned by members of the national elite, and even when they have little or no relevant experience. However, our next example further illustrates our core claim in this chapter: that indigenization policies are captured by elites who capitalize on the indigenization policy for private gain. The 2006 mini oil block round illustrates this.

The 2006 oil block allocation was pursued in response to the failures of the 2005 round. The mini round "was designed to fulfill promises of blocks made to China,

---

[60] Specifically, Vines et al. states,

> Curiously, ONGC was initially partnered with the same Equator. It seems that Nigeria had played India against South Korea to achieve the best deal on downstream projects. The structure of their bids was different. For this round, ONGC bid as an upstream company with no strings attached. By contrast, KNOC led a consortium, which meant it was better prepared as an infrastructure provider.... In addition, although ONGC was prepared to pay the same signature bonus as KNOC, it appears that the Indian cabinet's delay in agreeing the bid price contributed to ONGC's losing out. Although India tends to be more cautious about spending public money in foreign acquisitions than, say, the Chinese, in this case prior discussions with Nigeria had led India to believe that these blocks were in the bag. The Indian government was so displeased at the outcome that it complained directly to President Obasanjo about what it described as 'unfair treatment meted out to the oil major.

> *Id.* at 15.

[61] "The ad-hoc committee found that the minister was prepared to subvert the due process because of the commitments contained in a MoU dated July 25, 2005 which he signed with KNOC." *See* Ezeamalu, *supra* note 57.

[62] Dino Mahtani, *Nigeria Finds Shortfall of $1.5bn After Oil Bid Round*, FINANCIAL TIMES (Feb. 13, 2006), www.ft.com/content/726fbda4-9cb6-11da-8762-0000779e2340.

[63] For example, in the context of the payment of KNOC's signature bonus, "it was discovered that KNOC had not paid the full signature bonus on its blocks acquired in 2005. While KNOC has since argued that it had been given a discount by President Obasanjo, there was no record of this in NNPC, DPR or presidency files. The discount given to KNOC, probably orally during the South Korean President's visit, is a good example of Obasanjo's idiosyncratic style of government." VINES ET AL., *supra* note 53, at 22.

India and Taiwan" as they had missed out on the 2005 round.[64] One of the ANOCs, Taiwan's CPC, a state-owned company, was in a joint venture with Starcrest Nigeria Energy. Starcrest was owned by a powerful national figure, Emeka Offor.[65] For reasons that were not made public, Taiwan CPC requested to be granted two oil blocks (OPLs 292 and 226) instead of a different one (OPL 291) that it had been previously granted. This then paved the way for Starcrest to sell 72.5 percent of the stake in OPL 291 to Addax, a Western transnational corporation operating in Nigeria. The local content vehicle in the consortia was also jointly owned by Mr. Emeka Offor, and a certain Emmanuel Ojie, who was a close associate of President Obasanjo.[66] Starcrest's almost immediate sale of a majority of its stake in OPL 291 to a multinational corporation illustrates one of the ways that national elites have captured indigenization policies, through corporate structures, for their own private gain.

Many of the indigenous companies that took up the 10 percent equity stake in the 2006 oil licensing rounds were nonexistent at the time of the awards. Where they existed, they lacked the expertise and financial capacity to meet their signature fees. These indigenous companies acquired interests in the oil blocks at reduced signature bonuses and then sold them to multinationals at much higher prices that deprived Nigeria of the much-needed earnings. This goes to show that local elites, just like multinational corporations, use shell or paper companies to siphon off public assets.

As these examples illustrate, indigenization efforts in oil licensing were open to abuse by national elites with access to power.[67] These indigenization efforts were also the backwater against which complex corporate families were created through lawful processes that then facilitated elite profiteering from the disposition of public assets.

CONCLUSION

The chapter has argued that analysis of attribution of multinational enterprises' conduct ought to take into account the broader context within which these multinational enterprises legitimize their activities in alliance with domestic elites. By taking this context into account, it becomes possible to unearth the relationships between domestic elites and multinational enterprises. The involvement of domestic elites within the multiple corporate structures of multinational enterprises complicates attribution analysis and illustrates its tangible consequences.

---

[64] This was evident from the list of companies that were already pre-qualified: CNPC, ONGC Videsh, BG Sahara, ONGC Mital, Global Steel Holding, INC Natural Resources Exploration, Clean Waters Consortium, NAOC/Lotus, CPC Star Crest Energy, Transnational Corp., and Ni-Delta United Oil Company.

[65] *Id.* at 17.

[66] "NEITI officials confirmed that there were serious irregularities about this deal. Starcrest was only registered just before the round; it had no history and no credibility as an oil company." *Id.*

[67] Abati, *supra* note 51.

First, quite often domestic elites are powerful political actors who use their influence to block investigations in the first place. For example, during the privatization of Telkom Kenya, a shadowy company, whose owners have never been disclosed, made a windfall. Efforts to find its beneficial owners so that they could be held responsible were unsuccessful. Second, this involvement of domestic elites in complex corporate entities can divert funds intended for public coffers. For example, the oil block allocation examples from Nigeria show how the involvement of political leaders in indigenization efforts legitimizes the creation of complex corporate families that become the gateway to siphoning private profits from the sale of public assets. This chapter has, therefore, made the case for contextualizing attribution analysis and lifting it out of the abstraction of bare-bone doctrinal discussions by accounting for the role of domestic elites.

Another takeaway from this chapter is that the relationships between multinational enterprises and African governments have not been fixed but have been shifting over the last several decades. In particular, as multinational enterprises sought to reinvent themselves in the postcolonial period as agents of modernization and development rather than agents of imperialism, they adopted a strategy of hiring African officers and directors. This strategy of legitimization has continued to date. Our claim is that attribution analysis of multinational enterprises cannot be divorced from the fact that elites in developing countries are embedded within these multinational enterprises as officers and directors. In this sense, therefore, questions about attribution ought ideally to extend beyond doctrinal queries to examining the roles of a variety of actors – especially domestic elites – which in turn complicates pathways for establishing multinational enterprise liability. This is especially the case when questions arise about the potential liability of these entities in relation to illicit financial flows and the sale of public assets.

7

Transnational Blame Attribution

The Limits of Using Reputational Sanctions
to Punish Corporate Misconduct

Kishanthi Parella

INTRODUCTION

When corporations engage in misconduct, we rely on two types of sanctions to discipline them: legal and reputational. Legal sanctions are familiar. They include lawsuits against misbehaving companies that result in significant monetary damages and other remedies for the victims of misconduct. They also include monetary fines and penalties paid to government actors for similar misconduct. Unfortunately, these types of sanctions may not always accompany misconduct because of the challenges associated with extraterritorial application of laws, available causes of action, and lack of information concerning the mechanisms and perpetrators of harm. When legal sanctions fail to punish corporate conduct, we may then turn to reputational sanctions to discipline corporate conduct. But reputational sanctions are also limited in achieving these goals because (a) information gaps reduce the likelihood of blame attribution; (b) characteristics of the corporation and stakeholders reduce the likelihood of punishment for misconduct, and (c) features of reputational mechanisms reduce the likelihood of meaningful organizational change.

Due to the limitations of each independently, this chapter argues that the combination of legal and reputational sanctions can help to improve the effectiveness of each of these. For example, legal sanctions through lawsuits and government fines can trigger reputational sanctions that can unleash a subsequent wave of monetary costs because the publicity associated with the lawsuit or government fine can lead a corporation's stakeholders to reevaluate their opinion of it and their willingness to continue their relationship with it. Alternatively, legal rules can facilitate the operation of reputational markets by increasing information flows and thereby improving attribution of conduct to particular companies.

LIMITS OF LEGAL SANCTIONS

One way of disciplining corporations is through the use of legal sanctions. The problem is that these do not always accompany corporate misconduct. Consider the limitations to imposing legal sanctions through litigation. The first difficulty is the territorial limitation. Many corporations organize their functions globally, including raw material production, manufacturing, research and development, customer service, marketing, and sales.[1] This means that the injuries that a corporation causes may occur in a different jurisdiction than the one that seeks to hold the corporation accountable. For example, in the United States, a number of victims of corporate misconduct abroad have tried to hold corporations accountable using the U.S. Alien Tort Statute (ATS). The ATS "is a federal law first adopted in 1789 that gives the federal courts jurisdiction to hear lawsuits filed by non-U.S. citizens for torts committed in violation of international law."[2] However, the U.S. Supreme Court has held that the presumption against extraterritoriality applies to the ATS.[3]

The second challenge is that victims may not have a cause of action for the harms they suffered. Over the years, victims of corporate misconduct in the United States have attempted to bring their claims under international law, state common law, and consumer protection statutes, among others. For example, the U.S. Supreme Court "limited federal courts to recognizing causes of action only for alleged violations of international law norms that are 'specific, universal, and obligatory.'"[4] Plaintiffs have also encountered difficulties when alleging claims under state common law, such as contracts and torts, because of a lack of a legally recognized duty that the defendant corporations owe to the victims of the misconduct. The consequence is that victims often lack the legal vocabulary to articulate the harms they suffered from corporate misconduct. Alternatively, courts are unwilling to acknowledge that our current legal vocabulary also applies to the injuries sustained by these victims. Either way, the result is harms without legal redress.

A final challenge relates to identifying the party and the mechanisms for the perpetration of harms. Corporate identity can prove challenging to parse because of the complexity of corporate structures involving parent and subsidiary companies and associated entities.[5] This challenge grows in the transnational space in which it is challenging to show the links in the chain of accountability. It may prove difficult for plaintiffs and ultimately the court to ascertain what conduct was perpetrated by a domestic versus a foreign corporation when the two entities share common operations. This task grows even more complex in the supply chain context when economic production is maintained by dozens or hundreds of different entities spanning multiple jurisdictions. It can prove difficult to categorically state that a given product originated through a particular supply chain pathway. But difficulties also arise even if we can trace the harm to a particular supply chain site. For example, if a factory

---

[1]   Samuel J. Palmisano, *The Globally Integrated Enterprise*, 58 FOR. AFF. 127 (2006).
[2]   The Alien Tort Statute: Protecting the Law that Protects Human Rights, Center for Constitutional Rights, https://ccrjustice.org/home/get-involved/tools-resources/fact-sheets-and-faqs/alien-tort-statute-protecting-law-protects (April 17, 2013).
[3]   *Kiobel v. Royal Dutch Petroleum Co.*, 569 U.S. 108, 124 (2013).
[4]   *Kiobel*, 569 U.S. at 117; *Sosa v. Alvarez-Machain*, 542 U.S. 692, 732 (2004).
[5]   Carliss Chatman, *Corporate Family Matters*, 12 U.C.I. L. REV. 1 (2021).

fire occurs at a production site overseas, who is to blame when the fire resulted from a violation of health and safety standards? Is it the managers of the overseas factories who have control over facilities operations? Is it the local safety inspectors who failed to identify the risks, or local emergency personnel who could not manage the blaze? Or is it the companies who purchased the products from that site at prices that made it virtually impossible for the local managers and workers to maintain adequate health and safety controls? If it is the latter, then which of the dozens of buyers are responsible when multiple companies sourced from that site? What happens when the production site manufactured intermediate goods that are purchased by dozens of other companies and then incorporated into finished products by dozens of others? Which of these is to blame? And what blame attaches to the end consumer who keeps purchasing the finished product even while fully aware of the risks of fires, building collapses, and labor violations that plague the supply chain for these goods? In these complex production and consumption networks, who is to blame?

Even if we can identify the responsible actors, courts may be unwilling to recognize the *mechanisms* by which corporations perpetrated the harm; this unwillingness can shield companies from liability even if we know who is to blame. For example, in *Nestle v. Doe*, the U.S. Supreme Court explained that general corporate decision-making, like mere corporate presence, is insufficient to establish a sufficient domestic focus under the ATS.[6] This is "[b]ecause making 'operational decisions' is an activity common to most corporations, [and] generic allegations of this sort do not draw a sufficient connection between the cause of action respondents seek – aiding and abetting forced labor overseas – and domestic conduct."[7] But consider the facts as alleged by respondents:

- "Every major operational decision regarding Nestlé's U.S. market, including the sourcing and supervision of its supply chain in the Ivory Coast, is made or approved in the United States.[8]
- Petitioner offers both financial and technical assistance to the cocoa farmers.... Petitioner controls the terms and conditions by which plantations produce and supply cocoa.[9]
- Through exclusive supplier and buyer relationships, Petitioner dictates the terms by which the plantations produce and supply cocoa, including the labor conditions under which the cocoa beans are [] produced.[10]
- Training and quality control visits occur several times per year and require frequent and ongoing visits to the farms by Petitioner and their agents.[11]

---

[6] *Nestlé USA, Inc. v. Doe*, 141 S. Ct. 1931, 1937 (2021).
[7] *Id.*
[8] Brief in Opposition for Respondent at 4, *Nestlé USA, Inc. v. Doe*, 141 S. Ct. 1931 (2021) (No. 19-416).
[9] *Id.*
[10] *Id.* at 4–5.
[11] *Id.* at 5.

- Petitioner disseminates this on-the-ground reporting to U.S. offices so U.S.-based decisionmakers can assess what actions take place in the Ivory Coast.[12]
- Supplies provided by Petitioner include fertilizers, tools and equipment, as well as personal spending money to maintain farmers' loyalty as exclusive suppliers."[13]

A failure to recognize the domestic focus of that conduct speaks of a failure of attribution. By stating that the alleged acts occurred *there*, the Court fails to acknowledge what happened *here*. Specifically, this is an unwillingness to recognize causation between the types of corporate decision-making that occurred in the United States and the harms suffered elsewhere. And this case is not singular. Instead, there are other examples in which U.S. courts are unwilling to recognize the causal nexus between a corporation's seemingly routine acts, such as choosing contracting terms, and the harms that result from those terms.[14]

REPUTATIONAL SANCTIONS: CHARACTERISTICS OF A CORPORATE REPUTATION

Given the challenges with legal sanctions, and the apparent difficulty in overcoming them through legal reform, we may turn to reputational sanctions to try to discipline corporate conduct. According to reputation expert Charles Fombrun, "[a] corporate reputation is a collective assessment of a company's attractiveness to a specific group of stakeholders relative to a reference group of companies with which the company competes for resources."[15] Corporate reputation, therefore, consists of "(1) collective assessments (2) of a company's attractiveness (3) to a defined set of stakeholders (4) relative to a reference group of other companies."[16] Corporate reputations are built from information from (a) "personal experiences that stakeholders have with an organization,"[17] (b) "the corporate initiatives and communications that managers make to strategically influence stakeholder perceptions,"[18] and the (c) "specialized coverage the organization receives from influential intermediaries, such as analysts, journalists, and other central gatekeepers."[19] Additionally, the media also plays an important role in reputation building because their "coverage influences the information held and interpretations made by stakeholders about the validity and merits of the firm's initiatives and communications."[20]

---

[12] *Id.*

[13] *Id.*

[14] *Rahaman v. J.C. Penney Corp., Inc.*, CA. No. N15C-07-0174, 2016 WL 2616375 (Del. Super. Ct., May 4, 2016); *Doe I v. Wal-Mart Stores*, 572 F.3d 677 (9th Cir. 2009).

[15] Charles Fombrun, *The Building Blocks of Corporate Reputation, in* THE OXFORD HANDBOOK OF CORPORATE REPUTATION 100 (Michael L. Barnett & Timothy G. Pollock eds., 2012).

[16] *Id.*

[17] *Id.* at 103.

[18] *Id.*

[19] *Id.*

[20] *Id.*

A corporation's reputation matters to itself and to the various actors with whom it may interact. A reputation matters to a corporation because it influences its relationships with multiple stakeholders. Like all organizations, a corporation is not self-sufficient; it relies on resources provided by a variety of actors. Investors provide financial capital, employees provide human capital; consumers provide revenue, suppliers provide access to important raw materials and production capacities, government actors create a favorable regulatory environment, and local communities provide the "social license to operate." Corporations rely on these resources (and the actors who provide them) to aid their functions in various markets and more generally in society. A corporate reputation influences whether actors will provide these resources and, if so, the terms. For example, consumers may be unwilling to pay premium prices once they learn the product is defective. Shareholders may be unwilling to invest in companies that are unlikely to return a profit. Employees may avoid companies that do not provide a favorable employment environment. A corporation relies on its reputation to persuade these and other groups to supply (and continue to supply) the resources that it needs. In these different ways, various corporate stakeholders – consumers, investors, and employees – exercise their leverage in three distinct markets – the consumer market, the financial market, and the labor market. Stakeholders discipline companies by threatening to withhold the particular resources the corporation needs in order to thrive: revenue, financial capital, and human capital.

To exercise their leverage, these stakeholders rely on a corporation's reputation because they often do not have sufficient information to decide whether they should provide the needed resource to the corporation. For example, a consumer usually has limited information about the quality of a good or service before purchase; the company's reputation stands in for the incomplete information. A corporation's reputation is important to consumers and other stakeholders because it helps them "gauge the probable outcomes of interacting with a particular organization."[21] Stakeholders make two critical reputational judgments about companies: *capability* and *character*.[22] The former relates to the "quality and performance characteristics of a particular firm,"[23] while the latter concerns "the imputation that stakeholder groups make about the target organization's goals, preferences, and organizational values"[24] which "are used by stakeholders to make behavioral predictions and determine whether the target organization's goals and values are congruent with their own."[25] Both reputational judgments are used by stakeholders to address

[21] Yuri Mishina, Emily S. Block, and Michael J. Mannor, *The Path Dependence of Organizational Reputation: How Social Judgment Influences Assessments of Capability & Character*, 33 STRAT. MGMT. J. 459, 460 (2012).

[22] Id.

[23] Id. at 459–460.

[24] Id.

[25] Id.; E. Geoffrey Love & Matthew Kraatz, *Character, Conformity, or the Bottom Line? How and Why Downsizing Affected Corporate Reputation*, 52 ACAD. MANAG. J. 314, 316 (2009).

uncertainties they confront when interacting with a firm. Stakeholders use character judgments to deal with uncertainty relating to whether they expect the company
to treat them in an unfavorable manner.[26] Capability judgments address the issue
of the "lemons" problem where consumers risk overpaying for a product or service
because they cannot directly observe the characteristics of the company or products
ex ante.[27] Both types of evaluations have market consequences because they influence whether a stakeholder will want to associate or exchange with that company.

LIMITATIONS OF REPUTATIONAL SANCTIONS: INFORMATION, ENFORCEMENT, AND ORGANIZATIONAL CHANGE

Despite the importance of a reputation to a corporation, it may prove a blunt instrument with which to punish and change a corporation. This is because of three
particular difficulties. First, it may prove difficult to attribute blame to a corporation
because of a lack of information concerning what happened (harms), why it happened (causation), and by whose hand it happened (actors). Information deficits
regarding one or more of these can reduce the likelihood that a corporation's stakeholders will blame it for conduct. Second, even if stakeholders do possess this information, they may nevertheless decline to punish the corporation for the misconduct
because of its characteristics (brand), market characteristics (demand and supply),
or their own characteristics (lack of convergence between interest and leverage).
These limitations reduce the likelihood of enforcement through reputational sanctions, thereby making it unlikely that corporations will suffer penalties in their
relationships with their stakeholders. Finally, even when reputational sanctions are
used, they can be limited in effectiveness.

Attributing Blame: The Information Problem

We can only name and shame corporations if we first know what they have done
wrong. It is unlikely that those who intend to use shame as a tool of discipline
will have firsthand knowledge of the underlying misconduct. They must, therefore,
rely on another party to reveal that information. Media outlets may be effective in
revealing information and influencing the public agenda for change. For example,
consider the public scrutiny of labor conditions in supply chains that typically follows media exposure of "sweatshop conditions" in the overseas production facilities
associated with many brand names. Revelations of wrongdoing that make head-
line news, however, often require investigative journalism and significant resource
investment.[28] Such investment may be difficult to find at a time when journalists

---

[26] Mishina et al., *supra* note 21, at 460.
[27] *Id.* at 461.
[28] Roy Shapira, *Law as Source: How the Legal System Facilitates Investigative Journalism*, 37 YALE L. POLICY REV. 153, 200–201 (2018).

worry about the declining support for investigative journalism overall.[29] The risk to investigative journalism means that we may face a situation of underproduction of information; without this information, there may not be much to get the reputational mechanisms going.

The lack of information reduces the likelihood of attribution of blame for corporate misconduct in a number of important ways that relate to *harms, causes,* and *actors.* First, the public may never learn of the harms caused by the misconduct; therefore, they are unaware of the nature, severity, and scale of the injuries suffered by one or more individuals in society. Without this information, there may be no need for blame or attribution because those who would wield the reputational sanctions are unaware that wrongs have been perpetrated.

Second, knowledge of harm is not enough. In order to attribute blame, we need an understanding of causation to first identify the mechanisms by which the harm was perpetrated. It is not enough to know that a car malfunctioned or that private information was stolen. We also need to know how this happened because the reasons why a crisis occurred also impact the level of blameworthiness we attribute to those responsible.[30] According to research in crisis management, we can classify crises into the following three types, each with corresponding levels of blame attribution and reputational harm: *victim, accidental,* and *preventable.*[31]

In a "victim crisis," the company is viewed as a victim of the crisis; this category is associated with the lowest attribution of responsibility and mildest reputational threat.[32] In contrast, a preventable crisis is one in which stakeholders believe that "organization knowingly placed people at risk, took inappropriate actions or violated a law/regulation."[33] These types of crises are associated with strong attributions of responsibility and severe reputational threat.[34] We can, therefore, expect more significant reputational consequences for a company when stakeholders believe that the harm did not have to occur, but that the company chose to elevate its own interests above those of the victims and this caused the resulting harm. In contrast, a company may not suffer comparable reputational consequences when it can show that it had little control over the events that occurred.

We need information in order to classify a crisis into one of these three categories. Most people identify the type of crisis by using the frames provided by the media.[35]

---

[29] *Id.* at 163–67.

[30] W. Timothy Coombs, *Protecting Organization Reputations during a Crisis: The Development and Application of Situational Crisis Communication Theory,* 10 CORP. REPUTATION REV. 163, 166–68. (2007); W. Timothy Coombs, *An Analytic Framework for Crisis Situations: Better Responses from a Better Understanding of the Situation,* 10 J. PUB. REL. RES. 177, 182 (1998).

[31] Coombs, *Protecting Organization Reputations, supra* note 30, at 168.

[32] *Id.*

[33] *Id.*

[34] *Id.*

[35] *Id.* at 171.

We also need information in order to identify the actors responsible for the harms. Complex corporate structures, however, can frustrate the ability to make these attributions because the mechanisms are opaque or the relationship between different corporate entities is obscure.[36] The latter case results in a situation of partial attribution when we may blame (and subsequently sanction) one actor but spare another that is part of the same corporate family.[37]

Punishing Misconduct: The Enforcement Problem

Reputational sanctions may not occur even if the public has knowledge of the harms that occurred, the reasons for that occurrence, and the actors responsible. One reason for this is that public reactions to this information may depend on the salience of the underlying issues and vulnerabilities of the populations at risk.[38] It is not a given that a reported incident will sufficiently resonate with stakeholders so that they will be motivated to do something about it.[39]

Another reason that reputational sanctions can fail is that not all companies are equally vulnerable to shaming practices. Instead, some scholars have noted that consumer boycotts work best when the targeted corporation produces for end consumers.[40] Boycotts are also more effective when there is "the possibility of translating complex problems into neat story lines that can dramatically highlight responsibility and guilt."[41] Additionally, reputational sanctions vis-à-vis boycotts are also more effective when the targeted corporation derives much of its value from its brand. For example, companies such as Apple and Nike are known for their brand and their brand sustains much value to shareholders. Therefore, naming and shaming may pose significant risks to these companies because such practices may compromise the value of the brand. This is not equally true for all companies. Some companies do not sell to end consumers but instead produce intermediate components to other businesses; such companies are not as visible to consumers and are, therefore, more insulated from naming and shaming practices. Other companies do not rely on

[36] Chatman, *supra* note 5, at 30–40.

[37] *Id.*

[38] Kathryn Sikkink, *Codes of Conduct for Transnational Corporations: The Case of the WHO/UNICEF Code*, 40 INT'L ORG. 815, 823 (1986).

[39] *See, e.g.*, Teresa Johnson, *Public Shaming Will Not Solve The Lack Of Diversity On Corporate Boards*, FINANCIAL TIMES (June 8, 2019) (explaining reasons why information disclosure is unlikely to shame corporations into changing practices relating to diversity on corporate boards: "But 25 years as a corporate lawyer have taught me that this approach only works if the information that is disclosed grabs attention and prods stakeholders to action – simply disclosing information (however unflattering) does not move the needle.").

[40] Nicole Deitelhoff & Klaus Dieter Wolf, "Business and human rights: how corporate norm violators become norm entrepreneurs," 222, 228–29, *in* THE PERSISTENT POWER OF HUMAN RIGHTS (Risse et al., eds. 2013).

[41] *Id.* at 230.

their brand to sell their products or services, but instead market their products on other qualities, such as price.

The success of reputational sanctions also depends on factors that have less to do with the characteristics of a particular company as they relate to the broader market. For example, many boycotts occur in markets for consumer goods where demand is elastic and there are multiple substitution options. For example, if consumers learn that Acme Shoe produces its products through child labor and subsequently organize a boycott, then Acme Shoe is vulnerable because there are numerous substitution possibilities for its products; a consumer does not have to purchase the $700 shoe that Acme Shoe produces, but can instead purchase a similar product from one of its many competitors. Luxury goods are particularly vulnerable to shaming because they are products for which consumers pay a premium, and additional information about the retailer or manufacturer may affect consumers' preferences for the good or the premium they are willing to pay. Vulnerability to consumer shaming may dissipate when products are necessities or there are fewer substitution options in the market for those goods.

Finally, reputational sanctions also depend on the convergence between interest and leverage. When the party that is at risk of harm is the same as the one who imposes the sanction, then reputational sanctions may be very strong. For example, revelations of corporate fraud put shareholders on notice that their financial interests may be at risk; therefore, we are not surprised to see the stock price fall following such revelations. Revelations of consumer fraud similarly alert consumers that their financial (or material) well-being may be at risk if they keep doing business with the same organization; therefore, we can expect a fall in revenue. In both of these situations, the parties at risk of harm are important corporate stakeholders (shareholders, consumers) and they are motivated to levy reputational sanctions because they are the ones who may be harmed. They may not be similarly harmed by other types of corporate wrongdoing, such as environmental, labor, or human rights violations, which affect a different group of actors. These non-stakeholder groups lack leverage over the corporation and, therefore, have limited means to sanction them directly. And those with sanctioning power – such as shareholders and consumers – may lack the interest in exercising the leverage that they do possess when the harms produced by a corporation do not affect them. For these reasons, we may not be able to count on reputational sanctions to do the work of legal sanctions.

Limits of Reputational Sanctions

The previous section discussed why the public may not subject corporations to reputational sanctions for reasons such as lack of information, brand vulnerability, or stakeholder interest. The following section discusses limitations of reputational sanctions even when they are used.

Differences in Reputational Sanctions: Financial, Regulatory, Organizational, and Policy

Not all reputational sanctions are the same. In previous scholarship, I identified four distinct types of reputational sanctions: (a) financial sanctions from naming and shaming, (b) regulatory sanctions vis-à-vis the spillover effect, (c) barriers to entry, and (d) policy sanctions.[42] Each of these has different consequences for corporations and provides different types of incentives for corporations to change.

The classic reputational sanction is the *financial penalty* that follows from some form of public shaming, which is often accompanied by a consumer boycott. The public shaming leads stakeholders of a corporation, such as consumers, to stop doing business with the shamed corporation, resulting in the latter incurring some form of financial loss. Classic examples include the "anti-sweatshop movements" that attracted public attention concerning the labor practices of brand name companies in the United States and Europe.

Regulatory spillover sanctions occur when the misdeeds of one actor causes its industry peers or associated companies to also come under scrutiny.[43] For example, according to the CEO of Delta Airlines, Ed Bastian, "the airline industry is still 'traumatized' by the controversy surrounding the Boeing 737 Max aircraft after a spate of deadly accidents" and the accidents "left a major mark on the aviation industry as a whole."[44] And in 2018, Facebook and Cambridge Analytica came under scrutiny when the public learned that the latter obtained access to private information for more than fifty million Facebook users and that this information may have been used in connection with the 2016 U.S. presidential election.[45] The reputational crisis that resulted impacted more companies than just the primary parties involved, Facebook and Cambridge Analytica.[46] Following the scandal, the

---

[42] Kishanthi Parella, Reputational Regulation, 67 DUKE L. J. 907 (2018).

[43] *See* Michael L. Barnett, *Finding a Working Balance Between Competitive and Communal Strategies*, 43 J. MGMT. STUD. 1753, 1763 (2006) ("A single act by a single firm can spark a constituent mobilization that destabilizes the taken-for-granted status of an entire industry."); Michael L. Barnett & Andrew A. King, *Good Fences Make Good Neighbors: A Longitudinal Analysis of an Industry Self-Regulatory Institution*, 51 ACAD. MGMT. J. 1150, 1152 (2008) ("[W]hen new information is revealed about the characteristics of one firm, it reflects to some degree on all firms within its industry."); Tieying Yu & Richard H. Lester, *Moving Beyond Firm Boundaries: A Social Network Perspective on Reputation Spillover*, 11 CORP. REPUTATION REV. 94, 95 (2008) (explaining "reputational spillover"); Lori Qingyuan Yue & Paul Ingram, *Industry Self-Regulation as a Solution to the Reputation Commons Problem, in* THE OXFORD HANDBOOK OF CORPORATE REPUTATION 279 (2012) ("[R]eputations are 'intangible commons' because organizations share both the penalties and rewards associated with the reputation of their industries.").

[44] Rosie Perper and Rob Price, *Delta CEO Says Airline Industry is 'Traumatized' after Boeing 737 Max Scandal*, BUSINESS INSIDER (June 12, 2019).

[45] Issie Lapowsky, *Facebook Exposed 87 Million Users to Cambridge Analytica*, WIRED (Apr. 4, 2018, 5:43 PM), www.wired.com/story/facebook-exposed-87-million-users-to-cambridge-analytica [https://perma.cc/P4EM-SG8B].

[46] Alexandra Bruell, *Facebook to Boost Ad Spending as It Tries to Restore Reputation*, WALL ST. J. (June 14, 2019) ("Facebook is under intensifying government scrutiny.").

Senate Judiciary Committee invited the CEOs of both Twitter and Google, as well as Facebook CEO Mark Zuckerberg, to discuss the future of data privacy.[47] Given their participation in the tech industry, these companies share both the risk of public scrutiny over their own data collection practices, as well as the risk of heightened regulation that could affect them.[48]

It is also worth acknowledging that sometimes the lack of complete information can help to encourage corporate change. Reputational spillovers operate in a space of imperfect information. Specifically, these reputational mechanisms occur because the public learns *some* information regarding an incident but does not possess all the information concerning it. Therefore, the public is likely to blame all actors associated with the incident or attribute similar motivations and capacities to industry peers because it does not know everything about the incident and, therefore, cannot predict who is a risk and who is not. It is this combination of some information, on one hand, with absent information, on the other, that places a number of businesses at risk of reputational damage. It is this risk of reputational harm that may motivate these businesses to engage in steps to manage the risk of reputational spillover.

A *barrier to entry* sanction occurs when a reputational crisis threatens to delegitimize a particular type of organizational form. Specifically, incumbents or other market rivals may use a reputational crisis not only to shame a particular company but also to shame the very business model that the company uses; such de-legitimizing may not only affect the company under scrutiny but also other businesses that run on a similar model. For example, following the Cambridge Analytica scandal, Tim Cook used the crisis to distinguish Apple from Facebook and similar organizations by explaining that "[t]he truth is we could make a ton of money if we monetized our customer, if our customer was our product. We've elected not to do that."[49] Cook identified differences between the business model of the two companies and, by doing so, attempted to de-legitimize the way that Facebook does business, as well as any other company that "monetizes" customers.[50]

Finally, a *public policy sanction* occurs when a reputational crisis inhibits the ability of the corporation or industry under scrutiny to play a meaningful role in public policy debates concerning the issues that gave rise to the crisis. Like

---

[47] *See* Press Release, Office of Senator Chuck Grassley, Chairman Grassley Announces Hearing on the Future of Data Privacy in Social Media (Mar. 26, 2018), www.grassley.senate.gov/news/news-releases/chairman-grassley-announces-hearing-future-data-privacy-social-media   [https://perma.cc/5B8E-6689].

[48] Christopher Mims, *Apple, Amazon and Google Also Are Bracing for Privacy Regulations*, WALL ST. J. (Apr. 8, 2018, 8:00 AM), www.wsj.com/articles/apple-amazon-and-google-also-are-bracing-for-privacy-regulations-1523188801 [https://perma.cc/W7YX-VGLV].

[49] Ariana Brockington, *Apple's Tim Cook Slams Facebook: Privacy 'Is a Human Right,' 'A Civil Liberty,'* VARIETY (Mar. 28, 2018, 4:08 PM), https://variety.com/2018/digital/news/tim-cook-slams-facebook-privacy-1202738726 [https://perma.cc/7FG4-PFA].

[50] *Id.*

the scrutiny over tobacco companies and their involvement in health policy, corporations in the spotlight for their involvement in current issues may find themselves shunned or sidelined from a similar fear that they will undermine policy efforts.

These different reputational mechanisms matter because they offer different incentives to corporations to change their practices. Critically, some of these mechanisms may succeed in incentivizing while others may fail. However, a multitude of factors may determine whether a reputational crisis will lead to the initiation of one or more of these mechanisms; it is not a given that a scandal will produce all these different types of mechanisms and, if so, to the same degree.

Reactive

Another challenge with reputational mechanisms is that the change they encourage may not occur unless something bad has already happened – an event which may have already harmed innocent parties. Organizational change in the wake of such a crisis can help prevent similar harms to future victims, but occurs too late to help the victims of the crisis that triggers it. Additionally, the reactive focus – driven by reputational mechanisms – may also lead to inappropriate objectives for organizational change. Namely, if corporations are investing in organizational change in order to rehabilitate their reputations following a crisis, then there is a risk the primary goal of any organizational change is not prevention, but reputational rehabilitation. This creates the risk that any resulting organizational change is as much (or even more) of a public relations ploy than it is a meaningful commitment to compliance. Even if a corporation does invest in organizational change intended to prevent future harms, what are they preventing – risk to victims or risk to themselves? While these interests may overlap, they are not identical and can lead to divergent policies. This is because the risks to the business are not the same as the risks to the victims. While both groups may share a common interest in preventing those risks from crystallizing, the policies needed to manage those risks may be different.

For example, a triggering event – such as a product accident – poses risks to both the victims of that accident, such as consumers, and the corporation who may suffer reputational losses associated with the crisis. Such a crisis may also invite a regulatory response or future lawsuits against the corporation, which may impose additional harms like reputational and financial penalties on the corporation.[51] Those harms are different than the harms suffered by the victims of the product accident. If it is the risk to the corporation that drives preventative organizational change, then a corporation may invest in policies to decrease their own risk in a future accident without meaningfully decreasing the risk of harm to future parties.

---

[51] *See, e.g.,* Sinead Baker, Airlines say the grounding of the 737 Max will cost them hundreds of millions of dollars, and they 're ready to pursue Boeing for the money, Business Insider (Apr. 2019) ("US and European airlines say the grounding of the 737 Max has already cost them hundreds of millions of dollars, and they're ready to take on Boeing to get compensation.").

ORGANIZATIONAL OUTCOMES: CHALLENGES
OF SIGNALING AND INCENTIVES

If a corporation engages in organizational change for reputational reasons, how does it distinguish its response from that of its peers? This is the signaling problem that accompanies a corporation's efforts to distinguish itself in the market for corporate social responsibility. This problem accompanies both *ex ante* and *ex post* organizational change.

In *ex ante* situations, how does a corporation communicate its compliance efforts from that of its peers? Consider two companies that boast sustainability statements on their website. Company A provides a flashy downloadable brochure that lists its various core values (that all sound good) and references one or more company policies that it claims incorporates those values (note that direct links to those policies are not available). Its statement of values may be sufficient to satisfy a consumer base that may only care about the identity that company presents to the world. Now, consider Company B, which has not only invested in a statement of values and an accompanying set of company policies, but has gone further to turn values into action. Company B integrates company policies into operating procedures, develops metrics to track and evaluate the effectiveness of those policies, and regularly communicates with stakeholders about its evaluation and plans for improvement. Company B's policies and practices are certainly more costly than Company A's efforts, but how is that costliness communicated to consumers and stakeholders so that they reward the latter more than the former? The average consumer may be unable to distinguish between these efforts, because they all sound good and reflect a general commitment to sustainability. Therefore, Company A's efforts combine with Company B's efforts in a pooling equilibrium in which the latter's costlier efforts do not stand out.

In the *ex post* situation, corporations often invest in voluntary information disclosure following a crisis. Organizational change can serve as a form of information disclosure that communicates information from the corporation to the public in an effort to restore the reputation of the former. This stage of organizational change, however, also suffers from the risk of pooling, so that one corporation's efforts are indistinguishable from another corporation's efforts. If consumers know that there is some level of falsity or misrepresentation present in these pooling corporate statements, then there is a risk they may discount all such efforts, including those associated with a bona fide compliance system, because they cannot distinguish between these two types of companies.[52]

The signaling problem leads to an incentive problem: if "cheap talk" corporate social responsibility ("CSR") efforts are indistinguishable from meaningful

---

[52] David Hess & Thomas W. Dunfee, *The Kasky-Nike Threat to Corporate Social Reporting: Implementing a Standard of Optimal Truthful Disclosure as a Solution*, 17 BUS. ETHICS Q. 5, 17–20 (2007).

compliance processes, then why would a company invest in the latter? Let's return to Company A and Company B. Each of these companies invests in CSR efforts to receive a corresponding reward in the market from consumers who value these efforts and will choose their products. These efforts, however, do not cost the same. Company B's efforts are far more costly, but it does not have a way to sufficiently communicate that costliness to its consumer base to differentiate its efforts from Company A. As such, consumers will reward Company A and Company B equally. Company B will receive comparable reputational rewards (and market benefits) ex post as Company A, which invests in less costly efforts. In such a situation, why would Company B invest in more costly efforts ex ante than Company A, if both companies receive the same rewards ex post? This risk of pooling equilibrium creates downward pressure on CSR efforts that we may expect of companies since they would invest just enough to gain the reputational benefits (Company A's baseline) without doing more.

The signaling problem also influences incentives once a crisis has occurred. Imagine that Company A and Company B invest in the same types of efforts as above, but in response to a crisis, and in an effort to address the reputational damage that has resulted. If Company A's efforts are sufficient to achieve these objectives, why would Company B invest in more? If Company A's efforts are not sufficient – identified and dismissed by the public as insincere – then how does Company B distinguish its own efforts so that it does not suffer the same fate?

HYBRID SOLUTIONS: BUNDLING LEGAL AND REPUTATIONAL SANCTIONS

The previous sections discussed the limitations of using either legal sanctions or reputational sanctions to punish corporations for misconduct, but the choice is not always between the two. Instead, we can "bundle" the two types of sanctions to help independently address the limitations of each. The following discussion explains how legal sanctions through monetary fines can facilitate the creation of reputational sanctions that levy a second round of financial penalties for the companies involved. In this way, reputational sanctions create a magnification effect for legal sanctions that can help improve their effectiveness. The reverse may also occur, so that legal rules and sanctions can improve the operation of reputational sanctions by improving access to information.

Using Reputational Sanctions to Improve Legal Sanctions: The Magnification Effect

In 2016, the Consumer Financial Protection Bureau (CFPB) fined Wells Fargo for "the widespread illegal practice of secretly opening unauthorized deposit and credit card accounts"[53] in which "employees boosted sales figures by covertly opening accounts and funding them by transferring funds from consumers' authorized accounts without their knowledge or consent, often racking up fees or other charges."[54] The CFPB estimated that, according to Wells Fargo's own analysis, "employees opened more than two million deposit and credit card accounts that may not have been authorized by consumers."[55] The CFPB fined Wells Fargo $100 million, with additional fines imposed by the Office of the Comptroller of the Currency ($35 million), and City and County of Los Angeles ($50 million).[56] These fines were eclipsed by the projected losses that Wells Fargo expected to lose as a result of the reputational scandal, as consumers thereafter reevaluated their willingness to bank with Wells Fargo. A survey conducted of primary 1500 customers of the top 10 retail banks found that 85 percent of respondents were aware of the scandal and that the percentage of respondents with positive views of Wells Fargo decreased from 60 to 24 percent following the scandal.[57] Even while only 3 percent reported being affected by the scandal, 14 percent of respondents were projected to switch banks in the subsequent year.[58] The result of the reputational hit was an estimated loss of $99 billion in projected deposits and $4 billion in projected revenue – significantly more than the $100 million the bank was fined by CFPB.[59]

These losses are not surprising. Research reveals "that over 90 percent of the penalties imposed on firms committing private frauds reflects lost reputation"[60] and that "[o]nly a small portion of the financial penalties imposed on such firms is due to criminal or civil penalties and other court-imposed costs."[61] Scandals can also have *distributional effects* within the broader industry. Reputations often go up or down based on how a particular corporation performs compared to its peers. When the disgraced corporation is the "bad apple," we can imagine that the corporation's competitors may benefit from the former's lost business. For example, the customers unhappy with Wells Fargo had to go somewhere and, in this case, the beneficiaries of the scandal were community and regional banks, followed by a number of competitors of Wells Fargo that gained billions of dollars in additional projected deposits.[62] But these spillover effects are not always positive, as "reputational contagion"

---

[53] Consumer Protection Financial Bureau, *Consumer Financial Protection Bureau Fines Wells Fargo $100 Million for Widespread Illegal Practice of Secretly Opening Unauthorized Accounts* (Sept. 8, 2006), https://bit.ly/3j2gwgD.

[54] *Id.*

[55] *Id.*

[56] *Id.*

[57] CG42, WELLS FARGO MINI-STUDY 5 (Oct. 2016).

[58] *Id.* at 7.

[59] *Id.* at 8.

[60] Jonathan Karpoff, John Lott, and Eric Wehrly, *The Reputational Penalties for Environmental Violations: Empirical Evidence*, vol. XLVIII J. L. ECON. 653, 655–56 (2005).

[61] *Id.*

[62] CG42, WELLS FARGO MINI-STUDY 8 (Oct. 2016).

can occur, where peer companies suffer reputational losses based on the conduct of one of the industry's actors.[63] This risk is particularly high when similarities between organizations inhibit the ability of stakeholders to differentiate between industry actors.[64]

So, what factors may have contributed to Wells Fargo experiencing significant losses from their misconduct? First, there is high convergence between those at risk of harm and those who are empowered to levy reputational sanctions: customers. The scandal notified banking customers of the types of sales practices the bank permitted that had the consequence of placing customers at risk. Customers began to turn away from Wells Fargo because the scandal revealed the risk of harm to them from the bank's practices; they were the primary victims of the bank's wrongdoing. It is, therefore, unsurprising that customers would minimize the risk to themselves once they learned this information and reconsider their relationship with the bank. This reconsideration imposed financial costs on the bank, as current customers contemplated switching and new customers shied away.

Second, the quality of information was high because the information about Wells Fargo's practices came from a reputable source: the CFPB.[65] The CFPB not only shared information about Wells Fargo's practices but also publicly punished the bank because of it. This makes the information revealed credible, elevating it on an information landscape that is also occupied by messaging from Wells Fargo (and other banks), intermediaries, and the personal experiences of banking customers. Without this authentication feature, customers could dismiss the new information and decline to update their beliefs. The fine also received a great deal of media coverage that increased the level of awareness, notifying more customers of the risks to themselves and increasing the possibility of switching.[66]

Using Legal Rules to Improve Reputational Sanctions: Mandatory Information Disclosure Laws

Legal institutions may improve the operation of reputational sanctions through mandatory disclosure laws that can supply many of the absent information functions. These laws can aid in information revelation by requiring corporations to disclose information they may not otherwise want to share with the public. Mandatory disclosure laws reveal information to stakeholders that they otherwise may not

---

[63] Yue & Ingram, *supra* note 43, at 279; Michael L Barnett & Andrew J Hoffman, *Beyond Corporate Reputation: Managing Reputational Interdependence*, 11 CORP. REPUT. REV. 1, 2 (2008).

[64] Barnett, *Finding a Working Balance between Competitive and Communal Strategies, supra* note 43, at 1763.

[65] Consumer Financial Protection Bureau, *Consumer Financial Protection Bureau Fines Wells Fargo $100 Million for Widespread Illegal Practice of Secretly Opening Unauthorized Accounts* (Sept. 8. 2016), https://bit.ly/3efoLEz.

[66] Bill Chappell, *Wells Fargo Fined $185 Million over Creation of Fake Accounts For Bonuses*, NPR (Sept. 8, 2016), https://n.pr/3tvo6oQ.

possess by requiring corporations share information they possess about their operations, risks, and impacts. This information is highly credible because corporations could face significant legal sanctions for sharing inaccurate information.

Through revelation and authentication, mandatory disclosure laws add to the aggregate body of knowledge available about a corporation. Armed with this information, stakeholders update their beliefs about a corporation concerning its capabilities or character. These changed beliefs can also result in changed behavior: Consumers may be unwilling to pay a premium for a product once they learn of the environmental impact imposed by the production process. Investors may also be less willing to purchase shares if they learn that the company's operations create long-term reputational, litigation, or regulatory risks. In these ways and more, the audiences for mandatory information disclosure update their beliefs about a company based on the information disclosed; which also leads them to potentially change their behavior, including their willingness to interact with the corporation.

It is this changed behavior by the audience for mandatory disclosure laws that creates reputational sanctions (or rewards). When the audience changes its behavior, so too does the speaker (in anticipation of the former's changed conduct). We can anticipate this both on an organizational and an individual level. Companies may alter their practices in order to disclose information that places them in a favorable light. According to Hillary Sale, the information-forcing substance theory ties disclosure obligations to substantive change:

> Categories of required disclosures mean that an issuer with nothing to report in a particular category will stand out relative to its peers. To avoid that outcome, issuers implement systems to produce disclosures like those of their peers. Thus, the required disclosure of information results in substantive corporate decision-making and action by directors and management.[67]

If corporate executives anticipate a consumer backlash once consumers learn of the environmental or labor consequences of a product, they will most likely change their behavior to ameliorate the consumer reaction. Corporate executives may not make such changes if the time horizon is long, when there is a significant gap of time between action and revelation. Mandatory disclosure laws, however, close this gap so that consumers learn of the underlying acts closer in time to when the action occurred. This is important because a shorter time gap suggests that the individual executives involved in decision-making are still present, thereby making it more likely they will bear the cost of the decision.

The likelihood of behavioral change by the speaker, however, depends on the prospect of behavioral change by the audience. These changes are dependent on information dissemination and intermediation. Without dissemination, the information disclosed may not reach the audience that can wield reputational sanctions;

---

[67] Hillary A. Sale, *Disclosure's Purpose*, 107 GEO. L.J. 1045, 1050 (2019).

if this audience is not armed with information, then the corporation faces minimal reputational threat and is less inclined to change its conduct. While some stakeholders may seek out the disclosed information, others may not invest the time and resources to do so.

Over the past few years, a number of mandatory disclosure laws were introduced to improve transparency in supply chains regarding human rights violations by corporations. For example, the California Transparency in Supply Chains Act of 2012 requires that covered companies disclose their policies and practices concerning verification, audits, certification, internal accountability, and training regarding human trafficking and slavery.[68] It does not, however, set a substantive floor for compliance but instead requires information about what companies do. A company may comply with this law by simply stating that it does not take any steps to perform human rights due diligence. Similarly, the UK Modern Slavery Act requires that covered companies provide an annual statement of the measures that they take to eradicate slavery from their supply chains.[69] Specifically, Section 54 of the Act requires that covered companies produce a slavery and human trafficking statement that consists of "the steps the organisation has taken during the financial year to ensure that slavery and human trafficking is not taking place – (i) in any of its supply chains, and (ii) in any part of its own business, or (b) a statement that the organisation has taken no such steps."[70] This statement must also be signed and approved by the company's leadership, such as a director or partner.[71] The company must also publish the statement on its website in a prominent place if the company maintains a website.[72]

The objective of these laws is to improve corporate conduct in supply chains by forcing these companies to reveal information about their conduct to the public. The idea was that consumers would reward high-performing companies and, therefore, trigger a race to the top. Unfortunately, despite the additional information supplied by these laws, this race to the top did not seem to occur. From 2016–2018, the Business and Human Rights Resource Centre (BHRRC) evaluated company statements under the Modern Slavery Act (MSA), provided by Financial Times Stock Exchange (FTSE) for 100 companies, representing the largest companies in the United Kingdom.[73] The BHRCC found that companies persistently fell short of both reporting requirements and underlying performance.[74] What is worse is that even if companies improve their reporting, they may not be improving their underlying

---

[68] Cal. Civ. Code § 1714.43 (West 2012).

[69] Legislation.gov.uk, *Modern Slavery Act 2015*, https://bit.ly/3n12Bd1.

[70] *Id.*

[71] *Id.*

[72] *Id.*

[73] Business & Human Rights Resource Centre, FTSE 100 & the UK Modern Slavery Act: From Disclosure to Action 14 (2018).

[74] *Id.* at 14–23.

practices; according to the Corporate Human Rights Benchmark (CHRB), human rights due diligence is a key weakness for most companies.[75] The CHRB report also found that many companies are not improving their practices over time, thus "indicating that there have been insufficient incentives for them to change."[76]

So, what went wrong? Why did the improvement of the information landscape not improve the practices of corporations in their supply chains? One problem was the lack of an intermediation function in the transparency laws. Information needs to be analyzed before it can be made useful, so intermediation is essential. Specifically, audiences need to evaluate a corporation's conduct against some form of metric – a baseline, peer performance, or prior performance. In some markets, various intermediaries perform these functions by collecting the disclosed information from a large group of actors, developing metrics from it, comparing performance against these metrics, and then sharing the conclusions from their analyses. Intermediaries, however, are not present in all markets. Even when they are present, intermediaries may not be very effective when they cannot (a) determine which companies must disclose, (b) collect and search through disclosures, and (c) compare the disclosures of various companies.

Consequently, to maximize the prospect of reputational sanctions, mandatory transparency laws should include the following elements. First, a public list of all companies that are required to disclose; this will allow intermediaries to identify non-compliant companies.[77] Second, government actors should also publicize the disclosure requirements so that intermediaries can similarly identify non-compliance.[78] Third, mandatory disclosure laws should provide legal sanctions for non-compliance with the reporting requirements.[79] All these elements will expand the universe of available information so that intermediaries can remain confident they are "seeing the whole picture." Other measures are designed to improve the comparability of information disclosed so that intermediaries can gauge one company's performance against another to identify "leaders and laggards." For example, mandatory transparency laws should also establish a central database of disclosed statements so the public can compare peer performance (company to company) and prior performance (year to year). Similarly, mandatory disclosure laws should also require a standard reporting format that uses common metrics so that it is easier to compare disclosure statements across companies. Finally, by developing metrics, government actors also help intermediaries and stakeholders identify what they should be looking for in these disclosures and how to assess performance.

---

[75] Corporate Human Rights Benchmark, 2019 KEY FINDINGS 7 (2019).

[76] *Id.*

[77] Business & Human Rights Resource Centre, FTSE 100 & THE UK MODERN SLAVERY ACT: FROM DISCLOSURE TO ACTION 5 (2018).

[78] *Id.*

[79] *Id.*

CONCLUSION

This chapter has explored how both legal and reputational sanctions can fail to punish corporate conduct. Some causes of this failure are common to both types of sanctions. For example, it is difficult to operationalize sanctions when there are challenges with attribution concerning the mechanisms and perpetrators of harm – challenges that are exacerbated by complex entity relationships and global supply chains. Other challenges arise from particular types of sanctions. For example, it may be difficult to impose legal sanctions when corporate misconduct occurs abroad. Given the challenges with each independently, it is sometimes beneficial to combine these two types of sanctions to address some of the weaknesses of each. When reputational sanctions accompany legal sanctions, the former can trigger a second round of monetary penalties that magnify the costs of the misconduct, thereby (hopefully) encouraging companies to alter their conduct for the better going forward. The reverse may also prove true: legal rules can facilitate the operation of reputational markets by increasing information flows regarding corporate conduct, thereby enabling stakeholders to distinguish between company's efforts and punish or reward accordingly.

8

Mind the Agency Gap in Corporate Social Responsibility

Dalia Palombo

INTRODUCTION

In 1953, Howard Bowen defined the economic notion of corporate social responsibility (CSR) as the obligation of businessmen to act in the interest of society. The
Committee for Economic Development went a step further and defined the relationship between business and society as a social contract.[1] The romanticized idea of
the social contract works well to describe the economic rationales that bring society
to first invest in and second attempt to control companies: society empowers companies and, therefore, companies shall act in the interests of society. But, to ensure that
companies act in society's interest, a certain level of societal control over corporate
activities is necessary. Societal control is required in order to attribute responsibility
to corporations for various activities and harms. The problem, which CSR has been
unable to address, is how society should exercise such "control." Most of the debate
has focused on two alternatives: naming and shaming or legal liability.

Some commentators believe CSR is about corporations being "nice" to society and nothing more, while others believe corporations have the responsibility
to respect human rights, and such responsibility should be, or arguably already
is, reflected in the law.[2] A pivotal turn in this debate has been the movement
from the CSR framework to that of "business and human rights." While CSR is
depicted as pure voluntarism, business and human rights attempts to combine

---

[1] HOWARD R. BOWEN, SOCIAL RESPONSIBILITIES OF THE BUSINESSMAN (1953). The Committee
for Economic Development defined the social contract between society and business in
COMMITTEE FOR ECONOMIC DEVELOPMENT OF THE CONFERENCE BOARD (CED), SOCIAL
RESPONSIBILITIES OF BUSINESS CORPORATIONS 16 (1971).

[2] *See, e.g.,* Giovanni Esposito & Anna Carobolante, *Imporre o Invitare? Le Politiche Di Corporate
Social Responsibility Alla Ricerca Di Un'identità Europea*, 8 IANUS-DIRITTO E FINANZA 5 (2013)
https://orbi.uliege.be/bitstream/2268/171809/1/ianus%208_2013.pdf; Sorcha Macleod, *Reconciling
Regulatory Approaches to Corporate Social Responsibility: The European Union, OECD and United
Nations Compared*, 13 EUR. PUB. L. 671 (2007); ANNA BECKERS, ENFORCING CORPORATE SOCIAL
RESPONSIBILITY CODES: ON GLOBAL SELF-REGULATION AND NATIONAL PRIVATE LAW (2015);
ARCHIE B. Carroll, *A History of Corporate Social Responsibility: Concepts and Practice, in* THE
OXFORD HANDBOOK OF CORPORATE SOCIAL RESPONSIBILITY (Andrew Crane, et al., eds., 2009).

corporations' voluntary responsible conduct with states' duties to protect stake-holders against corporate human rights abuses.[3] However, in most cases, states' obligations to ensure that corporations respect human rights are neither imple-mented nor enforceable, generating an accountability gap.[4] The ineffectiveness and inability of current laws to regulate corporate conduct depend, to a great extent, on globalization and privatization, which together have fundamentally altered the relationship between corporations and society. Being "nice" to society has become increasingly difficult for companies now that "society" has expanded to include people living in any country where an enterprise conducts business. A multinational enterprise could be potentially obligated toward an incalculable number of individuals affected by its activities in multiple jurisdictions.[5] At the same time, extensive privatization of the production of commodities that were once provided by states has made the question of the control that society should exercise over corporations acutely pressing. It is increasingly difficult to exercise control over corporations that run large sectors of everyone's life, including the economic, financial, societal and political spheres.[6]

This chapter argues that the terms of the debate over whether CSR should com-prise soft law responsibility or legally binding obligations are inadequate to address the legal relationship between corporations and society. The debate over CSR overlooks the fundamental gap between the *economic* agency problem and *legal* agency, or attribution. The former is the problem of potential divergence of inter-ests between a principal and an agent, and the latter concerns the laws regulating the relationship between a person and his or her representative. CSR is meant to respond to the first of these – the economic agency problem – which scholars have

---

[3] John Gerard Ruggie, *The Construction of the UN "Protect, Respect and Remedy" Framework for Business and Human Rights: The True Confessions of a Principled Pragmatist*, 2 EUR. HUM. RTS. L. REV. 127 (2011); John Gerard Ruggie, *Report of the Special Representative of the Secretary-General on the Issue of Human Rights and Transnational Corporations and Other Business Enterprises*, 29 NETH. Q. HUM. RTS. 224(2011); Susan Ariel Aaronson & Ian Higham, *Re-Righting Business: John Ruggie and the Struggle to Develop International Human Rights Standards for Transnational Firms*, 35 HUM. RTS. Q. 333 (2013); Nicola Jägers, *UN Guiding Principles on Business and Human Rights: Making Headway Towards Real Corporate Accountability*, 29 NETH. Q. HUM. RTS. 159 (2011); Astrid Sanders, *The Impact of the "Ruggie Framework" and the United Nations Guiding Principles on Business and Human Rights on Transnational Human Rights Litigation, in* THE BUSINESS AND HUMAN RIGHTS LANDSCAPE: MOVING FORWARD, LOOKING BACK (Jena Martin and Karen E Bravo, eds., 2015).

[4] Florian Wettstein, *Betting on the Wrong (Trojan) Horse: CSR and the Implementation of the UN Guiding Principles on Business and Human Rights*, 6 BUS. HUM. RTS. J. 312 (2021); Olivier De Schutter, *The Accountability of Multinationals for Human Rights Violations in European Law, in* NON-STATE ACTORS AND HUMAN RIGHTS (Ph. Alston, eds., 2005); NICOLA JÄGERS, CORPORATE HUMAN RIGHTS OBLIGATIONS: IN SEARCH OF ACCOUNTABILITY (2002); GWYNNE SKINNER ET AL., THE THIRD PILLAR: ACCESS TO JUDICIAL REMEDIES FOR HUMAN RIGHTS VIOLATIONS BY TRANSNATIONAL BUSINESS (2013).

[5] PETER MUCHLINSKI, MULTINATIONAL ENTERPRISES AND THE LAW (3rd ed. 2021).

[6] JOHN BRAITHWAITE, REGULATORY CAPITALISM: HOW IT WORKS, IDEAS FOR MAKING IT WORK BETTER (2008).

analyzed at length.[7] However, the legal structures needed to address attribution and accountability are still far from established. We could define our time as the prehistory of corporate social *accountability*. It is the time when we need to develop an attribution framework that can appropriately address the legal agency problem. In other words, we need to couple CSR with corporate social accountability.

Against this background, this chapter investigates the gap between economic and legal agency with respect to two fundamental precedents that will serve as case studies: the formation of states and the incorporation of companies. The conceptual prehistories of both states and corporations – the logics that produced these institutions – have a lot to teach us. They shed light on how to establish a legal framework that could properly address the economic agency problem between society as principal and corporations as agents. In particular, a pivotal element of both states and corporations is their separate legal personality: they are separate persons from their shareholders and citizens. The creation of these separate persons resolved collective action problems and organized the actions of shareholders and citizens.

The chapter considers whether establishing a new legal person could be the appropriate tool to address the collective action problems that stakeholders now face vis-à-vis corporations. It acknowledges that such a proposal entails several normative limitations. Specifically, separate legal personality is a tool that can be used to either empower or oppress. Thus, the chapter suggests focusing not on *how* to build an attribution framework but rather on *who* should build such a framework. The issue here is to define society vis-à-vis multinational enterprises. The term "society" should overcome the traditional dichotomy between the public and private sectors. It should incorporate the complex relationships incurring between a wide variety of stakeholders that are affected by the states and the corporations' activities on a global scale.

RELATIONSHIP BETWEEN ECONOMIC AND LEGAL AGENCY

An agency relationship occurs when a principal owns some assets but s/he has no relevant expertise, time, and ability to manage them. Thus, s/he hires an agent to manage the assets. Agency relationships typically raise two different kinds of problems: economic agency problems and legal agency problems. The following example will illustrate the problems and their differences.

Assume that Sally, the principal, owns an apartment she would like to rent but has no time or expertise to rent it on her own, so she hires a real estate agent, Mary. At a

---

[7] Carroll, *supra* note 2; Archie B. Carroll, *Corporate Social Responsibility: Evolution of a Definitional Construct*, 38 Bus. Soc. 268 (1999); Eric C. Chaffee, *The Origins of Corporate Social Responsibility* 85 Univ. Cin. L. Rev. 347 (2017); Ute Schmiel, *Corporate Social Responsibility: A Fake Already According to the Theory of the Firm?*, 30 Mgmnt. Rev. 154 (2019); Jennifer A Zerk, Multinationals and Corporate Social Responsibility: Limitations and Opportunities in International Law (2006); Reinier Kraakman, et al., The Anatomy of Corporate Law: A Comparative and Functional Approach 29–47 (3rd ed. 2017).

first look, Sally and Mary have the same interest: to rent the apartment. However, at a closer look, their interests diverge on a number of fundamental points. Sally wants to rent the apartment long-term, for a high monthly price, to a reputable lessee who will not damage the property. The real estate agent, Mary, wants to rent the flat as soon as possible to get paid, become successful, and obtain more apartments for rent in the future. She is less interested in the exact monthly price of the apartment, as she will only get paid a commission of a single month of rent, no matter the length of the rental contract. Therefore, a slight rise in price will make no substantial difference to Mary but will be important to Sally, who will benefit from the rent increase for a number of months. Mary instead makes more money if she is able to turn the apartment over, renting on a short-term basis to numerous lessees one after another. Sally wants a reliable lessee who will always pay the rent on time, while Mary is not interested in reliability but rather in renting the apartment as soon as possible to receive her payment. This hypothetical illustrates an economic agency problem, which arises from the divergence of interests between the principal Sally and the agent Mary. The economic agency problem raises the question of incentives: How can Sally ensure that Mary has the appropriate incentives to act in Sally's interest and not in her own?

A separate issue is what legal duties Mary owes Sally and to what extent Mary can represent Sally. For example, can Mary sign a lease agreement on behalf of Sally if she finds an appropriate lessee, or should she just propose the rental to Sally, who will ultimately make the final decision? If Mary finds a lessee who is willing to pay the rent but may be insolvent in a few months, does she have an obligation to communicate such possible insolvency to Sally? Should Mary obtain proof of the lessee's income or employment before proposing a contract to Sally? These various questions are a matter of law. They derive from the underlying economic agency problem because if Sally and Mary's interests were perfectly aligned, the law would have little role to play in regulating the relationship between principal and agent. However, these legal questions are profoundly different from the economic agency questions. These legal questions implicate the responsibility of the agent toward the principal, rather than whether their economic interests are aligned.

The agent's duties and liabilities are the objects of study in several areas of law. For example, the duties Mary owes toward Sally could originate from the contract signed between them, from tort because Mary may have a duty of care toward Sally, or a regulatory code of ethics for real estate agents. These legal agency questions originate from the attribution of the agent's conduct to the principal (such as Mary's ability to sign a rental contract on behalf of Sally) and the related duties that the agent owes to the principal (such as the duty of care).

Therefore, economic and legal agency present two separate issues: the former is a question of incentives, while the latter is a question of attribution and related accountability. Economic agency articulates the problems arising from the divergence of

interests between principal and agent. Legal agency attempts to regulate the relationship between principal and agent by establishing appropriate rights and duties.

CORPORATE SOCIAL RESPONSIBILITY: AN
ECONOMIC AGENCY PROBLEM

At its core, CSR is an attempt to solve an *economic* agency problem. This problem could be defined as facing either society and corporations or shareholders and
stakeholders.

According to the so-called concession, fiction, and real entity enterprise theories,
CSR arises from an agency problem facing society as principal and corporations
as agents. According to these theories, states create companies and grant them a
number of privileges, such as limited liability and reduced taxation, with the understanding that companies exercise the fundamental function of providing goods and
services to society in the most efficient way.[8] The competition between various companies ensures that the quality of services and goods is the highest available on
the market. A monopolized state market would lower the quality of products and
services because of the lack of competition between various enterprises. One could
think about the extreme example of communist regimes, such as the Soviet Union,
where production was centralized at the state level, and private economic activities
were, to a larger extent, nonexistent. Since the collapse of the Soviet Union, privatization has increased all around the world, and the private sector is now producing
and providing the great majority of goods and services to society. In contrast, the
role of states in the production of goods and as a service provider has decreased.
However, the more society allows corporations to take control of production, the less
it can control such a process. The risk is to have corporations that act solely in their
self-interest and not in the interest of society. Some scholars have even argued that,
in recent years, corporations have increasingly exercised regulatory powers instead
of states.[9] Against this background, CSR is the responsibility that the agent, the
corporation, owes to the principal, society: with greater control of production comes
greater responsibility.

There are alternative views that justify the origins of corporations outside of the
state rather than as concessions or creations of the state. The most accepted of such
theories is the nexus of contracts or aggregate thesis. According to this theory, a corporation combines several contractual relationships between its various members or
shareholders. The aggregate theory does not consider CSR to be the responsibility
that corporations have toward society because companies owe nothing to society but

---

[8] Luh Lan & Loizos Heracleous, *Rethinking Agency Theory: The View from Law*, 35 ACAD. MGMNT.
REV. 294(2010); Michael J. Phillips, *Reappraising the Real Entity Theory of the Corporation*, 21 FLA.
ST. UNIV. L. REV. 1061 (1994); Bowen, *supra* note 1; Committee for Economic Development, *supra*
note 1.

[9] Braithwaite, *supra* note 6.

rather owe duties to their members. In this sense, CSR could be perceived as a form of charity rather than responsibility.[10] However, suppose one understands the nexus of contracts in broader terms as the multiple relationships between shareholders, directors, and stakeholders (including suppliers, consumers, creditors, and employees). In that case, one could interpret CSR as part of the agency problem between some of these actors – that is, between the stakeholders and the shareholders, while directors assume a balancing role between these multiple interests.[11]

To sum up, CSR is a question of incentives, which one can articulate in different terms. Either "how can society delegate the production of goods and services to corporations while at the same time ensuring a certain level of control over their activities?" or, alternatively, "how can society incentivize corporations to strike a fair balance between the multiple interests of various constituencies (including both shareholders and stakeholders)?" These questions both relate to the economic agency problem.

THE LACK OF A CORPORATE ACCOUNTABILITY FRAMEWORK

While CSR addresses the economic agency problem of incentives, there is no *legal* framework that regulates the relationship between society and corporations. As a result, the role that lawyers should play in the CSR debate is uncertain. Typically, legal scholars and practitioners specializing in CSR fall into two main camps: those who believe CSR is an economic doctrine that could be used to convince corporations to positively impact society as this would be in their long-term interest (CSR without the law);[12] and those who are attempting to use the existing fragmented legal framework to hold companies to account (accountability through current laws, including the business and human rights framework).[13] Each of these approaches

---

[10] Schmiel, *supra* note 7; Carroll, *supra* note 2; Chaffee, *supra* note 7.

[11] Kraakman et al., *supra* note 7, at 29–47, 110–119; Lawrence Ponoroff, *Enlarging the Bargaining Table: Some Implications of the Corporate Stakeholder Model for Federal Bankruptcy Proceedings*, 23 Cap. Univ. L. Rev. 441, 465–74 (1994); Alan Schwartz, *The Default Rule Paradigm and the Limits of Contract Law*, 3 S. Cal. Interdisc. L. J. 389, 411–13 (1993); Phillips, *supra* note 8.

[12] Esposito & Carobolante, *supra* note 2; Leyla Davarnejad, *In the Shadow of Soft Law: The Handling of Corporate Social Responsibility Disputes under the OECD Guidelines for Multinational Enterprises*, 2011 J. Disp. Resol. 351 (2011); Ashley L. Santner, *A Soft Law Mechanism for Corporate Responsibility: How the Updated OECD Guidelines for Multinational Enterprises Promote Business for the Future*, 43 Geo. Wash. Int'l L. Rev. 375 (2011); Macleod, *supra* note 2; Ruggie, *supra* note 3; Aaronson & Higham, *supra* note 3; U.N. OHCHR, Human Rights Council, Promotion and Protection of All Human Rights, Civil, Political, Economics, Social and Cultural Rights, Including the Right to Development, Protect, Respect and Remedy: A Framework for Business and Human Rights (2008) A/HRC/8/5.

[13] Liesbeth Enneking, Foreign Direct Liability and Beyond: Exploring the Role of Tort Law in Promoting International Corporate Social Responsibility and Accountability (2012); Susan Farbstein et al., *The Alien Tort Statute and Corporate Liability*, 160 U. Pa. L. Rev. 99 (2011); Richard Meeran, *Tort Litigation against Multinational Corporations for Violation of Human Rights: An Overview of the Position outside the United States*, 3 City U. H. K.

includes numerous currents that are beyond the scope of this chapter. However, I briefly summarize below the problems that each approach entails.

Corporate Social Responsibility without the Law

The main problem with the CSR approach is its failure to recognize that without laws imposing appropriate duties on corporations, only a limited number of companies will voluntarily act for the benefit of society when that societal benefit brings corporate costs (e.g., internalizing externalities).[14] This is not because companies are evil entities, but because the cost and benefit analysis rarely points to CSR. This is particularly true in a globalized world because the social norms that could encourage companies to act in the interest of stakeholders in far-flung locations are increasingly attenuated. As a result, stakeholders detrimentally affected by industrial activities have lost power vis-à-vis corporations.

For example, workers, who have traditionally been the most involved stakeholders in the industrial process, have lost the ability to organize their actions in an increasingly globalized labor market. First, the delocalization of enterprises that were traditionally large-scale industries based in one country has made the organization of labor movements and collective bargaining difficult. Trade unions, typically supported by left-wing parties in their home countries, no longer have a unified political home. Second, the flexibility of work has resulted in an increasing number of non-traditional short-term contracts. This has created a generational division between young workers, who are willing to accept worse working conditions to obtain a job, and senior workers with secure, standard employment contracts. It is objectively difficult for short-term workers to get actively engaged in trade unions given that their contract will cease. At the same time, the fewer the young workers that become involved in collective action, the more trade unions will focus on preserving the interests of their senior members with long-term traditional contracts. Third, the competition that both states and companies face to attract investments has worsened working conditions. Multinational enterprises have been able to engage in social dumping, moving to cheaper jurisdictions when their home countries impose demanding environmental or labor laws. At the same time, companies that guarantee good working conditions are often not competitive in the global market because they have to compete with low prices offered by others in the industry.

L. Rev. 1 (2011); Beckers, *supra* note 2; Philipp Wesche & Miriam Saage-Maaß, *Holding Companies Liable for Human Rights Abuses Related to Foreign Subsidiaries and Suppliers before German Civil Courts: Lessons from Jabir and Others v. KiK*, 16 Hum. Rhts. L. Rev. 370 (2016).

[14] Milton Friedman, *The Social Responsibility of Business Is to Increase Its Profits*, in Corporate Ethics and Corporate Governance (Walther Ch Zimmerli et al., eds 2007); Florian Wettstein, *Normativity, Ethics, and the UN Guiding Principles on Business and Human Rights: A Critical Assessment*, 14 J. Hum. Rts. 162 (2015); Magda B. L. Donia et al., *The Theorized Relationship between Organizational (Non)Compliance with the United Nations Guiding Principles on Human Rights and Desired Employee Workplace Outcomes*, 12 Sustainability 2130 (2020).

Both states and companies willing to provide good conditions of work risk being considered too costly on the global market.[15]

Given the difficulties confronting trade unions and other traditional labor organizations, stakeholders have increasingly attempted to interact with companies through alternative means, such as multi-stakeholder initiatives.[16] The objectives of such fora are various: they include the settlement of disputes between enterprises and people detrimentally affected by them, as well as establishing rules that regulate future industrial relations between companies and various stakeholders. While multi-stakeholder initiatives could seem appealing because they theoretically allow people to frame their relationships with industries as they see fit, these instruments have been assessed as highly ineffective.[17] For instance, a study points out the asymmetries between the resources of corporations and other participants in these multi-stakeholder initiatives; the failure of these initiatives to appropriately represent the interests of their various right holders; the lack of appropriate legal, monitoring, and remedial frameworks ensuring that companies respect human rights; and the inability of multi-stakeholder initiatives to move beyond corporate voluntarism, with the ultimate result of furthering the interests of business instead of people.[18]

In sum, the race to the bottom seems relentless without an appropriate accountability framework that not only encourages but also requires companies to act responsibly.

Corporate Accountability with Current Laws: Business and Human Rights

The shift from CSR to the business and human rights rhetoric has not addressed the accountability gap described above. While the Human Rights Council has adopted

[15] REBECCA GUMBRELL-MCCORMICK & RICHARD HYMAN, TRADE UNIONS IN WESTERN EUROPE: HARD TIMES, HARD CHOICES (2013); Pedro Mendonça & Dragoș Adăscăliței, *Trade Union Power Resources within the Supply Chain: Marketisation, Marginalisation, Mobilisation*, 34 WORK EMP. SOC. 1062 (2020); John Addison, *The Consequences of Trade Union Power Erosion*, 68 IZA WORLD LAB. 1(2014); Jörg Flecker et al., *Divide and Serve: The Labour Process in Service Value Chains and Networks*, 17 COMPET. CHANGE 6 (2013); Pamela K. Robinson & Helen Rainbird, *International Supply Chains and the Labour Process*, 17 COMPET. CHANGE 91 (2013).

[16] After the collapse of the Rana Plaza Building in Bangladesh, multi-stakeholder initiatives were put in place to avoid further tragedies and ameliorate workers conditions. These stakeholder consultations brought the Accord for Fire and Building Safety and the Alliance for Bangladesh Workers' Safety. Naila Kabeer et al., *Paradigm Shift or Business as Usual? Workers' Views on Multi-Stakeholder Initiatives in Bangladesh*, 51 DEV. CHANGE 1360 (2020).

[17] *What Are MSIs?*, MSI Integrity, www.msi-integrity.org/what-are-msis/ (last visited Mar. 14, 2023); INTERNATIONAL COMMISSION OF JURISTS, EFFECTIVE OPERATIONAL-LEVEL GRIEVANCE MECHANISMS, www.icj.org/wp-content/uploads/2019/11/universal-grievance-mechanisms-publications-reports-thematic-reports-2019-eng.pdf.

[18] MSI Integrity, *Not Fit-for-Purpose: The Grand Experiment of Multi-Stakeholder Initiatives in Corporate Accountability*, in CORPORATE ACCOUNTABILITY HUMAN RIGHTS AND GLOBAL GOVERNANCE (2020), www.msi-integrity.org/not-fit-for-purpose/ (last visited Apr. 2, 2021).

the United Nations Guiding Principles on Business and Human Rights (UNGPs), which enshrine corporate responsibility to respect human rights alongside states' duty to protect human rights from abuses committed by businesses, the UNGPs have not modified in any way the laws applicable to either enterprises or states.[19]

However, attempting to hold multinationals to account with current laws is problematic. International human rights law is not directly applicable to corporations but only to states, although it establishes internationally recognized standards that could potentially be implemented worldwide.[20] Domestic law applies to companies, but it has a limited territorial reach. Therefore, it is not always applicable to companies incorporated in foreign countries, even when those companies belong to a multinational enterprise with domestic headquarters.[21] There is an additional hurdle: the combination of limited liability and separate legal personality allows companies to incorporate, undercapitalize, and own subsidiaries while not being responsible for their conduct. This essentially means that if a subsidiary detrimentally affects a person or a community, it will be liable only to the extent of the assets it owns, which are limited by the will of the parent company.[22]

Against this background, creating a legal framework of liability implies combining international human rights with CSR to establish a possible standard of conduct for businesses and connect such a standard with causes of action in domestic law. This operation is complex, and its success depends on a number of technicalities pertaining to the various legal systems of the jurisdictions where companies are incorporated. The result is a fragmented system of liability where companies can be held to account sporadically only in countries with receptive domestic systems able to adapt their causes of action to new challenges, such as business and human rights. Only a limited number of cases make it past the jurisdictional stage, and it is extremely rare to obtain a decision on the merits. In addition, there are difficulties in terms of cost, enforcement, and timing of complex cross-border litigation.[23]

For instance, in the United States, the Alien Tort Statute (ATS) litigation against multinationals was often unsuccessful. Human rights litigators proposed to use the ATS, a jurisdictional statute from 1789, as a tool to hold multinational enterprises to account for transnational violations of the Law of Nations (i.e., some customary

---

[19] See UNGPs, General Principles, which specify: "Nothing in these Guiding Principles should be read as creating new international law obligations, or as limiting or undermining any legal obligations a State may have undertaken or be subject to under international law with regard to human rights." Wettstein, *supra* note 4.

[20] Markos Karavias, Corporate Obligations under International Law (2013).

[21] Enneking, *supra* note 13.

[22] Phillip I. Blumberg, *Limited Liability and Corporate Groups*, 11 J. Corp. L. 573 (1985); David W. Leebron, *Limited Liability, Tort Victims, and Creditors*, 91 Colum. L. Rev. 1565 (1991); Gwynne Skinner, *Rethinking Limited Liability of Parent Corporations for Foreign Subsidiaries' Violations of International Human Rights Law*, 72 Wash. Lee L. Rev. 1769 (2015).

[23] Gwynne Skinner et al., *supra* note 4; Dalia Palombo, Business and Human Rights: The Obligations of the European Home States (2020).

international law rules). However, the U.S. Supreme Court rejected the jurisdiction of U.S. courts over a number of these cases.[24] In the UK, litigators have filed cases against UK holding companies liable for extraterritorial torts committed by their foreign subsidiaries. These cases have been increasingly successful on jurisdictional grounds, and recently, the UK Supreme Court ruled that the UK courts, in principle, have jurisdiction over such extraterritorial cases. However, it is yet to be seen how courts will rule on the merits of such claims.[25] In the Netherlands, victims from Nigeria won a transnational case against Shell. This is a rare business and human rights case decided on the merits in the victims' favor.[26]

In developing countries, it has also been difficult to hold multinational enterprises to account for human rights abuses. For example, in Bangladesh, the Rana Plaza Building, where thousands of workers were manufacturing clothes for multinationals, was unsafe and collapsed, killing more than a thousand people. Victims filed a number of complaints in Canadian and U.S. courts that were barred, under the applicable Bangladeshi law, by an extremely low statute of limitation (one year). Parallel criminal proceedings are still ongoing in Bangladesh.[27]

As much as these litigation efforts are commendable from the standpoint of vindicating human rights claims, it is clear that a patchwork of CSR, international human rights standards, and domestic laws cannot establish an appropriate legal framework of accountability and attribution for corporate harms in the context of globalized business. The current legal framework looks more like a Swiss cheese full of legal holes than a robust architecture to couple legal accountability with the economic doctrine of CSR. Moreover, some scholars have raised an additional problem: even if one could imagine lifting these barriers to justice, only a limited number of people detrimentally affected by multinationals will be able to bear the time and cost of transnational litigation. However, the structural inequalities between people and companies would persist.[28]

---

[24] *Kiobel v. Royal Dutch Petroleum Co.*, 569 U.S. 108 (2013); *Jesner v. Arab Bank, P.L.C.*, 138 S. Ct. 1386 (2018); Giannini et al., *supra* note 13; Ross J. Corbett, *Kiobel, Bauman, and the Presumption against the Extraterritorial Application of the Alien Tort Statute*, 13 Nw. J. Int'l Hum. Rts. 50 (2015).

[25] *Okpabi v. Royal Dutch Shell Plc* [2021] UKSC 3; *Vedanta Resources PLC v. Lungowe* [2019] UKSC 20 (appeal taken from Eng.); Suzanne Chiodo, *UK Supreme Court Rules That English Companies Can Be Sued for Actions of Foreign Subsidiaries in the Interests of "Substantial Justice:" Vedanta Resources v Lungowe* [2019] UKSC 20, 38 Civ. Just. Q. 300 (2019); James Goudkamp, *Duties of Care and Corporate Groups*, 133 L. Q. Rev. 560 (2017).

[26] Lucas Roorda, *Wading through the (Polluted) Mud: The Hague Court of Appeals Rules on Shell in Nigeria*, Rights as Usual (Feb. 2, 2021), https://rightsasusual.com/?p=1388.

[27] *Das v. George Weston Limited*, 2017 ONSC 4129 (Can.); *Rahaman v. J.C. Penney Corp.*, No. N15C-07-174MMJ, 2016 WL 2616375 (Del. Super. Ct. May 4, 2016); Dutia Raam & Erol Abdurrahman, *Background Paper – Rana Plaza: Legal and Regulatory Responses*, Doing Business Right Blog, Asser Institute (Apr. 11, 2018), www.asser.nl/DoingBusinessRight/Blog/post/background-paper-rana-plaza-legal-and-regulatory-responses-by-raam-dutia-and-abdurrahman-erol.

[28] Grietje Baars, *"It's Not Me, It's the Corporation": The Value of Corporate Accountability in the Global Political Economy*, 4 London Rev. Int'l L. 127 (2016); Grietje Baars, The Corporation, Law and Capitalism: A Radical Perspective on the Role of Law in the Global Political Economy (2019).

BASES FOR A NEW LEGAL FRAMEWORK

We are currently living in the prehistory of corporate social accountability. At the moment, scholars have correctly identified and analyzed the economic agency problem between society and corporations but are still struggling to figure out how to establish a framework of accountability. This generates a number of difficult situations where people detrimentally affected by corporations are left without a remedy, and corporations lack legal certainty as to whether their conduct could be considered legal.

Given the complexity of the economic agency problem-facing, on the one hand, a group of various stakeholders (such as employees, indigenous communities, people affected by environmental degradation, and consumers) and, a variety of corporations (including both small businesses and multinational enterprises with income comparable to the GDPs of states) on the other, it is increasingly obvious that, in order to have a meaningful impact on the behavior of corporations, stakeholders would have to organize their actions collectively. An open question is how to address such a pivotal collective action problem. This chapter investigates how to organize the collective action of stakeholders based on two conceptual precedents that will serve as case studies: the incorporation of companies and the formation of states. In both cases, an economic agency problem – between shareholders and directors, and between people and the government – has been addressed by establishing a legal agency framework constructed around a separate legal person: the corporation and the state.

The Corporation

Corporate scholars have theorized three economic agency problems: the first agency problem, between shareholders as principals and directors as agents; the second between minority shareholders as principals and majority shareholders as agents; and the third, which is the CSR agency problem described above, between stakeholders and corporations.[29] In corporate law, there is a legal framework specifically addressing the questions of attribution and responsibility arising from the first and second agency problems. As explained above, no legal framework addresses the third agency problem of CSR that is traditionally studied only from the economic perspective, and not the legal one. Understanding the connections between the first and second economic agency problems, and the respective legal frameworks that regulate the relationship between directors and shareholders and majority and minority shareholders, is fundamental to creating a legal framework regulating the relationship between corporations and society. For the purpose of this chapter, I will focus solely on the first agency problem (between shareholders as principals

---

[29] Kraakman et al., *supra* note 7, at 29–47.

and directors as agents), but an analogous analysis could also be conducted on the second agency problem.

Economic Agency Problem

The first agency problem arises when a corporation's stock is widely held, with no shareholder able to control the company. In this scenario, shareholders are typically rationally apathetic, meaning they do not actively engage in the company's life but are just interested in making profits. Directors are the only ones in charge of the company and able to understand its real value, profitability, and future perspectives. This puts directors in a position of power because they have the relevant information and expertise to manage the company, while shareholders tend to be disinterested in the life of the company as long as they make reasonable profits. Therefore, the interests of shareholders and directors diverge: shareholders are typically interested in the short-term profitability of the company, while directors' interests are more diversified. They range from the long-term interest of the company to the use of their position to gain personal advantages (such as determining their own salary, self-dealing, or taking business opportunities that would otherwise belong to the company).[30]

Various jurisdictions address this economic agency problem in different ways. For example, the United Kingdom is known to be a jurisdiction emphasizing shareholder primacy: Company law rules tend to give extensive power to the shareholders in order for them to be able to control the board that would otherwise become too powerful.[31] By contrast, Delaware, one of the most prominent U.S. jurisdictions as it pertains to corporate law, takes the opposite approach: it empowers directors while limiting the rights of shareholders. The rationale of this division of powers is that directors are able to understand the value of the company and its long-term profitability. Therefore, they should rightly have more power than shareholders in order to make the right decisions on behalf of the company.[32]

Legal Agency Problem

No matter the approach, the law of various jurisdictions always uses a legal fiction, the company, to balance the rights and duties of shareholders and directors. The shareholders have rights over the company, while the directors owe duties of loyalty and care to the company. The directors are the company's legal agents,

---

[30] DAVID KERSHAW, COMPANY LAW IN CONTEXT: TEXT AND MATERIALS 171–588 (2nd ed. 2012); PAUL L. DAVIES, GOWER AND DAVIES' PRINCIPLES OF MODERN COMPANY LAW 365–646 (8th ed. 2008).
[31] *Id.*
[32] Del. Code Ann. tit. 8, § 141 (West, Westlaw through ch. 5 of the 152nd General Assembly 2023–2024); Thomas C Lee, *Limiting Corporate Directors' Liability: Delaware's Section 102(b)(7) and the Erosion of the Directors' Duty of Care*, 136 UNIV. PENN. L. REV. 239 (1987); Kershaw, *supra* note 30, at 171–588.

and the actions of the board are attributable to the company.[33] Furthermore, in both the United Kingdom and the United States, any shareholder has a right to sue the directors for breach of duties on behalf of and for the benefit of the company.[34]

Therefore, the subjects of the agency relationship are different in the economic and legal agency problems. The economic agency problem faces shareholders (principals) and directors (agents), while in legal terms, the company is the principal and the board of directors is the agent. A fundamental question often overlooked in this regard is why a conflict between shareholders and directors is addressed by creating rights and duties directors bear toward the company, a fictional entity.[35] The probable answer is that the use of a fictional entity addresses a collective action problem. In other words, it ensures a balance between opposing interests.[36] For instance, if directors owed duties directly toward each individual shareholder, a number of difficult questions would arise: How to define this group of people? Who would act on behalf of the shareholders? Who would determine their interests? The shareholders of a company may include a variety of persons, ranging from an investment bank to a pensioner during his first experience as a shareholder. When the legislator thinks about the duties of a director, should it frame them around the pensioner or the investment analyst? It would be difficult to accommodate the variety of interests that shareholders may have. The reference to the company, instead, addresses all of these problems. The company, a legal fiction, is the only entity that all shareholders have in common. The legislator assumes that if a person buys a share, s/he would be interested in the success of the company. Therefore, directors owe their duties to the company, and they must aim at its success.

The State

Although the date of birth of states is contested, a fundamental international recognition of their existence was the Peace of Westphalia, where European nations signed several treaties recognizing each other's sovereignties in 1648. It would take

---

[33] Note that although the directors are the company's agent, the origins of the duties of directors are the subject of debate. Agency is only one of the possible foundations of directors' duties. DAVID KERSHAW, THE FOUNDATIONS OF ANGLO-AMERICAN CORPORATE FIDUCIARY LAW (2018). For the relation between agency and attribution, *see* Susan Watson, *How the Company Became an Entity: A New Understanding of Corporate Law*, 120 J. BUS. L. (2015); Sarah Worthington, *Corporate Attribution and Agency: Back to Basics*, 133 L. Q. REV. 118 (2017).

[34] Andrew Keay, *Assessing and Rethinking the Statutory Scheme for Derivative Actions under the Companies Act 2006*, 16 J. CORP. L. STUD. 39 (2016); Arad Reisberg, *"Shareholders" Remedies: The Choice of Objectives and the Social Meaning of Derivative Actions*, 6 EUR. BUS. ORG. L. REV. 227 (2005); Kershaw, *supra* note 30, at 589–645.

[35] Some scholars pointed out at the discrepancy between the subjects of the economic and legal agency problems and proposed alternative agency theories, *see* Lan & Heracleous, *supra* note 8; Watson, *supra* note 33.

[36] KIRK LUDWIG, FROM PLURAL TO INSTITUTIONAL AGENCY (2017).

more than three hundred years to also recognize the sovereignty of states outside of Europe that were previously part of colonial empires. Westphalia is also often considered a fundamental moment in the early life of states because it coincides with the publications of Hobbes and Grotius, who theorized the foundations of states.[37] Hobbes expressed the necessity to establish states through the concept of a social contract. In a state of nature, people have unlimited power toward each other, which inevitably brings conflict. Therefore, people, being rational human beings, understand that the only way to ensure peace and stability in their lives is to agree on a social contract: people renounce some of their powers to gain some rights toward each other. The road to ensure that the social contract works is to delegate the power of the people to a sovereign government that establishes the appropriate rules of conduct everyone in the state shall abide by. Therefore, the power of the government originates from the social contract people accept, but once such a contract is finalized, the government becomes the authority that is able to establish laws and sanction those who do not comply with them.[38]

The Economic Agency Problem

Hobbes' theory describes and solves an economic agency problem. People, the principals, want to organize their lives peacefully. Therefore, they give up part of their powers and freedoms to empower a government, the agent, which becomes the sovereign. Every state is based on a social contract and has to face the economic agency problem: how can people incentivize government officials to act in their interest? One of the main incentives in liberal democracies is the competition between various political parties in elections. Despite this common approach, the constitutional rules that determine how the people elect their government officials are various.[39] For instance, the United States and France are presidential democracies, where people elect a president representing the state and separately a congress or parliament.[40] By contrast, numerous European countries, such as the United Kingdom, Italy, Spain, and Germany, are parliamentary democracies where people elect the members of parliament, who then vote for a prime minister or chancellor.[41] These various constitutional systems establish different ways to incentivize the government to act in the people's interest. The idea behind these incentives comes from Locke and Rousseau's conceptions of the social contract, according to which

---

[37] Gerry Simpson, *International Law in Diplomatic History*, in THE CAMBRIDGE COMPANION TO INTERNATIONAL LAW (2012); Catherine M. Brölmann & Janne Elisabeth Nijman, *Legal Personality as a Fundamental Concept for International Law*, in CONCEPTS FOR INTERNATIONAL LAW: CONTRIBUTIONS TO DISCIPLINARY THOUGHT (J. D'Aspremont & S. Singh eds., 2017); ROLAND PORTMANN, LEGAL PERSONALITY IN INTERNATIONAL LAW (2010).

[38] THOMAS HOBBES, LEVIATHAN (1651).

[39] TOM GINSBURG & ROSALIND DIXON, COMPARATIVE CONSTITUTIONAL LAW (2011).

[40] U.S. CONST. art. II CONST. DE LA RÉPUBLIQUE FRANÇAISE, Titre 2 (1958).

[41] Ginsburg & Dixon, *supra* note 39.

the constitutional laws established by a state limit the power of government.[42] Other states adopt a different approach. For instance, the Chinese Constitution recognizes that the power of the government rests in the people of China, who delegate that power to the National People's Congress. China adopts the so-called democratic centralism, according to which the communist party rules the country through its congress.[43] Essentially, in that system, people have limited control over the government's actions, and this is believed to improve efficiency and stability.

The Legal Agency Problem

Despite the different domestic mechanisms adopted to address the economic agency problem (i.e., incentivize the government to act in the people's interest), China, the United States, and all European countries are, under international law, equally sovereign over their territories and people. The common ground is that people have agreed to establish a separate fictional entity – the state – to govern their lives.[44] Vattel theorized the concept of the state as a subject with its own will. He agreed with Hobbes and Grotius that the foundation of states is the social contract, but he went further in establishing the state as a separate legal person and source of authority independent from the people signing the social contract.[45] Therefore, in terms of legal agency, the state is the principal and the government its agent. The government represents the state vis-à-vis its people in the national and international arena. Establishing the state as a separate legal entity avoids direct relationships between people and government officials. No individual, not even in well-functioning democracies, has a direct legal relationship with its government officials. People may file complaints against the state when the government breaches their rights, but they cannot hold the prime minister to account if s/he does not fulfill the promises s/he made during his or her political campaign. The state is the only entity that is able to hold the government to account. Examples of such proceedings are, for instance, impeachment in the United States allowing Congress to impeach the President[46] or the motion of no confidence that the UK Parliament can express against a government.[47]

Therefore, also as it pertains to states, the subjects of the agency relationship are different in the economic and the legal problem. The economic agency problem faces people as principals and the government as agents, while, legally, the state is the principal and the government the agent. One could ask why the people, who are

---

[42] Samantha Besson, '*Sovereignty*' MAX PLANCK ENCYCLOPEDIA OF PUBLIC INTERNATIONAL LAW (2011).

[43] XIANFA ARTS. 1, 2, 3 (1982) (China).

[44] CATHERINE BRÖLMANN, THE INSTITUTIONAL VEIL IN PUBLIC INTERNATIONAL LAW: INTERNATIONAL ORGANISATIONS AND THE LAW OF TREATIES 35–9 (2007); Besson, *supra* note 42; Ludwig, *supra* note 36.

[45] Portmann, *supra* note 37, at 35–41.

[46] U.S. CONST. art. 1 § 2-3, art. 2 § 4.

[47] Fixed-term Parliaments Act 2011, c. 14 § 2 (UK).

party to the social contract, do not have a direct legal relationship with their government and are not able to file complaints against government officials. The answer to this question is that the function of a government is to mediate between opposing interests in order to run a state and, therefore, it cannot be taken hostage by individual complaints.[48] However, when a government acts in a way that is contrary to the social contract signed with its people, constitutional law establishes a number of procedures to ensure that other state institutions can hold the government to account. In essence, this distance between the people and their government ensures the functioning of the state.

The Collective Action Problem

In both companies and states, the gap between economic and legal agency is filled by a fictional entity. Once the separate legal person is established, attribution is only one aspect of a complex set of legal issues gravitating around legal personality. The question of attribution boils down to the terms under which the agent (the director or government official) represents the principal (the company or state) and to what extent the conduct of such director or government official is imputable to the company or state.[49] A different set of questions concern the economic agency relation, such as the incentives for government officials or directors to care about the people's or shareholders' interests. The economic agency problems may be between shareholders and directors in corporations and between people and government officials in states. Nevertheless, the legal agency is only established between the company and its directors in corporate law and the state and its government in constitutional law. In other words, the subjects of the agency relationship change between the two kinds of agency, economic and legal. Why is this the case?

It shall be recalled that the institution of a separate legal person is not always necessary to establish the agent's legal duties and liabilities toward the principal. Getting back to the initial example of the relationship between Sally and Mary, the subjects of the economic and legal agency relationship are always the same: the apartment owner and the real estate agent. This could be defined as a simple relationship where Sally wants to incentivize Mary to act in her interest (economic agency), and the law establishes the legal duties that Mary owes to Sally (legal agency).

However, the situation changes when the economic agency problem faces two groups of people, rather than individuals, such as shareholders and directors or people and government officials. In that case, the economic agency relationship encompasses a collective action problem. The citizens of a state and shareholders

---

[48] On the contrary, in many states, government officials enjoy immunity from various lawsuits to ensure that their capacity to govern is not curtailed. *See, e.g.,* Const. de la République Française arts. 67, 68 (1958).

[49] Brölmann & Nijman, *supra* note 37.

of a company may have divergent, and even opposite, personal interests and beliefs. Likewise, government representatives or directors may also be people with diverse sensitivities, interests, and approaches to governance. In addition to such a variety of personal interests, there is also the interest of the group itself. Such an interest may be different, and sometimes opposite, to some citizens' or shareholders' personal interests. In this context, establishing a separate legal person (the state or the company) focuses these various divergent interests on a specific purpose: the smooth functioning of the state or the success of the company.[50]

Is the establishment of a separate legal person the only way to address a collective action problem? It is not. For instance, an enterprise does not necessarily need to become a company in order to address the collective action problem of its members; it could be organized as a partnership, in which actions are imputable to the partners. As already mentioned, companies could be considered as nexuses of contracts, meaning that all a corporation does could be established via contractual relationships between its various members, directors, management, and labor.[51] At the same time, the relationship between government and people existed way before states were established as legal persons. In Europe alone, one could refer in different centuries to the Greek poleis, the Roman Res Publica, the Catholic Church, or the Holy Roman Empire competing to regulate the lives of people in the middle age. Outside of Europe, the Global South was divided into empires until the second part of the twentieth century. Yet, in these earlier eras, emperors, princes, dukes, governments, and churches regulated the lives of people, including their rights and obligations, without the need to establish a separate legal person.[52]

Why was it necessary to create states and corporations as separate legal persons with their rights and obligations? For the purpose of this chapter, I will point to two opposing rationales in order to provide a sense of the academic debate around the creation of state and corporate institutions.

First, the institution of a separate legal person could serve to empower people so that they can act collectively in an effective way. One could indeed regulate the relationship between business partners, managers, and workers via a nexus of contracts, but it is more efficient to establish a separate legal person. Efficiency is an empowering tool for businesses because it allows them to fulfil their purposes in a profitable way. The corporation is a useful tool to facilitate business; to allow, through limited liability, people who may be able to invest a small sum of money to become shareholders without risking a loss of their personal assets; and to ensure that a business can pass on to the next generation without the complications related to wills and estates. The corporate form (and specifically the protection of limited

---

[50] Ludwig, *supra* note 36.

[51] *Id.* 213-40; Phillips, *supra* note 8.

[52] Portmann, *supra* note 37; Minda Holm & Ole Jacob Sending, *States before Relations: On Misrecognition and the Bifurcated Regime of Sovereignty*, 44 REV. INT'L STUD. 829 (2018).

liability) enables an unlimited number of shareholders to invest in a business, furthering innovation and creativity and, ultimately, boosting the economy.[53] The creation of states may also be analyzed as an emancipatory tool. It is true that people give up part of their freedoms to establish a state. However, in return, the state would guarantee peace and security while granting people a number of rights.[54] This state of peace empowers people to pursue their personal and societal goals instead of fighting each other for survival; at the same time, a well-functioning state allows people to act collectively to ensure proper representation of their interests at both the political and societal levels.

Second, an alternative view portrays states and corporations as tools of domination aimed at oppressing the weakest parties engaging in the collective action process.[55] The first corporations were chartered companies established by imperial nations, such as the United Kingdom, to administer their commercial interests in the colonies. They exercised both imperium, that is, public authority over the population, and dominium, that is, private ownership and control of their assets. Thus, they could be considered primary examples of tools of domination.[56] Even outside of the colonies, in the United States, corporations were chartered and established as an extension of the power of the state in the commercial field.[57] Furthermore, as some argue, even non-chartered companies have been used as tools of domination to further the interest of the bourgeois entrepreneurial class in controlling the labor market.[58] As it pertains to states, the institutions guaranteeing democratic participation of every citizen appear as a step forward in comparison with the absolute tyranny of a monarch, but they are, in fact, established to exercise power over people. The institution of the state entails its monopoly on violence, restricting the possibility for people to change the status quo.[59] It limits the political aspirations of oppressed classes to a number of rights that can be exercised within the institutional system of the state. This mechanism ensures that the impact of the people's collective action is tempered by institutional rules that determine how these people may act. In addition,

---

[53] Max Gillman & Tim Eade, *The Development of the Corporation in England, with Emphasis on Limited Liability*, 22 INT'L J. SOC. ECON. 20 (1995); Kershaw, *supra* note 30, at 5–29.

[54] JOHN LOCKE, ET AL., SOCIAL CONTRACT: ESSAYS BY LOCKE, HUME, AND ROUSSEAU (1960); Adrian Merfu, *Rousseau's General Will and the Notion of Collective Action*, in MODERN DILEMMAS: UNDERSTANDING COLLECTIVE ACTION IN THE TWENTY-FIRST CENTURY (2015).

[55] Claus Offe & Helmut Wiesenthal, *Two Logics of Collective Action: Theoretical Notes on Social Class and Organizational Form*, 1 POL. POWER & SO. THEORY 67 (1980).

[56] Erika George, *Incorporating Rights: Empire, Global Enterprise, and Global Justice*, 10 UNIV. ST. THOMAS L. J. 917 (2013); Martti Koskenniemi, *Sovereignty, Property and Empire: Early Modern English Contexts*, 18 THEORETICAL INQUIRIES L. 355 (2017); DOREEN LUSTIG, VEILED POWER: INTERNATIONAL LAW AND THE PRIVATE CORPORATION 1886–1981 (2020).

[57] Kershaw, *supra* note 33, at 285–308.

[58] Offe & Wiesenthal, *supra* note 55.

[59] Andreas Anter, *The Modern State and Its Monopoly on Violence*, in THE OXFORD HANDBOOK OF MAX WEBER (E. Hanke & others eds. 2019); ANTHONY GIDDENS, THE NATION-STATE AND VIOLENCE (1987).

such institutions function on the basis of sophisticated knowledge, such as law or economics, which the oppressed are often unable to access. As a result, the state and corporate machineries may be considered as instruments of oppression that allow the ruling class to maintain power and limit or even stop the collective actions of weaker classes.[60]

From these opposing views, it is clear that the effect of separate legal personality is neither unambiguously positive nor negative. The legal concept is a tool that can be used to address collective action problems in an effective way or to oppress the weakest members of society in order to limit their collective action. The likelihood of these different outcomes (finding solutions to collective action problems or suppressing collective action) ultimately depends on who is shaping such legal persons. Who are the shareholders or citizens and the directors or governments behind the legal persons?

SHIFTING THE PARADIGM: THE WHO RATHER THAN THE HOW

In the twelfth-century book *De Monarchia*, Dante Alighieri analyzed whether the Holy Roman Empire or the Church should govern the lives of Europeans.[61] Very much like in the middle age, humanity is at a crossroads. We are wondering whether, in a globalized world, our lives should be governed by the public or private sector. Recent events have made us acutely aware of such critical questions. Is it the job of corporations or states to produce lifesaving vaccines or drugs to ensure public health? Is it the job of corporations or states to determine whether we can share our opinions on social media? Is it the job of corporations or states to tackle climate change? If the answer to these questions is "states," we are entrusting states to regulate corporations in a way that meets our moral standards so that society benefits and does not suffer from industrial activities. If, instead, the answer is "corporations," we need to ensure that the social contract between people and companies is respected through proper economic and legal agency frameworks. Obviously, in most cases, the answer will not be black or white but rather grey: it is the job of both states and corporations.

One attempt to address these questions has been public-private partnership agreements that allow states and corporations to work together on specific projects, such as, for example, big infrastructure projects. From a legal perspective, the relationship between the involved states and corporations is regulated by contractual agreements. These partnerships are extremely diverse. The nature of the partnership agreements depends on the different states, corporations, and projects involved. Thus, it is difficult to analyze public-private partnerships in the abstract. On the one hand, private

---

[60] Offe & Wiesenthal, *supra* note 55; Lustig, *supra* note 56.
[61] DANTE ALIGHIERI & DIEGO QUAGLIONI, MONARCHIA. TESTO LATINO A FRONTE (2021); Iris Marion Young, *Responsibility and Global Labor Justice*, 12 J. POL. PHIL. 365 (2004).

law and economic scholars have often criticized these partnerships as inefficient.[62] Their main argument is that the private sector would be able to deliver the same infrastructures without the state's participation in a cheaper and more efficient way. On the other hand, other scholars consider them to be a successful avenue for the public and private sectors to collaborate.[63] In the future, one could envisage, as a development of public-private partnerships, the institution of public-private separate legal entities that work not on specific projects but on a regular basis. For example, a future public-private entity could be established to address global pandemics or climate change.[64] It shall be recalled that, to a certain extent, corporations developed as separate legal entities from contractual agreements between commercial partners. It is now possible for the public and private sectors to strike up partnerships through contractual agreements. In the future, such partnerships could develop into separate legal persons.

However, this proposal does not resolve the *who* question. Even if we develop public-private separate legal persons, the pivotal question would be who is in charge of such a new legal instrument. As described above, institutions are tools that may be created, shaped, and used for the interests of some and at the expense of others. One of the most significant criticisms of states and corporations is that they were created, established, and shaped by a ruling class: the European nobility, bourgeois, and entrepreneurs. They have gracefully established a number of rights for the rest of the people to exercise within the institutional order they framed. These rights provide people with hope for a better future and, at the same time, reinforce the institutional fundamentals of states and corporations. In essence, these institutions, or separate legal persons, are structurally deficient because they were designed to perpetuate the inequalities between a ruling class and the rest.[65] Thus, if we are to learn from past experiences, we shall consider the "who" question from a perspective of inclusivity and equality. We shall ensure that a future framework establishing the accountability of corporations toward society will be actually shaped by society and not by corporations and states alone. However, how do we define society? CSR has helped to reframe the terms of the debate around the corporation's responsibility to society but has not defined society. A pivotal question is whether we shall refer to a "global society" given that corporate activities are now globalized.

In essence, who would be the "shareholders" of a future separate person, and what place would the environment have in this relationship? At the moment, the

---

[62] Dejan Makovšek & Marian Moszoro, *Risk Pricing Inefficiency in Public-Private Partnerships*, 38 Transp. Rev. 298 (2018).

[63] Graeme A. Hodge & Carsten Greve, *On Public-Private Partnership Performance: A Contemporary Review*, 22 Pub. Works Mgmt. Pol. 55 (2017).

[64] A few examples of similar partnerships are already available in the medical sector, for example, public-private partnerships in relation to treating HIV. Ute Papkalla & Gesa Kupfer, HIV-Related Public-Private Partnerships and Health Systems Strengthening (2009), https://data .unaids.org/pub/report/2009/jc1721_publicprivatepartnerships_en.pdf.

[65] Offe & Wiesenthal, *supra* notes 55.

only members of public-private partnerships are corporations and states, but there is an increasing demand for other actors to take a role. In this context, the relevance of states is limited because states would reflect national, rather than global, interests. If one imagines establishing a separate legal person representing the various interests of stakeholders in society vis-à-vis corporations, this separate legal person will certainly not be the state. States represent citizens, but not a global society affected by multinational enterprises.

The UNGPs focus on three actors: states owning duties, corporations voluntarily accepting responsibilities, and victims who shall be entitled to remedies. The fact that the UNGPs mention victims was considered an important innovation as compared with the traditional understanding, which contemplated only the relationship between states and corporations. However, this reference is not enough to address the problem of corporate social accountability. Stakeholders cannot be reduced to victims. They include, first, communities, families, and individuals – who are more likely to consider themselves activists rather than victims vis à vis states and corporations; second, associations such as trade unions, non-profits, and non-governmental organizations, which organize at both the local and global level; and third, socially responsible companies that want to provide alternative solutions to traditional business models based solely on profit. These stakeholders want to act collectively and are increasingly representing interests and values that can be distinct from those of states and corporations. For example, global campaigns for climate justice sometimes draw a contrast between their views and those of both states and corporations. In these cases, the divide is no longer between the public and private sectors but rather between economic and environmental interests.

Therefore, it is necessary to reconceptualize our idea of society to truly understand CSR in light of globalization and privatization. Only by having all stakeholders affected by business activities take part in the construction of a new attribution framework could we ensure effective corporate accountability. Otherwise, we could end up with suboptimal solutions providing cosmetic changes that do not empower the collective action of stakeholders but rather institutionalize and justify oppressing those living at the margins of globalization. A separate legal person could be the tool to address stakeholders' collective action problem, but only if it is constructed and shaped by all stakeholders.

Domestic Attribution

9

To Whom Should We Attribute a Corporation's Speech?

Sarah C. Haan

INTRODUCTION

Over the past hundred years, American law has gradually – and controversially – expanded the speech rights of corporations. Over the same period, corporate speech has become pervasive, and now dominates most major channels of communication.[1] Corporate speech ranges from anodyne commercial appeals to expressions of ethical values to campaign finance payments. To whom should the law attribute corporate speech? To the corporation as a free-standing speaker? Doing so would respect the traditional bounds of the corporate entity, while presenting the firm as analogous to an individual human speaker. Or, should the law attribute a corporation's speech to its to managers – either its board of directors, the top decisionmakers in the corporate hierarchy, or a designee of the board, like a board committee, officer, or employee? The law might attribute a corporation's speech to its "owners," a word often used to describe its shareholders, an approach that has deep historical roots in American constitutional law.[2] Taking a broader, stakeholder approach, the law could ascribe a corporation's speech to all of the people who animate it – its community of workers, managers, shareholders, creditors, suppliers, and customers, whose collaborative association within the corporation might be said to generate its expression.[3]

This chapter focuses on speech attribution in the law. Of course, outside of the law, individuals routinely come across corporate expression and must make sense of its authorship and origin. Because of the great volume of corporate expression in

---

[1] *See id.* at 738 (noting the "changing practices of expression now dominated by organized rather than individual speech").

[2] Many scholars have critiqued the idea that shareholders "own" the corporation. *See, e.g.,* Eugene F. Fama, *Agency Problems and the Theory of the Firm,* 88 J. POL. ECON. 288, 290 (1980).

[3] Relevant here is "team production" theory. *See* Margaret M. Blair & Lynn A. Stout, *A Team Production Theory of Corporate Law,* 85 VA. L. REV. 247 (1999) (describing the corporation as the organizational structure encompassing "the enterprise-specific investments of all the members of the corporate 'team,' including shareholders, managers, rank and file employees, and possibly other groups, such as creditors").

modern life, ordinary people have significant experience and expertise at this. They value corporate speech – whether on political, persuasive, or artistic terms – according to their lay understandings of *whose expression it is*. As a result, corporate speech attribution in law is deeply intertwined with extra-legal ideas about knowledge production, truth, and democratic sovereignty. Ideas about speech authorship shape our understanding of the world around us, including our relationship to fact and opinion, and our ability to engage in self-government. It also suggests that there is a limit to how far legal speech attribution can diverge from ordinary persons' understandings of authorship and continue to retain legitimacy in the eyes of the citizenry.

Why does the law attribute corporate speech? It does so for two basic purposes. Where speech causes harm the law sometimes looks for a party to hold accountable, criminally or civilly. In other cases, speech is protected from government regulation – as, in the United States, by the First Amendment. Where speech enjoys protection from government regulation, the scope of that protection can turn on the identity of the speaker. This is so, for example, in American campaign finance law, which prohibits certain kinds of speech and spending by "foreign" speakers. In a more complex example, the power of the State to mandate a commercial disclosure may turn on whether the mandate violates the speaker's conscience, causing us to ask: Who is the speaker? Whose conscience is violated?

This Chapter argues that, for speech attribution purposes, the most important difference between a corporate speaker and a human one is the *process* that produces the speech. The corporate speaker expresses itself through acts that are structured by corporate governance law – typically, in the United States, a mix of state and federal law, and private ordering – while a human actor's expression is the product of organic processes that are insulated from law. Corporate speech is derivative, and its production formalized and observable; human expression is germinal, and its production obscure and mysterious. Accordingly, this Chapter argues that corporate speech attribution should, in nearly every case, take its cues from the governance that determines the production of speech. That is, corporate speech attribution should give attention to corporate governance law and practices. This is not how speech attribution always works now – but it is how speech attribution already works in many cases.

Strengthening this governance-focused approach would be beneficial for several reasons. First, it dispenses with the fiction that corporations are meaningfully analogous to humans as speakers. They are not. Although legal scholarship has explored the differences that exist between humans' production of speech and that of organizations, First Amendment law has failed to cognize them. Yet, these differences are self-evidently relevant to an understanding of the value of speech to speakers and listeners, and increasingly important in our commercialized, post-truth information environment.

Second, by putting emphasis on the power of actors within the firm to determine the firm's expressive acts, the approach places *control* at the center of attribution – an objectively fair approach. (It is also an approach that justifies greater transparency about corporate control.) Third, it allows speech-related legal doctrines to create and refine incentives for the individuals who make corporate speech choices. The creation of socially beneficial incentives for corporate decision-makers is an important purpose of law. Modern corporate law has been designed primarily to reduce the agency costs that arise from conflicts of interest among corporate managers and other constituencies within firms. Oddly, however, speech law has largely ignored these same conflicts. It has not been sensitive to governance dynamics that create conflicts among corporate participants – that allow, for example, some corporate decision-makers to expropriate the private benefits of control *by means of* the corporation's expressive activity.

This chapter first sketches a taxonomy of ways in which American law could attribute corporate speech, noting where the various approaches are reflected in real-world law. It then explores the major problems that arise in corporate speech attribution. These are: the problem of "freedom" in "freedom of speech"; the problem of corporate personhood; the problem of "other people's money"; and the problem (or myth) of corporate democracy. Finally, it advocates a governance-focused approach and notes the benefits and drawbacks of such an approach in light of the foregoing analysis.

A TAXONOMY OF ATTRIBUTION POSSIBILITIES

A corporation's speech is the product of decisions and acts by individual persons. (This is true even of the relatively new "autonomous" corporation, which originates in the design choices of an individual or group of individuals.[4]) A corporation lacks a "mind" or conscience that stands apart from those of the individuals who animate it, and cannot act except through its agents. Thus, the threshold question in corporate speech attribution is whether to treat the corporation as a stand-alone speaker, or to attribute authorship to the firm's human agents.

If the choice is to attribute the corporation's speech to its human participants, a second-order determination must be made: *who* within the firm is responsible for the corporation's speech? Three primary options exist: (1) the corporation's legal managers (its board and the board's delegates); (2) the corporation's shareholders; and (3) the corporation's entire community of participants. As a matter of corporate governance, the descriptively accurate choice is the first one – legally, the corporation's managers have authority over the corporation's expressive acts.[5] In addition, corporate governance law sets the ground rules for board action – the board acts as a single body through a vote, with each director receiving one vote – and for shareholder action – shareholders act collectively through a vote in which each shareholder holds as many votes as shares. However, corporate governance does not provide any framework for action by any broader, stakeholder-based constituency.

---

[4]   *See, e.g.*, Carla Reyes, *Autonomous Corporate Personhood*, 96 Wash. L. Rev. 1453 (2021); Nathan Tse, *Decentralised Autonomous Organisations and the Corporate Form*, 51 Victoria U. Wellington L. Rev. 313 (2020).

[5]   *See, e.g.*, Del. Gen. Corp. L. § 141.

The Corporation as a Stand-Alone Speaker

Treating the corporation as a stand-alone speaker extends the corporate "fiction" of legal personhood to the domain of speech and expression. Its great advantage is simplicity – the other approaches, outlined below, are all more complex. The stand-alone speaker approach is simple for courts to apply and simple for corporate participants to understand. It also aligns the corporation's speech interests with the professional obligations of the corporation's lawyers, who avoid conflicts of interest that would arise if, for example, an officer or employee could be held individually liable for the corporation's speech.

On the other hand, the stand-alone approach justifies holding only the corporation, as an entity, responsible for speech harms – thereby foregoing the use of the law to constructively incentivize the behavior of the corporation's agents. If the corporation's agents know that only the corporation will be held liable for speech harms, its agents may take risks and generate harms or costs that get externalized to the community. Even with regard to speech rights, the stand-alone approach tends to obscure the fact that, since corporate speech originates with one or more individuals, restrictions of corporate speech may have little to no impact on the proverbial "marketplace of ideas," because those individuals remain free to articulate the same ideas in their individual capacities.[6]

The stand-alone approach is also meaningfully out-of-touch with how most people think of corporate speech, implicating issues of legitimacy and trust. Americans don't think of corporations as authentic "speakers" like human beings, and thus, the stand-alone speaker approach contradicts intuitive ideas about who is speaking when a corporation produces speech. Widespread cynicism about the value of corporate speech – especially in the face of facile conventions treating corporations as analogous to human speakers – likely undermines the persuasive effect of corporate speech on recipients and may even contribute to Americans' broader suspicion of information found in mainstream channels of communication.[7]

The Corporation's Management Is the Speaker

The corporation is managed by its Board of Directors, who delegate some areas of responsibility to the corporation's officers.[8] (In turn, the officers may delegate some

---

[6] *Accord* Bill Shaw, *Corporate Speech in the Marketplace of Ideas*, 7 J. CORP. L. 265, 282 (1982) (noting, for example, that "[i]n Consolidated Edison the directors of the utility [were] perfectly capable of expressing their views on nuclear energy as individuals").

[7] *See, e.g.*, Ronald Collins, Mark Lopez, Tamara Piety, and David Vladeck, *Corporations and Commercial Speech*, 30 SEATTLE U. L. REV. 895, 917 (2007) ("The simple fact is that corporate speech now drowns out all other speech.").

[8] *See* Del. Gen. Corp. L. § 141(a) ("The business and affairs of every corporation organized under this chapter shall be managed by or under the direction of a board of directors...").

speech-related tasks to employees. For example, the corporation's political speech may be delegated to a "Head of Government Relations.") Although the chief executive officer may be viewed as speaking "for" the corporation, the ultimate decision-making authority about the corporation's speech rests with the Board.

Decision-making authority is a factor in speech attribution under many speech-related laws, such as prohibitions against securities fraud. In federal securities law, for example, a person may be liable for a corporation's misstatement of material fact if the person "directly or indirectly" controlled the party liable for the violation – that is, the corporation itself.[9] The U.S. Supreme Court stated in 2010 that, for purposes of Rule 10b-5, which prohibits securities fraud,

> the maker of a statement is the person or entity with ultimate authority over the statement, including its content and whether and how to communicate it. Without control, a person or entity can merely suggest what to say, not "make" a statement in its own right.[10]

This approach, which is found in other statutory schemes, justifies attributing the speech of a widely held corporation to its board of directors.

In fact, as I have written elsewhere (with Faith Stevelman), twenty-first century board governance has been trending toward "information governance" that is focused primarily on communication oversight.[11] The board engages in information governance through communicative action, which involves overseeing the firm's informational infrastructure and communications functions. The corporation's communications – its speech – include formal, legally mandated reporting, public relations speech and advertising, and political expression, including the now common statements of corporate values and political commitments. In April 2021, for example, hundreds of American companies expressed opposition to a newly enacted law that restricted voting rights, staking out a political position on a matter that did not directly concern their business operations.[12]

In recent years, corporate law itself has ratcheted up expectations for the Board's role in firm communications, increasing the case for viewing the Board as the command center of the corporation's speech.[13] Thus, not only does the management approach accurately reflect the corporate governance processes that produce corporate speech now, but it also reflects cutting-edge, twenty-first century corporate governance and anticipates a currently evolving trend that tends to place greater responsibility for the corporation's speech activities on the board of directors.

---

[9]   15 U.S.C. § 78t(a) (2006 ed., Supp. IV); *see also Janus Capital Group, Inc. v. First Derivative Traders*, 564 U.S. 135 (2010).

[10]   *See Janus Capital*, 564 U.S. at 142.

[11]   *See* Faith Stevelman & Sarah C. Haan, *Boards in Information Governance*, 23 U. PA. J. BUS. L. 179 (2020).

[12]   *See, e.g.*, David Gelles & Andrew Ross Sorkin, *Hundreds of Companies Unite to Oppose Voting Limits, but Others Abstain*, N.Y. TIMES, Apr. 14, 2021, www.nytimes.com/2021/04/14/business/ceos-corporate-america-voting-rights.html.

[13]   *See* Stevelman & Haan, *supra* note 12, at 179.

The Corporation's Shareholders Are (Collectively) the Speaker

Traditionally, American First Amendment law has analyzed a corporation's speech rights as if the corporation is an association of its shareholders. Under this long-standing approach, reflected in cases like *First National Bank of Boston v. Bellotti*[14] and *Citizens United v. FEC*[15], the corporation's speech rights are presented as derivative of its shareholders' speech rights. Indeed, the majority opinion in *Citizens United v. FEC* assumed that shareholders play a nontrivial role in the production of corporate political speech.[16] Somewhat paradoxically, however, speech harms are only rarely attributed to a corporation's shareholders, in recognition of the bedrock corporate law principle of limited liability, which insulates shareholders from liability for the corporation's debts and obligations.[17]

The shareholder approach is property-based and sensitive to issues of corporate control. Where a corporation has a controlling shareholder or group, that controller probably has sufficient power to influence the corporation's expression. Even though the Board legally "manages" the corporation, the board is accountable to the shareholders, and a controlling shareholder stands in a position to strongly influence the board's decisions. For this reason, some areas of speech law, such as campaign finance law, treat corporate control – that is, voting or ownership control – as the crux of speech attribution.[18]

Where a corporation is widely held, however – that is, where it has a large number of shareholders, none of whom owns a controlling share of stock – shareholders do not exercise meaningful control over a corporation's speech. In the widely held firm, corporate managers alone determine the corporation's speech.[19]

The Corporation's Entire Community of Participants Are (Collectively) the Speaker

A corporation includes many more participants than just its managers and shareholders. The people who perform the daily functions of a corporation include its workers – a group that generally gets left out of rights-based speech attribution, even though an employee can be held individually liable for speech harms arising

---

[14] 435 U.S. 765 (1978).

[15] 558 U.S. 310 (2010).

[16] *Citizens United v. FEC*, 558 U.S. 310, 362 (discussing the effectiveness of shareholder objections to a corporation's political speech through "the procedures of corporate democracy").

[17] *See generally*, Frank H. Easterbrook & Daniel R. Fischel, *Limited Liability and the Corporation*, 52 U. Chi. L. Rev. 89 (1985).

[18] *See* 52 U.S.C. § 30121(a)(1); 11 C.F.R. § 110.20(i) ("A foreign national shall not direct, dictate, control, or directly or indirectly participate in the decision-making process of any person, such as a corporation … with regard to such person's Federal or non-Federal election-related activities, such as decisions concerning the making of contributions, donations, expenditures, or disbursements…").

[19] *See, e.g.*, Lucian A. Bebchuk & Robert J. Jackson, Jr., *Corporate Political Speech: Who Decides?*, 124 Harv. L. Rev. 83, 87–89 (2010).

from corporate speech. For example, the 2020 COVID-19 Consumer Protection Act makes it illegal for any company to make false claims in advertisements for the treatment, prevention, or diagnosis of COVID-19, among other offenses.[20] An individual agent of a corporation, such as an employee, may be held personally liable for the corporation's violation of the FTC Act if that person participated directly in the deceptive practices or had authority to control those practices, and had (or should have had) knowledge of the deceptive practices.[21]

Creditors are also often understood as important participants in the firm. Corporate participants other than managers and shareholders are often called *stakeholders* in the corporate literature. No American speech attribution paradigm currently attributes a corporation's speech to all of its stakeholders, or even to the most obvious subset of stakeholders, the corporation's workers. However, the corporate law trend that favors adding stakeholders' interests to the group of interests served by the corporation – its corporate purpose – could easily be extended to speech attribution. Popular writing suggests that workers, especially, feel that a corporation's speech reflects on them – a sort of extra-legal, informal speech attribution.[22]

* * *

These four approaches are the most obvious choices for a corporate speech attribution regime. However, it is important to recognize that a one-size-fits-all approach might not work across all speech areas. It is not necessary to choose one of the four approaches above for all speech purposes; nor is that how speech attribution currently works. The paragraphs below suggest that attribution could be assigned differently across several axes: (1) closely held vs. widely held companies; (2) the type of speech in question; and (3) the purpose of the speech-related law.

Closely Held versus Widely Held Companies

State corporate law and federal securities law sometimes distinguish between small, closely held corporations and larger, publicly held ones – a distinction that often matters for attribution. Thus, corporate law itself provides clues for untangling corporate attribution issues. The Supreme Court relied on a similar distinction in *Burwell v. Hobby Lobby* when it suggested that the rules of corporate religious exercise might be different for closely held corporations than for widely held ones.[23]

---

[20] *See* COVID-19 Consumer Protection Act of the 2021 Consolidated Appropriations Act, Pub. L. No. 116-260, Title XIV, § 1401(b)(1).

[21] *FTC v. Ross*, 743 F.3d 886, 892 (4th Cir. 2014).

[22] *See, e.g.*, Shirin Ghaffary, *"I'm Deeply Ashamed": Another Facebook Employee Resigns in Protest over the Company's Handling of Trump's Posts*, Vox, June 5, 2020, www.vox.com/recode/2020/6/5/21281745/facebook-mark-zuckerberg-trump-post-employee-resigns.

[23] 573 U.S. 682 (2014).

However, corporate law offers an imperfect basis for resolving speech attribution. Corporate law is mostly enacted at the state level, which means that state-by-state differences exist. And because state corporate law has not developed for the purpose of allocating speech responsibilities and rights, it might not offer the optimal attribution regime.

Types of Speech/Tiers of Scrutiny

Another possible way to resolve attribution is by reference to the *kind* of speech in question. In the United States, a doctrinal practice evolved at the end of the twentieth century in which the level of scrutiny a speech restriction (or compelled speech mandate) receives in judicial review is determined by its content. American law distinguishes in meaningful ways among political speech, commercial speech, securities disclosure, campaign finance contributions (which are considered speech), etc. Political speech receives the highest level of protection – strict scrutiny – while commercial speech is somewhat easier to regulate, receiving either intermediate review under *Central Hudson* or even laxer *Zauderer* review.[24] Campaign finance disclosure laws receive "exacting scrutiny."[25] Securities laws that burden speech receive virtually no scrutiny.[26]

Organizations, including for-profit corporations, produce all of these kinds of speech. Thus, it might make sense to analyze speech attribution differently depending on the kind of speech involved. For example, we might decide that all of a corporation's commercial speech is attributed to the corporation itself, while its

---

[24] *See* Cent. *Hudson Gas & Elec. Corp. v. Pub. Serv. Comm'n of New York*, 447 U.S. 557, 566 (1980) (requiring that commercial disclosure mandates "directly advance[]" a "substantial" governmental interest without employing a means "more extensive than necessary to serve that interest"); *CTIA – The Wireless Ass'n v. City of Berkeley, California*, 928 F.3d 832, 842 (9th Cir.), *cert. denied*, 140 S. Ct. 658 (2019) ("We apply the intermediate scrutiny test mandated by *Central Hudson* in commercial speech cases where the government acts to restrict or prohibit speech, on the ground that in such cases intermediate scrutiny appropriately protects the interests of both the speaker (the seller) and the audience (the purchaser)."); *Zauderer v. Office of Disciplinary Counsel of Supreme Court of Ohio*, 471 U.S. 626, 651 (1985).

[25] *See Buckley v. Valeo*, 424 U.S. 1, 64, 68 (1976) (defining exacting scrutiny as requiring "a 'relevant correlation' or 'substantial relation'" between the governmental interest and the information required to be disclosed," and noting that campaign finance disclosure requirements "appear to be the least restrictive means of curbing the evils of campaign ignorance and corruption").

[26] *See, e.g.*, Amanda Shanor, *First Amendment Coverage*, 93 N.Y.U. L. REV. 318, 320–21, 325 (2018) ("Many activities that are colloquially considered 'speech' are not subject to constitutional challenge, let alone review or decision … [such as] large swaths of the administrative state, including antitrust, securities, and pharmaceutical regulation...."); *Nat'l Ass'n of Mfrs. v. S.E.C.*, 748 F.3d 359, 371–72 (D.C. Cir. 2014), *adhered to on reh'g sub nom. Nat'l Ass'n of Manufacturers v. S.E.C.*, 800 F.3d 518 (D.C. Cir. 2015) (refusing to analyze a conflict minerals disclosure mandate under securities disclosure law, suggesting that the latter category may be subject only to rational basis review); *cf. Ohralik v. Ohio State Bar Ass'n*, 436 U.S. 447, 456 (1978) ("Numerous examples could be cited of communications that are regulated without offending the First Amendment, such as the exchange of information about securities....").

political speech and spending are attributed to the individuals within the firm who make speech decisions. Although this approach would nicely complement existing First Amendment doctrine, that doctrine has been widely criticized. Speech categories are murky and overlapping, producing confusion for lawmakers and speakers. It is not always possible to distinguish between one type of speech and another. For example, in *National Association of Manufacturers v. S.E.C.*, the D.C. Circuit rejected Congress's design of a disclosure mandate as securities disclosure, but ultimately could not decide if it was commercial or political speech (and analyzed the regulation using both strict and intermediate scrutiny, in the alternative).[27] Because speech regulations targeting corporations increasingly involve potentially overlapping categories of speech – for example, ESG disclosure mandates – a "tiers of scrutiny" approach that ties corporate speech attribution to speech *type* may not be workable.

Speech Harms versus Speech Rights

Another alternative is to look to the *purpose* of attribution in law – is it to assign liability or responsibility for harmful speech? Or is it to protect potentially beneficial speech, for example, through First Amendment doctrine? It might make sense to attribute speech differently for these two different purposes.

Where the law seeks to attribute harmful corporate speech for liability purposes, it makes sense to allow the law to hold culpable actors responsible in order to incentivize better decision-making within the firm's structure. On this reasoning, laws that assign responsibility for harmful corporate speech should be finely tuned to reach the individual human decision-maker behind the corporation's expression or speech act, in order to encourage that person or persons to make better decisions.

Where the law in question protects speech from State restriction (or compulsion), it may be less important to identify the specific human actor within the firm who is responsible for the speech. Particularly if one adopts a listener-focused perspective, the identity of the individual corporate agent responsible for a speech act may be largely irrelevant to questions about the value of the speech to its recipients. On the other hand, treating a corporation as a stand-alone speaker analogous to an individual human expresses a societal judgment about the role and importance of corporations in a given setting. Thus, for example, when the speech in question is political speech, an approach that treats the corporation as a speaker on par with a human actor expresses the normative judgment that corporations and human actors are functionally equal, at least when it comes to expressive acts of political participation. Corporate political speech goes well beyond payments that fall within the statutory

---

[27] *Nat'l Ass'n of Manufacturers*, 800 F.3d at 518.

categories of "contributions" and "expenditures" and includes "'issue' advertising or 'institutional' advertising, 'grass roots' campaigns with respect to referenda or legislation, free use of company employees or facilities, and payments to outsiders to lobby or to campaign."[28]

***

Perhaps this section has raised more questions than it has answered. By providing four potential forms of attribution, and describing three different axes upon which attribution decisions might turn, it has identified a range of possible attribution approaches. The next section examines in greater detail four common problems that have arisen with corporate speech attribution in the United States.

FOUR PROBLEMS

Four main problems have plagued corporate speech attribution since corporations first started expressing themselves. One concerns the basis for protecting corporate speech: commentators and jurists have long asserted that "free speech" exists to promote human freedom, and thus has little, if any, salience for corporate speakers. If this is true, the question of speech attribution takes on special importance because the constitutional value of corporate speech may turn, in the first instance, on whether it is attributed to specific human actors within the firm.

A second major problem relates to the corporate personhood debate, and the question of when it is appropriate for law to treat corporations as analogous to humans. When applied to speech and expression, corporate personhood reflects a judgment that the speech of corporations and natural persons are similar in worth – a normative view with frankly political implications.

A third sub-part looks at the problem of "other people's money." This is the idea, famously expressed in a 1914 book by Louis D. Brandeis, who would later join the U.S. Supreme Court, that corporate managers are spending shareholders' money when they make expenditures for things like corporate speech. The problem of "other people's money" suggests that corporate speech should be understood to create potential conflicts of interest and agency costs.

Finally, a fourth major problem is the oft-expressed but mistaken idea that a corporation's speech is produced through "corporate democracy." The Supreme Court has suggested that corporate democracy protects shareholders from harms. Corporate democracy is also sometimes interpreted to suggest that the corporation's speech is really the shareholders' own expression in some meaningful way. As I show, this idea has rhetorical appeal but is essentially false.

---

[28] Victor Brudney, *Business Corporations and Stockholders' Rights under the First Amendment*, 91 YALE L. J. 235, 238–39 (1981).

The Problem of "Freedom" in "Freedom of Speech"

American law protects expression mainly because of its importance to "speakers," those who produce expression.[29] More broadly, the First Amendment canon recognizes three critical free speech values: producing "knowledge and 'truth' in the 'marketplace of ideas'"; facilitating individual self-expression, autonomy, and self-fulfillment; and contributing to self-government and democracy itself.[30] Among the three, some have argued that the second – "communication as a means of self-expression, self-realization, and self-fulfillment" – is the most important value, but is absent for corporate speech.[31] Corporations do not enjoy human autonomy, have no real selves, and cannot achieve "fulfillment."[32] As Tamara Piety has explained,

> [A] corporation lacks the expressive interests related to self-actualization and freedom that human beings possess by virtue of being human. Human beings are moral subjects and ends in themselves. Corporations are not.[33]

If this is true, then the constitutionally cognizable value of corporate speech must be found (exclusively) in the other two values – corporate speech must contribute to knowledge and truth, and/or to democratic self-government. And because the corporation is not itself a member of the political community (a citizen), the benefits of corporate speech for democratic self-government are benefits for other parties – for a group of people that may (or may not) include corporate insiders but is certain to include numerous people who are outside it. This is so, unless we attribute the corporation's speech to an individual person (or group of people).

While majority opinions in early cases that extended speech rights to corporations, such as *First National Bank of Boston v. Bellotti* and *Pacific Gas & Electric Co. v. Public Utilities Commission*, ignored differences between human and corporate speakers, dissenting judges focused on those differences. In *Bellotti*, decided in 1978, the Supreme Court invalidated a Massachusetts law that prohibited a corporation from spending money to influence a ballot initiative addressing matters unrelated to

[29] Since at least the 1970s, the First Amendment has been understood to protect the interests of listeners. *See Virginia State Bd. of Pharmacy v. Virginia Citizens Consumer Council, Inc.*, 425 U.S. 748 (1976).

[30] *See, e.g.*, Robert Post, *Participatory Democracy and Free Speech*, 97 VA. L. REV. 477, 478 (2011) (the First Amendment extends only to speech that implicates the values of "(1) the creation of new knowledge; (2) individual autonomy; and (3) democratic self-government"); KATHLEEN M. SULLIVAN & GERALD GUNTHER, CONSTITUTIONAL LAW 987 (15th ed. 2004).

[31] *First Nat'l Bank of Boston v. Bellotti*, 435 U.S. 765, 804–05 (White, J., dissenting) (joined by Justices Brennan and Marshall) ("what some of have considered to be the principal function of the First Amendment, the use of communication as a means of self-expression, self-realization, and self-fulfillment, is not at all furthered by corporate speech"); *see* Tamara R. Piety, *Against Freedom of Commercial Expression*, 29 CARDOZO L. REV. 2583, 2646–49 (2008).

[32] James D. Nelson, *The Freedom of Business Association*, 115 COLUM. L. REV. 461, 511 (2015) ("for-profit businesses are not generally bound up with deep ties of identity and attachment," and therefore should not be viewed as associational for First Amendment purposes).

[33] Piety, *supra* note 32, at 2646.

the corporation's business. Justice White, dissenting from the majority – and joined by Justices Brennan and Marshall – argued that "corporate expenditures designed to further political causes lack the connection with individual self-expression which is one of the principal justifications for the constitutional protection of speech provided by the First Amendment."[34] The communications of "profitmaking corporations" "do not represent a manifestation of individual freedom or choice," he wrote.[35] The *Bellotti* dissenters focused on whether a corporation's speech furthered "the desires of individual shareholders," but gave no consideration to governance mechanisms that would have made the furtherance of shareholders' desires possible.[36] White noted merely that "[i]n the case of corporate political activities, we are not at all concerned with the self-expression of the communicator."[37] This seems correct, not least because a corporation's individual shareholders and managers retain the right to speak as individuals, even if the corporation is completely silenced.[38]

Almost a decade later, in a dissent in *Pacific Gas & Electric Co. v. Public Utilities Commission*, Justice Rehnquist emphasized differences between natural persons and corporations in the context of compelled speech. "Extension of the individual freedom of conscience decisions to business corporations strains the rationale of those cases beyond the breaking point," he wrote.[39] "To ascribe to such artificial entities an 'intellect' or 'mind' for freedom of conscience purposes is to confuse metaphor with reality."[40]

Thus, both liberal and conservative Justices raised these concerns, though the concerns did not shape the dominant First Amendment doctrine as it evolved. In academia, legal scholars too theorized about those differences and proposed First Amendment approaches that would take them into account.

At the end of the twentieth century, law dean and First Amendment scholar Randall Bezanson attempted to map the constitutionally cognizable differences between the speech of individual persons and what he called "institutional speech."[41] (The term itself had been deployed, somewhat cautiously, by the majority in *Bellotti*.[42]) Bezanson argued that institutional speech is "authorless speech" and has "no speaker – no point of human origin in the voluntary communicative intention of an individual who can be identified and through whom such critical

---

[34] *Bellotti*, 435 U.S. at 807.

[35] *Id.* at 805.

[36] *Id.* at 805.

[37] *Id.* at 806 n.6.

[38] *See, e.g.*, Brudney, *supra* note 29, at 244 (a corporate officer's freedom of speech is not burdened "by denying him the opportunity to [express himself] with other people's money, or, more particularly, by denying him the use of corporate funds to cause the corporation to speak for him").

[39] *Pacific Gas & Elec. Co. v. Public Utilities Comm'n*, 475 U.S. 1, 33 (1986) (Rehnquist, J., dissenting).

[40] *Id.*

[41] Bezanson, *supra* note 1, at 735.

[42] *Bellotti*, 435 U.S. at 793.

questions as purpose, intent, and meaning can be answered."[43] Core to the protection of "free speech," in Bezanson's view, was the author's liberty:

> The protection of individual speech—of speaking—is important to the preservation of human liberty at both the individual and societal level. It facilitates the capacity of the individual to give meaning to conscious life, and fosters the critical capacity to enrich that meaning by communication with other similarly situated individuals. The act of speaking is itself an expression of freedom.[44]

As Bezanson pointed out, whether something is speech in the first place is commonly determined, in part, by whether "an intent to convey a particularized message was present," an inquiry that assumed the existence of a speaker with intent.[45] Bezanson argued that the requirement of a discernible speaker was important for two reasons:

> First, without a speaker no sensible idea of liberty or individual freedom would exist under the First Amendment. Second, without a speaker speech could not be seen as an intentional act (as the Supreme Court sees it), and the speaker's intent could not be used as a standard by which to judge otherwise ambiguous questions of meaning, effect, and harm.[46]

Bezanson went so far as to argue that, because they "possess no mind or free will," "institutions cannot speak for purposes of the First Amendment." "They may produce speech that is relevant to First Amendment policies," he wrote, "but its constitutional protection would rest on considerations *other than liberty or individual freedom.*"[47]

After *Citizens United* was decided, Bezanson concluded that the Supreme Court had "wiped clean from free-speech jurisprudence" the status of the author of speech.[48] Notwithstanding the Supreme Court's turn in *Citizens United*, powerful questions remain about the relationship between corporate speech and long-recognized First Amendment values, such as self-actualization and freedom. By treating corporations and natural persons as roughly equivalent speakers, the Supreme Court appears to have gradually demoted these values in our constitutional scheme.

Speech Attribution and Corporate Personhood

Corporate speech attribution runs headlong into the debate about corporate "personhood." The concept of corporate "personhood" originated with the legal right to

[43] Bezanson, *supra* note 1, at 739.
[44] *Id.* at 776.
[45] *Id.* at 750 (quoting *Texas v. Johnson*, 491 U.S. 397, 404 (1989)).
[46] *Id.* at 750.
[47] *Id.* at 756.
[48] Randall P. Bezanson, *No Middle Ground—Reflections on the* Citizens United *Decision*, 96 Iowa L. Rev. 649, 650–51 (2011).

sue and be sued, and expanded fairly quickly until it had rendered the corporation a rights-holder, like a natural person.[49] However, the "personhood" debate is mostly semantics; as explored above, there is little basis to argue that the corporation – or any organization, for that matter – is truly analogous to a natural person when it comes to speech and expression. Moreover, as Victor Brudney observed, "[c]orporations are accorded 'personality' in order to create a mechanism for saving transaction costs in business dealings, not to create autonomous beings."[50]

Courts generally employed an associational theory of the corporation in the nineteenth century, an approach that led the Supreme Court to recognize some corporate constitutional rights.[51] However, by the end of the century, the associational theory had become a poor fit for a burgeoning group of large, public companies.[52] "By about 1910," Margaret Blair and Elizabeth Pollman write, "a sizable class of very large, branded, publicly traded corporations had emerged, and for these entities, it was no longer credible that they would be seen as proxies for the interests of a well-defined and identifiable group of individual investors or other participants."[53] Since Congress had passed the Tillman Act in 1907, prohibiting corporate political spending, issues related to corporate political speech would not come to the fore for another sixty years or so. Thus, questions about whether the corporation plausibly functioned as a proxy for the *speech interests* of participants did not receive attention until the 1970s.

The Supreme Court's decision to give First Amendment protection to commercial speech in *Virginia Pharmacy* was a watershed moment because it virtually ensured that much speech by corporations would now be analyzed through the lens of individual rights.[54] *Citizens United v. FEC* is among the latest major First Amendment cases addressing corporate speech, and it endorsed an approach that viewed the corporation as a "person" for speech purposes. A whole section of the majority opinion argued that the First Amendment does not permit discrimination against speakers, employing language that tended to make corporations seem no different from natural persons. *Agency for International Development v. Alliance*

---

[49] Two good overviews of this evolution include ADAM WINKLER, WE THE CORPORATIONS: HOW AMERICAN BUSINESSES WON THEIR CIVIL RIGHTS (2018), and Margaret M. Blair & Elizabeth Pollman, *The Derivative Nature of Corporate Constitutional Rights*, 56 WM. MARY L. REV. 1673, 1676–77 (2015). Theories of corporate personhood also relate to blame attribution when corporations cause criminal or tortious harm. For an exploration of corporate personhood in these contexts, see generally, For an exploration of corporate personhood in these contexts, see generally, Mihailis E. Diamantis, *Corporate Identity, in* EXPERIMENTAL PHILOSOPHY OF IDENTITY AND THE SELF (Kevin Tobia ed., 2022).

[50] Brudney, *supra* note 29, at 240.

[51] *See, e.g., San Mateo v. S. Pac. R.R.*, 13 F. 722, 730 (C.C.D. Cal. 1882) ("Private corporations are, it is true, artificial persons, but with the exception of a sole corporation, with which we are not concerned, they consist of aggregations of individuals united for some legitimate business.")

[52] Blair & Pollman, *supra* note 50, at 1676–77.

[53] *Id.* at 1678–79.

[54] 425 U.S. 748 (1976).

for Open Society International, Inc., decided in 2020, drew a bright line between American and foreign corporations for the purpose of recognizing First Amendment rights.[55] By recognizing a formal, legal separation between American-incorporated organizations and their foreign-incorporated affiliates for free-speech purposes, holding that foreign entities "have no First Amendment rights," and declining to recognize that the foreign corporations' speech could be attributed to the American organizations' in any meaningful way, the Court strengthened the "personhood" analogy.[56] The dissenting Justices could only protest that the Court "attribute[s] speech across corporate lines all the time."[57]

When it comes to political speech, the corporate "personhood" concept is particularly strained. Ordinarily, the dignity of a human person would at least open for debate questions about the person's participation in the political system. However, corporations stand in a different relationship with democracy than individuals do – corporations can never be citizens or elected officials. In fact, the only way that corporations participate in democracy – other than being *acted upon*, as subjects of laws or acts by the executive, or orders of the judiciary – is through expressive acts, such as lobbying and campaign finance. Yet, there is no question that whole categories of expressive acts by corporations that relate to democratic government can be completely prohibited. For example, current federal law categorically prohibits corporations from making contributions to candidates for federal office.[58]

In the end, the conceit of corporate personhood works poorly for speech attribution, because corporations share few of the characteristics of human persons that are relevant to speech production. Laws addressing speech harms commonly recognize this and provide liability to individual firm actors who participated in or controlled the corporation's speech. Yet, American First Amendment law persists in treating corporations as stand-alone, personalized speakers for purposes of constitutional analysis, an approach that obscures how corporations actually produce speech. It also contradicts the popular view of many Americans that a corporation is *not* a person in the ways that matter for expression and speech. The tension between the legal view and the popular view may undermine people's trust in information broadly, especially where information originates from corporate sources. Courts would do well to resist applying corporate personhood concepts in the context of speech rights.

The Problem of Other People's Money

Louis Brandeis's 1914 book, *Other People's Money*, highlighted a concern about the corporation that has animated corporate speech discourse for more than a

---

[55]   140 S.Ct. 2082 (2020).
[56]   *Id.* at 2088–89.
[57]   *Id.* at 2096 (Breyer, J., dissenting).
[58]   *See* 11 C.F.R. § 114.2.

century: When corporate resources are deployed for speech, aren't its managers spending "other people's" money?[59] What if someone within the firm disagrees with the speech? What right do corporate managers have to spend "other people's money" to express the managers' own views, especially if dissenters exist? Sometimes framed as the problem of the dissenting shareholder, this concern arguably extends beyond shareholders' interests to implicate the interests of creditors and workers.[60]

The problem has several dimensions. There is a debate in corporate theory about the extent to which the corporation's funds "belong" to any particular constituency, at least insofar as such a characterization sheds light on corporate speech. At the time the First Amendment was written, however, there is little question that Americans would have considered the corporation's assets and cash to belong to its "owners," the shareholders. A corporation's political and charitable expenditures were still viewed through a strict property rights lens at the end of the nineteenth and beginning of the twentieth centuries. For example, in Fall River, Massachusetts, in 1872, a mill corporation's shareholders rejected a proposed charitable donation to a religious organization; one shareholder argued that it was "robbery" to "take the smallest fraction of her property without her consent."[61] More recently, some corporate law scholars have argued that shareholders are not the only investors or residual claimants in the firm, suggesting that other dissenting stakeholders might have a legitimate, property based complaint when the corporation's managers make controversial expenditures.[62]

Putting this debate to the side, Brandeis's question invokes one of the major issues in corporate law: agency costs.[63] In the case of corporate speech, agency costs are generated when managers make corporate expenditures that benefit the managers personally, in an act of expropriation. For example, a CEO might decide to spend the company's money on advertisements that feature her own accomplishments, building her name recognition and reputation in the community. Corporate law professors have long raised concerns that corporate political expenditures are a form of agency cost, and empirical research has tended to

[59] *See* LOUIS D. BRANDEIS, OTHER PEOPLE'S MONEY AND HOW BANKERS USE IT (1914); *see also* Brudney, *supra* note 29, at 235. A line in Adam Smith's *Wealth of Nations* observed that corporate directors were "the managers rather of other people's money than their own," and suggested that they exhibited less "vigilance" over the money for this reason. ADAM SMITH, AN INQUIRY INTO THE NATURE AND CAUSES OF THE WEALTH OF NATIONS 334 (Edinburgh 1850) (J. R. McCulloch, ed., 4th edition).

[60] *See generally*, David Min, *Corporate Political Activity and Non-Shareholder Agency Costs*, 33 YALE J. ON REG. 423 (2016).

[61] Miscellaneous, BOSTON INVESTIGATOR, Feb. 19, 1873 at 5.

[62] *See, e.g.*, Douglas G. Baird & M. Todd Henderson, *Other People's Money*, 60 STAN. L. REV. 1309, 1310–11 (2008); Lynn A. Stout, *Bad and Not-So-Bad Arguments for Shareholder Primacy*, 75 S. CAL. L. REV. 1189, 1192–95 (2002).

[63] *See generally*, Adam Winkler, *"Other People's Money": Corporations, Agency Costs, and Campaign Finance Law*, 92 GEO. L.J. 871 (2004).

confirm that a company's political donations match the political preferences of its leaders.[64]

Another concern is that corporate speech distorts the "marketplace of ideas" when it amplifies managers' expression at the expense of other firm participants with different viewpoints. This is so because the expenditure does not reflect the actual strength of human opinion supporting the speech; rather, it reflects the fact that the individual (or group) at the top of the corporate hierarchy has authority over the corporate treasury – while others within the firm, who may be more numerous and hold differing opinions, lack this authority. If corporate speech is distorted in this way, then the failure to accurately attribute corporate speech to the corporation's managers undermines the citizenry's ability to engage in truth-seeking, individual self-actualization, and democratic self-government. Noting that the Supreme Court had endorsed listeners' rights in *Virginia Pharmacy*, Victor Brudney asserted that listeners cannot be "enriched" by speech "unless willing and able speakers exist."[65]

First National Bank of Boston v. Bellotti involved a Massachusetts law that had prohibited corporations from spending money to influence a state referendum. The law in question would have allowed a corporation to seek to influence a ballot initiative materially related to its business, property, or assets, but the referendum at the center of the case concerned an issue that all the parties had agreed was *not* so related: individuals' taxes. Massachusetts's legislature had perhaps reasoned that a corporate political expenditure on a matter unrelated to its business would be more likely to reflect managerial self-dealing. The Supreme Court invalidated the law by treating the corporation as no different from an individual human speaker.

Corporate Democracy

It has become common for the Supreme Court to discuss "corporate democracy" as a justification for corporate speech rights. Corporate law professors have resisted these claims since the Supreme Court first used the term "corporate democracy" in 1978, in *First National Bank of Boston v. Bellotti*.[66] But even before the 1970s, business experts had been debating the extent to which corporate democracy accurately

---

[64] Researchers have even found that managers' political affiliations help explain their corporate management choices. *See* Irena Hutton, *Danling Jiang & Alok Kumar, Corporate Policies of Republican Managers*, 49 J. FIN. QUANT. ANALYSIS 1279 (2014) (finding that "Republican managers who are likely to have conservative personal ideologies adopt and maintain more conservative corporate policies").

[65] *Id.* at 245 ("In short, contrary to Justice Powell's implication, the interests of the listener and the public in the exchange or circulation of views are cumulative upon, but not independent of, a speaker's ability and desire to speak."); *see also id.* at 247 n.60 ("Justice Blackmun initiated his discussion of listeners' rights under the First Amendment in [*Virginia Pharmacy*] with the observation that '[f]reedom of speech presupposes a willing speaker.'").

[66] *See, e.g.*, Daniel D. Dykstra, *Political Contributions*, 4 J. CORP. L. 460, 473 (1979) (describing the Court's argument that shareholders are "presumed competent to protect their own interests" in part through "corporate democracy" as valid only for majority interests).

described real-world governance. In an early example, Jerome Frank declared in 1933 that corporate democracy "has vanished or is vanishing."[67] More recently, several corporate theorists have challenged the normative view that corporate democracy is desirable.

"Corporate democracy" describes a social movement that began to emerge during the Great Depression as a grassroots shareholder response to problems that had long challenged American corporate capitalism. In the 1940s and 1950s, the term was widely adopted, especially by business leaders, in a rhetorical trend that sought to connect corporate capitalism to American democracy in the global fight to defeat communism.[68] Within corporate law, the term has an ambiguous meaning. Early users of the phrase employed it to suggest that small stockholders should wield substantially the same power as large stockholders to influence corporate policy.[69] Later, advocates of corporate democracy, such as Lewis D. Gilbert, used it to describe a robust role for shareholders in corporate governance.[70] After the middle of the century, some users whittled down its meaning further, to the notion that directors were chosen "at least with the consent of" shareholders.[71]

In the 1950s, shareholder meetings grew in size and were increasingly analogized to "town halls," a metaphor that emphasized the public company as a political body. It was a false analogy, in part because attendance at meetings remained low in proportion to the total number of a company's stockholders; in addition, the proxy system (and intermediation) disenfranchised numerous beneficial holders. Nonetheless, the myth was popular and may have helped shape the "marketplace of ideas" concept that was emerging simultaneously in First Amendment jurisprudence. (The term "marketplace of ideas" was first used in a concurrence by Justice William O. Douglas in 1953.[72]) The marketplace metaphor suggested that individuals' market decisions could function as votes, leaving open the possibility that consumers, shareholders,

---

[67] Jerome Frank, *Book Review: The Modern Corporation and Private Property*, 42 YALE L. J. 989, 989 (1933).

[68] *See, e.g.*, LEWIS D. AND JOHN J. GILBERT, EIGHTEENTH ANNUAL REPORT OF STOCKHOLDER ACTIVITIES AT CORPORATION MEETINGS, DURING 1957 196 (N.Y.: Gilbert & Gilbert, 1958) (quoting a speech by New York Stock Exchange President G. Keith Funston about corporate democracy); JANICE M. TRAFLET, A NATION OF SMALL SHAREHOLDERS: MARKETING WALL STREET AFTER WORLD WAR II 88–109 (Johns Hopkins U. Press, 2013) (describing the New York Stock Exchange's campaign in the 1950s to sell Americans on stockholding in order to strengthen democracy).

[69] *See, e.g.*, WILLIAM Z. RIPLEY, MAIN STREET AND WALL STREET 38 (Little, Brown & Co. 1927) ("the very essence of corporate democracy" is "that all members of the company shall stand upon an even footing one with another").

[70] *See, e.g.*, LEWIS D. GILBERT, DIVIDENDS AND DEMOCRACY (1956).

[71] *See, e.g., Essex Universal Corp. v. Yates*, 305 F.2d 572, 575 (1962) (the "most fundamental principle of corporate democracy" is "that management must represent and be chosen by, or at least with the consent of, those who own the corporation"). J. A. Livingston, an early, public critic of corporate democracy, defined it narrowly "as the shareholder's right to speak, congregate, communicate with other shareholders, and to know what is going on." J. A. LIVINGSTON, THE AMERICAN STOCKHOLDER 76 (J. B. Lippincott Co., 1958).

[72] *United States v. Rumely*, 345 U.S. 41, 56 (1953) (Douglas, J., concurring).

and others could use market transactions to weigh in on a company's political and social positions – which were expressed, of course, through its communications. This idea transferred nicely to shareholders' investment decisions and was reinforced by the informal "Wall Street Rule," which held that dissenting stockholders should sell their stock (exit) rather than exercise "voice" within firm governance.[73]

At the same time, federal securities law itself evolved to give the Securities and Exchange Commission the power to decide which topics the shareholders could debate fully, and which were off limits. At the end of 1952, the SEC codified a rule allowing companies to silence shareholder proposals that primarily concerned "general economic, political, racial, religious, social or similar causes."[74] For more than twenty years thereafter, the rule foreclosed any real "town hall" discussion of racial policy reforms at public companies that would have included shareholders. This was hardly democracy in action.

In *Buckley v. Valeo*, the Supreme Court famously held that money is, at least for some purposes, speech. The decision laid the groundwork for modern political speech doctrine, which has accorded significant speech rights to corporations. Importantly, the Supreme Court's majority opinion adopted the logic of a dissenting opinion in the case below, which had been authored by a judge of the D.C. Circuit Court of Appeals, Edward Allen Tamm.[75] A few years before he wrote that dissenting opinion, Tamm had written the majority opinion in a different case, *Medical Committee for Human Rights v. Securities and Exchange Commission*, which had controversially articulated a robust case for corporate democracy and would have strengthened the role of shareholders in shaping a corporation's expressive acts.[76] However, when given the chance in 1972 to endorse this robust case for corporate democracy, the Supreme Court balked; it first granted a writ of certiorari and then dismissed the case on grounds of mootness.[77] As a result of this history, the Supreme Court essentially adopted Tamm's idea that money (and thus corporate expenditures) can be speech, but failed to endorse Tamm's complementary view that corporate shareholders should have strong governance rights to weigh in on political expenditures. Two years after *Buckley*, writing for the 5–4 majority in *First National Bank of Boston v. Bellotti*, Justice Powell asserted that:

> Ultimately shareholders may decide, through the procedures of corporate democracy, whether their corporation should engage in debate on public issues. Acting through their power to elect the board of directors or to insist upon protective

---

[73] *See, e.g.*, Elliott Weiss, *Proxy Voting on Social Issues: A Growth Industry*, BUS. SOC. REV. 16, 16 (1974) (describing the Wall Street Rule as "vote with management or sell").

[74] Amendment of Proxy Rules, SEC Securities Exchange Act of 1934, Release No. 4775 (Dec. 11, 1952), 1952 SEC LEXIS 121, at *2.

[75] *See* Sarah C. Haan, *Civil Rights and Shareholder Activism: SEC v. Medical Committee for Human Rights*, 76 WASH. LEE L. REV. 1167, 1196 n.135 (2019).

[76] *See id.* at 1194–96.

[77] *See id.* at 1198–1206.

provisions in the corporation's charter, shareholders normally are presumed competent to protect their own interests. In addition to intracorporate remedies, minority shareholders generally have access to the judicial remedy of a derivative suit to challenge corporate disbursements alleged to have been made for improper corporate purposes or merely to further the personal interests of management.[78]

Powell suggested that dissenting shareholders needed no protection in speech law because corporate governance law gave them tools to protect their interests. But the implication was that shareholders *participated* in the production of corporate speech – they were the deciders. The dissenting justices did nothing to clear this up. Justice White drew a line between a corporation's commercial speech and its political speech; dissenting separately, Justice Rehnquist challenged the idea that the First Amendment applied to corporations at all. A little more than thirty years later, it was still possible for the Supreme Court – now with all new members – to repeat, in *Citizens United v. FEC*, the myth that "the procedures of corporate democracy" were available to shareholders who wanted to weigh in on corporate political speech.[79]

In that controversial decision, the Supreme Court went even further to not only treat the corporation as a stand-alone speaker for First Amendment purposes, but also justified its holding, in part, on an assumption that shareholders would learn about the corporation's political expenditures through disclosure. This assumption turned out to be unjustified – as Justice Kennedy later acknowledged.[80] If shareholders can't even learn about a corporation's political spending, how can they be understood to assent to it? The disclosure deficiencies that emerged after *Citizens United* underscored the myth of "corporate democracy" in the real world.

ATTRIBUTION AND THE RISE OF INFORMATION GOVERNANCE

The four problems discussed above implicate issues of attribution. If corporate speech is misattributed, two groups are potentially harmed. First, as we have seen, people *within* the corporation itself are prejudiced. Corporate stakeholders may be harmed financially, if corporate speech creates significant agency costs, leaving less money for workers and shareholders. In those cases, corporate speech is a drain on the firm akin to corporate "waste," though the standard for corporate waste has traditionally been very high. We might also observe that giving corporate managers free rein to expropriate the corporation's funds for speech creates a whole set of incentives and activities by managers that the corporate economy, at least, would do

[78] 435 U.S. at 794–95.
[79] 558 U.S. 310, at 361–62 ("There is, furthermore, little evidence of abuse that cannot be corrected by shareholders 'through the procedures of corporate democracy.'") (*quoting Bellotti*, 435 U.S. at 794).
[80] *See, e.g.*, Francis Wilkinson, Commentary, *Super PACs Spoil Justice Kennedy's Fantasy*, CHICAGO TRIBUNE, Nov. 4, 2015 (reporting that Justice Kennedy told an audience at Harvard Law School that corporate political spending disclosure was "not working the way it should").

well to discourage. Corporate stakeholders may experience expressive harms, too, when the organization with which they affiliate as workers or shareholders engages in speech acts that violate the stakeholders' own interests and consciences.

Separately, the public itself is harmed from misattribution. As we have seen, attributing a corporation's speech to the corporation as a stand-alone "person" can distort the marketplace of ideas by obscuring the identities of the real people whose viewpoints are being expressed – and by promoting what are, in truth, minority viewpoints, held by a small percentage of the corporation's stakeholders. This sleight of hand may cause ordinary citizens to misunderstand the meaning and origin of corporate political expression.

These observations suggest that the process through which corporate speech is produced is critical for understanding how to attribute authorship.

Since the corporate speaker expresses itself through acts that are structured by corporate governance law, it makes sense for corporate speech attribution to take important cues from the governance that determines the production of speech. That is, corporate speech attribution should give attention to how corporate governance law and practices structure the speech-production process, and should realistically identify the human actors who play important roles in that process.

In previous work, I have argued with Faith Stevelman that the twenty-first century public-company boards engage in "information governance," in which the board's job is to oversee the firm's knowledge and communication systems in order to build its strategic, organizational, and ethical identity.[81] In this paradigm, coordinated action is catalyzed inside the organization by the board's decisions about "what the firm will measure, value, and communicate, internally and externally."[82] These decisions are deeply intertwined in the modern corporation, where information governance has emerged as the primary way in which boards add value to the corporate enterprise. Our work to reconceptualize board governance as "communicative action" highlights the governance structures *behind* the speech, drawing a tight connection between speech production and organizational decision-making processes.

A governance-focused approach to speech attribution would obviate the much-criticized fiction that corporations are meaningfully analogous to humans as speakers. They are not. In addition, by putting emphasis on the power of actors within the firm to determine the firm's expressive acts, the approach places *control* at the center of attribution – an objectively fair approach. Individuals who control a firm's speech should be understood to have produced the speech. This approach is advantageous because it allows speech-related legal doctrines to create and refine incentives for the individuals who make corporate speech choices, particularly where potential speech harms, such as fraud, libel, and incitement are involved. The approach

---

[81] *See generally*, Stevelman & Haan, *supra* note 12.
[82] *Id.* at 183.

would be consistent with current legal trends favoring greater transparency about the identities of those who control corporations.

Finally, this approach would help resolve a tension that has long existed in corporate speech law. The reduction of agency costs has long been understood as an important – to some, the most important – purpose of modern corporate law. Those agency costs arise from conflicts of interest among corporate managers and other constituencies within firms, mainly shareholders. Speech law's failure to cognize these same agency costs in the context of corporate speech is remarkable, as well as problematic. However, acknowledging that corporate managers – or, in some cases, controlling shareholders – are the real "faces" behind corporate speech choices can put speech law on the path to identifying and addressing expressive agency problems. In some cases, requiring a corporation to document, or even disclose, the process used to produce the corporation's speech, in order to get the benefit of a legal presumption, might be especially helpful to courts trying to resolve attribution questions. And it would sharpen the focus of corporate decision makers on that process in ways that would be likely to reduce agency cost problems.

CONCLUSION

The idea of the corporation as a legitimate political actor has been renewed with the occurrence of extraordinary recent events – a pandemic, a racial justice crisis, the #MeToo movement, market turmoil, and a challenge to democracy itself. Corporations have responded to these events with an unprecedented surge of speech: value statements, pledges, political speech, and donations, much of it designed to create an identity and make connections with its stakeholders. These efforts embody "information governance," and reflect a new paradigm in which the corporate board commands the corporation's communication systems, including its public speech. From an internal perspective, a corporation's speech is best attributed to its board. This chapter has argued that, from an external perspective, corporate speech attribution in law should recognize and reflect the information governance paradigm. The *process* of speech production inside the firm – one structured through the information-governance framework emerging in corporate law and theory – is the key to the puzzle. Corporate speech attribution must be deeply informed by the system of firm governance that produces the speech. A candid recognition that corporate speech is, ultimately, the product of board-level decisions would improve our understanding of corporate speech and protect knowledge production, truth, and democratic self-government, at a critical moment in our history.

10

What Is a Corporate Mind?

Mental State Attribution

Benjamin P. Edwards

INTRODUCTION

Many laws apply to natural persons and business entities alike. Yet, corporations, limited liability companies, and other entities differ from humans in many significant ways. Business entities do not breathe. They do not walk our streets. And they do not have minds of their own capable of thinking up corporate thoughts. Humans actually do – or at least enable – all of the things we attribute to these legal entities. If we attribute some mental state to a corporation, the thoughts and intentions attributed must be drawn from some external sources: a human, a collection of humans, or perhaps records of some form.

Attributing mental states to business entities requires law to embrace a double fiction. We must first deem these entities to "exist" even though they lack corporeal substance and are only described in documents. Then, we must somehow attribute mental states to these fictional entities – not because we believe them to have minds but because we need to do it for the law to work. Unsurprisingly, courts struggle to attribute mental states to business entities and mostly default to *respondeat superior* and attribute some human's mental state to the entity.[1] Attributing human acts and intentions remains a relatively new affair; for centuries corporations were not viewed as capable of acting or possessing mental states.[2]

For entities with many diverse shareholders, members, officers, employees, subsidiaries, and affiliates, attributing some mental state to the entity poses a particular challenge. This chapter probes how we attribute mental states to business entities by focusing on how we attribute scienter or fraudulent intent to business entities in securities cases.

---

[1] See Mihailis E. Diamantis *Corporate Criminal Minds*, 91 NOTRE DAME L. REV. 2049, 2050 (2016) (explaining that courts mostly use "an antiquated gimmick–respondeat superior–for holding corporations vicariously responsible for the crimes of their employees").

[2] See W. Robert Thomas, *How and Why Corporations Became (and Remain) Persons under the Criminal Law*, 45 FLA. ST. U. L. REV. 479, 486 (2018) ("for centuries it was understood that corporations were incapable of satisfying even the minimum requirements of criminal law, which generally involve a proscribed act (actus reus) carried out concurrently with a proscribed attitude (mens rea)").

Attribution matters because it allows for application of criminal and civil laws. American laws often define unlawful conduct by pairing some act with a particular mental state. In the criminal law context, we often refer to these components as the *actus rea* and *mens rea* requirements.[3] We also often see mental state requirements in the civil law context to apportion liability for any harm caused by a respondent's actions.

Reviewing mental state attribution in the context of securities fraud claims offers an entry point to thinking about attribution more broadly. Courts have struggled with attributing fraudulent intent to business entities for some time because these entities often create and issue securities. Intention plays a key role in securities fraud claims and may transform an innocent mistake into an odious fraud. For almost half a century, intention has also been a key requirement for claims under Rule 10b-5, the primary anti-fraud regulation for securities transactions.[4] Today, "scienter" generally describes conduct to be more than merely negligent and "connotes intentional or willful conduct designed to deceive or defraud investors."[5]

Yet how does a court attribute a "scienter" to a business entity? Imagine the simplest and most straightforward case for attribution; a corporation's board of directors would meet and unanimously pass a resolution directing the corporation's officers to lie to investors. The unanimous resolution would specifically recognize that the board knew that all of the statements the corporation would make would be false. It would also recognize that these false statements were plainly material to investors and designed to dupe them into purchasing securities. Perhaps, the board would pass a resolution declaring an intent to deceive. In reality, the humans operating business entities do not document their deceptions so plainly. Courts must struggle to attribute intent to the entity on other evidence. For example, a court might consider what the entity's leadership knew and how those facts differed from what they told investors.

Scholars have long struggled with these issues, and this chapter benefits significantly from past work. Over a decade ago, Patricia S. Abril and Ann Morales Olazábal worked to identify "where corporate scienter resides" and argued that we should extend attribution beyond the mechanical application of *respondeat superior*.[6] In recent years, Mihailis Diamantis has probed the area with a focus on corporate minds, corporate knowledge, the possibility of a corporate insanity defense,

---

[3] *See* Erica Beecher-Monas & Edgar Garcia-Rill, *Actus Reus, Mens Rea, and Brain Science: What Do Volition and Intent Really Mean?*, 106 Ky. L.J. 265, 267 (2018) ("Every law student is taught that criminal law is based on two concepts, actus reus and mens rea"). The U.S. Supreme Court has explained that "[c]rime, as a compound concept, generally constituted only from concurrence of an evil-meaning mind with an evil-doing hand." *Morissette v. United States*, 342 U.S. 246, 251, 72 S. Ct. 240, 244, 96 L. Ed. 288 (1952).

[4] *Ernst & Ernst v. Hochfelder*, 425 U.S. 185 (1976) (imposing scienter requirement).

[5] *Id.* at 199.

[6] Patricia S. Abril & Ann Morales Olazábal, The Locus of Corporate Scienter, 2006 *Colum. Bus. L. Rev.* 81, 83 (2006).

and other related topics.[7] Their work lays a strong foundation for understanding the challenges inherent in attributing a mental state to a mindless legal fiction.

This chapter proceeds in three parts. It first surveys some philosophical challenges which complicate conceptualizing a corporate mind and attributing any mental state to it. The second section considers how American courts have attributed intent to business entities in securities fraud cases. Finally, the third part argues that we should not limit courts to simply attributing an intention from an identified human to the entity.

PHILOSOPHICAL CHALLENGES

Attributing some mental state to a business entity poses many of the same challenges as attributing intent to individual humans, only with even more challenges. All of the problems associated with applying a mental state framework to humans simply grow larger in the business entity context.

What Are Minds?

At the outset, the concept of a mind itself has puzzled philosophers for generations. Consider the difficulties inherent in identifying how a mind arises from the body – or even what makes a mind. Are minds physical things or immaterial things?[8] Plato, Aristotle, and Descartes were dualists who all believed minds to be somehow immaterial.[9] In contrast, physicalists believe that minds exist in the physical world.[10] Is a mind a particular collection of neurons? If a traumatic accident damages some neurons, when does the mind cease its existence? If a person functions with the aid of a neural implant, do they have a mind? With the difficulties in identifying a mind, how do we cleanly determine some internal mental state? Ultimately, we must arrive at workable answers for a legal system to apportion liability.

Charting the boundaries for corporate minds may be even more difficult. One approach might require a particular human mind with some relationship to a business entity to have a mental state before attributing it to the entity. Yet, this approach suffers from real flaws because business entities now execute transactions without any human mind ever specifically considering the transaction. Many financially sophisticated entities now rely on algorithms to evaluate data and make trading

---

[7] Mihailis E. Diamantis *Corporate Criminal Minds*, 91 NOTRE DAME L. REV. 2049, 2050 (2016); Mihailis E. Diamantis, *The Extended Corporate Mind: When Corporations Use Ai to Break the Law*, 98 N.C. L. REV. 893, 900 (2020); Diamantis, Mihailis, *The Corporate Insanity Defense* 111 J. CRIM. L. CRIMINOLOGY 1 (2020).

[8] *See* Brian L. Frye, *The Lion, the Bat & the Thermostat: Metaphors on Consciousness*, 5 SAVANNAH L. REV. 13, 26 (2018) (reviewing different theories of consciousness).

[9] *Id.*

[10] *Id.*

decisions. Could a corporate entity be held liable for an algorithm's actions if no human mind directed acts amounting to insider trading or market manipulation? The answer depends on how we attribute mental states to business entities.

Mihalis Diamantis has argued for an expanded conception of the corporate mind, which would sometimes attribute some mental state to a business entity even if no human affiliated with the entity ever possessed the requisite mental state.[11] His argument relies on the extended mind thesis recognizing that minds may extend beyond the boundaries of brains.[12] If a corporation's algorithm uses a database to make decisions, it may be appropriate to attribute knowledge of the database's content to the corporation.

As Diamantis formulated it, the extended mind theory would apply when three criteria are met:

1. The information is available, and the employee/algorithm (on behalf of the corporation) typically invokes it;
2. the employee/algorithm (on behalf of the corporation) more or less automatically endorses the information upon retrieval; and
3. the employee/algorithm (on behalf of the corporation) can easily access the information.[13]

Only attributing mental states actually possessed by actual humans to corporations could cause real problems. For example, a business entity might profit by issuing false and misleading statements and duping people into transactions. Should this conduct be legally permissible so long as no human knows about the false statements? If we require some human to possess a particular intention, modern technology may now effectively free business entities from responsibility for their actions whenever businesses remove humans from decision processes.

The Free Will Assumption

Our law implicitly requires an assumption that individuals have free will and that they could have freely chosen to act in some other way. As commonly understood, to say someone has "free will" means that their minds somehow or to some extent sit outside the ordinary chain of causal determinism governing ordinary things, such as billiard balls.[14] A billiard ball has no choice but to spin across the felt when struck.

---

[11] Diamantis, *The Extended Corporate Mind, supra* note 7, at 900 (arguing "that the law could and should recognize that corporate minds extend to algorithms fulfilling roles that were once occupied only by human employees. By extending the corporate mind in this way, the law could bring corporate accountability into the twenty-first century").

[12] *Id.* at 912.

[13] *Id.* at 921.

[14] *See* Stephen J. Morse, *Criminal Responsibility and the Disappearing Person*, 28 CARDOZO L. REV. 2545, 2547 (2007) ("free will is sometimes taken to mean a distinctively human ability or capacity to act independent of the causal processes of the universe that had been operating on the agent until he or she acted").

To say that humans have free will means that humans may decide on their own when to move and to act instead of responding mechanically when jostled by forces within their immediate environment.[15]

Yet, we know that many individuals often act and move without free will. Routine medical examinations test human bodies for simple motor reflexes by striking below the knee with a mallet. When in good working order, human legs predictably kick forward.[16] Similarly, we do not consciously choose whether to dilate our pupils in response to changes in environmental light. Our bodies simply react to the stimulus. Advances in neurotechnology and medical science may eventually undercut the assumption that humans act with free will as our understanding of human anatomy grows. It may eventually become possible to trace a causal chain of environmental factors leading to decisions in a way that undercuts the free will assumption.

Mental state requirements often mean that law does not hold a person accountable if we understand that a person lacked free will and could not have chosen to do otherwise. The law generally does not hold a person accountable when their hand was forced to action by some external cause. The Seventh Circuit explained the issue as follows:

> In the narrowest sense, every crime must be the product of defendant's free will; it must reflect his choice to perform the criminal act. If the act itself was the result of a mere reflex, or muscular spasm, or was caused by physical duress or compulsion, even the narrowest intent would be absent and the defendant would be innocent of crime; indeed, it could be said that he did not act at all.[17]

For humans, factual showings which undercut the assumption of free will often mitigate or entirely excuse a human from legal responsibility. Notably, the Supreme Court, in limiting the use of the death penalty, recognized "the diminished culpability of juveniles" when it found that "the penological justifications for the death penalty apply to them with lesser force than to adults."[18] The ruling may be read as implying that juveniles lack the "free will" necessary to subject them to capital punishment. We also understand that as juveniles age, they tend to better regulate their behavior.

Courts may hesitate to extend this line of reasoning to exonerate corporations for their actions on some showing the corporation lacked free will even if a court would excuse a human for the same action. Consider two similar scenarios: (i) Alice drafts and mails a fraudulent prospectus because Bert physically holds her hand and forces her to; and (ii) Alice, Inc. issues a fraudulent prospectus because Alice, Inc. may only act through Bert. Although neither has freely chosen to send

---

[15] Philosophical debates about the nature and extent of free will have raged for centuries. I will not attempt to cover all the varied positions.
[16] Medical Dictionary for Regulatory Activities (MedDRA), § 4.32 Reflex Activity.
[17] *United States v. Cullen*, 454 F.2d 386, 390–91 (7th Cir. 1971).
[18] *Roper v. Simmons*, 543 U.S. 551, 571, 125 S. Ct. 1183, 1196, 161 L. Ed. 2d 1 (2005)

a fraudulent prospectus, Bert's fraudulent intent will only be attributed to Alice, Inc. and not to Alice.

Alice and Alice, Inc. differ in significant ways. Alice would, if not for Bert's intervention, make decisions for herself. Alice, Inc. does not actually exist in any corporeal form.

Information versus Knowledge

Attributing a mental state to a corporation may be difficult because simply showing that a corporation possessed information may not always mean that it knew something. If I told you that you had $2.34 in your left pocket, $1.27 in your right pocket, and $1.34 in your hand, most humans would not immediately know whether they had more or less than $5. It takes some quick arithmetic to calculate that you have $4.95 on you. Simply possessing information does not always mean that a person knows its meaning.[19]

For corporations, information may be stored across various places: a third-party-operated server space, executive craniums, and dusty paper files in a Topeka, Kansas warehouse. A corporation may possess information without being fairly characterized as knowing the information in its possession. Imagine three different corporate employees have three distinct pieces of information. If no corporate agent aggregates the information, it may not be fair to charge the corporation with knowledge – even though its agents operated in possession of the information.

Large, multinational corporations may face particular challenges. In some instances, key knowledge may reside in the cranium of a particular, low-level employee. If the knowledge does not move from that individual to significant corporate decisionmakers, the knowledge might nevertheless be attributed to the entity – even though the persons who would have been in a position to use the knowledge never possessed it when making decisions.

CURRENT METHODS OF ATTRIBUTION

Courts now regularly attribute mental states to corporate actors under agency theory.[20] In the securities fraud context, courts have struggled through different approaches, including (A) *respondeat superior*; (B) apparent authority; and (C) collective scienter.[21]

---

[19] *See* Mihailis E. Diamantis, *Functional Corporate Knowledge*, 61 WM. MARY L. REV. 319, 322 (2019) ("Corporate law has yet to grapple with this intuitive distinction between information and knowledge").

[20] Thomas Lee Hazen, § 12:58. Pleading and Proving Scienter – Corporate Scienter, 3 Law Sec. Reg. § 12:58 ("the law of agency will allow the scienter of corporate officials acting on behalf of the corporation to be imputed to the corporation").

[21] *See, e.g., Makor Issues & Rights, Ltd. v. Tellabs Inc.,* 513 F.3d 702, 708 (7th Cir. 2008) ("doctrines of *respondeat superior* and apparent authority remain applicable to suits for securities fraud").

Attributing scienter to business entities plays a pivotal role in U.S. securities fraud litigation. The Private Securities Litigation Reform Act of 1995 (PSLRA) requires that plaintiffs "state with particularity" facts that support a "strong inference" that a defendant possessed the required state of mind.[22] The exercise requires courts to consider whether particular facts warrant attributing fraudulent intent to the corporation at an early stage in the litigation. In essence, attribution becomes a key battleground at the outset.

The Private Securities Litigation Reform Act (PSLRA) also limits discovery until a plaintiff successfully alleges this strong inference of scienter. Functionally, this often means that unless a plaintiff can attribute scienter to the entity in some way at the motion to dismiss stage, the case will never proceed to discovery which might uncover facts sufficient to establish some other basis for attributing scienter to the entity. The entire inquiry becomes more complicated because instead of establishing scienter for a human, a plaintiff must usually somehow attribute scienter to a corporation.[23]

The procedural requirements imposed by PSLRA create a layered attribution challenge. Some courts consider attribution under the same theories at the pleading stage as at proof. Here, narrow standards functionally free business entities from both responsibility and costly legal fees. In other instances, courts sometimes shift their lens when moving from pleading to proof, embracing one set of attribution principles at the pleading stage and another at proof. More expansive attribution standards at the motion to dismiss stage may allow cases to proceed, simultaneously increasing costs for defendants and the potential deterrent effect of the anti-fraud laws.

Respondeat Superior

Respondeat superior provides the most time-honored method for attributing corporate intent. The Restatement (Third) of Agency formulates the broad doctrine as subjecting an employer to liability "for torts committed by employees while acting within the scope of their employment."[24] The phrase "scope of employment" encompasses a broad range of behavior. Under the Restatement's formulation, an employee operates within the scope of employment when "performing work assigned by the employer or engaging in a course of conduct subject to the employer's control."[25] Employee activities fall outside the scope of employment when they occur "within an independent course of conduct not intended by the employee to serve any purpose of the employer."[26]

---

[22] 15 U.S.C. § 78u-4(b)(2).
[23] *See* In re Omnicare, Inc. Sec. Litig., 769 F.3d 455, 473 (6th Cir. 2014) ("This analysis can become much more complicated when the defendant is a corporation because there is the additional question of whose knowledge and state of mind matters.").
[24] Restatement (Third) Of Agency § 2.04 (2006).
[25] *Id.* § 7.07.
[26] *Id.*

Courts considering a business entity's mental state often first look to the mental states of the humans involved.[27] In most instances, federal circuits will *only* attribute scienter under *respondeat superior* and will not consider any other attribution theories. For example, the Fifth Circuit has declared that it will

> look to the state of mind of the individual corporate official or officials who make or issue the statement (or order or approve it or it's making or issuance, or who furnish information or language for inclusion therein, or the like) rather than generally to the collective knowledge of all of the corporation's officers and employees acquired in the course of their employment.[28]

In essence, the Fifth Circuit will only attribute scienter to a corporate entity when it believes that a particular human had scienter. The Fourth Circuit follows the same approach at the pleading stage.[29]

But the doctrine certainly has real flaws and may be both underinclusive and overinclusive. *Respondeat superior* may attribute mental states to a corporation where the overwhelming majority of the corporation's agents act without fraudulent intent. Consider a situation where a corporation employs a hundred different sales-focused employees and charges them all with selling shares. If only one acts with an intention to commit fraud on the corporation's behalf by duping investors, rote application of *respondeat superior* might attribute fraudulent intent to the corporation even though the overwhelming majority of its agents operated lawfully and without fraudulent intent. Relying on *respondeat superior* would attribute a single employee's fraudulent intent to the entity even if all the shareholders, directors, and senior management intended to operate honestly.

Relying exclusively on *respondeat superior* for attributing corporate intent may also allow a corporation to escape liability for acts which, if made by a single natural person, would almost certainly lead to an inference of scienter.[30] For example, a series of persons at a large corporation may make a series of sloppy mistakes, causing the corporation to issue false and misleading statements to its benefit, even though no individual person within the corporate hierarchy intended for the corporation to lie to the public. If the same series of actions had been undertaken by a single

---

[27] For example, *Zhengyu He v. China Zenix Auto Int'l Ltd.*, No. CV21815530KMJAD, 2020 WL 3169506, at *9 (D.N.J. June 12, 2020) ("[entity's] knowledge is imputed through principles of respondeat superior, so its scienter necessarily depends on the knowledge of its employees")

[28] *Southland Sec. Corp. v. INSpire Ins. Solutions, Inc.*, 365 F.3d 353, 366 (5th Cir.2004).

[29] *Teachers' Retirement System of Louisiana v. Hunter*, 477 F.3d 162 (4th Cir. 2007) ("if the defendant is a corporation, the plaintiff must allege facts that support a strong inference of scienter with respect to at least one authorized agent of the corporation, since corporate liability derives from the actions of its agents.").

[30] *Makor Issues & Rights*, 513 F.3d at 707 ("the hierarchical and differentiated corporate structure makes it quite plausible that a fraud, though ordinarily a deliberate act, could be the result of a series of acts none of which was both done with scienter and imputable to the company by the doctrine of respondeat superior.").

individual, it would be simple to infer that the person speaking and acting under such circumstances had intent. Yet, it may not be possible to hold the entity account-able for fraud if no person with fraudulent intent could be identified.

Evidentiary issues may also give a corporate actor the ability to evade liability for acts which, if made by a human transacting business, would almost certainly result in liability. If a human made false statements tending to deceive investors despite having ample information in her possession that the statements were not true, it would be a simple thing to infer that the human intended to deceive. Yet, a corpo-rate actor may behave in largely identical ways, and courts, rigidly bound to *respon-deat superior*, may not be able to attribute fraudulent intent to the entity in instances where it cannot be cleanly established that some person held a fraudulent intent.

Apparent Authority

Corporate scienter may also be established through apparent authority which attri-butes the act of an apparent agent to the entity.[31] The doctrine recognizes the "power held by an agent or other actor to affect a principal's legal relations with third par-ties when a third party reasonably believes the actor has authority to act on behalf of the principal and that belief is traceable to the principal's manifestations."[32] The "traceability" requirement means that the principal must have somehow signaled that the apparent agent possessed authority to act on the principal's behalf. The "reasonableness" requirement limits the scope of the authority to what a reasonable person would believe about the scope of the agent's authority.

Courts have relied on apparent authority to attribute an apparent agent's scienter in the securities fraud context. In *Holloway v. Howerdd*, the Sixth Circuit attributed an unfaithful agent's scienter to the corporation for the plaintiffs who did not know that the agent acted outside the scope of his authority.[33] Notably, plaintiffs who did know that the agent exceeded his authority were unable to recover.[34]

Mental state attribution through apparent authority means that law may attribute a mental state to a corporate entity even when no employee, officer, director, or shareholder ever possessed the mental state. It also raises the possibility that a cor-porate entity may be simultaneously the victim of a crime and rendered a criminal because of the act. An unfaithful agent may both betray a principal and subject it to liability at the same time. The doctrine of apparent authority makes this pos-sible because agents acting outside the scope of their actual authority may still bind

---

[31] *See Am. Soc. of Mech. Engineers, Inc. v. Hydrolevel Corp.*, 456 U.S. 556, 567, 102 S. Ct. 1935, 1943, 72 L. Ed. 2d 330 (1982) (describing apparent authority).

[32] Restatement (Third) Of Agency § 2.03 (2006).

[33] 536 F.2d 690, 696 (6th Cir. 1976).

[34] *Id.* (explaining that the court "relieved TSI from liability to the knowledgeable plaintiffs and held TSI liable to those plaintiffs who were without knowledge of limitations on the agent's authority").

their principles so long as third parties do not have reason to suspect the agent has exceeded her authority. It may also attribute a mental state to a corporate entity even when *respondeat superior* would not permit attribution because an employee acted outside the scope of employment.

For example, the Ninth Circuit relied on apparent authority to impute scienter to a corporate entity "even though [the CEO]'s looting of the corporate coffers was adverse to [the corporation]'s interests."[35] The CEO, Ron Chan, founded ChinaCast Education Corporation (ChinaCast) in 1999.[36] After conducting public offerings, Chan "'transferred' $120 million of corporate assets to outside accounts that were controlled by him and his allies," pledged corporate assets to secure loans unrelated to the business, and allowed other alleged financial misconduct.[37] Eventually, ChinaCast's board removed Chan as Chairman and CEO once it discovered his interference with an audit.[38]

ChinaCast attempted to avoid liability by arguing that Chan's fraudulent intent should not be imputed to it because he plainly acted against ChinaCast's interests in committing his fraud.[39] Relying on Donald Langevoort's analysis, the Ninth Circuit rejected the argument because, even though an "act[ing] against ... interests" exception to the general rule will sometimes limit imputation, the exception to that exception is triggered when a third party is involved: "'the principal is charged with even the faithless agent's knowledge when an innocent third-party relies on representations made with apparent authority.'"[40]

Notably, the Ninth Circuit found that imputing intent under these circumstances cohered with "the public policy goals of both securities and agency law."[41] It explained that imputation created an incentive for "close and careful oversight of high-ranking corporate officials to deter securities fraud."[42]

Other courts have also imputed scienter to corporate entities under an apparent agency theory. The Third Circuit explained that "a swindler may still act with apparent authority, even if he is acting for his own benefit."[43] Similarly, the Tenth Circuit has recognized that "[t]he scienter of the senior controlling officers of a corporation may be attributed to the corporation itself to establish liability as a primary violator of § 10(b) and Rule 10b–5 when those senior officials were acting within the scope of their apparent authority."[44]

---

[35] In re ChinaCast Educ. Corp. Sec. Litig., 809 F.3d 471, 472 (9th Cir. 2015).

[36] *Id.* at 473.

[37] *Id.*

[38] *Id.* at 474.

[39] *Id.* at 476.

[40] *Id.* at 477 (quoting Donald C. Langevoort, *Agency Law Inside the Corporation: Problems of Candor and Knowledge*, 71 U. Cin. L. Rev. 1187, 1214 (2003)).

[41] *Id.* at 478.

[42] *Id.*

[43] *Belmont v. MB Inv. Partners, Inc.*, 708 F.3d 470, 496 (3d Cir. 2013).

[44] *Adams v. Kinder-Morgan, Inc.*, 340 F.3d 1083, 1106 (10th Cir. 2003), as amended on denial of reh'g (Aug. 29, 2003).

Collective Scienter

Collective scienter differs from both *respondeat superior* and apparent authority because it provides an independent basis for corporate scienter without deriving it from a particular agent's scienter. Under this type of approach, it may be possible to draw a strong inference of corrupt corporate intent – at least at the pleading stage – without ever identifying any particular individuals who had the intent.[45]

The Seventh Circuit opened the door to this approach when it gave the following hypothetical:

> Suppose General Motors announced that it had sold one million SUVs in 2006, and the actual number was zero. There would be a strong inference of corporate scienter, since so dramatic an announcement would have been approved by corporate officials sufficiently knowledgeable about the company to know that the announcement was false.[46]

Although the magnitude of some lies may indicate that scienter must exist in the mind of some humans, real-world instances of staggering and unbelievable falsehoods may be rare. Indeed, as lies grow larger, the likelihood that any investor would actually believe them may diminish.

Courts may also apply different approaches to attribution depending on the stage of litigation. For example, the Second Circuit may permit a case to proceed past a motion to dismiss based on collective allegations while still requiring a plaintiff to locate a particular human skull that contained the relevant intent to recover at trial.[47] This approach allows a plaintiff to establish a "strong inference" of scienter in some presently unknown human based on collective corporate conduct without identifying the particular human at the pleading stage.[48] Still, establishing ultimate liability in the Second Circuit requires a plaintiff to "prove that an agent of the corporation committed a culpable act with the requisite scienter, and that the act (and accompanying mental state) are attributable to the corporation."[49] The Ninth Circuit may also follow this approach.[50] Other Circuits have

---

[45] *Makor Issues & Rights*, 513 F.3d at 710 ("it is possible to draw a strong inference of corporate scienter without being able to name the individuals who concocted and disseminated the fraud").

[46] *Id.*

[47] *See Teamsters Local 445 Freight Div. Pension Fund v. Dynex Capital Inc.*, 531 F.3d 190, 195 (2d Cir. 2008) ("it is possible to raise the required inference with regard to a corporate defendant without doing so with regard to a specific individual defendant").

[48] *See id.* ("When the defendant is a corporate entity, this means that the pleaded facts must create a strong inference that someone whose intent could be imputed to the corporation acted with the requisite scienter.").

[49] *Id.*

[50] *See* In re NVIDIA Corp. Sec. Litig., 768 F.3d 1046, 1063 (9th Cir. 2014) ("[T]here could be circumstances in which a company's public statements were so important and so dramatically false that they would create a strong inference that at least some corporate officials knew of the falsity upon publication.") (*quoting Glazer Capital Mgmt., LP v. Magistri*, 549 F.3d 736, 744 (9th Cir. 2008)).

declined to take a position on collective scienter.[51] Some have flatly rejected collective scienter.[52]

In some instances, courts adopt hybrid standards allowing courts to expand their view before reaching a conclusion about corporate scienter. The Sixth Circuit leads with an approach that will attribute scienter to business entities by looking at whether the management-level employees engaged in misconduct.[53] After rejecting the narrow *respondeat-superior*-only approach first embraced by the Fifth Circuit, the Sixth adopted the following approach first proposed by Professors Patricia S. Abril and Ann Morales Olazábal:

> The state(s) of mind of any of the following are probative for purposes of determining whether a misrepresentation made by a corporation was made by it with the requisite scienter under Section 10(b): ...
>
> a. The individual agent who uttered or issued the misrepresentation;
> b. Any individual agent who authorized, requested, commanded, furnished information for, prepared (including suggesting or contributing language for inclusion therein or omission therefrom), reviewed, or approved the statement in which the misrepresentation was made before its utterance or issuance; or
> c. Any high managerial agent or member of the board of directors who ratified, recklessly disregarded, or tolerated the misrepresentation after its utterance or issuance.[54]

The expanded approach aims to limit the ability of corporations to evade "liability through tacit encouragement and willful ignorance, as they potentially could under a strict *respondeat superior* approach."[55] Even if high-level executives lack an intention to mislead investors, they may signal that subordinates should not bring them bad news or otherwise cause the corporation to make overly optimistic or untrue statements without ever knowing that their statements were false.

---

[51] *Smallen v. The W. Union Co.*, 950 F.3d 1297, 1314 (10th Cir. 2020) ("We have neither accepted nor rejected [the collective scienter] theory of corporate scienter"); *Martin v. GNC Holdings, Inc.*, 757 F. App'x 151, 155 at n. 24 (3d Cir. 2018) (declining to "decide whether the "corporate" or "collective" scienter doctrine is a viable theory because the allegations in the complaint are insufficient to establish GNC's scienter.").

[52] *Southland Sec. Corp. v. INSpire Ins. Solutions, Inc.*, 365 F.3d 353, 366 (5th Cir.2004) (rejecting "generally to the collective knowledge of all of the corporation's officers and employees acquired in the course of their employment."); *see also Phillips v. Scientific–Atlanta, Inc.*, 374 F.3d 1015, 1018–19 (11th Cir.2004) (implicitly adopting this approach).

[53] *See, e.g., Employees Ret. Sys. of Puerto Rico Elec. Power Auth. v. Conduent Inc.*, No. CV198237SDWSCM, 2020 WL 3026536, at *8 (D.N.J. June 5, 2020) ("Amended Complaint also alleges corporate scienter through an inference based on alleged misconduct that is attributable only to management level corporate officials").

[54] *In re Omnicare, Inc. Sec. Litig.*, 769 F.3d 455, 476 (6th Cir. 2014) (quoting from Patricia S. Abril & Ann Morales Olazábal, *The Locus of Corporate Scienter*, 1 COLUM. BUS. L. REV. 81, 83 (2006)).

[55] *Id.* at 477.

ATTRIBUTION FOR ALGORITHMIC ENTITIES
AND DISTRIBUTED INTELLIGENCES

Current methods for attributing intention to corporate entities all suffer from one critical flaw – they all require that some humans be meaningfully involved in the entity's affairs. Yet, developments in law and technology now enable entities to act in increasingly sophisticated ways without any human ever directing their actions.

Organizations Now Act without Human Direction

As Mihailis Diamantis has recognized, corporations now regularly act without any human specifically directing and ordering their actions.[56] This happens with increasing frequency in securities trading, credit-evaluation, price-setting, and in automotive transport.

As humans fade from decision-making processes, attributing intentions derived from humans becomes increasingly challenging. Despite this, law's application often requires some link to a particular human's intention. Functionally, Diamantis recognized that this means that "corporations will become increasingly immune to liability as their operations require less and less human intervention."[57]

Current attribution doctrines may also create perverse incentives to structure an entity's affairs in ways that frustrate efforts to hold entities accountable for actual activities. If liability may be diminished by distancing humans from decisions, corporations will likely accelerate transitions to automation without fully grappling with the dangers the digital delegation may unleash.[58]

Consider the possible outcomes if an insurance company delegated payment decisions to some sophisticated artificial intelligence. Some machine learning algorithms might be tasked with making determinations about whether to approve or deny claims. Human oversight and intervention might only enter into the process when insured persons appeal initial determinations to the company. In addition to distinguishing between the legitimate and bogus, a machine-learning algorithm might learn to strategically deny claims made by persons least likely to appeal the decision. In this circumstance, no human would have intended to deny claims by persons most vulnerable and likely to accept an insurance company's abuse. The insurance company would reap a substantial profit, and the risk of liability for intentional bad faith conduct might be almost entirely eliminated. Yet, if a human acted in the same way, the insurance company would likely face liability for acting in bad faith. Ultimately, increasing automation may allow entities to neatly sever intention from effect.

---

[56] *See* Diamantis, *The Extended Corporate Mind, supra* note 11, at 895 ("advanced algorithms utilizing big data and artificial intelligence are rapidly reshaping every corner of modern business").

[57] *Id.* at 899.

[58] *Id.* at 899–900 ("legal loophole[s] left by *respondeat superior* incentivizes an unpalatable form of corporate gamesmanship. Corporations keen to manage their liabilities will seek the safe haven of algorithmic misconduct rather than chance liability for misconduct by human employees").

Entirely Autonomous Entities May Have No Humans Involved

Much has changed since Lawrence Solum first speculated about legal personhood for artificial entities.[59] About six years ago, Shawn Bayern recognized the possibility that "certain types of business entities" may now "serve as legal 'containers' for autonomous systems, such as computer programs or robots."[60] Essentially, an algorithm in control of a limited liability company enjoys functional legal personhood and the ability to contract with and interact with natural persons.

Lynn Popucki has also considered the issue and argued that these entities might pose significant threats to humanity and enjoy significant comparative advantages in criminal activities.[61] Artificial algorithmic entities need not fear prison because they may simply self-replicate or spawn subsidiaries and affiliates carrying copies of their code. Lacking mirror neurons, they will feel no empathy and may "not recoil at the necessity to do violence to humans."[62]

Persons creating and launching independent, algorithmic entities free from their subsequent control may not face significant liability for the entity's later actions because prosecutors may struggle to show that some curious initiator of these entities possessed any specific intent that the entity would later engage in some harmful activity.[63] Indeed, it may be difficult, if not impossible to predict an algorithmic entity's future behavior. After all, our society does not hold parents accountable for the acts of their children once they become independent legal persons.

Applying current laws to these entities may be a challenge if we may only attribute intentions to them by deriving them from some human. Fully autonomous, algorithmic entities act without any human first intending their actions.

Future Attribution Challenges

Some thought experiments might suggest an alternative approach. Advances in technology may soon restore movement to limbs after paralysis or significant nerve damage. Neural implants seeded into the brain may soon allow persons who would

[59] *See* Lawrence B. Solum, *Legal Personhood for Artificial Intelligences*, 70 N.C. L. Rev. 1231 (1992) ("No existing computer program currently possesses the sort of capacities that would justify serious judicial inquiry into the question of legal personhood.").

[60] Shawn Bayern, *The Implications of Modern Business-Entity Law for the Regulation of Autonomous Systems*, 19 Stan. Tech. L. Rev. 93, 94 (2015); Shawn Bayern, *Of Bitcoins, Independently Wealthy Software, and the Zero-Member LLC*, 108 Nw. U.L. Rev. Online 257, 268 (2014) ("it appears remarkably straightforward to set up a perpetual LLC that has no members in its final, planned operational state.").

[61] *See* Lynn M. Lopucki, *Algorithmic Entities*, 95 Wash. U.L. Rev. 887, 891 (2018) ("Unfortunately, AEs' greatest comparative advantage would be in criminal enterprise.").

[62] *Id.* at 892.

[63] *Id.* at 901 ("If the algorithm later directed the commission of a crime, prosecutors may be unable to prove the intent necessary to convict the initiator of that crime (as opposed to the lesser charge of reckless initiation).").

otherwise be locked inside their craniums to recover complete control over their bodies.[64] If these augmented folks used technological aids to commit crimes, our civil and criminal laws would hold them accountable for their behavior – as we would if an ordinary person used a stick, automobile, or other devices to act.

Yet, we can also imagine circumstances where these augmented persons might do significant damage and not incur any legal liability. Imagine if a faulty software update, hacker, or some other external cause disrupted the ordinary control these persons had over their neural implants. Evidence that many similarly situated persons found their bodies lurching about and malfunctioning in similar ways at the same time would appropriately cause us to infer that the person lacked any intent to commit a particular act. Even if the behavior, standing alone, would have ordinarily caused us to attribute intentions to their actions, the broader circumstances would stop us from attributing a mental state and from holding them accountable for actions undertaken by a malfunctioning neural implant.

In many circumstances, we might seek to hold some other human accountable for the damage caused by an augmented person with malfunctioning neural implants. If a software company executive, with an eye toward bonus season, recklessly rushed an unfinished and untested software update out, our law would likely hold him accountable for the damage caused by recklessness. Similarly, if a human hacker took control of an augmented person's body and used it to commit crimes, our law could attribute the augmented person's puppet-like acts to the hacker holding malicious intent and hold the hacker accountable.

Yet, how would our law address an algorithmic entity seizing control of an augmented person? The augmented person would walk our streets, breathe our air, and perhaps take actions we would deem to be securities fraud if they were to be committed by an ordinary human. Ordinary attribution principles – *respondeat superior* and apparent agency – might not attribute any mental state to the entity.

As technology advances, our ability to readily differentiate between an augmented person and an ordinary human may diminish. An algorithmic entity might simply grow a human corpus in a vat or assemble one with a three-dimensional printer. If and when these entities walk our streets, we will not likely excuse them from all responsibility for their actions if they reveal their true nature. We will either abandon the human-centric mental state framework or somehow attribute intentions to these entities.

It seems most likely that we would treat these entities as we do any other human. After all, without cracking skulls, we could not truly know whether another person in the room is controlled by an algorithmic entity or not. When we deal with humans, statutes often instruct us to simply make an inference and attribute an intention to

---

[64] *See* Hannah C., *Can Elon Musk's Neuralink Overcome the Complexities of the Human Brain?*, THE SCIENCE TIMES (Aug. 30, 2020, 11:18 PM), www.sciencetimes.com/articles/27101/20200830/elon-musk-neuralink-complexities-human-brain.htm (discussing neural implant technology).

other persons – even though we can never truly know with absolute certainty what another person's intentions were. For example, Delaware's statute instructs that a "defendant's intention, recklessness, knowledge or belief at the time of the offense for which the defendant is charged may be inferred by the jury from the circumstances surrounding the act the defendant is alleged to have done."[65] It tells a jury to "consider whether a reasonable person in the defendant's circumstances at the time of the offense would have had or lacked the requisite intention, recklessness, knowledge or belief."[66] If we treat an entity as we would a human, we would simply infer intentions based on the surrounding circumstances.

Thus far, we have considered how to attribute intention when a single augmented human or simulacrum operates under the control of a single intelligence – be it human or an algorithmic entity. Yet our future likely holds other, stranger possibilities. Algorithmic entities might pay for the privilege of driving about in human bodies, much as sharing economy services now allow us to rent transportation, lodging, and office space. In these circumstances, we would most likely apportion responsibility by temporal control. After all, we do not hold a human responsible for what the next driver does with the rental car.

But not all intelligences function as we humans do. Consider an octopus, for example. The creature possesses a large and complex nervous system.[67] Unlike us mammals, the octopus does not centralize its nervous system to the same degree. Most neurons sit inside tentacles. Some experiments have shown that an octopus's tentacles may move both at the direction of its brain and entirely independent of it. Moreover, tentacles communicate information to each other without it ever reaching the centralized brain.[68] Do octopi possess mental states? How would we know? We would likely attempt to infer it based on their actions. If an octopus were outfitted with neural implants and granted control over an augmented human (perhaps by some curious, scientifically inclined algorithmic entity), we would likely attribute a mental state to the augmented human's octopoid operator – even if it were predominantly operated by the octopus's tentacles and not its centralized brain.

Business entities today often behave more like octopi than humans with centralized nervous systems. Although some centralized decision-making groups such as officers and directors may exist, much of the actual activity occurs without any conscious direction from the centralized decision-making structure. Tentacles and lower-level personnel also communicate substantial information among each other

---

[65] Del. Code Ann. tit. 11, § 307(a) (West).

[66] *Id.*

[67] Peter Godfrey-Smith, *The Mind of an Octopus: Eight smart limbs plus a big brain add up to a weird and wondrous kind of intelligence*, SCIENTIFIC AMERICAN (Jan. 1, 2017), www.scientificamerican .com/article/the-mind-of-an-octopus/.

[68] Michelle Starr, *Octopus Arms Are Capable of Making Decisions without Input from Their Brains*, SCIENCEALERT (June 26, 2019), www.sciencealert.com/here-s-how-octopus-arms-make-decisions-without-input-from-the-brain.

without ever involving the centralized core. When information passes between lower-level agents, important context and information may be lost. One employee may make statements that another employee knows to be false. As it stands now, our law makes it unlikely that any mental state would be attributed to an entity for these acts – even though we would likely attribute intentionality if we understood the entity to function as a whole.

CONCLUSION

Mental state requirements may be too deeply entrenched in legal systems to be eliminated. If we do not abandon the mental state framework for allocating civil and criminal liability, additional fictions to attribute appropriate intentions may be necessary.

But establishing reasonable attribution principles will be challenging. Consider the dangers of simply presuming that entities always intend the consequences of their acts. In cases where false statements deceive investors, the presumption would simply attribute scienter to the entity. This crude method would render entities liable for any simple mistake committed by their agents. Merely issuing a false statement would subject an entity to liability for securities fraud. This dynamic would likely cause businesses to fear making any statements at all or to over-invest in ensuring accuracy. On balance, it would likely deter economic activity and create far too much liability.

But we should not continue to excuse entities from responsibility simply because we cannot successfully tie intentions to specific individuals. We must consider entities as we do other humans and attribute mental states to them when appropriate – even if no single human mind possesses the requisite intent. This means making inferences about them by looking at the entire circumstances surrounding their actions – in fact, it means treating them like people.

11

Who Is a Corporation?

Attributing the Moral Might of the Corporate Form

Catherine A. Hardee

INTRODUCTION

Moral values – like a belief in following the dictates of a higher power, ethical claims about the proper treatment of our fellow human beings, or the moral worth of responsible stewardship of the planet – have driven human action for millennia. In recent years, there has been increasing pressure on corporate entities to engage in moral or ethical decision-making. Given the immense economic and political power of modern corporate entities, it becomes critical to determine the origin point of these ethical decisions, both to ensure that corporations are held responsible for their moral choices and to tether corporate moral decision-making power to the appropriate group, or groups, of human beings. Determining to whom corporate morality should be attributed is not an easy task, however, and requires consideration not just of the people involved in the corporation but also of the role the corporation plays within a representative democracy. Ultimately, inquiry into the attribution of a corporation's moral judgments may best be seen as fluid and context-dependent. That is, it should examine both the way the corporation is structured and the importance of representation for the moral choices of corporate stakeholders.

One way to approach this attribution inquiry is to begin with the nature of the corporation. "What is a corporation?" is a question that has puzzled courts and scholars for well over a century. Scholars have posited many theories of the nature of a corporation: a mere nexus of contracts,[1] an association of individuals,[2] an entity created by the state,[3] or a team of people bound together by a shared goal to produce a good or service,[4] to name just a few. In the United States, the U.S. Supreme Court

---

[1] See Frank H. Easterbrook & Daniel R. Fischel, *The Corporate Contract*, 89 COLUM. L. REV. 1416 (1989).

[2] See, e.g., Morton J. Horwitz, *Santa Clara Revisited: The Development of Corporate Theory*, 88 W. VA. L. REV. 173 (1985).

[3] Whether the entity is "real" or a "fiction" is subject to debate. See, e.g., Mark M. Hager, *Bodies Politic: The Progressive History of Organizational "Real Entity" Theory*, 50 U. PITT. L. REV. 575, 587 (1989).

[4] See, e.g., Margaret M. Blair & Lynn A. Stout, *A Team Production Theory of Corporate Law*, 85 VA. L. REV. 247 (1999).

has been consistent only in the inconsistency with which it treats the question.[5] In some cases, it has treated the corporation as an entity, in others as an association of individuals, and in still others, it has only superficially engaged with the corporate identity question, treating it as an afterthought. At times, the conception of a corporation motivating the Court's analysis appears to change even within a single opinion, and at no point has the Court expressed a coherent theory of what a corporation is under the law.

By the late twentieth century, the debate over the nature of a corporation had somewhat fizzled out in the United States, with some scholars questioning whether it really matters what a corporation is in an abstract sense. This *détente* was upended in the early twenty-first century when the U.S. Supreme Court began giving deeply personal rights to corporations, divorced from profit motives, starting with the freedom of speech and moving into the freedom of religion.[6] These decisions lean strongly on an associational theory of corporations, but never fully embrace it. In response, members of the legal academy took to their computers with a renewed furor, with literally thousands of articles discussing the cases.[7] The nature of a corporation has once again become a hot topic.

Alongside this debate over the legal status of corporations, a corollary discussion has reemerged over the purpose of corporations. The U.S. political left has long championed socially responsible corporations that put social goods – like environmental welfare and human rights – over, or at least alongside, profit.[8] This movement has experienced a resurgence in the past two decades. In recent years, however, the expansion of corporate purpose beyond profit has found an unlikely ally in the religious right. "Conservative corporate theory" of profit maximization is no longer *en vogue* with many political conservatives who have argued that corporate purpose should be expanded to include religious motivations – an argument embraced by the Supreme Court's conservative wing.[9] In this increasingly partisan world, surprisingly, it appears that there is widespread agreement that corporations – whatever they are – should be norm-generating entities.

---

[5] *See* Elizabeth Pollman, *Reconceiving Corporate Personhood*, 2011 UTAH L. REV. 629 (2011).

[6] The decisions of the United States Supreme Court are used in this chapter to help illustrate the difficulty of attributing morality to artificial corporate entities. While United States law is used as the example, scholars outside the United States have long grappled with similar issues relating to artificial entities. *See, e.g.*, Ron Harris, *The Transplantation of the Legal Discourse on Corporate Personality Theories: From German Codification to British Political Pluralism and American Big Business*, 63 WASH. LEE L. REV. 1421 (2006) (describing the European origins of American corporate law theory).

[7] At the time of publication, there were nearly 5,000 law review articles citing *Citizens United v. Fed. Election Comm'n*, 558 U.S. 310 (2010), and nearly 2,000 law review articles citing *Burwell v. Hobby Lobby Stores, Inc.*, 573 U.S. 682 (2014).

[8] *See* Douglas M. Branson, *Corporate Social Responsibility Redux*, 76 TUL. L. REV. 1207 (2002).

[9] *See* Leo E. Strine, Jr. & Nicholas Walter, *Conservative Collision Course?: The Tension between Conservative Corporate Law Theory and Citizens United*, 100 CORNELL L. REV. 335 (2015); *see also Burwell*, 573 U.S. at 711–12 (rejecting profit as the only proper purpose of a corporation).

Despite these pressures for corporations to become moral agents, it is difficult to attribute the creation of moral frameworks to corporations. Even in granting religious rights to corporations, the Supreme Court stopped short of attributing religious beliefs or sincerity to the corporations themselves. Instead, the Court employed linguistic slights of hand to attribute to entities the personal beliefs of those associated with the corporation. Moreover, corporate moral commitments, especially by public corporations, bump up against profit maximization in ways that leave serious questions about whether corporate morality is sincere or simply an effective marketing tool. If corporations are to engage in true moral expression, it would seem there must be a person or people to whom these morals can be attributed. This suggests that the real question should not be *"what* is a corporation," but rather *"who* is the moral conscience of the entity." Attribution becomes a central question. That is, to whom in the corporation should this moral agency be attributed?

In answering this question, it may be tempting to turn to corporate law's default – the shareholders. While that is the route the Supreme Court has taken, at least with respect to corporate religion, it is hardly the only option. Shareholders are arguably a good fit to speak for the profit-making aspects of corporate governance, as they are the holders of the residual profits of the company. There is far less reason, however, why shareholders' capital investment should give them status as the moral soul of the corporation.

Given the predominance of the profit maximization theory in corporate law, searching for the "whom" to which to attribute the moral soul of a corporation is an exercise that at times feels like hammering the proverbial square peg in a round hole. Alongside the rise in calls for broader corporate purpose, however, a rich literature has arisen advocating for a broader conception of corporate stakeholders. Whether through stakeholder theory, communitarianism, or team production, scholars have described the ways that various groups should be, or already are, central to corporate decision-making.[10] In considering to whom corporate morality should be attributed, this chapter lends additional support to the call for a more inclusive conception of corporate actors.

A fresh look at who should be considered "the corporation" with respect to corporate morality, ethics, and religion – matters of a profoundly different nature than economic return – leads to a variety of potential groups of people, apart from shareholders, to which corporate morality might be attributed. Management, employees, and consumers all potentially can claim a connection with the corporation that justifies attributing the corporation's morality, at least in part, to them. In examining each group's claim to moral relevance, one must consider whether the corporation's

[10] *See, e.g.*, Blair & Stout, *supra* note 4; Robert M. Ackerman & Lance Cole, *Making Corporate Law More Communitarian*, 81 Brook. L. Rev. 895 (2016); P.M. Vasudev, *The Stakeholder Principle, Corporate Governance, and Theory: Evidence from the Field and the Path Onward*, 41 Hofstra L. Rev. 399 (2012) (describing stakeholder theory and surveying U.S., U.K., and Canadian corporations).

moral claim necessarily arises from within the corporation – for example, moral claims that purport to ground the sincerity requirement for religious exemptions – or whether the corporation's moral claim is a reaction to the ethical choices of market participants outside the corporate structure, like consumers.

An additional, and critical, factor to consider is the role that corporate ethics play *vis-a-vis* state norm generation. Corporate ethics designed to supplant democratically imposed norms may require heightened concern for true corporate democracy, while corporate morality working within democratically set limits may raise fewer representation concerns. That is, if corporate ethics are used to seek an exemption from generally applicable laws, this may create more concerns than other targets of corporate ethics. Further, where failings in democratic institutions leads to corporations taking the place of governments, we should be especially concerned about whether corporations' normative stances are representative of those of the broader public, and especially those members of the public who are impacted by the corporate enterprise. As history has shown, when corporations step into the breach left by governments with little concern regarding their responsiveness to the people they "govern," the result is not just antidemocratic, but ultimately unsatisfactory, even for those in power.[11] One possible reason for the increased calls for corporate morality may be a loss of faith in democratic institutions to truly represent the beliefs of their constituencies. If corporations are to step into the role of norm generation, traditional forms of corporate governance, which arose to accommodate profit maximization, may be insufficiently representative. It may be time to rethink *who* is a corporation.

This Chapter proceeds in three parts. Part I considers whether attribution of the traditional loci of corporate control – to the corporation itself or to its shareholders – is appropriate for moral attribution. Part II argues that a broader set of corporate stakeholders should be considered as potential loci of a corporation's moral values, including management, employees, and consumers. Finally, Part III examines the way a corporation's role with respect to the state impacts the attribution question.

WHOSE MORALITY?

The argument that corporations can, and should, generate and act upon moral principles raises an important question: When we say a corporation holds some moral belief, or makes a moral claim, whose morality are we talking about? This question is of fundamental importance because corporate morality can have an enormous

---

[11] *See generally* Doreen Lustig, *The Enduring Charter, Corporations, States, and International Law, supra* chapter 4. Prof. Lustig chronicles the rise and fall of corporate control over British colonies, which eventually ended in the state taking over the formal power to govern from early corporations. As Prof. Lustig points out, however, corporations maintained their influence in the colonies and reaped the financial benefits.

impact on corporate stakeholders, communities, and the world at large. When a corporation asserts a religious belief in the sanctity of life at the time of conception, thousands of employees can lose their statutory right to contraceptive coverage.[12] Whether corporations follow through on their environmental commitments can have world-altering consequences.[13] Given the broad impact corporations have, it is necessary to be able to hold accountable those whose moral compass is directing corporate action. It is also desirable to ensure that those who are impacted by corporate moral decision-making have a voice in the creation of the corporation's moral code.

The Corporation Itself

One potential answer to the question, to whom corporate morality should be attributed, could be the corporation itself. Such an answer would be in line with the fundamental corporate law principle that the corporation is a separate entity that stands separate and apart from the human beings who create and maintain it.[14] Whether corporate entities themselves are capable of creating and using a moral compass, however, is debatable.

Corporations can without doubt engage in moral behavior. Corporate structures may even be put into place that require the corporation to follow a particular moral code even if no one within the corporation shares that moral belief. A compelling example of this phenomenon is "zombie" religious corporations, which are required by contract to abide by the religious code of a former business partner who is no longer associated with the entity.[15] The corporation must continue to engage in these religious activities even if no one in the company – shareholders, management, or employees – hold the governing religious views. Such corporations raise questions of moral philosophy similar to arguments regarding whether artificial intelligence can be a moral actor.[16]

---

[12] *See Burwell v. Hobby Lobby Stores, Inc.*, 573 U.S. 682, 702 (2014) (noting that defendant Hobby Lobby employs 13,00 people).

[13] *See* Peter Eavis & Clifford Kraus, *What's Really behind Corporate Promises on Climate Change?*, NY Times, Feb. 22, 2021, www.nytimes.com/2021/02/22/business/energy-environment/corporations-climate-change.html (describing the difference between corporate commitments and their continued environmental impacts).

[14] *See* Leo E. Strine, Jr. & Nicholas Walter, *Originalist or Original: The Difficulties of Reconciling Citizens United with Corporate Law History*, 91 Notre Dame L. Rev. 877, 887 (2016) ("A business corporation is not simply 'individual men and women': it is a distinct entity that is legally separate from its stockholders, managers, and creditors.").

[15] *See* Elizabeth Sepper, *Zombie Religious Institutions*, 112 Nw. U. L. Rev. 929 (2018) (discussing this relatively common phenomenon that results from mergers and break ups between religious and secular hospitals).

[16] *See, e.g.*, Joshua P. Davis, *Law without Mind: Ai, Ethics, and Jurisprudence*, 55 Cal. W. L. Rev. 165, 170 (2018). *See also*, Benjamin P. Edwards, *What Is a Corporate Mind? Mental State Attribution*, supra chapter 9 (analyzing attribution for algorithmic entities).

Outside the realm of moral philosophy, when it comes to moral decision-making, especially involving personal moral decisions, there is a disconnect between the idea of morality and the profit-making imperative of for-profit corporations. This discomfort is evident in the U.S. Supreme Court's language granting religious exemptions to corporations. Despite giving the corporations at issue the religious exemptions they sought, the Supreme Court has consistently attributed religious beliefs to *people* associated with the corporation rather than the corporation itself. In *Burwell v. Hobby Lobby*,[17] the religious belief that life begins at conception was attributed to the families who run the corporations – "the owners" – rather than the corporations themselves, despite the fact that the corporations were the entities supplying the contraceptive insurance to employees.[18] In *Masterpiece Cakeshop*,[19] when discussing whether the petitioner's religious or speech rights were violated by the state's decision to fine the company for refusing to bake a cake for a gay wedding, the Court consistently referred to the sincere beliefs of "the baker" rather than the corporate party.[20] The concurrence by Justices Thomas and Gorsuch, which reached the merits of the petitioner's free speech claim, focused on the expressive acts of the individual petitioner *as a baker* and discussed *his* religious belief that marriage is between a man and a woman.[21] The concurrence only mentioned the corporate party seeking relief to note the baker's "control over the messages that Masterpiece sends."[22]

---

[17] 573 U.S. 682 (2014). The *Hobby Lobby* case involved three for-profit corporations who objected to the Affordable Care Act's contraceptive mandate, which gave employees a right to no-cost contraceptive coverage. The shareholders of the three closely-held corporations objected to certain contraceptives as abortifacients and challenged the mandate under the Religious Freedom Restoration Act ("RFRA"). A majority of the Supreme Court found for petitioners and held that the corporations at issue were entitled to an exemption from the mandate.

[18] *See* Catherine A. Hardee, *Who's Causing the Harm?*, 106 KENTUCKY L. J. 751, 774, n.158 (listing references to shareholders' beliefs in the *Hobby Lobby* opinion).

[19] 138 S. Ct. 1719 (2018). The petitioners in *Masterpiece Cakeshop* were: (a) one of two shareholders in a closely held corporation that owned and operated a bakery, and (b) the corporation itself. The individual petitioner had refused to bake a wedding cake for a gay couple. The petitioners were found to be in violation of Colorado's anti-discrimination statute, and petitioners appealed, claiming the statute violated both their religious freedom and their free expression rights under the First Amendment. The Supreme Court, in a divided opinion, narrowly held that the Colorado Civil Rights Commission had displayed religious animus in its decision-making and therefore vacated its ruling. The decision produced three concurring opinions and a vigorous dissent by Justices Ginsberg and Sotomayor.

[20] *See, e.g., Masterpiece Cakeshop*, 138 S. Ct. at 1723 ("The reason and motive for the baker's refusal were based on his sincere religious beliefs and convictions."); *id.* at 1724 (describing Jack Phillips' religious beliefs regarding gay marriage); *id.* at 1728 (describing petitioner's claim as "implicat[ing] his deep and sincere religious beliefs"). Although the corporation had two shareholders, the Justices only referred to the named petitioner and omitted any discussion about the other shareholder's religious beliefs. *See* Catherine A. Hardee, *Schrodinger's Corporation: The Paradox of Religious Sincerity in Heterogeneous Corporations*, 61 BOSTON COLL. L. REV. 1763, 1776 (2020).

[21] *See, e.g., Masterpiece Cakeshop*, 138 S. Ct. at 1743–44 (Thomas J. concurring) (describing the expression involved in designing and baking the cake and noting that forcing Phillips to make same sex wedding cakes forces him to convey "the precise message he believes his faith forbids").

[22] *Id.* at 1745; *see also id.* at 1734 (Gorsuch J. concurring) (focusing on "Mr. Phillips's sincerely held religious beliefs" while never mentioning the corporate party).

The Court has had no such qualms attributing religious beliefs religious entities, whether they be for-profit or non-profit entities. In *Hobby Lobby*, the belief that life begins at conception was directly attributed to the Mennonite Church.[23] In *Obergefell v. Hodges*,[24] the Supreme Court reaffirmed its respect for the sincere religious convictions of "religious organizations and persons."[25] This linguistic turn is most prominent in *Little Sisters of the Poor v. Pennsylvania*.[26] In that opinion, the majority and concurring opinions attribute religious beliefs directly to the religious, non-profit entity, The Little Sisters of the Poor.[27] Justice Alito's concurring opinion reaches the question of whether the exemption for for-profit entities, including public entities, is required under the Religious Freedom Restoration Act. Here, the opinion's language shifts and religious beliefs are attributed to an "employer" with sincere religious beliefs, a word whose definition includes both people and companies who employ.[28] This linguistic sleight of hand situates the reader in a more comfortable position of associating religious conviction with human beings rather than the corporate entity.[29]

The court's avoidance of attributing morality to the corporate entity is not merely a matter of linguistics. The Court's holdings require the individuals associated with the corporate parties to prove their religious sincerity, but not the corporation itself.[30] This is markedly different from previous cases where non-human "persons," like churches or religious corporations, were subject to a test of legitimacy

---

[23] See *Hobby Lobby*, 573 U.S. at 700 ("The Mennonite Church opposes abortion and believes that the fetus in its earliest stages ... shares humanity with those who conceived it.") (quotation omitted).

[24] 576 U.S. 644 (2015). The *Obergefell* decision is the landmark case where the Supreme Court held that the right to marry is a fundamental right that cannot be denied to same sex couples.

[25] 576 U.S. 644, 679 (2015).

[26] 140 S. Ct. 2367 (2020). The opinion addresses the State of Pennsylvania's challenge to the Trump administration's regulations exempting "religious employers," including for-profit and even public corporations, from the contraceptive mandate in the Affordable Care Act.

[27] See *id.* at 2376 ("[T]he Little Sisters hold the religious conviction 'that deliberately avoiding reproduction through medical means is immoral.'"); *id.* at 2386 (noting that the Little Sisters are "motivated by a religious calling"); *see also id.* at 2391 (Alito, J. concurring) ("It is undisputed that the Little Sisters have a sincere religious objection to the use of contraceptives.").

[28] *Id.* at 2391 (Alito, J. concurring) (noting that the mandate impacts "any employer who, like the Little Sisters, has a sincere religious objection" to it "and a sincere religious belief" opposing compliance with the accommodation).

[29] Although the Supreme Court is hesitant to attribute sincerely held religious beliefs to the entities themselves, the federal regulations at issue in *Little Sisters of the Poor* occasionally do. *See, e.g.*, Religious Exemptions and Accommodations for Coverage of Certain Preventive Services Under the Affordable Care Act, 83 F.R. 57536-01 ("The rules are necessary to expand the protections for the sincerely held religious objections of certain entities and individuals."). The regulations even allow that unions or multi-employer health plans might have sincerely held religious beliefs. *See id.* at 57560. At times, however, when discussing specific religious beliefs, the language is narrowed to the religious beliefs of human beings. *See id.* at 57554 ("The Departments do not take a position on the scientific, religious, or moral debates on this issue by recognizing that some people have sincere religious objections to providing contraception coverage on this basis.").

[30] See Hardee, *Schrödinger's Corporation*, *supra* note 20, at 1777–80 (describing the Court's focus on religious sincerity of individuals, not corporate entities).

rather than sincerity.[31] While sincerity is a subjective test that examines the veracity of an individual's religious beliefs, legitimacy is an objective test that is "based on the organization's creation, purpose, function, activity, and self-expression to the community."[32] Under the legitimacy test, it is not sufficient to demonstrate that the individuals who comprise the organization hold particular religious beliefs; the organization itself must be organized primarily for a religious purpose rather than a secular purpose, such as a profit motive.[33] The fact that for-profit organizations categorically fail the legitimacy test suggests that courts have been unwilling to consider such corporate entities as the root of religious beliefs.

The Supreme Court's hesitancy to attribute morality to for-profit entities is not limited to religious beliefs. Attribution differs in the free speech context depending on the nature of the speech, with at least some Justices looking to the individual, rather than the corporation, when questions relating to personal moral choices are at issue. When dealing with corporations, the Court usually respects the entity form and looks to the corporate entity for purposes of attribution. This is best seen in the corporate speech arena where the Court looked to the "procedures of corporate democracy" to determine who speaks for the corporation.[34] Corporate speech, at least campaign-related speech, was attributed to the corporation. That holding stands in contrast with Justice Thomas' concurrence in *Masterpiece Cakeshop*, which reached the free expression claim involving the creation of a cake for a same-sex wedding.[35] In his concurrence, joined by Justice Gorsuch, the focus was on the role of the petitioner as employee – as baker – rather than shareholder, and the corporate entity was altogether ignored.[36] The moral beliefs motivating the speech are attributed to the baker – an individual.[37] For at least some Justices, it appears that the closer the rights at issue are tethered to the adoption of a moral claim, the less willing the Court is to attribute them to the corporation.

---

[31] *See* Richard Carlson, *The Sincerely Religious Corporation*, 19 MARQ. BENEFITS & SOC. WELFARE L. REV. 165, 179 (2018) ("Before *Hobby Lobby*, the courts had adopted two separate tracks for evaluating the credibility of religions persons. Human persons claiming religion were subject to questions about sincerity. Non-human persons, such as churches, religious schools, and other religious organizations were subject to a test of legitimacy.").

[32] *Id.* at 185 (discussing the test for organizations under Section 702 of Title VII of the Civil Rights Act (42 U.S.C. § 2000e-1(a) (2012))).

[33] *See, e.g., EEOC v. Townley Eng'g & Mfg. Co.*, 859 F.2d 610, 619 (9th Cir. 1988) (holding that a mining company is not primarily religious despite its use of corporate funds to support religious purposes and religious owners because the corporation is primarily a for-profit mining operation).

[34] *Citizens United v. Fed. Election Comm'n*, 558 U.S. 310, 362 (2010) (finding that "corporate democracy" would determine what speech the corporation chooses to engage in) (quoting *First Nat. Bank of Bos. v. Bellotti*, 435 U.S. 765, 794 (1978)).

[35] *Masterpiece Cakeshop*, 138 S.Ct. at 1740 (Thomas, J., concurring).

[36] *See, e.g., id.* at 1742 (noting that petitioner "considers himself an artist" and describing in detail the process of designing and creating the cake).

[37] *See, e.g., id.* at 1744 (arguing that forcing the petitioner to create a wedding cake for a same sex wedding would violate his personal faith).

Outside Supreme Court religious exemptions jurisprudence, there is much skepticism regarding moral claims by a corporation. Claims that a corporation "cares about the environment" or "believes in equality" are often met with concerns that corporations are merely reacting to market forces – holding moral positions only to the extent that they provide more profit than the contrary moral position. The term "greenwashing" is a commonly referenced example of this phenomenon, where corporations claim to hold strong environmental values but only do so in response to market forces and only to be followed through with as the market requires.[38] In recent years, the term "woke-washing" has been coined to describe this same phenomenon regarding corporate commitments to social justice movements, such as the Black Lives Matter movement.[39]

This reluctance to see a corporation itself as generating sincere moral beliefs suggests that when we say a corporation is exercising moral agency, what is more likely meant is that we recognize that some person or constellation of people associated with that corporation holds those beliefs. Thus, the *corporation's* morality is better attributed to that set of human beings than the corporation itself. The question of whose beliefs are attributed to the entity is crucially important because it could determine who has a say in the process of forming the corporation's moral framework, or, at the very least, to whom the corporation is answerable for its moral decision-making.

The Shareholders

Given the shareholder primacy model in the United States, the obvious group of people to whom to attribute corporate morality in this context would be corporate shareholders. That is who the Supreme Court tapped to determine a corporation's religious beliefs.[40] In colloquial terms, shareholders are often thought of as the "owners" of the corporation.[41] In closely held corporations, shareholders frequently run the company directly themselves. In larger entities, including public corporations, shareholders elect the board of directors, who are the ultimate decision-makers for the company. It follows that shareholders may feel connected to the corporation in ways that make them feel morally responsible for corporate actions.

---

[38] *See* Miriam A. Cherry, *The Law and Economics of Corporate Social Responsibility and Greenwashing*, 14 U.C. Davis Bus. L.J. 281, 282–83 (2014) (providing history and definitions of the term "greenwashing").

[39] *See* Owen Jones, *Woke-Washing: How Brands Are Cashing in on the Culture Wars*, The Guardian, May 23, 2019, *available at* www.theguardian.com/media/2019/may/23/woke-washing-brands-cashing-in-on-culture-wars-owen-jones.

[40] Although the question of which shareholders' religious beliefs are attributable to the corporation, and under what circumstances, is still open for debate. *See* Hardee, *Schrodinger's Corporation, supra* note 20.

[41] The U.S. Supreme Court, for example, exclusively refers to the shareholders in *Hobby Lobby* as the "owners" of the corporation rather than as shareholders. *See, e.g., Hobby Lobby*, 573 U.S. at 691 ("The owners of the businesses have religious objections to abortion…").

This standard response, however, ignores many of the nuances of corporate governance and papers over the distinctions between types of corporations. It is hotly debated whether it is accurate to refer to shareholders as the "owners" of a corporation.[42] In addition, shareholder power is greatly constrained, especially in public companies.[43] This limited power is further diluted by the fact that most shareholders own their stocks through intermediaries, such as in mutual funds and through retirement accounts, and thus have no direct control over shareholder votes.

Despite these limitations, there is a trend toward shareholder activism, even in public corporations. Shareholders of public companies are increasingly instigating and voting in favor of shareholder proposals that encourage management to commit the corporation to engage in socially responsible behavior based on the shareholders' moral framework.[44] The growth of socially responsible investment funds demonstrates that even when investing through an intermediary, some shareholders expect their capital to carry with it their moral values. All this suggests that shareholders in public corporations likely differ in whether they believe that the moral actions taken by the corporations in which they invest can (or should) be attributed to them.

The picture becomes even more complex when taking different types of corporations into account. The obvious distinction between publicly held and private corporations can mask the differences within each group. When thinking of publicly held corporations, entities with broad, diffused public shareholders spring to mind. But there are also a large number of publicly held corporations with majority or controlling shareholders or shareholder families.[45] Controlling shareholders, even in public corporations, might feel more responsibility for the corporation's moral choices than shareholders in a public corporation with no controlling shareholder.

There are also great variations among "closely-held corporations" or "privately held corporations." The term "closely-held corporation" can apply to both venture capital backed companies and family run enterprises; to both small businesses and massive entities with tens of thousands of employees; and to entities with a single shareholder or hundreds, depending on the state of incorporation. These differences mean that the relationship between shareholders and the corporation can vary dramatically, including whether the shareholder directs, or is likely to identify with, the moral choices of the entity.

[42] *See, e.g.,* Margaret M. Blair, *On Models, Metaphors, Rhetoric, and the Law,* 41 TULSA L. REV. 513 (2006) (discussing limitations of the ownership model).

[43] *See, e.g.,* Stephen M. Bainbridge, *Director Primacy and Shareholder Disempowerment,* 119 HARV. L. REV. 1735 (2006).

[44] *See* Faith Stevelman & Sarah C. Haan, *Boards in Information Governance,* 23 U. PA. J. BUS. L. 179 (2020).

[45] *See* Lucian A. Bebchuk & Assaf Hamdani, *Independent Directors and Controlling Shareholders,* 165 U. PENN. L. REV. 1271, 1279 (2017) (noting that "a sizable minority of large, publicly traded firms" have controlling shareholders).

The lack of consistency regarding shareholders' roles in corporate moral decision-making is perhaps why the Supreme Court has been reluctant to attribute religious sincerity to shareholders in *all* corporations. This suggests that in the Court's view share ownership does not automatically come with the right of moral determination for the corporation. In other words, it is not necessarily a feature of share ownership in any type of corporation that it conveys the right to decide corporate morality in the way that share ownership typically conveys the right to vote for the board or for the residual profits of the company. Rather, it is some constellation of actions or beliefs on the part of particular types of shareholders that can provide the justification for attributing the moral acts of the corporation to them.

The Supreme Court has never explicitly outlined what feature of shareholding, or what shareholding context, conveys the ability for shareholders to claim the moral soul of the corporation. Despite this, the Court's precedent regarding corporate religious beliefs can be of assistance in sketching out some factors that may lead to a conclusion that shareholders are closely enough aligned with the company to be its moral center. A careful reading of the Court's corporate religion opinions exposes some commonalities the Justices have deemed relevant to their inquiry, including:

(1) *Whether the shareholder is the decision-maker regarding the moral choices of the corporation.*[46] This factor tracks the idea that individuals are responsible for the choices they make. It makes a certain measure of logical sense to attribute decisions to the decision-maker.

(2) *Whether the shareholders' money is funding the corporate behavior.*[47] Much like being the ultimate decision-maker, providing the funding for an action creates a feeling of responsibility for the consequences of that decision.

(3) *Whether the shareholder's personal morality is impacted by the corporation's moral choices.*[48] Corporate action that is in direct conflict with the

---

[46] The fact that the petitioner shareholders are the decision-makers for the corporation is crucial in *Hobby Lobby* and *Masterpiece Cakeshop*. In both cases the Court takes pains to point out that the petitioner shareholders "own and operate" the corporation at issue and made the corporate decisions at issue based on their personal morality. See *Hobby Lobby Stores*, 573 U.S. at 700–01, 702–03; *Masterpiece Cakeshop*, 138 S. Ct at 1724.

[47] The majority in *Hobby Lobby* noted repeatedly that the issue in the case was that plaintiffs were required to "fund contraceptive methods that violate their religious beliefs." 573 U.S. at 730; *see also id.* at 726 (noting that plaintiff's "assert that funding the specific contractive mandate at issue violates their religious beliefs").

[48] The clearest example of this factor is found in *Masterpiece Cakeshop*, where the baker/shareholder would have been required to meet with customers and bake a cake for a wedding to which he objected on religious grounds, thus creating a conflict with his personal morality. See 138 S. Ct. at 1724. There is a more attenuated impact on shareholders when complicity-based claims are asserted, as in *Hobby Lobby*. The basis of the complicity-based claims is that a corporate decision, such as the one to provide contraception coverage, enables employee decisions that conflict with the shareholders' morality, that is, using covered contraception, and thus impacts the shareholders. See Douglas Nejaime & Reva B. Siegel, *Conscience Wars: Complicity-Based Conscience Claims in Religion and Politics*, 124 YALE L.J. 2516 (2015).

shareholder's choices can create a conflict between share ownership and the shareholder's moral beliefs.

(4) *Whether the shareholder identifies strongly with the corporation.*[49] A corporation is not supposed to be the alter ego of its shareholders, but that does not stop some shareholders from feeling as if the company is part of who they are and an expression of themselves.

These factors can combine to strengthen the argument that corporate morality is attributable to shareholders. For example, the more decisions within the corporation the shareholder makes, the more the shareholder may identify with the corporation. This can lead to a chicken and egg dilemma: Do shareholders feel responsible for the moral decisions of the corporation because they are the decision-makers, or should shareholders be the decision-makers regarding corporate morality because they feel a personal responsibility for the corporation's actions?

Regardless, shareholders are not the only people who engage in these activities *vis-a-vis* corporations, even in closely held corporations. Management is frequently the group making the moral decisions for the corporation. Employees' personal moral choices can be impacted by the corporation's moral stance.[50] The money used to fuel corporate behavior can be seen as coming from consumers, as much as, if not more than, from the shareholders. Members of any of these groups may identify closely with the corporation. As the group is entitled to the corporation's residual profits, it makes sense that shareholders would have the biggest (and perhaps only) say in decisions that further the corporation's *profit* motive. But shareholders are neither the only people implicated in the *moral decision-making* of the corporation, nor the only group impacted by that morality.

A FRESH PERSPECTIVE

A fresh perspective on the question of the attribution of corporate morality requires taking into account ways in which corporate morality differs from the profit motives of a corporation. If the right to determine the corporation's moral choices is not inherent in the "bundle of sticks" that comprise share ownership, but rather arises from some constellation of decision-making, funding, impact, and/or identification, then a more careful look at the people involved with these aspects of the corporation is necessary. This inquiry requires a more thoughtful analysis of where these choices originate and whom they impact.

---

[49] The best evidence that shareholder unity with the corporation plays a significant role in the Court's decisions is the fact that the Justices ignore the corporate form entirely, and thus, assume a unity of identity. *See* Hardee, *Who's Causing the Harm?*, *supra* note 18, at 751.

[50] For example, the employees in *Hobby Lobby* lose their contraceptive coverage due to the religious exemption granted based on the morality of the companies' shareholders.

Management

When considering who makes the decisions that cause a company to engage in moral actions, corporate management – the board of directors and officers – must be discussed. After all, the board of directors is the ultimate decision-maker for most matters of corporate policy, and corporate officers create and impose that corporate policy.[51] But does, or should, the board make decisions based on the moral beliefs of the individual directors?

The traditional view in corporate law is that directors act on behalf of, and are beholden to, the shareholders in a fiduciary relationship, and thus must put the interests of the shareholders first.[52] As such, perhaps it could be argued that this fiduciary relationship extends beyond financial return to morality as well. In this rendering, the board would be required to adopt the moral position of shareholders rather than enacting its own morality. In a closely held corporation with a limited number of homogenous shareholders, such a director-as-shareholder-agent rule might reflect the practical reality of corporate governance. In publicly held corporations or private corporations with heterogeneous shareholders, however, it is neither likely that the shareholders share a unified moral view, nor is it likely that the board has a strong sense of the shareholders' dominant views on a particular issue. A growing number of shareholder proposals by socially responsible investment funds are giving boards a better sense of the values some shareholders hold and of the strength of those values among the shareholder class.[53] But these proposals are often limited to particular questions and do not generally provide information to the board about how the shareholders as a class wish to balance the social benefit and their desire for profit.[54] In addition, boards may be called upon to act on social issues before coordinating feedback from shareholders. For example, after the murder of George Floyd in the summer of 2020, corporate boards and management were pressured to make swift and decisive statements in support of the Black Lives Matter movement.

Even if management is unable to ascertain a shareholder consensus (or, under an alternate theory, are agents of the corporation only and not its shareholders, and therefore, not required to be responsive to shareholder values), it does not follow that managers are free to enact their own moral judgments. They are at least agents of the corporation itself, and thus, still required to act in the best interests of the

---

[51] It is also reasonable to assume that directors and officers identify with the corporations they serve, perhaps even more so than shareholders, as they are generally the public face of the corporation.

[52] *See* Henry Hansmann & Reinier Kraakman, *The End of History for Corporate Law*, 89 Geo. L.J. 439, 441–42 (2001). This is a debated proposition, with many modern scholars rejecting the shareholder primacy framework. *See, e.g.,* Stephen M. Bainbridge, *Director Primacy in Corporate Takeovers: Preliminary Reflections*, 55 Stan. L. Rev. 791, 795 (2002).

[53] *See* Stevelman & Haan, *supra* note 44, at 216 (documenting the rise of ESG investor-activism and its impact on boards).

[54] Even shareholders who favor a particular position – for example, reduction of carbon emissions – might differ greatly on how much, if any, profit they are willing to forego in pursuit of that goal.

corporation. Under a profit maximization theory, management should ascertain what morality consumers are willing to pay for and align the corporation to those values to the extent that they are profitable. In that circumstance, it is consumers' moral beliefs that are ultimately driving corporate morality.

If the profit maximization theory is rejected, or management is not an agent of, and thus not beholden to, the shareholders, management is arguably left to develop a moral compass for the corporation. This outcome is not necessarily better than a shareholder as principal model. The result is to entrust an elite minority, which is notoriously unrepresentative of the public, with the power to decide the moral impact of immense resources under its control.[55] While this seems like a potentially poor policy, it may be an accurate description of practice. Even if boards claim to be following the moral commitments of their consumers or their shareholders, they are allowed such great latitude in making decisions that their own personal moral preferences are likely to play a heavy role in determining corporate practice.

Employees

Even in circumstances where the answer to the corporate morality attribution question must involve a belief that originates within the corporation, there is no reason why that belief must originate from the more elite groups of shareholders or management. These groups are not the only decision-makers in the corporation, especially when one considers the difficulty in identifying a single decision-maker in any given corporate context. For example, if the CEO of a pharmacy decides to carry the prescription for Plan B without objection from the board of directors, the local branch manager stocks the store, and the pharmacist fills a customer's prescription, who is the decision-maker regarding the "corporate pharmacy's" decision to sell Plan B to that customer? Was it the non-objecting board, the CEO, or the lower-level employees who did not dissent?

In addition, while employees do not contribute capital to the corporation, their labor contributions to the corporation create corporate wealth in much the same fashion as shareholders' capital contributions do. Corporate expenditures arguably arise from employees' contributions of labor – just as they do from shareholders' contributions of capital – and employees can thus be viewed as facilitating corporate moral action in much the same way as shareholders are. This contribution of labor has led to an increasing interest by employees in the ethical commitments of their employer. Employers attempt to attract top talent by promising a just workplace aligned with employee values, thus using this employee desire to work for a moral

---

[55] See *Missing Pieces Report: The Board Diversity Census of Women and Minorities on Fortune 500 Boards: 6th ed.* 18, DELOITTE (June 8, 2021), *available at* www2.deloitte.com/us/en/pages/center-for-board-effectiveness/articles/missing-pieces-board-diversity-census-fortune-500-sixth-edition.html (finding that, in 2020, of the Fortune 500 companies only 26.5 percent of board seats were occupied by women and only 17.5 percent of board seats were occupied by racial minorities).

employer in their favor and binding the workforce to its employer through moral identification.

Perhaps most importantly, employees are often the ones whose personal moral choices are most impacted by the corporation's moral stance. Corporations claiming religious exemptions have increasingly made complicity-based claims that the corporation is facilitating moral choices made by employees with which the shareholders do not agree.[56] The most prominent example of such complicity-based claims is the various suits objecting to the contraceptive mandate in the Affordable Care Act, including the suits at issue in the *Hobby Lobby* decision. In these suits, several corporations argued that providing government-mandated employee health insurance that includes contraceptive coverage to all employees violates the religious rights of the corporation and its shareholders. While the Court focused on the rights of the shareholders to determine a corporate policy, it paid little attention to the impact corporate morality had on the personal moral choices of employees.[57] These claims, however, necessarily involve the corporation infringing on the moral autonomy of employees.

Significant support for the argument that corporate morality impacts employees comes, ironically, from a corporate religion case brought by the corporate owner – *Masterpiece Cakeshop.*[58] The claim of the baker/owner focused almost entirely on his actions as an employee, not as a shareholder. The majority and concurrences discussed the impact on the baker's religious and expressive rights of having to meet with a gay couple, design a cake to celebrate their union, and bake the cake for a wedding to which he objected.[59] All of these actions – interacting with customers and creating a product – are actions taken by the baker as *employee* of the bakery. It is difficult to see how the same arguments would not also apply to any employee of a bakery who is forced to bake and decorate a cake to which they had a moral objection – or alternatively, to a baker forced to refuse to bake a cake for a gay couple in opposition to their sincerely held religious beliefs about love and equality. This recognition of employee morality finds support in the so-called "conscience clauses" in virtually every state, which allow medical professionals to refuse delivery of reproductive care that violates their personal or religious beliefs.[60]

Even outside of religious exemptions, moral decisions made by the corporation can have an impact on employees' moral autonomy. Henry Ford infamously used

---

[56] *See* Nejaime & Siegel, *supra* note 48, at 2516.

[57] *See id.* at 2580 (countering the Court's assertion that accommodating the shareholders' religious beliefs would have "precisely zero" impact on the corporation's female employees).

[58] 138 S. Ct. at 1719.

[59] *See, e.g., id.* at 1724 (creating a wedding cake); 1742–43 (Thomas, J. concurring) (describing the process of creating the cake).

[60] Elizabeth Sepper, *Taking Conscience Seriously*, 98 VA. L. REV. 1501, 1504 (2012). Nevertheless, most states also allow medical facilities to "assert moral positions against certain treatments and refuse to provide them," which employees must follow "even when they conflict with their individual consciences." *Id.*

his company to impose a moral code on his factory employees. While known best in the law for taking a stand against shareholder profit maximization,[61] Ford also believed that he could use the corporation to force employees to behave according to his vision of American values, down to mandating church attendance, the way employees dressed, and even to how they furnished their homes.[62] More recently, the company WeWork, as a part of its environmental commitment, created a policy that employees would only be reimbursed for vegetarian meals while travelling on company business.[63] Employees' decision-making autonomy could end up a casualty as companies seek to create change in the world.

Like shareholders in a closely held corporation, employees often make decisions necessary to implement corporate moral choices, provide the labor necessary to fund the corporation's actions (thus solidifying their identification with their employer), and are impacted by the corporation's moral commitments. As such, there is a strong argument that corporate morality can be attributed to employees, and this argument compares favorably to the claims by shareholders or management. Thus, when considering religious exemptions to the law, if courts are going to consider the moral beliefs of the shareholders, they should look to the employees' beliefs as well. This may be difficult to do as employees are likely to have heterogeneous beliefs. The difficulty, however, should not allow employees' moral beliefs to be pushed aside. If both shareholders and employees have conflicting claims to the corporation's moral identity on a religious exemption impacting employee rights, a return to a legitimacy test that focuses on the purpose of the entity may be more appropriate. Outside of the religious exemption context, corporations that claim to be furthering a moral end should provide a mechanism for employees to play a part in developing the moral compass of the corporation.[64]

One argument against attribution to employees is that employment is often temporary and employees may simply change jobs if they disapprove of the corporation's moral stance. While it is true that many employees are mobile, this does not distinguish employee status from share ownership, as share ownership in most corporations is also mobile. The real question is whether employees should be entitled by another way to impact corporate morality besides changing employment. After all, while shareholders have the ability to influence corporations by selling shares, they are also given a limited right to impact the corporation while remaining

---

[61] *Dodge v. Ford Motor Co.*, 204 Mich. 459 (1919).

[62] *See* Leo E. Strine, Jr., *A Job Is Not a Hobby: The Judicial Revival of Corporate Paternalism and Its Problematic Implications*, 41 J. CORP. L. 71, 81 (2015).

[63] David Gelles, *Memo From the Boss: You're a Vegetarian Now*, NY TIMES, July 20, 2018, www.nytimes.com/2018/07/20/business/wework-vegetarian.html.

[64] For example, consider the dual boards structure of governance under German corporate law, which mandates employee representation on the supervisory board. *See* Vahid Dejwakh, *The Directorist Model of Corporate Governance: Why a Dual Board Structure for Public Corporations Is Good for Shareholders, Entrepreneurs, Employees, Capitalism, and Society*, 8 WM. MARY POL'Y REV. 57, 66 (2016) (describing German corporate governance).

shareholders through their voting power. Employees arguably should be given a similar mechanism to influence the corporation's moral commitments.

Consumers

While some expressions of corporate morality legally require the ethical determination to originate *within* the corporation – such as from its shareholders, management, or employees – most do not. Outside the context of religious decision-making that requires an exemption from the law, it is irrelevant, from a legal perspective at least, whether anyone within the corporation sincerely believes in the corporation's moral choices. As such, attribution of the corporation's moral choices to the appropriate individual-level source is not a legal requirement in most contexts. It does not follow, however, that attribution questions outside that context should not be answered. Attributing moral choices to a particular individual or group ensures both accountability and that the power to make moral decisions for the corporation is in the correct hands. In situations where attribution of a moral choice to an individual or group within the corporation is *not* required by law, corporate morality can still be attributed to individuals or groups inside the corporation – but it can also be attributed to an outsider: the consumer.

Many, if not most, moral positions taken by corporations are in response to market pressure from consumers. It is tempting to dismiss these choices as not properly "ethical" at all, but rather some variation of "greenwashing" or "woke-washing." If a corporation commits to supporting the LGBTQ+ community, for example, but only because its managers have determined that this support will make consumers more inclined to purchase their products and thus increase profits, the corporation might face accusations of woke-washing. In these situations, no one within the corporation necessarily needs to share a moral belief that it is right to support the LGBTQ+ community. Moreover, the corporation's morality will likely change if market morality changes, and so potentially decouple itself from the beliefs of corporate insiders. Ultimately, the notion that morality can be profit-driven feels like a corruption of the term "morality."

Looking outside the corporation, however, there *is* morality at work in these market-driven processes. It is the morality of *consumers* that drives the decision-making of corporations taking profit-driven stances. Increasingly, consumers are tying their spending decisions to their personal moral beliefs.[65] These consumer choices drive corporations to make certain decisions regarding corporate morality. As such, the moral weight of those decisions can be attributed to their consumers. One problem with woke-washing, or greenwashing, is that the company's

---

[65] *See* Sarah Dadush, *Identity Harm*, 89 U. Colo. L. Rev. 863, 870 (2018) ("Studies consistently find that consumers are increasingly willing to pay a premium for goods sold by companies whose sustainability values align with their own.").

commitment is only surface level. The corporation will only do whatever consumers require and will attempt to hide any corporate actions that violate its public commitments. It does not necessarily follow that morality is not at play, however; merely that the market or legal regulations may be doing a poor job of informing consumers of the reality of corporate positions and, more importantly, of corporate actions.

Even in corporations or contexts where ethical decision-making comes from within (from shareholders, management, or employees), there is reason to take the moral choices of consumers seriously in attributing corporate morality. Consumers' spending drives the company regardless of its ownership model. Money comes into the corporation from consumers and cycles through capital holders back into the corporation, which employees use to create products that consumers buy, and the cycle continues. All groups – shareholders, employees, and consumers – engage in moral decisions regarding their contributions in this economic cycle.

All this suggests that corporate morality can be attributed, at least in part, to consumers as well as shareholders. Recognizing that consumers are a significant driver of corporate morality might suggest regulatory changes to provide more information or control to consumers. At present, consumers can make purchasing decisions based on their moral beliefs, but these are not necessarily well-informed decisions. Corporations have no legal obligation to disclose whether their actions are in line with their public moral commitments and consumers have little to no enforcement mechanism if corporations act in opposition to their stated moral positions. Just as there are calls for more information and accountability for public shareholders making socially responsible investments, a similar disclosure regime could benefit consumers as well.[66] Given the diffused nature of stock ownership and the weak power of shareholders, consumers may be able to vote more easily with their spending dollars than their retirement funds.

CORPORATION VERSUS STATES

In addition to considering all corporate stakeholders, another important dimension of corporate morality is the role that corporations play in norm generation, and the entity's relationship to state power. One facet of that relationship is whether the corporation's moral actions are in compliance with democratically enacted regulations, or serve to resist those. Most corporate action is constrained by the democratic process – either by statute or government regulations that place limits on corporate behavior. Environmental regulations, for example, provide a floor for how a corporation's actions may impact the environment. The corporation may willingly exceed that baseline if it commits to do so, but it may not drop below the standard set by

---

[66] *See also*, Sarah Dadush, *The Law of Identity Harm*, 96 WASH. U.L. REV. 803 (2019) (advocating for a cause of action for conscious consumers under tort, contract, and state consumer law).

the law without facing a penalty. If societal norms change and the standard is raised, corporations must abide by the norms set by the democratic process.

When the public democratic process provides a baseline for corporate ethics, there may not be a concern that corporate democracy provides a mechanism for taking the views of all corporate constituents into account. To the extent that employees are unhappy with corporate ethical decision-making, they can respond through the democratic process. For example, if a majority of voters believe that corporations should be required to provide health insurance to employees, they may vote for representatives who will require that through state regulation.

When corporations thwart the public democratic process on the basis of corporate morality, however, it may raise a concern that there be some measure of true corporate democracy to take the place of democratically developed regulations. This thwarting occurs, for example, when corporations claim exemptions to the law on moral grounds, such as religious exemptions. In these instances, there is no democratic "check" on corporate moral decision-making. As such, it becomes significantly more important that the internal structure for determining a corporation's morality embraces a broader theory of attribution. Otherwise, those who help create and are impacted by corporate morality may see their moral agency reduced with little recourse.

Another facet of the relationship between corporations and the state to consider is whether corporations have taken over the functions typically performed by the state. One way to view the increased pressure on corporations to act morally or "do the right thing" is as a response to the government's failure to respond to popular demands for regulation. In the modern era, corporate power has traditionally been reined in by external state regulations rather than by any internal corporate mechanism or morality.[67] In recent years, democratic institutions in the United States have failed to respond to public will on a wide range of issues. Corporate lobbying has played a significant role in diverting the legislative process away from regulatory efforts, even those called for by the public at large. Proponents of corporate morality in the United States may be seeking a solution to legislative gridlock and unresponsive representatives by asking corporations to voluntarily do that which the majority believes the government should require.[68]

To be fair, some corporations do appear more responsive than governmental entities, at least on the surface. For example, banks and retail outlets responded quickly against gun manufacturing and sales following the school shooting in Parkland,

---

[67] *See* Elizabeth Pollman, *Constitutionalizing Corporate Law*, 69 VAND. L. REV. 639 (2016).

[68] The ultimate irony is that governments may have become unresponsive to the people in part because of corporate spending to thwart government regulation. *See,* Leo E. Strine, Jr., *Corporate Power Ratchet: The Courts' Role in Eroding "We the People's" Ability to Constrain Our Corporate Creations,* 51 HARV. C.R.-C.L. L. REV. 423 (2016). Forcing corporations to take into account the views of a broader constituency when making moral decisions, which might include lobbying, could wind up helping to address legislative gridlock.

Florida, in 2018, while Congress has consistently failed to take meaningful action on gun control.[69] Regardless of why corporations take these moral positions, the fact that they do can weigh heavily in the creation of a society's moral fabric. If corporations are to step in to the breach left by government failures, those driving corporate ethics should be representative of more than just an elite few.

With respect to corporate morality, we may be asking corporations – and corporate law – to take on roles that do not suit them. Arguably the first-best solution would be to return to a functioning democratic process that is responsive to the majority, creating baselines for corporate behavior that align with public sentiment. Corporations could then be left largely to focus on profit-making within a more stringent regulatory framework. If governments fail to respond adequately to citizens' calls to rein in the negative externalities of corporate power, however, the next best option is to reconsider who has the power to shape corporations into moral entities.

CONCLUSION

In the end, the question of attribution of corporate morality is not an easy one to answer. One must push past metaphors like corporate personhood and the linguistic slights of hand designed to obfuscate attribution more than to illuminate it and actually consider the attribution claims for various corporate constituencies and the roles that corporations play within society. The result is that there is no one answer to attribution questions that is rational and satisfactory for every corporation in every instance. Rather than striving for a unifying theory of corporate morality attribution, one might be better served taking a utilitarian or consequentialist approach, examining the impact corporate morality has on society and whether attribution to a particular set of people in a given situation furthers important societal goals.

Such an inquiry may lead to disparate attribution rules in disparate circumstances. For example, in a functioning state with a regulatory baseline that is representative of majority views, taking into account the moral beliefs of corporate constituents in the attribution inquiry may be of less importance as everyone has the ability to alter the corporation's moral baseline through the legislative process. Even in a functioning state, however, when a corporation seeks a moral exemption to democratically enacted regulations, meaningful attribution of moral identity takes on new importance. To avoid giving an elite few the power to control the morality of other corporate constituencies, the attribution inquiry should consider not just shareholders but also employees whose moral choices are impacted by corporate morality and whose labor helps finance corporate action. If expanding that inquiry to reflect the moral

---

[69] See *Factbox: Recent U.S. Corporate Responses to Gun Violence*, REUTERS, Sept. 3, 2019, www.reuters.com/article/us-usa-shooting-guns-companies-factbox/factbox-recent-u-s-corporate-responses-to-gun-violence-idUSKCN1VO2LT.

choices of all employees is too cumbersome for courts to manage, the solution is not to ignore the moral choices of tens of thousands of employees. Rather, courts could revert to the legitimacy test discussed earlier in this chapter, under which an organization's moral choices may be credited only if the organization itself is organized primarily for a moral or religious purpose.

When the public democratic process is failing and there is reason to be concerned that public regulations are not representative of majority will, the corporate morality attribution question takes on its greatest importance. If corporations are the de facto norm-generating entities for society, then it should be of paramount importance that corporate morality is formed through true corporate democracy. The focus should be on finding meaningful ways for disaggregated shareholders and employees to participate in corporate governance and to ensure that consumers are informed and have legal mechanisms to hold corporations to their moral commitments. Only in that circumstance would there be alignment between the true moral agents – the consumers, employees, and others who help drive and fund corporate moral choices – and the power to make ethical decisions for the corporation.

PART IV

Conceptual Origins and Lineages

12

The Juridical Person of the State

Origins and Implications

David Ciepley

INTRODUCTION

When one speaks today of a "corporation," one invariably means a business corporation. In lay usage, there is no other referent. Yet, long before the business corporation, there were monasteries, cathedral chapters, bishoprics, confraternities, cities, universities, hospitals, guilds, and more, all of which were allowed use of the corporate form – that is, allowed to organize their activities around a corporate "person" that owns all the property, makes all contracts, and appears in court in its own name rather than in the name of natural persons. But of all the diverse applications of the corporate form to date, only one has had a world-transformative impact rivaling that of its application to business enterprise, and that is its application to the state.

An important and growing body of historical scholarship focuses on the influence of the corporate concept on the state's *constitutional order* – the locus of its sovereignty, and its governmental structure.[1] The present chapter attends instead to a separate question regarding the role of the corporation in bequeathing to the state its *juridical personhood* – its capacity to own and contract in its own name – a feature of all modern states, regardless of constitutional order, that vastly augments their power and makes possible the current international state system.

DISTINGUISHING THE ORGANIZATIONAL STATE AND THE JURIDICAL STATE

Among social scientists today, "the state" is most commonly understood along the lines advanced by Max Weber: "a ... political organization [that] successfully

---

[1] BRIAN TIERNEY, RELIGION, LAW AND THE GROWTH OF CONSTITUTIONAL THOUGHT 1150–1650 (1982); J.P. CANNING, THE POLITICAL THOUGHT OF BALDUS DE UBALDIS (1987); Mary Sarah Bilder, *The Corporate Origins of Judicial Review*, 116 YALE L. J. 502 (2006); DANIEL LEE, POPULAR SOVEREIGNTY IN EARLY MODERN CONSTITUTIONAL THOUGHT (2016); David Ciepley, *Is the U.S. Government a Corporation? The Corporate Origins of Modern Constitutionalism*, 111 AM. POL. SCI. REV. 418 (2017); QUENIN SKINNER, FROM HUMANISM TO HOBBES (2018).

upholds the claim to the monopoly of the legitimate use of physical force" within a territory.[2] It roughly aligns with what Americans call "the government."

This is a useful definition of the state for certain kinds of comparative work. But, it obscures what is most distinctive about the form of the state developed in Europe, which is that, alongside this organizational state there developed a juridical state – the state conceived as a legal individual (or "person") distinct from the sitting government, that owns the property used by the government and that is the underlying legal party to treaties and other contracts made by the government.[3] James Wilson, the leading participant in the U.S. Constitutional Convention and an inaugural member of the Supreme Court, provides a particularly clear articulation of the concept:

> By a "state," I mean a complete body of free persons united together for their common benefit.... It is an artificial person. It has its affairs and interests; it has its rules; it has its rights; and it has its obligations. It may acquire property distinct from that of its members. It may incur debts to be discharged out of the public stock, not out of the private fortunes of individuals. It may be bound by contracts, and for damages arising from the breach of those contracts.[4]

In this passage, Wilson, following early modern political theory and iconography, figures the state as an "artificial person," a multitude united into one "body" – a "body politic," as distinct from a body natural. An approximate figuration of what Wilson has in mind is depicted on the frontispiece of Hobbes' *Leviathan*, although Wilson would deny the body needed a sovereign head. The united body of citizens – the People, or state – is, Wilson avers, itself "SOVEREIGN," although it can only act when in constitutional assembly.[5]

It is notable that this figuration exactly follows how the law figured ordinary corporations. "Corporation" is the English translation of *"universitas,"* the medieval Latin word for an incorporated group, which connotes a plurality that has been turned (*verto*) into one (*unum*). *Uni-vers-itas*. The English carried the figure forward. As defined in an early English treatise on corporate law, "A Corporation ... is a Body framed by Policy or Fiction of Law, and it's therefore called a Body Politick; and it's called an Incorporation or Body Incorporate, because the Persons are made into a Body which endureth in perpetual Succession; and are of capacity to grant, sue or be sued, and the like."[6] However unfamiliar the figuration today, what is clear is that Wilson's state – with rights and duties, property and liabilities, and even interests and purposes, wholly separate from those of the citizens figuratively composing it – is not the state described by Weber, making no reference to institutional

[2]   MAX WEBER, ECONOMY AND SOCIETY 54 (1978).
[3]   David Runciman, *Is the State a Corporation?*, 35 GOV'T AND OPPOSITION 90 (2000).
[4]   *Chisholm v. Georgia*, 2 U.S. 419, 455 (1793).
[5]   *Id.* at 454. On the seventeenth-century debate over whether state sovereignty lay in the head or the body of subjects, *see* QUENTIN SKINNER, FROM HUMANISM TO HOBBES 34 (2018).
[6]   AUTHOR UNKNOWN, THE LAW OF CORPORATIONS 1–2 (Facsimile Publisher 2015) (1702).

machinery. We may call it a "juridical state," as distinct from the "jurisdictional and organizational state" of governmental apparatus (legislature, courts, executive, agencies and bureaus, etc.).

In this usage, an organizational state, or government, is not only distinct from the juridical state but acts on its behalf as its legal agent – collecting taxes, incurring debts, negotiating treaties, making contracts – all of which are the revenues, debts, treaties, and contracts of the state, which subsequent officeholders are obliged to honor. Yet again, a corporation presents an exact parallel. Its government (e.g., its board) acts in the name of the juridical person of the corporation, which bears the legal consequences, including legal obligations that must be honored by succeeding boards. The similarity, as we shall see, is not coincidental.

State personhood is no small thing. Placing the property and liabilities of the organizational state with an undying juridical entity, rather than with natural persons, fundamentally transforms the state, as it does the business firm. It allows property to be amassed at a scale well beyond what normally rests in the hands of an individual. It also allows this property to be dedicated to, and credibly committed to, multigenerational projects (including the multi-generational repayment of debt, the basis of modern money creation and banking).[7] And it shifts liability from natural persons to the entity, altering the risk-tolerance and incentives of organizational actors.

What is more, having all property owned by a legal entity rather than natural persons dramatically alters what is possible in the way of governance norms and governance structures. Because the entity owns, those who control the entity's property and personnel must do so on some basis other than ownership. Leadership can, thus, be recruited from outside the ranks of the wealthy and selected through varied and inclusive procedures, from lottery to election. Also, this separation transforms rulership into an office. The ruler controls but does not own. The ruler, thus, becomes a fiduciary, with a presumptive duty to use the property for common ends beyond the ruler's personal or familial interests. Owner autocracy thus gives way, at least potentially, to constitutional orders with a prescribed arrangement of offices, limitation on the authority of these offices, and limitation on the tenure of officeholding so as to introduce accountability.

Finally, contracts and treaties made in the name of the state bind successor governments, adding new stability to domestic and international orders. The United Nations state system, as well as ancillary interstate systems based on treaties and trade agreements, is predicated not only on the existence of states in the sense of bounded national territories, but also, and even more fundamentally, on the existence of states as juridical persons. In sum, constitutional democratic states, robust developmental and welfare states, and the current international system of states, would be unlikely or impossible without state personhood that decouples control and ownership.

---

[7] CHRISTINE DESAN, MAKING MONEY: COIN, CURRENCY, AND THE COMING OF CAPITALISM (2015).

DISTINGUISHING JURIDICALITY, JURISDICTIONALITY, AND CONSTITUTIONALITY

Having a state with juridical personhood converts the ruler into an officeholder. But the converse is not true. The Islamic sultan and the Roman Emperor can meaningfully be said to have occupied offices, for example. But in both cases, all associated property formally belonged to the ruler, not the office, whatever were the norms imposed by the office on the property's use.[8] Likewise, contracts were with the ruler, not the office. This put them at risk. As Accursius, the great Glossator of the thirteenth century, emphasized (in his gloss of *Digest*, 1.3.31),[9] the emperor is not bound by the laws of his predecessors or even by his own laws.[10]

It would be quite impossible to enter into meaningful contractual relations with such a Proteus, so it is not surprising to see medieval lawyers distinguishing between legislation and contracts (including feudal contracts) and holding the latter to be inviolable under the *ius gentium* (the "law of peoples," a branch of the law of nature), which binds even the emperor. "God has subjected the laws to him, but has not subjected contracts to him."[11] But this did not solve the problem of transgenerational obligation, since a contract with an emperor, king, or sultan is a contract with a specific mortal. Feudal vows, for example, had to be renewed whenever the king or his vassal died.[12]

The nonobvious solution ultimately struck upon was to posit an undying juridical person as the subject of contracts and endow it with property to bond its contracts. This is the juridical person of the state. I have suggested that it was patterned after the corporation. However, to trace its conceptual roots accurately, a distinction, already alluded to, must be drawn, the strict observance of which is a leading contribution of this essay.

The corporation has two distinct traits that sets it off from other forms of organization. First, it is treated in law as a legal individual, or "juridical person," that owns and contracts in its own name. In the Roman jurist Ulpian's lapidary formulation, "[a] debt to a corporation is not a debt to individuals and a debt of a corporation is not a debt of individuals."[13] We may call this the corporation's "personhood," or individuality (although this is a metaphor and should not imply agency or anything beyond contracting and ownership rights).

Second, because it cannot itself act, the corporation needs a natural person or group of persons to act on its behalf. That is, it needs a government. Furthermore,

---

[8] P.W. Duff, P. W., Personality in Roman Private Law 51–61 (1938); Walter J. Jones, *The Early History of the Fiscus*, 43 L. Q. Rev. 43 499, 502–03 (1927).

[9] Digest (Theodor Mommsen & Paul Krueger eds., Alan Watson trans., 1985) [hereinafter Justinian's].

[10] Kenneth Pennington, *Law, Legislative Authority, and Theories of Government, 1150–1300*, in Cambridge History of Medieval Political Thought 431 (J.H. Burns ed., 1988).

[11] Canning, *supra* note 1, at 84.

[12] Carl Stephenson, Medieval Feudalism 23–24 (13th ed. 1956).

[13] Justinian's, *supra* note 9, at 3.4.7.

unlike other voluntary associations, corporations are granted jurisdictional authority – a right to make rules for its members (and for any others within its jurisdiction)
that, unlike the rules of purely private associations, are binding in court (so long
as they do not contradict the law of the land). This is the feature of corporations
that modern, contractual accounts of the corporation miss. Towns pass ordinances;
universities erect campus regulations; and business corporations make by-laws and
work rules. Indeed, securing this power was long regarded as the primary advantage
of incorporation. "The general Intent and End of all ... incorporations is, for better
Government."[14]

A corporation has a *constitutional* government, in that those exercising authority
do so not as owners but as officeholders and fiduciaries. Most commonly, a corporation's leading offices (e.g., a corporation's board) are established by charter (or,
in the modern era, by a charter in conjunction with a general incorporation law
to which the charter makes reference), the provisions of which specify the structure of offices, their powers, the procedures for filling them, and the purposes that
their incumbents are authorized to pursue. Actions outside of this are *ultra vires*,
"beyond powers" of the corporation and subject to being voided in court. The charter thus serves as the corporation's constitution.[15] In the case of Church corporations, which typically lack charters, these offices are established and regulated by
canon law – today, codified as a single chapter, which in essence operates as a general incorporation law for Church corporations and functions as their constitution,
or fundamental law.[16]

The recent flowering of scholarship on the corporate underpinnings of the
European and American state has focused on this second trait of the corporation – its constitutionalism – and its influence on the constitutionalism of the
state. This includes the corporate underpinnings of popular sovereignty,[17] medieval and early modern mixed constitutionalism,[18] and the modern constitutional
republic.[19]

---

[14] AUTHOR UNKNOWN, *supra* note 6, at 2; *see also* WILLIAM BLACKSTONE, COMMENTARIES ON THE
LAWS OF ENGLAND (1765–1769), https://avalon.law.yale.edu/18th_century/blackstone_bk1ch18.asp.
Were corporations purely private associations, such rules, to be binding, would require the contractual
consent of all parties, that is, unanimity, which would make them largely ungovernable. But corporations are not purely private creations, receiving their "personhood" and jurisdictional authority from
the public authority, via charter or statute, making them enforceable in court. David Ciepley, *Beyond
Public and Private: Toward a Political Theory of the Corporation*, 111 AM. POL. SCI. REV. 139 (2013).

[15] Ciepley, *supra* note 1, at 420–22, 424.

[16] Vatican, *Code of Canon Law*, www.vatican.va/archive/cod-iuris-canonici/cic_index_en.html (last visited March 6, 2023).

[17] CANNING, *supra* note 1; LEE, *supra* note 1; Quentin Skinner, *A Genealogy of the Modern State*, 162
PROCEEDINGS OF THE BRITISH ACADEMY 325 (2009).

[18] TIERNEY, *supra* note 1.

[19] JOHN PATERSON DAVIS, CORPORATIONS: A STUDY OF THE ORIGIN AND DEVELOPMENT OF
GREAT BUSINESS COMBINATION (1905); Bilder, *supra* note 1; Ciepley, *supra* note 1; Nikolas Bowie,
Why the Constitution was Written Down, 71 STAN. L. REV. 1397.

But this story of the constitutionalization of the state on the model of the corporation (via shared application of the "body politic" metaphor) is distinct from the story of the "personification" of the state on the model of the corporation (via shared application of a "personhood" metaphor, among other metaphors). While state personhood implies at least a weak constitutionalism – because it converts the ruler into an officeholder – the converse is not true. England, for example, made wide use of corporate metaphors in constructing its constitutional order – for example, treating the king as head and lords as members of a corporate body (Parliament), whom the king was to consult on questions of taxation.[20] But, this was no guarantee that the king would view the taxes he received as anything other than payment of rent to his person by the tenants of his realm,[21] nor guarantee that he would submit to be bound by his contracts. In short, the governmental structure of a corporation can (and often did) inspire imitation without juridicality following in train. Narrating the "corporatization" of the state's organizational structure, therefore, does not necessarily illuminate how it acquired its personhood. This requires distinct treatment.

Indeed, it is a striking fact about England that its pervasive corporate construction of constitutional order did nothing to propel a corresponding personification of the state. F. W. Maitland notes the "sound thought" of the English Year Books (recording medieval court cases) "that the realm is 'a corporation aggregate of many,'" yet finds in the record no "admission that the corporate realm, besides being the wielder of public power, may also be the 'subject' of private rights, the owner of lands and chattels." "[T]his," he adds, "is the step that we have never yet formally taken."[22]

> Now and then it was necessary to distinguish between lands that [the king] held in right of his crown and lands which had come to him in right of an escheated barony or vacant bishopric. But in the main all his lands were his lands, and we must be careful not to read a trusteeship for the nation into our medieval documents.[23]

In short, we must distinguish the organizational, associational aspect of the corporation, which was drawn on to model and legitimize the state's *constitutional* order, from the abstract, juridical aspect of the corporation, which was drawn on to provide continuity to its property and contracts. Although the two aspects could readily be conjoined, as in Wilson, this was no logical necessity. Accordingly, the proliferation of "body politic" metaphors in medieval and early modern discussion of the English realm is not by itself good evidence that a juridical state has emerged. As Maitland suggests, the Continent is its true cradle, not England.

---

[20] Tierney, *supra* note 1; Skinner, *supra* note 1.
[21] Frederick Pollack & Frederic Maitland, The History of English Law Before the Time of Edward I (The Lawbook Exchange, Ltd. ed. 2013) (1898).
[22] F.W. Maitland, State, Trust and Corporation 34 (David Runciman and Magnus Ryan eds., 2003).
[23] *Id.* at 33.

THE STATE–CORPORATE ANALOGY, AND THE THREE-STEP
PROCESS OF EUROPE'S CONSTITUTIONALIZATION

It took no great imaginative leap for medieval Europe's emerging legal class – both civilian and canonist – to think of corporations and civil governments as analogous in the dimension of juridicality. Their central legal text, Justinian's *Digest* of Roman law (recovered in the second half of the eleventh century), had already drawn the analogy for them, noting that the corporation exists "on the model of the state" (*ad exemplum rei publicae*), which it illustrated with the observation that, like the state, the corporation has its own treasury.[24]

The perplexity was, Europeans did not at this point *have* states with separate treasuries. The treasury of the Roman republic, called the *aerarium* (and understood as the people's purse) was, under the empire, gradually absorbed into the emperor's purse.[25] In the barbarian kingdoms succeeding the empire in Europe, any meaningful distinction between the *patrimonium* and *fiscus* was abandoned, with fiscus coming to refer to "the whole aggregate of the king's possessions, whatever their nature or source."[26] Roman concepts of public authority, public law, and public property (*res publica*) simply evaporated in Europe, the very distinction between private and public, and between ownership (*dominium*) and rulership (*imperium*), being lost within feudalism, as *imperium* was attached to, and became one face of, *dominium*.[27]

Yet, this erasure of Roman categories of public and private would only deepen the impress of the corporation on the European state. Once Europeans had worked up the fragments of Roman law into a robust European corporation, the *Digest*'s corporation–state analogy invited them to use it to reverse-engineer what would be a juridical state.

Why, in their state-building efforts, did European jurists not adopt and adapt the public law of ancient Rome directly, rather than look to the rules of corporations for guidance? Because the public law of ancient Rome – law regarding religion, priests, magistrates, and things affecting the common utility[28] – was administrative in nature, never codified, and thus, did not come down to Europeans except in fragments. Instead, what Europeans received was the *Corpus Iuris Civilis* (including the *Digest*), the body of Roman civil law, or "private" law, regarding "the utility of individuals."[29] It was from selections out of these principles of Roman private law that

---

[24] Justinian's, *supra* note 9, at 3.4.1.
[25] Jones, *supra* note 8, at 500.
[26] *Id.* at 505–06.
[27] LEE, *supra* note 1, at 93–98.
[28] Justinian's, *supra* note 9, at 1.1.1.
[29] *Id.*; GAINS POST, STUDIES IN MEDIEVAL LEGAL THOUGHT: PUBLIC LAW AND THE STATE 1100–1322, 3–26 (1964) [hereinafter POST 1964]; Gains Post, *The Theory of Public Law and the State in the Thirteenth Century*, 6 Seminar (Jurist) 42, 47 (1948) [hereinafter Post 1948].

European jurists ultimately framed a new system of public law – a constitutional law, broadly speaking. But this transformation of private law rules into constitutional rules did not occur immediately or directly.

What one finds in case after case is that these principles of Roman civil law – principles such as *quod omnes tangit* (determining who must be consulted on certain decisions), and *plena potestas* (used in authorizing a corporation's legal agents) – were given their first exposition and application within the corporate bodies of the Church by canon lawyers, who developed them into a robust body of rules for the external and internal operation of corporate bodies – a procedural and constitutional law for corporations. These rules were then applied to the largest "corporate" bodies of all: the Church, the Empire, the commune, and the kingdom.

The "reverse engineering" of constitutional and juridical states in Europe was thus a three-step process. First, the Church applied the corporate form to its subordinate bodies; next, principles of Roman private law were constitutionalized within these corporations, and finally, the resulting constitutional law of the corporation was put to service as the constitutional law of Church and state, treated as corporations-writ-large.[30] In this circuitous manner, corporate practices of personification, officeholding, consent, delegation, election, and representation made their way into European government, giving it its distinctive corporate shape and color.

The present article is concerned with the first two of these corporate practices – personification and officeholding. The next section recounts the Church's application of the corporate form to its inferior bodies, which generated a new understanding of corporate "personhood" and officeholding. The following two sections document the use of the Church corporation in theorizing kingship in England and the Continent. This birthed state juridicality, at least in concept. The final section sketches the new form of constitutionalism pioneered by the American founders, which creatively resolves the longstanding tension between state sovereignty and state juridical personhood.

THE CHURCH APPLIES THE CORPORATE FORM

To reiterate, a corporation is a juridical person, owning property in its own name. The head of a corporation, who in many instances holds the position but temporarily, is self-evidently not the property holder. The corporation's property is wholly distinct from the head's property.

Beginning in the eleventh century, the Church began to construe its numerous semi-independent, semi-subordinate bodies as corporations. Church bodies were ready candidates for application of the corporate form because, as religious

---

[30] Brian Tierney was the first to articulate this dynamic which the present paper extends to the question of juridical personhood and property, which Tierney did not treat. *See* TIERNEY, *supra* note 1, at 23, 25.

institutions, they already distinguished between organizational and personal property. The property of Church bodies was sacred property (*res sacra*), "owned" in the
broadest sense by Christ, and sometimes, held to be owned more specifically by a
particular saint, and thus, not to be disposed of as the personal property of the prelate,
who was merely its steward (*dispensator*) and custodian (*custos*) with a fiduciary duty
to use it for the good of the Church community (*utilitas ecclesiae*).[31] Church bodies
thus naturally approximated to corporations. In the wake of the Investiture Conflict,
it was also an appealing proposition politically, for it bolstered the Church's case for
freedom from lay control of Church appointments (e.g., freedom from emperors
appointing popes and from great lords appointing bishops), since it is characteristic
of corporations that members, not outsiders, select the leadership.[32] With adoption
of the corporate concept, election by members became the normal and approved
means of filling high ecclesiastical offices, with cardinals electing the Pope, cathedral priests electing the bishop, and (already longstanding practice in the so-called
"free monasteries") monks electing the abbot.[33]

However, Church practices did bring about an important mutation in the corporate concept – a mutation that would have epochal consequences, yet which has
gone unexplained in the literature. In a Roman corporation, all rights lay with the
members, who might or might not institute a corporate *tutor*, or director, as they
saw fit. In contrast, an ecclesiastical corporation was held to require a head, and
certain corporate actions could only be undertaken by the head.[34] The difference
in approach stemmed from the fact that Church offices, including the offices of
Church corporations, with their powers and duties, were understood to be instituted
from above by the Church hierarchy, and ultimately by Christ.

The idea of a corporate office instituted, not by the members, but from above,
made it possible for canon lawyers to theorize and bring into being a new kind of
corporation – one without members. Following the Latin, we may call it an "incorporation of property," or "property corporation" (*universitas bonorum* or *rerum*), as
opposed to the original concept of an incorporation of people-and-property (*universitas personarum*), which we may call a "member corporation." First applied to
Church benefices, such as the bishopric, the property corporation was used to clarify
that the property of the benefice did not belong to the cleric, and thus, did not pass
to the cleric's kin at his death. The corporation included an office with prescribed
powers and duties, along with property dedicated to the purpose of the corporation
under the stewardship of the office holder. But it had no members.[35]

---

[31] Shael Herman, *Utilitas Ecclesiae: The Canonical Conception of the Trust*, 70 TULANE L. REV. 2239,
2244–45 (1996); HAROLD BERMAN, LAW AND REVOLUTION: THE FORMATION OF THE WESTERN
LEGAL TRADITION 239 (1997).

[32] BERMAN, *supra* note 31, at 218.

[33] *Id.* at 88, 97–98.

[34] *Id.* at 219.

[35] *Id.* at 239–40; POLLACK & MAITLAND, *supra* note 21, at 1503.

This development clarified the wholly abstract character of the corporate entity. The Romans (like English-speakers today) were constantly backsliding, despite their own practices, into the view that corporations are reducible to individuals in association.[36] The first wave of Italian commentators on the Roman law – the "Glossators" – by and large did the same. Accursius (c. 1182–1263), author of the "Great Gloss," famously wrote, "The corporation is nothing other than the men who are there."[37] Against this, the canon lawyers, arguably for the first time, articulated without equivocation or inconstancy the abstract, purely juridical existence of corporations,[38] which sometimes had members conjoined and sometimes did not. This was soon followed by the introduction of the metaphor that, for all its troublesome over-suggestiveness, did have the merit of underscoring the irreducibility of the corporation to its individual members. Medieval jurists began to denominate the corporation a "person" in its own right – although one only by "fiction," or "artifice," or "policy" – and thus, legally distinct from the members or officeholders of the corporation.[39]

These developments also changed the understanding of a corporation *with* members. In essence, the corporeal, "organological" understanding of the corporation as a collection of individuals with head and members, and the incorporeal understanding of it as an abstract legal entity, were conjoined. When the members gathered in assembly to deliberate and vote on corporate policy, they were the corporation incarnate. Their majoritarian will was considered the corporation's will. At the same time, in legal view, the legislation they passed and the acts they undertook with respect to property and contract were the acts of the corporation as an incorporeal person, and not the acts of individuals. These remained binding even as specific individuals comprising the corporation were replaced over time.[40] The corporation was thus *not* reducible to the distinct corporeal individuals comprising it. They were and were not the corporation. As Canning puts it, "[T]he members are the physical expression of the abstract entity of the corporation which acts through the instrumentality of these members who thus express not the wills of separate individuals but that of the corporation as a whole."[41] The canonists' favored image for capturing this duality of the member corporation, as both visible and invisible, corporeal and incorporeal, plural and unitary, propinquitous and successional, was to describe it as a *corpus misticum*, a "mystical body" analogous to Paul's figure of the Church as the mystical body of Christ with all the faithful (past, present, and future) as members.[42]

[36] Duff, *supra* note 8, at 80.

[37] Canning, *supra* note 1, at 186.

[38] Skinner, *supra* note 17, at 26–27.

[39] *Id.* at 27–28. In Roman law, only humans are "persons" and subjects of civil law. *Universitates* fell under public law. Jones, *supra* note 8, at 502. The farthest jurists went was to say that corporations in certain respects have the "function of a person." Justinian's, *supra* note 9, at 46.1.22, 4.2.9, 35.1.56; *see also* Duff, *supra* note 8, at 20–1.

[40] Canning, *supra* note 1, at 189.

[41] *Id.* at 188–89.

[42] Earnest Kantorowicz, The King's Two Bodies 193–232 (Reprint ed. 1997).

This canonist understanding and imagery was accepted also by the wave of civilian jurists who succeeded the Glossators – the Commentators, or Postglossators – including the most influential of them, Baldus de Ubaldis (1327–1400), who was both a canon lawyer and a civil lawyer. In a striking and illustrative passage, Baldus treats the populations of the independent Italian cities as canonist-style member corporations. In an express rebuttal of Accursius, Baldus writes that "separate individuals do not make up the people, and thus properly speaking the people is not men, but a collection of men into a mystical body (*corpus misticum*) and taken abstractly, the significance of which has been discovered by the intellect" rather than by the senses.[43] The aspect of the corporation receiving emphasis – whether the abstract and juridical, or the corporeal and governmental – depended upon the nature of the case. By the close of the fifteenth century, this dualistic corporate conception had made its way onto the English bench, with "corporation" generally used when highlighting the corporate group's unitary legal capacity (the corporation then sometimes described as a "person"), and "body politic" generally used when highlighting the group as a political community of natural persons.[44]

It will be noted that this corporate dualism matches Wilson's characterization of the American people as a body politic that is simultaneously a juridical person with its own property and contracts. The question thus becomes how this juridical side of the canonist conception of the corporation came to be applied to entire kingdoms, creating "states" in the juridical sense. It turns out, there was a ready avenue for this. Analogies between bishops and kings – between the princes of the Church and the princes of the Empire – pervade medieval political thought.[45] It is perhaps then not so surprising that, having "corporatized" the bishop's bishopric, jurists proceeded to corporatize the king's realm. The result was the transmission of juridical personhood from the one to the other.

THE ENGLISH CROWN AS JURIDICAL PERSON

We have seen Maitland observe that the corporate realm of England was no juridical state, no owner of Crown lands and chattels. The king owned these. Yet Maitland immediately cautions against holding this to have been "at any time a complete view." He notes, for example, the lawyers of Edward II's day (1307–1327) gathering ideas from the canon law and "co-ordinating the *corona* [Crown] with the *ecclesia* [Church]" to arrive at a notion of royal guardianship of the Crown.[46] Kantorowicz goes a step further, documenting the Crown's acquisition of full corporate character, including separate property. Unfortunately, he adduces from this no more than

---

[43] CANNING, *supra* note 1, at 187.
[44] Heinz Lubasz, *The Corporate Borough in the Common Law of the Late Year-Book Period*, 80 L. Q. REV. 228, 234–36 (1964).
[45] KANTOROWICZ, *supra* note 42, at 441.
[46] MAITLAND, *supra* note 22, at 33.

that it gave a public dimension to the king's rule,[47] seemingly not recognizing that these portions of his wide-ranging study evidence the emergence of the rudiments of a juridical state. Its juridicality would falter. Nonetheless, the case is instructive, confirming the appeal of a juristic gambit that would yield more lasting results on the Continent.

The Roman law books at many points draw a connection between the public and sacred spheres, and the medieval jurists followed them. But whereas Justinian treats the Church as a public thing,[48] the jurists – confronting a feudal world in which lordship has become a private thing – treat the kingdom as a Church-like thing, as a gambit to give it a public cast. The opening move was to impute to the property of the realm a purpose higher than the king's personal use. Then, the distinction drawn in canon law between the prelate's personal property and the property of his corporate benefice that he is to use for the good of the Church, is redeployed to distinguish between the king's *patrimonium* and the property of the corporate kingdom that he is to use for the good of the kingdom. Corporate theory was thus the means to subject the kingdom to public law by removing Crown land from the king's *dominium*, though it still remained under his control. This created what would become public property, the *res publica*, the material basis for a juridical state and public sphere.

Kantorowicz points out a twelfth-century development that prepared the ground for transplanting the corporate concept to the Crown. Namely, along one line of usage, the word "Crown" had become increasingly removed not only from the physical crown, but from the physical king. Spurred perhaps by the recovery of the Roman concept of *respublica*, it had become associated with the property and rights of the king that were to be used for the common utility.[49] The juridicality we are hunting poked out its head when these properties and rights associated with the Crown were fenced off from the *patrimonium*, or feudal possessions of the king, by a principle of inalienability. Behind this lay the bishop–king analogy.

During the high Middle Ages, papal legates commonly ordained bishops and crowned kings. As part of this, they administered oaths indebted to feudal fealty oaths (although true vassalage was rarely involved).[50] At the close of the twelfth century, indirect evidence shows that restrictions on reinfeudating or alienating Church lands and valuables without papal consultation were being appended to the ordination oaths of bishops and archbishops.[51] Later oaths further exacted a promise to revoke all previous alienations of rights and properties from the archbishopric.[52] These inalienables were *res sacrae*, sacred property and rights, dedicated to the maintenance of the bishopric.

---

[47] KANTOROWICZ, *supra* note 42, at 172.
[48] Justinian's, *supra* note 9, at 1.1.2.
[49] KANTOROWICZ, *supra* note 42, at 337–44; POST 1964, *supra* note 29, at 12–24.
[50] KANTOROWICZ, *supra* note 42, 348.
[51] *Id.* at 350.
[52] *Id.* at 351.

Famously, in 1216, a papal legate, evidently drawing on the usual ecclesiastical oath, administered a coronation oath with a similar non-alienability clause to Henry III (reigning 1216–1272). With this, a feudal oath of the bishop not to alienate Church property was transformed into an oath of the king not to alienate Crown lands.[53]

The oath stuck, perhaps because, while on its face a restriction, the English kings immediately found a way to put it to advantageous use, albeit at the price of further deepening the line between the estate of the king and the estate of the Crown. Henry II (reigning 1154–89) had labored to increase royal revenues by asserting rights over land that had been part of the king's estate under William the Conqueror – what came to be known as the "ancient demesne,"[54] a far more extensive territory than the existing royal demesne. Such rights included levying tallage and hearing the cases of villeins left unsatisfied by the court of the manor (and, all-importantly, collecting their court fees). The papal charge not to alienate things of the Crown, and even to revoke past alienations, not only rationalized this effort, but turned it into a duty. These rights, the king now argued, inhere in the Crown and, thus, cannot have been alienated even if the manors underneath were.[55] The great English jurist Bracton (1210–1268), in support of these claims, filled out the bishop-king analogy, asserting that these lands and rights were *res quasi sacrae*, "things quasi sacred," dedicated to the maintenance of the realm – the preservation of justice and of peace – and could no more be alienated by the king than could the *res sacrae* of the Church be alienated by the clergy.[56]

In short, their predecessors having for all practical purposes alienated these lands, kings were able to use the new principle of non-alienability to at least claw back a right to tax the land (functionally equivalent to charging a rental payment for its use) and to administer justice on the land. The price, however, was that these new revenues would be associated very tightly with the Crown rather than with the king's *patrimonium*, and, thus, were to be used for the common utility only.

This distinction between ancient demesne and personal *patrimonium* was administrative as well as normative. Since most of the ancient demesne was no longer in the king's estate, but in the estate of others, its properties and revenues had to be administered in a separate manner from the king's personal holdings, with its revenues earmarked to the fiscus. As already noted, in early medieval Europe the concept had lost its public dimension, being reduced to the king's purse. But during the thirteenth century, in light of the doctrine of the inalienability of the ancient demesne, the *fiscus* acquired an unprecedentedly public status, being removed from the king's full discretion and attached to the Crown. In the words of Bracton,

---

[53] *Id.* at 353–54; POST 1964, *supra* note 29, 493–512.
[54] Robert S. Hoyt, *The Nature and Origins of the Ancient Demesne*, 65 ENG. HIST. REV. 145, 170–74 (1950).
[55] *Id.* at 173.
[56] KANTOROWICZ, *supra* note 42, at 168, 362.

"[a] thing quasi-sacred is a thing fiscal, which cannot be given away or be sold or transferred upon another person by the Prince or ruling king; and those things make the Crown what it is, and they regard to common utility such as peace and justice."[57] Henceforth, the concepts of Crown and *fiscus* would develop together.[58]

Inalienability, it should be noted, does not automatically implicate the corporate concept. In the general case, corporate property is eminently alienable. But the trait of inalienability invited application of the corporate concept to the Crown in three ways. First, inalienability clearly distinguished a body of property from the personal (patrimonial) property of the ruler, and therefore, encouraged a search for new concepts of ownership and even new concepts of owners, including corporate concepts, to define its legal status.

Second, inalienability invites the corporate concept by way of its connection to "sempiternity." Scholastics operated with a three-fold scheme of temporality. Some things were mortal, having a beginning and end in time. Others were eternal, having no beginning or end in time. And still others were "sempiternal," having a beginning but no end in time. This last category paradigmatically included angels. It also included the Church and the Empire. And it included corporations, which "do not die."[59] The inalienability of the *res sacrae* of the Church (its property and rights) meant that they, too, will be sempiternal, since they will be with the Church always, held by Church's sempiternal corporations, such as friaries and bishoprics. The inalienability of the *res quasi sacrae* of the realm suggested they too must be sempiternal. Thus, like the *res sacrae*, they must be held by something that is sempiternal, such as a corporation.

Third, inalienability invites application of the corporate concept by way of its connection with guardianship. It was a well-established principle, then as now, that guardians are not allowed to alienate or diminish the property of their ward. For this reason, political moralists from Carolingian times described the kingdom as a minor placed by God under the care of the king as *tutor* (rather than as *dominus*), who was to preserve the rights of his ward, not despoil them.[60] Separately, it was a well-known trope of the age that children, madmen, and corporations cannot manage their own affairs except through a *tutor* or *curator* (guardian). Canon lawyers put these two ideas together to produce the doctrine that the bishop is a tutor and guardian of the corporate Church, and that the Church is a perpetual minor, enjoying the special legal protections of a minor, against which there is no prescription, and the property of which may not be alienated. The inalienability of Crown lands invited the bodily transfer of this canon law doctrine regarding bishoprics to the Crown, making the

---

[57] *Id.* at 173.

[58] *Id.* at 167, 186–87.

[59] *Id.* at 192, 386–87.

[60] J.P. Canning, *The Corporation in the Thought of the Italian Jurists*, 1 Hist. Pol. Thought 9, 24 (1980); Walter Ullmann, *Juristic Obstacles to the Emergence of the Concept of the State in the Middle Ages*, 12 Annali di Storia del Diritto 43, 49–51, 54–6 (1968–69).

king the guardian of a corporate Crown. And this transfer did occur, with jurists by the end of the century speaking of the Crown as a minor – unable to act on its own behalf, owning property that could not be alienated nor prescribed – and of the king as "guardian of the Crown."[61]

Bracton was familiar with corporation concepts in Roman and canon law,[62] and in characterizing the *fiscus*, he shows his familiarity specifically with the concept of an abstract incorporation of property. Both the *res sacrae* and *res quasi sacrae*, he states, are "property of none" (*bona nullius*), adding, "that is, they are not properly of any single person, but only property of God or the fisc."[63]

In describing the *res quasi sacrae* as "property of none," Bracton was applying a Roman law category that encompasses such sundry items as wild beasts, things abandoned, city walls, free men, and the *res publica* itself.[64] Kantorowicz singles out the last to argue that Bracton, in declaring the *res quasi sacrae* to be the "property of none," was reclaiming the legal status of the Roman *res publicae* for the English Crown.[65] This interpretation may be correct. But what Kantorowicz does not note is that Roman law also describes the property of *universitates* as "property of none,"[66] and that when Bracton reaches beyond the Roman law books to suggest that the inalienables of the Crown, as quasi-sacred things, are "property of God or the fisc," he evidences yet again that his legal model for the Crown was not the Roman republic, but the bishopric, the inalienables, of which, it would have been said, are "property of God or the bishopric." This is exactly the co-ordination of *corona* and *ecclesia* – or more precisely, of *corona* and *episcopatum* (bishopric) – that Maitland observed in the lawyers of Edward II, although seen here half a century earlier.

A government brings a juridical state into being and becomes its representative when it establishes an independent treasury and submits itself to contract law. In thirteenth-century England, the *fiscus* of the Crown became that independent treasury – a memberless corporation that "never dies" and owns property in its own name.[67] At the same time, as we have seen, natural law became a protector of contracts, which, outside of a state of emergency, the king is not to violate. Early evidence of the institutionalization of the division between king and Crown, and of the permanence of acts done in the name of the Crown, comes from 1240, when the king's clerk, though under orders from the king, refused to seal a charter, as

---

[61] Kantorowicz, *supra* note 42, at 180–85, 374–79; Maitland, *supra* note 22, at 33.

[62] Gains Post, *A Romano-Canonical Maxim, 'Quod Omnes Tangit,' in Bracton*, 4 Traditio 197, 213–220 (1946).

[63] Bracton on the Laws and Customs of England 57 (Woodbine ed., 1968) [hereinafter Bracton]; Kantorowicz, *supra* note 42, at 186.

[64] Bracton, *supra* note 63, at 41, 57;

[65] *Id.* at 187.

[66] Jones, *supra* note 8, at 502.

[67] Kantorowicz, *supra* note 42, at 177. The corporate interpretation of the fiscus was not unanimous, however, with some still regarding it as the purse of the king. *Id* at 179.

contra coronam domini regis.[68] It may not be too much to say, therefore, that in the thirteenth-century English lawyers conjured the rudiments of a juridical state. This state was the "Crown," become corporate and juridical by being modeled on the bishopric, with the *fiscus* as its treasury and the king as its guardian, a fiduciary to its corporate purpose of advancing the common utility.

The legal construction of the ancient demesne on the model of ecclesiastic property can thus be said to have brought forth from out of the old kingdom a new kind of kingdom, the two co-existing side-by-side – a feudal kingdom and a corporate kingdom, reigned over respectively by "feudal king" and "fiscal king."[69] The former, exercising *dominium*, managed relations between lord and vassal; the latter, exercising *jurisdictio*, managed the common utility – matters that "touched all." The former lived by *patrimonium*, with properties falling in and out by feudal and customary right; the latter lived by *fiscus*, with properties subject neither to alienation nor prescription. The former held authority (in part) through personal fealty; the latter by office, like bishop over bishopric. In fact, the latter was, in legal form, a bishopric writ large.

Despite these early developments, Maitland's verdict stands with respect to the longer run. State juridicality was quickly retracted in England, even as the distinction between feudal and fiscal king was preserved. It is speculative, but this may have followed from the events of 1308, when a group of barons revolted (unsuccessfully) against the king's favorite in the name of the Crown, setting the good of the Crown against the will of the king. It was thenceforth treated as political heresy – a "damnable and damned opinion" – to suggest that the Crown can be separated from, let alone opposed to, the king's person.[70] Crown and king were reattached, and the king theorized instead as having two distinct yet inseparable "capacities," one natural and one corporate.[71] The king as a natural person owned his *patrimonium*; the king as a corporate person – that is, as a "corporation sole" – owned the *fiscus* (more on this later). Not until the late eighteenth century was a juridical state effectively (if still not forthrightly) established in Britain when, with the king's credit in ruins, Parliament set afoot "the Publick" as owner of the National Debt.[72] For more enduring early concepts of a juridical state, the Continent is where one must look.

JURIDICAL PERSONHOOD ON THE CONTINENT

It is not surprising that some of the earliest and sharpest theorizations of the juridical state come out of the north Italian cities, where, from the twelfth century until

---

[68] *Id.* at 360.

[69] The seed of this idea can be found in Kantorowicz. *Id.* at 172. The phrase "corporate kingdom" is my own. But see Maitland on the "corporate realm." MAITLAND, *supra* note 22, at 34.

[70] POLLACK & MAITLAND, *supra* note 21, at 525; KANTOROWICZ, *supra* note 42, at 364–65.

[71] KANTOROWICZ, *supra* note 42, at 369.

[72] MAITLAND, *supra* note 22, at 39.

the mushrooming of tyrants in the fourteenth century, rule was generally by elected *podestà*. This landscape would have given the Italian jurists an especially clear notion of the distinction between office holder and office, and between the ruler's personal property and property of the city.

An existing line of scholarship locates the roots of the modern state concept in the Bartolist treatment of these cities.[73] The focus is on the city's right of self-government. *De jure*, Bartolus argues, the Italian cities remain subject to the emperor. But de facto, the emperor does not exercise authority there. Each city may, therefore, exercise jurisdictional authority – that is, may legislate – based on popular consent. What is more, his pupil Baldus adds, a people has the exceptional right, by the *ius gentium*, to incorporate without authorization by a superior.[74] This corporate whole – whether acting in general assembly or through an elected council – is the sovereign in the independent city, "the lord and *princeps* of its citizens" taken as individuals.[75]

Canning fairly describes Baldus as having thus provided one of the first theories of the sovereign state, understood as a source of authorization, allegiance, and obedience distinct both from the individual citizens who compose it and from the magistrate who derives his authority from it.[76]

But as this suggests, the notion of a sovereign corporate people, whether treated as a direct governing power or as an indirect authorizing power, properly belongs to the history of jurisdiction and constitutional order – that is, the governmental aspect of the state. This aspect of the state is (I emphasize again) distinct from its juridical personhood. Indeed, on its face, declaring the people sovereign cuts against it. As Roman law emphasized, a sovereign ruler, exercising *merum imperium* – which the *populus* did on the Bartolist account[77] – is not bound by statute, but is the "living law," whose pleasure "has the force of law."[78] This is not an auspicious basis for securing the state as a seat of stable possessions and obligations.

It is elsewhere that we must look for the contribution of the Italian jurists to the state's juridical personhood. We must turn from the city to the kingdom, and from the topic of jurisdictional independence and authority, to that of property and contract.

Property of the Corporate Kingdom: The Fiscus

Like the English, the Italians distinguished between *patrimonium* and *fiscus* and gave the *fiscus* an ever more public and corporate meaning. Azo of Bologna (1150–1230)

---

[73] CANNING, *supra* note 1; SKINNER, *supra* note 1, at 28–31; LEE, *supra* note 1.

[74] Canning, *supra* note 60, at 20–22.

[75] CANNING, *supra* note 1, at 199 (quoting Baldus at 204).

[76] *Id.* at 207.

[77] LEE, *supra* note 1, at 72.

[78] Justinian's, *supra* note 9, at 1.4.1.

(whose glosses on Roman law significantly influenced Bracton), offered a modified Roman view, conceding that the *fiscus* is the private right of the emperor, but categorizing it nonetheless as belonging to public law, adding the *fiscus* to Justinian's list of "religion, priests, and magistrates" as things affecting the common utility. His student Accursius (1182–1283), the towering glossator of the thirteenth century, went the rest of the way, forthrightly declaring the *fiscus* to be public. It is the treasury of the empire, not the patrimony of the imperial family.[79] Again, analogy to the Church was decisive. As Wahl notes, "Canonists had already determined that the Church did not belong to the pope so now it was easy to argue in a parallel fashion that the fisc did not belong to the Prince."[80] Like Church property, the fisc was declared to be inalienable; and imprescriptible – long possession by the king did not make it his;[81] and "eternal and perpetual ... for the fisc never dies."[82]

Bartolus, in a significant innovation among Continental jurists, added that fiscal powers do not belong to the empire uniquely (or to other polities by imperial concession only). They are also native to those cities, numerous in Italy, that recognized no superior.[83]

But, it was his student Baldus who, by conceding a fisc also to the kingdom and applying corporate concepts to it, developed perhaps the first clear concept of a juridical state – as can be extracted from Canning's important study of Baldus' jurisprudence. Baldus' treatment of the kingdom in most respects parallels his treatment of the city republic. Like a city, a kingdom in the empire may claim de facto sovereignty if, as in France and England, the emperor exercises no authority there. And on this ground it can, by custom or statute, establish a fisc.[84] Also like the city, the kingdom is held to be a corporation, and with a dual aspect. It has a corporeal aspect: the collective people who, at some past point, assembled as a corporate body and elected a king, alienating their powers to him. And it has an abstract aspect as an undying legal person, or state: the "person" of the *respublica* that "does not die."[85]

This latter is crucial, providing ground for the key step Baldus next takes. Because the kingdom is an undying legal person, the fisc could be declared one too, for the fisc belongs not to the king but to the corporate kingdom. Baldus, thus, took the lead among jurists in treating the fisc as a legal person – "*Fiscus est persona incorporalis.*"[86] This unambiguously separated fiscal property from the private property of the king. Indeed, it was the same legal device used to separate the property of the bishopric from the private property of the bishop. The fisc, like the bishopric, was

---

[79] Post 1948, *supra* note 29, at 180; KANTOROWICZ, *supra* note 42, at 180.

[80] J.A. Wahl, *Immortality and Inalienability: Baldus*, 32 MEDIEVAL STUDIES 308, 322 (1970); KANTOROWICZ, *supra* note 42, at 178.

[81] Wahl, *supra* note 80, at 320–22.

[82] KANTOROWICZ, *supra* note 42, at 180, 185 (citing Baldus).

[83] CANNING, *supra* note 1, at 120.

[84] *Id.* at 216.

[85] *Id.* at 211, 215–16.

[86] Wahl, *supra* note 80, at 211, 215–16.

an incorporation of property. Alternatively, when emphasizing the propertied side of the *respublica* – the *res* of the *publica* – the *fiscus* and *respublica* could be treated as synonyms.[87] The fisc was the property of the person of the incorporated republic – the property of the state. This rounded out the bishopric~kingdom analogy with respect to property. Like the bishop who is the tutor of the bishopric, managing it on behalf of the Church for the *utilitas ecclesia*, the king is but the tutor of the fisc, managing it on behalf of the state for the *utilitas publica*.[88] In essence, this corporatized (and tightened) the received notion of the king as a God-ordained guardian. It emphasized that the king is appointed most immediately by his subjects, not God, and strictly for the purpose of advancing their common good. And unlike the guardian of a wardship, who may take the proceeds of the ward's estate for himself so long as this does not diminish the underlying estate,[89] the officer of a corporation is to use its proceeds for the benefit of all.

Contracts of the Corporate Kingdom: In the Name of the *Dignitas*

Also, from the fisc's corporateness follows the obligation of royal contracts across reigns. "[S]ince the *respublica* and the *fisc* are … eternal and perpetual entities," Baldus argues, "it at once follows that the *respublica* of the kingdom and the *fisc* would be bound once and for all by a royal contract … the king can bind the *fisc* of his kingdom."[90]

This is a clear conceptualization of a juridical state, with separate property (the fisc) under contractual obligations. But this is not yet the whole story, for not all royal contracts involve the fisc. Those that do not will still bind across reigns if made in the name of the king's *dignitas*.[91] Before there was the "State," before even there was the "Crown," there was the "Dignity," which poured its contents into them.[92]

Of classical origin, the term, in the Christian era, became associated with ecclesiastical offices. It was not a description of the character or bearing of the occupant, but rather a personification of the office in its perfection and sempiternity – the *dignitas* that the bishop of Rome or other bishop or prelate assumed in ascending to the office. In early medieval iconography, it was signified by a square halo hovering over the prelate, marking him the bearer of a perpetual power derived from God.[93] Owing to Christological conceptions that long echoed within European kingship, this symbology readily passed to the emperor and king, who were also conceded *dignitates*.

---

[87] *Id.* at 320.

[88] *Id.* at 320.

[89] POLLACK & MAITLAND, *supra* note 21, at 1319.

[90] CANNING, *supra* note 1, at 217.

[91] Baldus also theorizes the Holy Roman Empire as a juridical state. For Baldus on the imperial fisc and *dignitas*, *see id.* at 89–90. But Baldus gave the royal *dignitas* fuller treatment.

[92] KANTOROWICZ, *supra* note 42, at 383.

[93] *Id.* at 82, at 338.

That each bishop at investiture donned the self-same *dignitas* as his predecessor gave rise to a new variant of the member corporation – an undying "corporation in succession," whose membership comprised all the past and future occupants of the seat, with the current bishop as its physical incarnation and instrument.[94] Grants made in the name of the Dignity, or made to a Dignity, therefore, did not expire with the death of the prelate.[95]

In England, which preferred its corporations "bodified," this was a welcome conceit. And thus arose that curious sixteenth-century English doctrine that the bishop, and also the king, has *two* bodies: a body natural and a body corporate, the corporate *dignitas* that he incarnates. "[The king] has not a body natural distinct and divided by itself from the office and dignity royal," opined the court, "but a body natural and body politic together indivisible."[96] In the terminology of later jurists, the latter made the king (like the bishop and parson) a "corporation sole." But this corporational king, because corporeal, failed to break free from the natural person of the king to become a separate and abstract "juridical person," or state.[97] Instead, it operated as one of two royal "capacities." When the king acted in his corporate capacity, he wielded the authority of the realm. But he did not do this as an officeholder acting on behalf of "the state." He did it as the king of his kingdom.

Baldus, meanwhile, made two important innovations in his treatment of the *dignitas* that together transformed it into a state concept. First, in keeping with his emphasis on the corporate people as the immediate source of authorization, Baldus did not source the royal *dignitas* to the godhead, but to the corporate people. "[I]t is true to say that the *respublica* does nothing for itself; the ruler of the *respublica*, however, acts in virtue of the *respublica* and the office [*dignitas*] conferred on him by the same *respublica*."[98]

Second, he gave the *dignitas* a more abstract corporate interpretation. As with the fisc, because the underlying *respublica* was an abstract, undying corporate person, the *dignitas* could be also. In Baldus' vocabulary, therefore, the king is not two bodies but two persons: a *persona personalis* and a "*persona idealis*, which is the Dignity."[99] This Dignity "miraculously perseveres forever, though not corporeally; for let the king be deficient with regard to his flesh, he nevertheless functions holding the place of *two* persons."[100]

As an emanation from the corporate kingdom, it is the *dignitas* that is, in legal view, the kingdom's true actor. In terms that startle the modern reader for their clean corporate logic, the *dignitas* is described repeatedly and consistently, across

[94] *Id.* at 387.
[95] *Id.* at 385–86.
[96] Maitland, *supra* note 22, at 35.
[97] Kantorowicz, *supra* note 42, at 446–49.
[98] Canning, *supra* note 1, at 215.
[99] Kantorowicz, *supra* note 42, at 400 n.293.
[100] *Id.*

varied contexts, as relating to the king as principal to agent. "[T]he Dignity," Baldus writes, "does not die, whereas the person is the instrument of that very Dignity without which the Dignity cannot act anything."[101] "Here we are aware of the Dignity as the principal [*principalem*], and of the person as the instrumental. Hence, the fundament of the [king's] acts is that very Dignity which is perpetual."[102] Speaking again of the natural king and the Dignity as two "persons," Baldus writes, "The king's person is the organ and instrument of that other person which is intellectual and public."[103] Exactly as principal-agent logic would suggest, the actions of the king are attributable to this public Dignity, because "[i]t is that intellectual and public person which principally causes the actions; for the mind is turned more to action, or to the principal power, than to the instrumental power."[104] The *dignitas* as the spiritually efficacious actor behind the bishop has been creatively reimagined as the legally efficacious actor behind the king.

Finally, more comprehensively than the fisc, the *dignitas* maintains the continuity of contracts across a change in kings. While contracts with a king as a person end with the person, "the contracts of kings ... pass on to the successor in the kingdom if they are quoted in the name of the Dignity."[105]

Pulling these threads together, we find in Baldus a "fisc that never dies" that is the property of the kingdom. This kingdom is conceptualized as an *universitas*, an incorporation of people and property, and the king is its officer, or head. This office bears the *dignitas*, which in a sense functions as a double of the king – the king's public persona – yet it is more than this, being something undying, emanating from the incorporated people, on behalf of which the king acts as a legal agent, placing the kingdom and its fisc under obligations that must be honored by the next king-as-agent. In sum, we have a separate treasury and contractual obligations that endure through changes in government. It is hard to deny that Baldus bequeathed Continental Europe a concept of a state as a juridical person, although it had yet to acquire its modern name. And although this is not the place to trace its inroads, it is relevant that Baldus was one of the most influential jurists of the Middle Ages, whose writings were esteemed into the seventeenth century – cited by Bodin and Grotius, for example.[106]

Of course, juridical personality does not by itself make for a state in the full modern sense. There are other prerequisites for this that were not yet in place, such as the peak authority within the *regnum* be both independent and supreme, with no rival law-making power above it (such as the emperor or Pope) or below it (such as

---

[101] *Id.* at 444.
[102] *Id.* at 441–42.
[103] *Id.* at 445.
[104] *Id.*
[105] *Id.* at 398.
[106] CANNING, *supra* note 1, at 228–29; for uptake of Baldus' arguments, *see* 4 OTTO VON GIERKE, DAS DEUTSCHE GENOSSENSCHAFTSRECHT 239 n.122, vol. 3 694 n. 19 (1868–1913).

feudal lords), and that it should be seen as constituted strictly for political purposes, and not also religious ones.[107] But this key feature of the modern state – juridical personhood – which distinguishes the Western concept from other versions of centralized rule, was already available by the high Middle Ages owing to the encounter with corporate theory. In both England and on the Continent, the bishopric served as the mediating institution in this encounter. Indeed, the state as a juridical person, one might say, is the corporate bishopric writ large; and our present-day world order, an international system of secularized bishoprics.

MODERN CONSTITUTIONALISM AND THE JURIDICAL STATE

But a problem remained, even after the state had cleared the field of rivals. Sovereignty and juridical personhood stand in obvious tension. *Princeps legibus solutus est* is the principle of sovereignty. "The sovereign is not bound by the law."[108] Until government (*administratio*) is separated from sovereignty (*imperium*), the government's obligation to contracts, which is central to juridical personhood, has no firm basis, either theoretically or institutionally. Recent scholarship emphasizes the importance of Bodin in theorizing this separation.[109] Yet, not until modern American-style constitutionalism were state sovereignty and juridicality squared both theoretically and institutionally. And this followed not from Bodin, but from the Americans' experience as corporate colonies.

Life under Parliament taught the Americans that even elected governments, when sovereign, can be arbitrary and tyrannical (as epitomized by the Navigation Acts). They preferred charter-limited government – familiar to them from their recent colonial past when the New England colonies were literal corporations of the Crown. Being incorporated, these colonies had juridical personhood, with treasuries and contracts distinct from those of their members.[110] But they did not have sovereignty. Rather, like all subordinate corporations, each had a limited jurisdictional authority exercised by a governing body limited by charter to specified governmental structures, procedures, and purposes. The Americans wished to retain such limits. But where could they find a replacement sovereign, more trustworthy than the king, to place charter limits on their *new* governments?

The Americans' great constitutional innovation was to wed the practice of corporate chartering with the Baldusian tradition of popular sovereignty. Just as a sovereign king could issue a corporate charter that founds a corporate government with a legally limited (charter-limited) jurisdiction, so could a sovereign People. The U.S. Constitution is that founding charter (*Federalist* 49 [Madison]). Indeed, all of the

---

[107] 2 Quentin Skinner, The Foundations of Modern Political Thought: The Age of Reformation 349–53 (1978).
[108] Justinian's, *supra* note 9, at 1.3.31.
[109] Richard Tuck, The Sleeping Sovereign (2016); Lee, *supra* note 1.
[110] Maitland, *supra* note 22, at 42–43.

things that we think of as American constitutional innovations – written constitutional charters, constitutional conventions, elected executives, judicial review, and charter amendment – represent a transfer of instrumentalities used for governing corporations to governing the state.[111]

In this new form of constitutionalism, the People is a Baldusian sovereign. In one guise, it is a corporeal body politic that, gathered in assembly, exercises sovereignty. This makes it a constituting (or "constituent") power, capable of erecting a government over its members as individuals. This is the "jurisdictional" People. But this People is also an abstract incorporeal person, or corporation in succession, which remains legally the same as its members come and go. This is the "juridical" People, which has its own treasury (or "fisc"), with its own property and contracts, which the government manages on its behalf.

The difference from Baldus is that the modern People conducts itself in a way that Baldus never imagined. The corporate People does not remain an active force in the government, as it did in the Italian city-republic, where its sovereignty put in question its juridicality. But neither does it alienate its sovereignty to a king or other ruler, disbanding itself as a capable corporate person. Instead, it does two things. First, it charters a government with a limited jurisdiction, reserving to itself sovereignty, and thus, a right to reconvene and reform or abolish this government. And then, just as notably, it goes to sleep. That is, until such time as it stirs itself to further constitutional action, the People is (in the evocative phrase of Hobbes revived by Richard Tuck)[112] a "sleeping sovereign," content (for better or worse) to leave the management of its affairs, its property, and contracts, to its steward, the government (which, in democratic incarnations, is animated by the electorate, the people as a multitude, not the people as sovereign). There was, thus, no need for the American founders to posit an undying *dignitas*, a principal behind the throne, to bind successive rulers. The People itself is this juridical person, this principal – the subject of state property and contracts, whose constancy (i.e., juridicality) is maintained through its slumbers.

It is this corporate People that Wilson and his generation referred to as the "state." To restate Wilson's tidy summary, the "state" is both a "body of free persons united together" (which he calls "Sovereign") and "an artificial person" with property and debts, contracts, and purposes "distinct from that of its members," which successive administrations, as its agent, are bound by the Constitution to honor and the courts to enforce (under the Contracts Clause, for example). Thus are state sovereignty (which is popular sovereignty) and state juridicality reconciled and institutionalized – a trick turned by dividing the People into an active phase and a passive phase, awake or asleep on the *ex ante* and *ex post* sides of its chartered government.

---

[111] Ciepley, *supra* note 1.
[112] Tuck, *supra* note 109.

This allows us finally to clear up a confusion in our current political lexicon. The juridicality of the state – the state as a legal person distinct from the persons of individual citizens – too easily slides into the notion that the state is something alien set against the People. Political science has exacerbated this confusion, introducing a Weberian conception of the state that conflates the state with the government. But properly understood, the state is the People themselves in corporate succession.[113] Government may become arbitrary and tyrannical. But this is not an action of "the state." It is done against the state and in betrayal of it.

---

[113] LEE, *supra* note 1, at 70, 77.

13

Corporate Personhood as Legal and Literary Fiction

Joshua Barkan

INTRODUCTION

The corporation plays a special role in discussions over legal personhood. Whereas advocates for human rights have turned to personhood to offer protection to the vulnerable, corporate personhood confers privileges on already powerful institutions. Nonetheless, attempts to distinguish corporate persons from other persons are beset by problems. In this essay, I suggest that instead of trying to find the truth of persons, such that we can distinguish real flesh and blood humans from the *persona ficta* of the corporation, we should take seriously the fictional nature of corporate personhood. I conclude by mapping out two different ways that corporate fictions operate, one in law and the other in literature. Whereas law tends to read the fictional dimensions of corporate personhood pragmatically, facilitating the ends that corporations were chartered to serve, the literary approach to the fictional nature of the corporation highlights the grave problems with this organizational form, while simultaneously prodding us to think about more just forms of collective life.

PARSING PERSONHOOD

The concept of legal personhood has long vexed legal scholars. Although seemingly self-evident as a figure of speech, questions concerning the extension of legal personhood to entities as diverse as the fetus, the dead, the comatose, the animal, the corporation, the river, or the artificially intelligent force legal scholars to grapple with the fundamental malleability, if not downright ambiguity, in the concept. At its most basic, the attribution of personhood is a means by which liberal legal systems ascribe rights to things or create rights bearing entities, be they animate or inanimate, individual or collective. Beyond that, however, scholars have found little consistency in the juridical notion of personhood, noting, "no coherent body of doctrine or jurisprudential theory exists" that firmly establishes the meaning of "this legal metaphor."[1]

---

[1] Dave Fagundes, Note, *What We Talk about When We Talk about Persons: The Language of a Legal Fiction*, 114 HARV. L. REV. 1745, 1746 (2001).

In response, legal scholars strived to establish some parameters around personhood that would allow jurists to bring the diverse discussion of personhood in line with some more foundational idea. This is particularly true in relation to the corporation whose legal personhood remains singularly troublesome. Whereas many debates over personhood concern questions about extending legal recognition to vulnerable entities relatively lacking standing, debates over corporate personhood concern some of the most powerful institutions in contemporary society. The rights conferred through personhood protect and immunize these powerful institutions from regulation and legal oversight, rather than solve the problems of the powerless. Debates over corporate personhood are like mirror images to the attempts to protect things such as natural environments as persons.[2] In the case of the recognition of the Whanganui River as a person[3] or the subsequent granting of personhood to the Ganga and Yamuna Rivers by the High Court of Uttarakhand,[4] courts and legislatures used legal personhood to protect the fluid dynamics of riverine ecosystems in their environmental, social, and spiritual dimensions. Whatever the limitations of these explicitly postcolonial turns toward personhood, such cases starkly contrast with questions about corporate personhood, in which the legal status of personhood enables corporations to limit the liability of shareholders, cross political boundaries, and engage in regulatory arbitrage.[5]

For this reason, in fields like human rights law, we see attempts to clearly demarcate corporate persons from other juridical entities. Because international human rights law is, in part, grounded in the "dignity and worth of the human person,"[6] human rights lawyers have expressed concern about how the language of personhood favors global corporate interests over others, making human rights just another component of corporate-led economic globalization.[7] As Upendra Baxi bluntly put it, "the paradigm of the Universal Declaration of Human Rights ... is ... being *supplanted* by that of trade-related, market friendly human rights ... under the auspices of contemporary globalization."[8] Although Baxi notes these legal changes involve both nation states and supranational institutions, such as the World Trade

---

[2] *See* CHRISTOPHER STONE, SHOULD TREES HAVE STANDING? LAW, MORALITY AND THE ENVIRONMENT (3rd ed. 2010); Isaac Davidson, *Whanganui River Given Legal Status of a Person under Unique Treaty of Waitangi Settlement*, N.Z. HERALD (Mar. 15, 2017).

[3] Te Awa Tupua (Whanganui River Claims Settlement) Act, NZL-2017-L-108218 (Mar. 20, 2017) (N.Z.).

[4] High Ct. of Uttarakhand at Nainital Dec. 5, 2016 & Mar. 20, 2017, *Mohd. Salim v. State of Uttarakhand & others*, Writ Petition (PIL) 126 (India) (stating that "Rivers Ganga and Yamuna are breathing, living and sustaining the communities from mountains to sea.").

[5] On these dimensions of corporate personhood *see generally* Morton Horwitz, *Santa Clara Revisited: The Development of Corporate Theory*, 88 W. VA. L. REV. 173 (1985); JOSHUA BARKAN, CORPORATE SOVEREIGNTY: LAW AND GOVERNMENT UNDER CAPITALISM 65 (2013).

[6] G.A. Res. 217 (III) A, Universal Declaration of Human Rights (Dec. 10, 1948).

[7] *See* UPENDRA BAXI, THE FUTURE OF HUMAN RIGHTS (2nd ed. 2006); ANNA GREAR, REDIRECTING HUMAN RIGHTS: FACING THE CHALLENGE OF CORPORATE LEGAL HUMANITY (2010).

[8] Baxi, *supra* note 7, at 234.

Organization, he treats corporations as both primary shapers and beneficiaries of the current rights regime. Baxi argues that securing rights to things such as health, food, sustainable development, political participation, and gender equality is increasingly conceptualized as achievable through the granting of privileges and protections to large corporations involved in industries including agriculture, techno-science, media, and pharmaceuticals.[9] Corporations, thus, are made the vehicles by which human rights are secured, while simultaneously being protected from owning up to their own violations.

As such, the intertwining of corporations within the human rights regime potentially upends the essential connection between right and person on which human rights depends.[10] In response, scholars invested in the progressive possibilities of human rights have suggested ways forward that hinge on distinguishing between the vulnerable bodies requiring the protection of human rights and powerful institutions like corporations. Inverting the common discourse of rights as a protection for persons, Anna Grear argues that it is the regime of human rights itself that needs protection from corporations. To do so, she argues, "human rights need *redirecting* toward the embodied, vulnerable human being, precisely in order to challenge the development of a form of corporate legal humanity."[11]

In a sophisticated theoretical reading, Grear locates the problem with corporate personhood in a pattern of "disembodied rationalism"[12] endemic to human rights. Because human rights emerged from a liberal tradition that prioritizes abstract, universal, and disembodied reasoning, it views the juridical subject of human rights in a similar light, obscuring the history and context that situate living human beings differently in relation to law and authority. Such rationalism is especially fraught, as it is the concrete events of history that render, say, the stateless person vulnerable, denied the protections of citizenship and left appealing to the protections of rights based on nothing more than their status as humans. For the corporation, however, this decontextualized and abstract reasoning is empowering, in that it enables corporations to claim rights as persons despite their extensive powers to act and shape the world. In this conceptualization, today's business corporations arguably represent archetypical liberal legal subjects in that, as aggregations of capital, they are pure expressions of instrumental economic rationality.

Recognizing as much, Grear advocates for a different conception of the subject of human rights; one grounded not in calculative or instrumental reason, but rather in embodied vulnerability, which she argues, "supplies a (possibly *the*) crucial distinction between the corporation and the human being for the purposes of human

---

[9] *Id.* at 256.
[10] For work moving in this direction, *see* Roberto Esposito, *The Dispositif of the Person*, 8 L., CULTURE & HUMAN. 17 (2012).
[11] GREAR, *supra* note 7 at 3.
[12] *Id.* at 42.

rights attribution."[13] Her contention is that the human body, unlike the corporate person, is "affectable" in terms of its ability to be made vulnerable and to feel pain and suffering.[14] Grear recovers an alternative line of development in the Universal Declaration of Human Rights that, as a response to Nazi atrocities, linked legal rights with discrete embodied vulnerabilities.[15] This framework, she suggests, can be more usefully applied to human rights cases, in that it differentiates human from corporate persons, and therefore, can more appropriately grasp "what is at stake between the parties" in human rights disputes.[16]

Thus, for Grear, "both *embodiment* and *vulnerability*" are categories which allow us to distinguish what legal persons are valid subjects of human rights. In other words, Grear includes the vulnerable bodies made to suffer within the human rights regime, while simultaneously excluding, for good moral and political reasons, corporations that, in some cases, bear responsibility for such suffering.[17] Moreover, Grear's conceptualization of embodied vulnerability is important because it attempts to establish, maintain, or expand the political efficacy of human rights in the protection of the poor and vulnerable, without resorting to biological essentialisms which only recognize flesh and blood human beings as rights bearing. Confronted, for instance, with the aforementioned claims to personhood for rivers and other ecosystems, Grear's theory of embodied vulnerability recognizes the fragility of socio-ecological relations as something worth protecting through a human rights framework.

Of course, the downside to this theory is that it could arguably be expanded to include the very corporations Grear wishes to exclude from the category of embodied vulnerable persons. After all, the social science literature on corporations in fields such as sociology, anthropology, and geography has demonstrated how corporations are embedded in the cultures, dispositions, and complexes of power and knowledge that course through these institutional forms.[18] Although stylized as rational, disembodied economic actors, this literature demonstrates that corporations

---

[13] *Id.* at 132.

[14] *Id.* at 131 (Stating "[t]he human body is 'affectable.' It can be radically compromised. We die if we cannot gain the necessary nutrients that our bodies require. We need to drink clean water. We suffer, and sometimes even die, if we cannot breathe sufficiently clean air. We can be killed. We can be made to suffer pain.").

[15] *See id.* at Ch. 7.

[16] *Id.* at 168.

[17] *Id.* at 131.

[18] In terms of the social embeddedness of economic action, *see* Karl Polayni, The Great Transformation (1944); Mark Granovetter, *Economic Action and Social Structure: The Problem of Embeddedness*, 91 Am. J. Soc. 481 (1985). For the diverse social science literature on the social construction of the corporation *see* Peter Miller & Nikolas Rose, *Governing Economic Life*. 19 Econ. Soc. 1 (1990); Erica Schoenberger, The Cultural Crisis of the Firm (1997); Phillip O'Neill, *Financial Narratives of the Modern Corporation*, 1 J. Econ. Geography 181 (2001); Phillip O'Neill & J. K. Gibson-Graham, *Enterprise Discourse and Executive Talk: Stories that Destabilize the Company*, 24 Trans. Inst. Brit. Geography 11 (1999); Karen Ho, Liquidated: An Ethnography of Wall Street (2009); Marina Welker, Enacting the Corporation: An American Mining Firm in Post-Authoritarian Indonesia (2014).

rely on and reproduce a whole host of social relations that are built through affective ties of trust, reciprocity, and tacit learning.[19] More recently, scholars working in the tradition of actor network theory extended these arguments to suggest that corporations are the outcomes of socio-technical assemblages.[20] In this framework, the corporation *is*, ontologically speaking, nothing more than the ability of diverse things—people, computers, factors of production, communicative networks of skill and expertise, regulatory regimes, etc. – to produce and preform various ritualized affects in one another. While we rarely think of corporations as "vulnerable" in the sense Grear suggests, both corporations themselves and the actor-networks producing the markets on which corporate stocks are traded are adept at employing the languages of vulnerability and loss—albeit in a particular, financialized tongue.[21]

None of which is to say that sociological, geographic, or actor-network conceptions of corporations – much less the self-descriptions of corporate managers or financial institutions – have some priority over Grear's framework. Rather, the attempt to parse personhood, with all of the nuance and anti-essentialism that marks Grear's project as exemplary, cannot fully resolve the problems of liberal personhood, which scholars writing on biopolitics have identified as internal to the very structure of liberal law.[22] By biopolitics, I refer to the tradition of thought, closely identified with the work of Michel Foucault, that considered the way life itself became the primary object of political concern and calculation in western modernity.[23] For thinkers like Giorgio Agamben and Roberto Esposito, what establishes the point of connection between liberal democracies and totalitarianism is that both regimes are founded on saving some portion of the population, qualifying some lives as worthy of political existence, while simultaneously exposing others to the potential of death.[24] As Esposito notes, the metrics and calculations adjudicating the ratios of life and death

---

[19] Understanding the ways these relational attributes structure the geography of economic innovation has been a major preoccupation of economic geographers and regional scientists. For an introduction, *see* ANNALEE SAXENIAN, REGIONAL ADVANTAGE: CULTURE AND COMPETITION IN SILICON VALLEY AND ROUTE 128 (1994); ANNALEE SAXENIAN, THE NEW ARGONAUTS: REGIONAL ADVANTAGE IN A GLOBAL ECONOMY (2007). For a review of the geographic literature, *see* Harald Bathet et al., *Clusters and Knowledge: Local Buzz, Global Pipelines, and the Process of Knowledge Creation*, 28 PROGRESS IN HUMAN GEOGRAPHY 31 (2004).

[20] See, for instance, Mika Viljanen, *Making Banks on a Global Scale: Management-Based Regulation as Agencement*, 23 IND. J. GLOB. LEGAL STUD. 425 (2016); *see generally* MICHEL CALLON, THE LAWS OF THE MARKETS (1998).

[21] *See* O'Neill & Gibson-Graham; *supra* note 18; Ho, *supra* note 18.

[22] See, in particular, the arguments on personhood in Esposito, *supra* note 10; GIORGIO AGAMBEN, HOMO SACER: SOVEREIGN POWER AND BARE LIFE (1998).

[23] MICHEL FOUCAULT, HISTORY OF SEXUALITY, VOL. 1: AN INTRODUCTION (1978). For an introduction to key philosophical texts in this tradition, *see* Timoty Campbell et al., BIOPOLITICS: A READER (Timothy Campbell & Adam Sitze, eds., 2013).

[24] See also, in this regard, Michel Foucault's arguments about state racism. Michel Foucault, Society Must Be Defended, Lecture at Collège de France (1975–1976) *in* SOCIETY MUST BE DEFENDED, LECTURES AT THE COLLÈGE DE FRANCE 1975–1976 (Mauro Bertani ed., David Macey trans., 2003).

are different within totalitarian and liberal democratic regimes. Yet, both forms of government are preoccupied with setting the line between those that can be saved and those that can be exposed to death in ways that benefit the social totality.[25]

This is also the reason that Agamben pays much attention to the *threshold* where sovereign power and bare life blur. Agamben's language of the threshold, which occurs throughout his writing, refers to this line between qualified political life and simple bare life. Agamben's arguments about bare life are often read in sociological terms, giving social scientists some way to conceptualize the relations between sovereign power and abandoned populations. On this read, bare life refers to specific empirical groups that are marginalized or exposed to the possibility of an unmarked death. And of course, it's a grim statement about contemporary socio-legal orders that we can all identify a litany of individuals and populations who are exposed to potential death through specific events – ranging from gun violence to environmental toxicity – along with more structural patterns of inequality shaped by the dynamics of political, economic, racialized, gendered, and sexual violence.[26] The list could go on and on.

Yet, Agamben makes clear that his argument is not just historical-empirical but ontological. Formulated in this manner, the argument is that *the potential* for designating bare life – for establishing the line or threshold where some element is legally excluded from law – resides as a permanent "fracture" in liberal legal orders.[27] As such, this potential sits within liberal legal orders, as a possiblity to be called on in emergencies or exceptional situations when the welfare of the state or public is at risk. If Agamben is correct, the implication is that there is no way to distinguish between persons included and excluded from the realm of human rights without becoming trapped in the relation where some part of the whole is legally excluded for the safety and salvation (in other words, the *salus*) of others.[28]

Grear, recognizes these issues, acknowledging that "Agamben's challenge must be taken up,"[29] while, nonetheless, attempting to recover the embodied vulnerability

[25] ROBERTO ESPOSITO, BIOS: BIOPOLITICS AND PHILOSOPHY (2008) and Roberto Esposito, *Totalitarianism or Biopolitics? Concerning a Philosophical Interpretation of the Twentieth Century*, 34 CRITICAL INQUIRY 633 (2008). For an attempt to insert the corporate person into this matrix, *see* Joshua Barkan, *Roberto Esposito's Political Biology and Corporate Forms of Life*, 8 L., CULTURE & HUMAN. 84 (2012).

[26] *See* ROB NIXON, SLOW VIOLENCE AND THE ENVIRONMENTALISM OF THE POOR (2011).

[27] On the permanence of the biopolitical "fracture," *see* GIORGIO AGAMBEN, HOMO SACER 114 (1995). On the ontological dimensions of Agamben's work, *see* his discussion of Antonio Negri and Aristotle. *Id.* at 42–48. *See also* MATTHEW ABBOTT, THE FIGURE OF THIS WORLD: AGAMBEN AND THE QUESTION OF POLITICAL ONTOLOGY (2014); Joshua Barkan, *Sovereignty, in* WILEY-BLACKWELL COMPANION TO POLITICAL GEOGRAPHY 48 (John Agnew et al., eds., 2015).

[28] On the ways these dimensions of right intersect with state sovereignty and the concept of the *salus publica*, *see* ADAM SITZE, THE IMPOSSIBLE MACHINE: A GENEALOGY OF SOUTH AFRICA'S TRUTH AND RECONCILIATION COMMISSION (2013).

[29] GREAR, *supra* note 7, at 155.

of the refugee from being ascribed to the realm of bare life. Human rights, in her formulation, act as a sort of salvation for the refugee. The problem remains, however, that attempts to care for the refugee through rights – even rights based on embodied vulnerability – rely on the same legal framework that has always powered the biopolitical machine. Agamben, for his part, makes this clear in a number of ways: for instance, by noting that Nazi thanatopolitics conceptualized and embodied vulnerability in nationalist and eugenic terms.[30] For those who would like to see law attend to the needs of the poor and vulnerable, the deeply disturbing implication of Agamben's argument is that Nazism conceived of the Holocaust in the same language of protecting the social body that we might look toward as an alternative framework for rethinking human rights.

This leaves critical and progressive approaches to human rights in a bit of a bind. If our best attempts to deploy the language of human rights on behalf of the poor, vulnerable, and needy are based on the same distinctions grounding corporate abuses, how then do we respond to these entanglements between the corporate person and the subject of human rights? What critical potential is there in rights language concerning corporate power? And, if the answer to such a question is that rights are limited in their ability to address corporate power, what other positions of critique could help us understand and challenge the roles of corporations in structuring the human rights regime while also, in many cases, being involved in violating the human rights of others?

GENEALOGIES OF CORPORATE PERSONS

Given these problems, one response would be to shift attention away from attempts to establish new frameworks of legal personhood that could resolve these issues, and toward understanding corporate personhood by charting its genealogy.[31] Doing so involves recognizing the connections between the corporation and political sovereignty, as well as the work that the legal designation of corporations as persons has accomplished in suturing this relationship within distinct historical and geographic contexts. Although the interweaving of corporations, sovereign power, and personhood are complex, the relations can be traced back to early modern formulations in Western law, where both entities were conceptualized as political bodies that united individuals into a collective entity.

A full genealogy of personhood is beyond the scope of this chapter, but the story of the role of personification in the formation of secular state sovereignty in the West is well known.[32] Historian Ernst Kantorowicz famously noted the ways the

---

[30] AGAMBEN, *supra* note 22, at 140.
[31] BARKAN, *supra* note 5.
[32] DAVID RUNCIMAN, PLURALISM AND THE PERSONALITY OF THE STATE (1997); MARK NEOCLEOUS, IMAGINING THE STATE (2003).

corporate body sacralized the emergence of the secular state.[33] For Kantorowicz, corporateness enabled legal scholars to conceptualize sovereignty as extending beyond the life of an individual ruler.[34] For Agamben, personification established the sovereign's right to compel the allegiance of individuals to the state, up to and including the power to expose them to potential death. Thus, as Agamben claims, "the great metaphor of the Leviathan, whose body is formed out of all the bodies of individuals, must be read in this light. The absolute capacity of the subjects' bodies to be killed forms the new political body of the West."[35]

Less commented on, however, is the significance of personification for other institutions in society – from churches to hospitals to educational institutions – that were also corporations. As I have argued elsewhere, these institutions are also derived from, and ontologically linked to, state sovereignty in that their existence was established through charters, legal "gifts" considered "not law but exemptions from law."[36] These exemptions made corporations powerful institutions, able to accomplish various ends of government. States found a decentralized mechanism in chartering corporations to provide for the education, health and welfare of the population (in other words, the *salus publica*), as well as, much later, coordinating transportation, trade, and manufacturing. At the same time, the liberties afforded corporations via chartered grants also empowered corporations in relations to states. Corporations were self-governing institutions, with rights against centralizing state authorities; for just this reason, they were often viewed as politically threatening to state sovereignty. Agamben provided a nice encapsulation of this dynamic when he noted (in a slightly different context) *"Corpus is a two-faced being, the bearer both of subjection to sovereign power and of individual liberties."*[37]

Moreover, a genealogical approach explains how the content of corporate personhood and its attendant privileges changed over time. Whereas early modern corporations were thought of as lesser political bodies in relation to emergent forms of national state sovereignty, the late nineteenth-century articulation of the corporate legal form in relation to capitalist production repositioned both the corporation, as an institution, and the larger discourse of personhood. In the U.S. context, for instance, much has been written about the way the end of slavery and the reconstruction amendments to the U.S. Constitution following the civil war transformed

[33] ERNST KANTOROWICZ, THE KING'S TWO BODIES: A STUDY IN MEDIEVAL POLITICAL THEOLOGY (1957); NEOCLEOUS, *supra* note 32; AGAMBEN, *supra* note 22; Foucault, *supra* note 24.
[34] KANTOROWICZ, *supra* note 33.
[35] AGAMBEN, *supra* note 22, at 125.
[36] BARKAN, *supra* note 5, at 37. The language of "exemption from law" is from THOMAS HOBBES, LEVIATHAN 200 (Richard Tuck ed., 1999) (1651) and his discussion of the charter. On the exemption from law, *see* GEORGIO AGAMBEN, STATE OF EXCEPTION (Kevin Attell trans., 2005).
[37] AGAMBEN, *supra* note 22, at 125 (italics in original). Agamben was writing of *habea corpus*, but, for interesting reasons, the argument stands equally valid for other political and politicized bodies, including corporations.

notions of citizenship and personhood.[38] This rise of a new national political economy and an attendant legal and regulatory system also restructured the content of
corporate personhood. As Morton Horwitz has shown, concepts of personhood were
crucial to limiting the liability of shareholders – arguably the most important advantage businesses could secure through the corporate legal form.[39] Personhood was
also central to the ability of capitalist corporations to extend their business ventures
beyond the boundaries of the states in which they were incorporated.[40]

A genealogical approach does not directly resolve the problem of corporate legal
humanity that Grear and Baxi identify, but it does help explain why and how states
and supranational institutions continue empowering corporations for projects of
national and economic development, while also viewing them with great trepida-
tion. For the state, corporations have their uses, but remain potential rivals, if not
totally ungovernable. A genealogical approach also helps us think about the double-
edged nature of corporate power in relation to the regulation, management, and
enhancement of life when examined under the rubric of biopolitics.[41] Although
corporate power has expanded, based on its potential to ameliorate life, it has also
been accompanied by the ability of corporations to abandon populations. More
specifically, once the corporation became the legal form for coordinating capitalist
commodity production, corporate institutions were also empowered to routinely
deny housing, clothes, food, work, and essential medicine, as well as to expose individuals and groups to unsafe living conditions and environmental hazards and to
push workers into more depoliticized forms of bare life, precisely in the name of
their (and our) collective salvation.

Thus, a genealogical approach is much less concerned with establishing a fixed
content of legal personhood in a way that clarifies future disputes than it is with
understanding how personhood changed in relation to the shifting uses of corporate
and state power. In this respect, the genealogical approach is consonant with the
argument that the pragmatist philosopher John Dewey made in regard to corporate personhood.[42] Dewey began his 1926 essay on corporate personality with the
memorable line that "put roughly, 'person' signifies what law makes it signify."[43]
Although the phrase is direct and seemingly straightforward, Dewey took pains to
make a nuanced philosophical point, namely that legal reasoning about personhood
does not require the establishment of a metaphysical essence. Adopting Charles

---

[38] *See, e.g.*, Barbara Young Welke, Law and the Borders of Belonging in the Long
Nineteenth Century (2010); Amy Dru Stanley, From Bondage to Contract: Wage
Labor, Marriage, and the Market in the Age of Slave Emancipation (1998).

[39] Horwitz, *supra* note 5.

[40] Barkan, *supra* note 5, at 87; Gerard Henderson, The Position of Foreign Corporations
in American Constitutional Law (1918).

[41] *See supra* note 23 and accompanying text.

[42] John Dewey, *The Historic Background of Corporate Legal Personality*, 35 Yale L.J. 655 (1926).

[43] *Id.* at 655.

Pierce's "pragmatist rule" that objects are best understood in terms of their effects,[44] Dewey argued that what was important about corporate personhood was what happened when the law treated a corporation as a "rights-and-duty-bearing unit."[45] As such, confusion engendered when calling a corporate entity a "person" ensnared the corporation's legal standing in various debates of morality, metaphysics, psychology, and biology that were, strictly speaking, non-legal – therefore, at least in terms of legal analysis, "irrelevant."[46] Over time, according to Dewey, these non-legal debates about personhood made their way into law, and thus, produced historically and geographically specific legal definitions that structured the development of juristic reasoning. In this manner, lawyers agonized over just what type of persons corporations were, variously describing them as real, artificial, fictitious, natural, a state grant, or concession, etc. In each of these debates, as Dewey explained, the key point was not as much how legal reasoning corresponded with metaphysical truth, but more about the practical effects produced by treating the corporation in one way versus another.[47]

If Dewey is correct, it means little can be gained by attempting to establish a new foundation for personhood. On this read, personhood – be it of corporations or of the vulnerable body – is, to echo Dewey's frankness, what law says it is. It might then be more fruitful to ask a different set of questions of the corporate person, focused less on the category of its personage and more on the way law conceptualizes what it is saying. Why, for instance, have legal scholars vacillated so much over the status of the corporate person? And why, for so long, did they attempt to accommodate corporations by describing corporations as persons, but then qualifying them as either fictional or, relatedly, artificial? If corporate persons are what law says they are, why does law require recourse to the status of fiction at all? Rather than defining personhood, such questions potentially open up a critique of the systems of law that ascribe rights to these entities in the first place.

LAW'S FICTIONS

To be sure, the fictional status of corporate personhood has been subjected to extensive analysis and nearly all accounts of corporate personhood dwell on the nature of legal fictions.[48] Likewise, discussions of legal fictions usually require some

---

[44] *Id.* at 661. *See also* PIERCE, CHANCE, LOVE AND LOGIC 45 (Morris Cohen ed., 1923) ("This logical method was first stated by Charles S. Peirce as the pragmatistic rule: 'Consider what effects, which might conceivably have practical bearings, we conceive the object of our conception to have. Then, our conception of these effects is the whole of our conception of the object.'").

[45] Dewey, *supra* note 42, at 661.

[46] *Id.* at 663.

[47] *Id.* at 664.

[48] The question of the fictional status of corporate personhood dominated the massive debate on the issue during the first three decades of the twentieth century. *See* Dewey, *supra* note 42; *see also* FREDERICK HALLIS, CORPORATE PERSONALITY (1930); ALEXANDER NEKAM, PERSONALITY

perfunctory comments on the personality of corporations.[49] Although their ubiquity in the law raises interesting questions, Anglo-American legal scholars long downplayed the importance of legal fictions, considering them, with some notable exceptions,[50] pragmatic contrivances that ease the machinery of legal decision-making. Thus, Lon Fuller argues, in one of the most extensive, if not systematic treatments of the topic,[51] "[a] fiction is either (1) a statement propounded with complete or partial consciousness of its falsity, or (2) a false statement recognized as having utility."[52] This account of legal fictions extends to his treatment of corporate personhood, which relies on both aspects of this definition. Thus, for Fuller, we at once recognize the falsity of the link between corporations and persons, while still holding onto the concept as legally useful. For this reason, Fuller described the fictional corporate person as an "abbreviatory device"[53] or "a matter of subjective convenience."[54]

Fuller, here, was simply reiterating the dominant approach to corporate personhood in Anglo-American law from the 1930s.[55] Although an extensive debate concerning the status of corporate personality roiled both the continental European and

CONCEPTION OF THE LEGAL ENTITY (1938); Arthur Machen Jr., *Corporate Personality*, 24 HARV. L. REV. 235, 347 (1911); Paul Vinogradoff, *Juridical Persons*, 24 COLUM. L. REV. 594 (1924); Max Radin, *The Endless Problem of Corporate Personality*, 32 COLUM. L. REV. 643 (1932). Fictional theories of corporate personhood were also examined by the defenders of the "real entity" theory of the corporation. *See* OTTO GIERKE, POLITICAL THEORIES OF THE MIDDLE AGES (F. Maitland trans. 1900); ERNST FREUND, LEGAL NATURE OF CORPORATIONS (1987); W. Jethro Brown, *The Personality of the Corporation and the State*, 21 L.Q. REV. 365 (1905).

[49] *See, e.g.,* LON FULLER, LEGAL FICTIONS 12 (1967); Anon., Note, *Lessons From Abroad: Mathematical, Poetic, and Literary Fictions in the Law*, 115 HARV. L. REV. 2234 (2002); William Twining, *Preface*, *in* LEGAL FICTIONS IN THEORY AND PRACTICE v (Maksymilian Del Mar & William Twining, eds., 2015); Aviam Soifer, *Reviewing Legal Fictions*, 20 GA. L. REV. 877 (1986); Maksymilian Del Mar, *Introducing Fictions: Examples, Functions, Definitions and Evaluations*, *in* LEGAL FICTIONS IN THEORY AND PRACTICE xi (Maksymilian Del Mar & William Twining, eds., 2015).

[50] Chief among the objectors is Jeremy Bentham, who (in)famously claimed in a critique of corruption in the special jury system that "In *Roman-bred* law in general – in the Scotch edition of it in particular – *fiction* is a *wart*, which here and there deforms the face of justice: in English law, *fiction* is a *syphilis*, which runs in every vein, and carries into every part of the system the principle of rottenness." *On the Art of Packing Special Juries*, *in* V JEREMY BENTHAM, THE WORKS OF JEREMY BENTHAM 92 (John Bowring ed. 1843). Part of the quotation is reproduced in FULLER, *supra* note 49, at 2. For discussions of Bentham's account of legal fictions, *see* Nomi Maya Stolzenberg, *Bentham's Theory of Fictions – A 'Curious Double Language'* 11 CARDOZO L. REV. 223 (1999); Robert Yelle, *Bentham's Fictions: Canon and Idolatry in the Genealogy of Law*, 17 YALE J.L. HUMAN. 151 (2005). For a more contemporary objection to the dependence on legal fictions, *see* Cass Sunstein, *Principles, Not Fictions*, 57 U. CHI. L. REV. 1247 (1990).

[51] I agree with Kenneth Campbell's sentiment that "it is difficult to detect an overall thesis" in Fuller's account. *See* Kenneth Campbell, *Fuller on Legal Fictions*, 2 L. PHIL. 340 (1983).

[52] FULLER, *supra* note 49, at 9.

[53] *Id.* at 82.

[54] *Id.* at 13.

[55] We should note that although Fuller's LEGAL FICTIONS was published in 1967, it was based on three law review articles from the early 1930s. Lon Fuller, *Legal Fictions*, 25 ILL. L. REV. 363 (1930); Lon Fuller, *Legal Fictions*, 25 ILL. L. REV. 513 (1931); Lon Fuller, *Legal Fictions*, 25 ILL. L. REV. 877 (1931).

Anglo-American legal academies at the turn of the twentieth century, by the 1930s, Anglo-American legal scholars became tired of the metaphysical speculation concerning what they viewed as a simple organizational tool for business enterprises. This exasperation was evident in Dewey and Fuller, but even more so in the writings of the comparative legal historian Max Radin, who likened the question of corporate personhood to an "interminable controversy."[56] For Radin, as with Dewey and Fuller, corporate personhood was simply a linguistic convenience that the law could use as a shorthand for a set of relations. Radin, with his vast knowledge of ancient Greek and Roman law along with the legal theories of the medieval glossators, scholastics, and canonists, recognized the etymological origins of the corporate fiction in the Latin terms of *fingere* and *persona*, as well as the Greek term *prosopon*. Yet, in terms of the debate over the reality of corporate personhood, he also averred, "it is doubtful whether all this playing with words serves any purpose."[57] For Radin, legal personality – dating back to the ancient *personae* and *prosopon*, which referenced the masks worn by actors, and thus, the roles they assumed – had always indexed a set of legal relations operating at a remove from the flesh and blood human being involved in those relations. Radin drew on Wesley Newcomb Hohfield's legal algebra to demonstrate the complex processes by which these relations were taken up in the law in ways that at once recognized the distinct nature of legal relations, while also grasping their connection to flesh and blood human beings. In terms of the corporation, this implied that corporate personality likewise referred to a discrete set of relations connected to human beings, but operating at a distance from those same individuals, be they managers, stockholders, or workers in a corporation.

Radin's argument, which viewed the fiction of corporate personality as convenient and necessary, while also the focus of interminable debate, was extraordinarily effective because of his ability to deeply engage the rich history associated with corporate personhood while also sidestepping and minimizing its importance. As the German political theorist and advocate of "realism" in discussion of corporate personhood Otto Gierke noted, the notion of the corporation as a *persona ficta* dated back to the writings of Pope Innocent IV in the mid-thirteenth century.[58] Frederic Maitland, Gierke's English translator and an important advocate for his theories in the Anglophone legal world, emphasized the fictional element here was the group-person, which could engage in distinct types of legal actions while simultaneously, due to lacking body and soul, "could commit neither sin nor delict."[59] Gierke argued it was Savigny that incorporated the Roman concept of the *persona ficta* into German law, doing so at the expense of what Gierke viewed as a more foundational German conception of associated or corporate legal status. As Maitland stressed, Gierke's primary conflict with the

---

[56] *See* Dewey, *supra* note 42; Radin, *supra* note 48, at 643.
[57] Radin, *supra* note 48, at 643, 645.
[58] *See* Maitland, *Translator's Introduction, in* GIERKE, *supra* note 48, at xix.
[59] *Id.*

Italian or Roman theory of corporate personhood was the claim that corporations' personalities were derived from and dependent upon the state and, by extension, positive law. Gierke sought to elevate corporations, arguing that long-standing German fellowships and associations preceded the establishment of the state, and thus were dependent on the state for legal existence. Maitland's translation of sections from the third volume of Gierke's monumental *Das deutsche Genossenschaftsrecht* ends with the vivid imagery of existential conflict between centralized state authority and other forms of collective life, ultimately resulting in the "exaltation of the Sovereignty of the State."[60] As Gierke wistfully concludes, "in the course of that struggle all intermediate groups were first degraded into the position of the more or less arbitrarily fashioned creatures of mere positive law, and in the end were obliterated."[61]

Thus, while we commonly think of the fiction in the *persona ficta* of corporate personhood as a reference to the corporation's intangible qualities, one thing that Gierke and Maitland make clear through their historical excursus is that the primary fiction, here, is much broader. For these advocates of the real entity theory of the corporation, the fictional dimensions of corporate personality are not exhausted by what U.S. Supreme Court Justice John Marshall famously referred to as "an artificial being, invisible, intangible, and existing only in contemplation of law."[62] Rather, the incorporation of the *persona ficta* into both Continental European and, later, Anglo-American law, also extended beyond the specific artificiality of corporations to the more general fiction of state sovereignty itself.

This, potentially, is the most important contribution of Gierke's reading of medieval political thought; not his emphasis on the reality of organic German associational life, which was precisely the debate that Dewey and Radin viewed as ridiculous, but his insistence that central state sovereignty rests on fictional grounds. Yet, it also nonetheless leaves us with questions about what it means to consider state sovereignty in such terms. Other contemporary scholars, such as David Runciman and Henry Turner, wrote about the fictional nature of the state and found a crucial hinge between fiction, personhood, and sovereignty in the work of Thomas Hobbes. Runciman, for instance, has argued the state itself is a "person by fiction."[63] In a series of detailed readings of *The Leviathan*, Runciman explains that, for Hobbes, personhood is connected with the ability to represent individuals and things.[64] Glossing Hobbes, Runciman argues, "to be a person is to speak and act in such a way as to require others to consider who you are speaking and acting for."[65] Hobbes famously

---

[60] GIERKE, *supra* note 48, at 98.

[61] *Id.* at 100.

[62] *Trustees of Dartmouth College v. Woodward*, 17 U.S. 636 (1819).

[63] David Runciman, *What Kind of Person Is Hobbes's State? A Reply to Skinner*, 8 J. POL. PHIL. 268 (2000).

[64] See RUNCIMAN, *supra* note 32; Runciman, *The Concept of the State: The Sovereignty of a Fiction, in* STATES & CITIZENS: HISTORY, THEORY, PROSPECTS 28 (Quentin Skinner & Bo Stråth, eds. 2003).

[65] Runciman, *supra* note 63, at 269.

divided natural persons who represent themselves from artificial persons who represent others.[66] Runciman also clarifies a distinction within artificial persons between those who "truly" represent others – implying that the "words and actions are truly owned by those whom they represent" – and those who represent others "by fiction."[67] Runciman contends that the corporate body of the Leviathan, which Hobbes presented as an "artificial person," was in fact a "person by fiction" in the sense that no precise individual is represented by the artificial person of the state. Rather, the state represents the newly constituted collectivity of the commonwealth, formed out of a multitude of individuals.[68] For Runciman, this makes the state complex and elusive. More than the sum of individuals who form it, the state is "a person in its own right, that person in whose name the sovereign speaks and acts."[69] But Runciman also notes, "the person of the state is nothing without its sovereign representative; it has no inherent authority, because it has no ability to speak and act for itself" and must rely on individuals to act on its behalf.[70] For this reason Runciman calls the state a fiction, referring to it in another echo of Hobbes's own discussion of the person-as-*prosopon*,[71] as "a kind of mask" that we generally agree to leave in place.[72]

Henry Turner extended Runciman's formulation of the Hobbesian state as a person by fiction in two ways.[73] First, he demonstrates that Hobbes's actual experience with imperial joint-stock companies, as a member of the Virginia Company and the Somers Islands Company, was central to the formulation of his theories of collective persons.[74] As Turner claims, Hobbes already recognized the continuity in form between commonwealths and joint-stock corporations in his earlier 1640 text, *The Elements of Law*, long before his extensive criticism of corporations in *The Leviathan*.[75] Second, Turner emphasizes the important role that theater played in Hobbes's understanding of personhood.[76] In particular, Turner argues that Hobbes's "theatrical analogy" was a way of concretizing or making real the "nominalist fiction" of sovereignty.[77] As Turner suggests, the theater gave Hobbes a way of conceptualizing the collective entity as "distinct from the members who make it up" yet still an entity that becomes ever more real as it acts, through its representatives, in the world.[78]

---

[66] HOBBES, *supra* note 36, at 111.

[67] Runciman, *supra* note 63, at 269.

[68] *Id.* at 272. *See also* HOBBES, *supra* note 36, at 115.

[69] Runciman, *supra* note 64, at 36.

[70] *Id.*

[71] HOBBES, *supra* note 36, at 112.

[72] Runciman, *supra* note 64, at 36.

[73] HENRY S. TURNER, THE CORPORATE COMMONWEALTH: PLURALISM AND POLITICAL FICTIONS IN ENGLAND 1516–1651 (Univ. of Chicago Press 2016).

[74] *Id.* at 215.

[75] *Id.* at 216, 219.

[76] *Id.* at 223. Runciman also notes the importance of the theater in the Hobbesian framework. RUNCIMAN, *supra* note 32, at 244.

[77] TURNER, *supra* note 73, at 223, 224.

[78] *Id.* at 224.

In recovering the notion of state as fiction, Runciman and Turner read Hobbes as recognizing some Gierkean truths about the plural and self-constituting sources of political authority in society – even while the Hobbesian political project in *The Leviathan* runs precisely in the opposite direction. Hobbes, the great theorist of the unified state, had to conceptualize the way individuals could come together to form a new order or system of authority that was real, but could only act through representatives. The Hobbesian project of *The Leviathan* was thus caught in a double bind: at once admitting the importance of corporate associational life while simultaneously attempting to downplay other forms of association besides the commonwealth. The degradation and obliteration of these lesser bodies was what Gierke lamented,[79] but as Turner explains, it also indicates an early modern conceptualization of corporateness that was much more expansive than the reduced notions of associational life offered by our contemporary notions of the corporation, which focus primarily on businesses and nation-states.

We can also contrast these accounts, focused on the question of the reality of group existence, with another narrative of the Hobbesian state as fiction that Michel Foucault offered in a 1975–1976 lecture series at the Collège de France. Foucault presents *The Leviathan* as a story whose fictional elements begin in the hypostatized state of nature. For Foucault, Hobbes's account of the war of all against all was not a real war but rather a "theater where presentations are exchanged."[80] Whereas real war would have quickly led to victory for one side and the emergence of new relations of domination and subordination, the relative equality of the state of nature meant that each individual was engaged in a performance of war. As Foucault argued, the state of nature was thus characterized by "presentations, manifestations, signs, emphatic expressions, wiles, and deceitful expressions; there are traps, intentions disguised as their opposite, and worries disguised as certainties."[81] Thus, for Foucault, the Hobbesian state of war is really "a sort of unending diplomacy between rivals who are naturally equal."[82] Moreover, Foucault argues this diplomacy extends beyond the state of nature into political society, as a "permanent backdrop"[83] of the Hobbesian commonwealth. Foucault chronicles multiple accounts of the state's formation in THE LEVIATHAN, in each case noting the way Hobbes's argument for state sovereignty served as an injunction to potentially warring parties to engage in politics rather than actual physical conflict. Thus, the fictional nature of the state sovereignty, for Foucault, masks the possibility that real conflicts could erupt at any moment.

Foucault goes on to find the inversion of conflict into politics not only in Hobbes, but also in a variety of other stories of suppressed conflicts: Sir Edward Coke's account

---

[79] GIERKE, *supra* note 48.
[80] Foucault, *supra* note 24, at 92.
[81] *Id.*
[82] *Id.*
[83] *Id.* at 93.

of the rights of Saxons, the fables of Franco-Gallia, the aristocratic histories of Henri de Boulainvilliers, the political pamphlets of the Levellers and Diggers, Abbé Sieyès's arguments on behalf of the Third Estate, and even in twentieth-century biopolitics. More interestingly, Foucault also finds discourses of suppressed conflict in literature and popular culture, noting, for instance, that accounts of the Norman Conquest were accompanied by "two heterogeneous sets of legends" with fables of Robin Hood's social banditry, on one side, and aristocratic tales of King Arthur, on the other. In summarizing the multiple accounts of state sovereignty as fiction we can note that, whereas Turner and Runciman direct us to the plural forms of social authority and the reality of group life behind the persona of the state, Foucault emphasizes a permanent and eradicable reality of conflict. For Foucault, there are not just multiple groups, but multiple groups seeking to dominate one another. Thus, the fables of political power should be understood as moments in a "silent war to reinscribe the relationship of force, and to reinscribe it in institutions, economic inequalities, language, and even the bodies of individuals."[84] Grappling with these fictions thus requires a different type of interpretive practice, one less sanguine about the law's fictions, less focused on the reality of group life, and more attentive to the role of fiction in what Foucault called "the techniques and tactics of domination"[85] – in other words, something like an ideological critique addressing the role of fiction in securing group or class power.

FICTION AND THE CORPORATION

It is hard to miss the ways the fictional presence of the corporation extends beyond the law to inhabit the imagination. Indeed, few figures are as ubiquitous in contemporary popular culture than the corporation, which has come to play a starring role in many genres exploring utopian and dystopian elements of real and imagined worlds. Indeed, whether it is the corporate control of artificial intelligence in William Gibson's *Neuromancer*; the burned out landscape of corporate-led genetic and ecological disaster in Margaret Atwood's *MaddAddam Trilogy*; the villainous multination E Corp in Sam Esmail's *Mr. Robot*; or even the Buy n Large megacorporation of Pixar's animated *Wall-E*, scarcely any speculative account of the future does not possess some vision of corporate control over work, the environment, thinking, and life in general.

In an attempt to understand a variety of these new corporate fictions, Ralph Clare suggested that they collectively represent anxieties about postindustrial economies that have come to be hegemonic across the advanced capitalist world since the 1970s.[86] As such, Clare reads texts, ranging from popular movies such as *Gung*

---

[84] *Id.* at 16.

[85] *Id.* at 34.

[86] Ralph Clare, Fictions Inc.: The Corporation in Postmodern Fiction, Film, and Popular Culture (2016).

Ho, *Ghostbusters*, *The Manchurian Candidate*, and *Michael Clayton* to the literature of Thomas Pynchon, Don DiLillo, William Gaddis, and Richard Powers, as
evincing a cultural dissatisfaction with neoliberal, globalized corporate capitalism.
As he puts it,

> America's ambivalent relationship with corporations reveals a deep discontent with
> the capitalist system itself, despite capital's promise of a future market utopia and
> complete freedom of consumer choice, and marks a preoccupation with the loss of
> individual rights and freedoms as well as the possibilities of resistance to corporate
> capitalism.[87]

Literature, then, offers a (however ideological)[88] way of understanding and critiquing corporate capitalism. The changing literary configuration of the corporation
over time reflects shifts in both the organization of economic life and resistance
to dominant forms of socio-economic relations. Using fiction to examine these
changes, Clare contrasts the account of industrial corporate power offered over
a hundred years ago in Frank Norris's book *The Octopus*, with the more diffuse
and ever-present form of corporate capitalism presented in Thomas Pynchon's *The
Crying of Lot 49*, noting the different ways corporate power and resistance are conceptualized in these two texts. Norris's critique of late nineteenth-century industrial
capitalism concerns the plight of farmers facing off against land acquisitions by a
giant railroad company backed by powerful financial interests. Clare recounts the
way that much of Norris's story comments on the ineffectual nature of traditional
forms of anti-corporate resistance – from legal struggles to unionization – before
ultimately returning to themes of naturalism and romanticism at the end of the
novel as a potential solution to the problems of industrialization. In a fascinating
reading, Clare suggests that this shift marks the ideological content of Norris's book.
Recognizing the difficulty of anti-corporate movements to stem the growth of rapa-
cious industrialization, *The Octopus* presents a fantasy where industrial capitalism's
contradictions are displaced without ever being fully resolved. This differs from the
ubiquitous corporate presence that suffuses Thomas Pynchon's *The Crying of Lot
49*. Engaging Fredric Jameson's famous presentation of postmodernism, Clare reads
Pynchon's late twentieth-century text as being structured by the lack of any point
outside of or beyond the corporate order from which to launch either critical or aesthetic critique.[89] Clare thus laments, "corporations and capital have attained such
a hold on American life that all avenues of resistance, already seen as troubled by

---

[87] *Id.* at 3.

[88] Clare makes clear in his readings that the egalitarian impulse in anti-corporate literature is never free
from the broader ideological matrix of society, quoting Fredric Jameson to argue that "the production
of aesthetic or narrative form is to be seen as an ideological act in its own right, with the function of
inventing imaginary or formal 'solutions' to unresolvable social contradictions." CLARE, *supra* 86, at
30 (quoting FREDRIC JAMESON, THE POLITICAL UNCONSCIOUS 79 (1981)).

[89] The one exception to this being the mysterious Tristero, which Clare reads as "in a sense, the abstract
possibility of resistance, the residue of a utopian way out of the current state of affairs." *Id.* at 46.

Norris, have apparently disappeared by the time of Pynchon."[90] Consequently, as
Clare's subsequent readings make clear, the dissatisfaction with the reigning corporate order evinced in postmodern literature is primarily ineffectual, swallowed up by
a corporate hegemony that has come to dominate even our fantasies of resistance.

Understandably, Fredric Jameson looms large in Clare's account, not only for
his discussion of postmodernism as the complete saturation of culture by capital,
but also for his writing on the utopian elements in speculative fiction. As Jameson
argues, utopian texts are less important for imagining and laying out real blueprints
for a future society than they are, as he puts it, for transformations "of our own
present into the determinant past of something yet to come."[91] Moreover, Jameson
suggests that what is politically important about this form of literature is its ability

> to bring home, in local and determinate ways and with a fullness of concrete detail,
> our constitutional inability to imagine Utopia itself: and this, not owing to any
> individual failure of imagination but as the result of the systemic, cultural and
> ideological closure of which we are all in one way or another prisoners.[92]

This inability can be understood in the ways that contradictions – in particular
between form and content; and between grand utopian plans and the concrete
details and events of utopian worlds – suffuse the genre as something like symptoms
of utopian failure.

As for the corporation, Jameson's account of utopia suggests it has a dialectical
relation to the present, exposing us to the limits of our current utopian imagination, while also promising something more to us in the future. Clare, recognizing as
much, reads this dialectic in postmodern literature as grappling with the promise of
a capitalist utopia and a boundless market that is ultimately oppressive, alienating,
and miserable, failing to ensure the common good. Because Clare only reads the corporation as a capitalist institution, he is ultimately pessimistic about the Jamesonian
dialectical project of finding the "ways in which the corporation might hint at the
utopian."[93] In the conclusion to his book, Clare considers the possibility of a socialist
or redistributive corporatism before contrasting it with an entirely new model of collectivity he derives from Michael Hardt and Antonio Negri's notion of the multitude,
referred to as a "coming incorporation." Clare describes the politics of this collectivity – in language that echoes Grear's account of embodied vulnerability – as the "very
possibility of the multitude's 'embodiment' or 'incorporation' as a collective" that
"affirms the corporeal yet resists hierarchical organization, and ... is composed of
singularities that share what they have in common – not a profit motive."[94]

[90] *Id.* at 14.
[91] Fredric Jameson, Archaeologies of the Future: The Desire Called Utopia and Other Science Fictions 288 (2005).
[92] *Id.* at 289.
[93] Clare, *supra* note 86, at 201. Clare derives the model for a socialist corporation from Kurt Vonnegut, Jailbird (1979).
[94] *Id.* at 203.

Yet, Clare's elevation of a mystical "coming incorporation" over and against the utopian aspects of a reformulated "socialist corporation" rests on a truncated version of the corporation's history and complexity. Given that Hardt and Negri's notion of the multitude derives from the constituting power of collectivities prior to their being subsumed by the Hobbesian state, Clare's assertion that "the multitude presents a new and different challenge" to corporate power is incorrect. Rather, as Runciman, Turner, and Gierke all noted, the multitude is the very foundation of corporate power, albeit one that undergoes significant transformations at the hands of the modern state and through the vicissitudes of capitalist development.

Another way of grasping this could be through the very same Jamesonian framework that Clare finds wanting, if we take it from a different starting point. For though Clare justifies his selection of Frank Norris's *The Octopus* as "one of the earliest fictional representations of a corporation in American literature," he might have also considered the equally important work of Edward Bellamy, whose massively popular 1888 utopian novel LOOKING BACKWARD was also a text centrally concerned with corporate power.[95] More crucially, Bellamy's writing transgressed the boundaries between fiction and politics through the creation of the "Nationalist" movement that sought to enact a Bellamyite form of utopian socialism focused on the nationalization of industrial production.[96]

Looking Backward nominally tells the story of Julian West, a wealthy, 30-year old Bostonian engaged to a woman named Edith Bartlett, who, on an early summer day in 1887, is mesmerized and put to sleep in a subterranean chamber by an "irregular" doctor and "Professor of Animal Magnetism" named Pillsbury.[97] West wakes up in autumn of the year 2000 in the house of a Dr. Leete, discovered by Leete's daughter during a rainstorm that flooded the basement. Upon rousing, West encounters a transformed Boston composed of "public buildings of a colossal size and architectural grandeur,"[98] unprecedented in his experience. Recognizing his new circumstances, West begins exploring his new environment through a series

---

[95] EDWARD BELLAMY, LOOKING BACKWARD 2000–1887 (Signet Classic ed. 2000) (1888). John Dewey, himself, asked by Edward Weeks, the editor of the ATLANTIC MONTHLY, in 1935 to list "the twenty five most influential books published since 1885" put LOOKING BACKWARD in second place behind Karl Marx's, DAS KAPITAL. *See* SYLVIA BOWMAN, EDWARD BELLAMY 26 (1986).

[96] On the Bellamyite Nationalist movement, *see* ARTHUR LIPOW, AUTHORITARIAN SOCIALISM IN AMERICA: EDWARD BELLAMY AND THE NATIONALIST MOVEMENT (2nd ed., 1991); EVERETT MacNAIR, EDWARD BELLAMY AND THE NATIONALIST MOVEMENT 1889 TO 1894 (1957). In the preface to the paperback edition, Lipow argues that not only was Bellamy's vision of socialism foundational to the U.S. socialist left through the 1930s, but that it also was central to the technocratic and corporatist vision of planning associated with the New Deal and, specifically, with Adolf Berle. Lipow avers the Bellamyite origins of Berle's recognition of the separation of ownership and management that he would articulate in his justifiably famous book with Garner Means, and also notes that Berle's father was a member of a Bellamyite club in Boston. *See* LIPOW at xviii.

[97] BELLAMY, *supra* note 95, at 16.

[98] *Id.* at 25.

of conversations and excursions with Dr. Leete and his daughter, Edith. These dialogues comprise the bulk of *Looking Backward*, giving Dr. Leete and Edith the opportunity to explain this utopian world to West. In terms of plot, little occurs to the main characters in the novel, outside of a budding romance between Julian West and Edith Leete, and the revelation that Edith Leete is the great-granddaughter of Edith Bartlett, to whom Julian was once betrothed. The book ends with Julian West awaking from a dream that he had returned to the nineteenth century, accepting his life in the new utopia as something of a religious salvation.

More interesting are the details of the utopian society that Bellamy articulates through the dialogues between West and the Leetes. Dr. Leete explains to West that problems of labor unrest and war that troubled the nineteenth century were quickly extinguished in the twentieth century through a process of "industrial evolution"[99] in which the concentration of capital that began with the nineteenth-century monopolies, trusts, and cartels was "completed by the final consolidation of the entire capital of the nation."[100] As Leete expounds,

> The industry and commerce of the country, ceasing to be conducted by a set of irresponsible corporations and syndicates of private persons at their caprice and for their profit, were entrusted to a single syndicate representing the people, to be conducted in the common interest for the common profit. The nation, that is to say, organized as the one great business corporation in which all other corporations were absorbed.[101]

This ultimate unification of state and capital results in transformations of almost all subsequent social relations: citizenship and military service are refocused into an industrial army, coextensive with society, that coordinates all work and service; distribution of goods no longer works on the basis of market exchanges mediated by money, but through state-run stores that ship goods across the city through pneumatic tubes; transgressions of law and order are medicalized, rather than criminalized; efficiencies in production encourage the flourishing of literature and the arts, while also being sustained by the state; heterosexual marriage and protestant religion persist, but framed around Bellamy's particular (nineteenth century) vision of equality and collectivism.

Bellamy rhapsodizes over the details of this new world, yet modern readers might not be struck only from the book's occasional prescience (its foreshadowing of things like credit cards and cable communications), but also by the frightening image of a nationalist state. Whereas Bellamy posits a benign evolutionary development from decentralized corporations to industrial cartels to an industrialized corporate-state managing all work, production, and consumption, readers, such as Arthur Lipow, chastened by experiences with Stalinism, present Bellamy as offering a "socialism

[99] *Id.* at 32.
[100] *Id.* at 37.
[101] *Id.*

from above" in which "a new class rules over a stratified economy in the name of socialism."[102] Put differently, if Hobbes saw the state as a unifying and totalizing entity, Bellamy offers a logical end-point of Hobbesian reasoning, as the boundaries between society and state are eliminated in the form of a new corporate Leviathan. The way that corporatized state and states-as-corporations have become the great figures of evil and malice in contemporary dystopian literature testifies to the notion that Bellamy's utopia confronts modern readers as not the best, but the worst of all possible worlds. Whereas for writers of an earlier era, such as Kafka or Orwell, the impersonal forces of the bureaucratic state were the seedbeds of totalitarianism and the primary threat to individual freedom, in more recent dystopias, beginning with Aldous Huxley, and moving on to Neil Stephenson, David Foster Wallace, and Margaret Atwood, corporations play this role.[103] In these dystopian texts, corporations are presented either as oligarchic entities supplanting democratic will with corporate will, or as entities whose power over life is so extensive that it threatens life itself, be it from the unintended consequences of technological development or through management of human sexuality, reproduction, and genetics. In either case, it is the antidemocratic nature of corporate decision-making, as well as corporate science, research, and development, that make corporations such worrisome figures.

But the Jamesonian framework here is important, as Jameson highlights the failure of utopian texts to point to certain impasses or contradictions in the present concerning our ability to conceptualize an alternative future. The dialectical reversal that Bellamy's utopia offers is the possibility of considering an alternative form of collective life, precisely in the way that *Looking Backward* disrupts our conception of the relations between the two fictional bodies of state and corporation. Unsurprisingly, Jameson himself has recognized the productivity of the limits and failures in Bellamy's utopian account. In his recent text, *An American Utopia*, Jameson anchors his vision of a utopian future to a "universal army" that mirrors the state as a dual power that serves collective functions.[104] Jameson's utopia not only directly references Bellamy's industrial army; it also highlights those aspects of corporations that have enabled them to serve as doubles to state sovereignty.[105] On this read, the fictional configurations of the corporation not only express anxieties and disaffections with capitalism, as Clare suggests, but they also express a radical dissatisfaction with the forms of collective life, prodding us to imagine the present as, in Jameson's dialectical imaginary, the past of some radically different social order yet to come.

---

[102] LIPOW, *supra* 96, at 1.
[103] FRANZ KAFKA, THE TRIAL (1925); GEORGE ORWELL, 1984 (1949); ALDOUS HUXLEY, BRAVE NEW WORLD (1931); NEIL STEPHENSON, SNOW CRASH (1991); DAVID FOSTER WALLACE, INFINITE JEST (1996); MARGARET ATWOOD, ORYX AND CRAKE (2003); MARGARET ATWOOD, THE YEAR OF THE FLOOD (2009); MARGARET ATWOOD, MADDADDAM (2013).
[104] FREDRIC JAMESON, AN AMERICAN UTOPIA: DUAL POWER AND THE UNIVERSAL ARMY (2016).
[105] On doubling of corporate and state, *see* BARKAN, *supra* note 5, at 4.

CONCLUSION

The focus on literary analysis might seem to take us far from the discussions of the attributions of rights to corporations laid out at the beginning of the chapter and in this book more broadly. Legal scholars, of course, recognize that law, like literary analysis, is an interpretive practice concerned with the meaning of texts. Yet, attribution is not only a question of interpretation, as it also is a generative and constitutive moment in which law creates and shapes the social order. Durkee makes this clear in the introduction to this book, when characterizing firms and states as "products of legal imagination ... constructed by laws, and laws assign their rights and responsibilities."[106]

Recognized as such, we can grasp the historical and conceptual contingency in the attribution of rights and responsibilities to fictional entities. We might also note the anxiety that the great debates over the fictional nature of corporate personhood index. As I've attempted to demonstrate, juridical fictions were made as contrivances to achieve particular ends but, once constituted, they have exercised an outsized effect on the legal imagination. They have not only shaped but also constrained subsequent legal experimentation as we try to constitute just orders within the scope of law's fictions.

Lawyers, of course, have responded with innovative arguments that attempt to establish some rational kernel within the framework of human rights that could realign corporate personhood to more beneficial ends. Yet, literary analysis might offer us a different response. Put simply, what a literary framework grasps about corporations, which the legal misses, is that central problems with corporations and corporate power are caused by, rather than resolved by, law. Whereas lawyers posit that simply getting a more accurate image of the corporate person will resolve problems about corporate abuses, literary analysis suggests it is something internal to the vision of legal order offered by today's dominant institutions that leaves us wanting.

---

[106] *See* Melissa J. Durkee, Introduction.

Index

Printed in the USA
CPSIA information can be obtained
at www.ICGtesting.com
LVHW051135240224
772720LV00004B/95

9 781009 334679